The Armenian Social Democrat Hnchakian Party

Armenians in the Modern and Early Modern World

Recent decades have seen the expansion of Armenian Studies from insular history to a broader, more interactive field within an inter-regional and global context. This series, *Armenians in the Modern and Early Modern World*, responds to this growth by promoting innovative and interdisciplinary approaches to Armenian history, politics, and culture in the period between 1500-2000. Focusing on the geographies of the Mediterranean, Middle East, and Contemporary Russia [Eastern Armenia], it directs specific attention to imperial and post-imperial frameworks: from the Ottoman Empire to Modern Turkey/Arab Middle East; the Safavid/Qajar Empires to Iran; and the Russian Empire to Soviet Union/Post-Soviet territories.

Series Editor

Bedross Der Matossian, *University of Nebraska, Lincoln, USA*

Advisory Board

Levon Abrahamian, *Yerevan State University, Armenia*
Sylvie Alajaji, *Franklin & Marshal College, USA*
Sebouh Aslanian, *University of California, Los Angeles, USA*
Stephan Astourian, *University of California, Berkley, USA*
Houri Berberian, *University of California, Irvine, USA*
Talar Chahinian, *University of California, Irvine, USA*
Rachel Goshgarian, *Lafayette College, USA*
Ronald Grigor Suny, *University of Michigan, USA*
Sossie Kasbarian, *University of Stirling, UK*
Christina Maranci, *Tufts University, USA*
Tsolin Nalbantian, *Leiden University, the Netherlands*
Anna Ohanyan, *Stonehill College, USA*
Hratch Tchilingirian, *University of Oxford, UK*

Published and Forthcoming Titles

The Politics of Naming the Armenian Genocide: Language, History and 'Medz Yeghern', Vartan Matiossian
Picturing the Ottoman Armenian World: Photography in Erzerum, Kharpert, Van and Beyond, David Low

The Armenian Social Democrat Hnchakian Party

Politics, Ideology and Transnational History

Edited by
Bedross Der Matossian

I.B. TAURIS
LONDON • NEW YORK • OXFORD • NEW DELHI • SYDNEY

I.B. TAURIS
Bloomsbury Publishing Plc, 50 Bedford Square, London, WC1B 3DP, UK
Bloomsbury Publishing Inc, 1385 Broadway, New York, NY 10018, USA
Bloomsbury Publishing Ireland, 29 Earlsfort Terrace, Dublin 2, D02 AY28, Ireland

BLOOMSBURY, I.B. TAURIS and the I.B. Tauris logo are trademarks
of Bloomsbury Publishing Plc

First published in Great Britain 2024
This paperback edition published in 2025

Copyright © Bedross Der Matossian, 2024

Bedross Der Matossian and Contributors have asserted their rights under the
Copyright, Designs and Patents Act, 1988, to be identified as Authors of this work.

Copyright Individual Chapters © 2023 Toygun Altıntaş, Kadir Akın, Yaşar Tolga Cora,
Richard G. Hovannisian, Yeghia (Yeghig) Jerejian, Varak Ketsemanian, Ümit Kurt,
Gerard J. Libaridian, Abel H. Manoukian, Vartan Matiossian, Gaïdz Minassian,
Garabet K. Moumdjian, Vahram L. Shemmassian.

For legal purposes the Acknowledgements on p. xii constitute
an extension of this copyright page.

Cover design: Adriana Brioso
Cover image: SDHP emblem, from Arsen Gidur, *Patmut'iwn S.D. Hnch'akean
Kusakts'ut'ean*, vol. I (Beirut: Tparan Shirak, 1962), 33.

All rights reserved. No part of this publication may be: i) reproduced or
transmitted in any form, electronic or mechanical, including photocopying,
recording or by means of any information storage or retrieval system without
prior permission in writing from the publishers; or ii) used or reproduced
in any way for the training, development or operation of artificial intelligence (AI)
technologies, including generative AI technologies. The rights holders expressly
reserve this publication from the text and data mining exception as per
Article 4(3) of the Digital Single Market Directive (EU) 2019/790.

Bloomsbury Publishing Inc does not have any control over, or responsibility for,
any third-party websites referred to or in this book. All internet addresses given
in this book were correct at the time of going to press. The author and
publisher regret any inconvenience caused if addresses have changed or sites
have ceased to exist, but can accept no responsibility for any such changes.

A catalogue record for this book is available from the British Library.

Library of Congress Cataloging-in-Publication Data
Names: Der Matossian, Bedross, 1978- editor.
Title: The Armenian Social Democrat Hnchakian Party: politics, ideology and
transnational history / Bedross Der Matossian.
Description: London; New York: I.B Tauris, 2023. | Series: Armenians in the modern and early
modern world | Includes bibliographical references and index. | Contents: Introduction: The
Social Democrat Hnchakian Party in the Course of History / Bedross Der Matossian – The
History of a Group Picture and the Foundation Date of a "Revolutionary Society" in Geneve
/ Abel Manoukian – The Hnchakian "Nay" to Young Turk Overtures, 1895-1908 / Garabet K.

Moumdjian – A Newly Discovered Letter of Sabah-Gulian to Paramaz / Yeghig Djeredjian – The Hnchakian Party and the First Republic of Armenia (1918-1920) / Richard G. Hovannisian – Armenians, Muslims, Citizens: Hnchak Pamphleteering in Central Anatolia / Toygun Altıntaş – Peasants, Pastoralists, and Revolutionaries: Hnchakians and Armeno-Kurdish Relations in Late Ottoman Eastern Anatolia / Varak Ketsemanian –The Hnchakian Revolutionary Party in Aintab: Founders, Ideology and Structure / Ümit Kurt – Absolute Monarchy: The Social Democrat Hnchakian Revolutionary Episode in Armenian Musa Dagh during the 1890s / Vahram Shemmassian – The Hnchakian Party in the Armenian Communities of South America: An Outline of its Early History / Vartan Matiossian – Ideology and Reality: Hnchakian Paradoxes at Birth / Gerard J. Libaridian – The Social Democrat Hnchakian Party and the Armenian Revolutionary Federation, Fraternal Twins or Semi-Identical Twins? / Gaïdz Minassian – The Istanbul Students' Union of the Social Democrat Hnchak Party and its Periodical Kaytz (1911-1914) / Yaşar Tolga Cora – In the Footsteps of Hidden History: The Roots of Socialism in the Ottoman Empire / Kadir Akın.
Identifiers: LCCN 2023011389 (print) | LCCN 2023011390 (ebook) | ISBN 9780755651375 (hardback) | ISBN 9780755651344 (paperback) | ISBN 9780755651368 (pdf) | ISBN 9780755651368 (epub) | ISBN 9780755651337
Subjects: LCSH: Sots'ial Demokrat Hnch'akean Kusakts'ut'iwn. | Political parties–Armenia–History. | Political parties–Turkey–History. | Armenia–Politics and government. | Turkey–Politics and government.
Classification: LCC JQ1759.3.A98 S67 2023 (print) | LCC JQ1759.3.A98 (ebook) | DDC 306.2/6094756–dc23/eng/20230323
LC record available at https://lccn.loc.gov/2023011389
LC ebook record available at https://lccn.loc.gov/2023011390

ISBN: HB: 978-0-7556-5137-5
PB: 978-0-7556-5134-4
ePDF: 978-0-7556-5136-8
eBook: 978-0-7556-5135-1

Series: Armenians in the Modern and Early Modern World

Typeset by Deanta Global Publishing Services, Chennai, India

For product safety related questions contact productsafety@bloomsbury.com.

To find out more about our authors and books visit www.bloomsbury.com and sign up for our newsletters.

Contents

List of figures	ix
List of contributors	x
Acknowledgements	xii
Note on transliteration	xiii

Introduction: The Social Democrat Hnchakian Party in the Course of
History *Bedross Der Matossian*   1

Section I From Inception to the First Republic of Armenia (1918–20)

1. The History of a Group Picture and the Date of the Formation of the 'Revolutionary Society' of Geneva *Abel Manoukian*   21
2. The Hnchakian 'nay' to Young Turk Overtures, 1895–1908
   Garabet K. Moumdjian (†)   38
3. A Newly Discovered Letter of Sabah-Gulian to Paramaz *Yeghig Jerejian*   56
4. The Social Democrat Hnchakian Party and the First Republic of Armenia (1918–20/21) *Richard G. Hovannisian (†)*   75

Section II Regional and Local Histories

5. Armenians, Muslims, Citizens: Hnchak Pamphleteering in Central Anatolia *Toygun Altıntaş*   87
6. Peasants, Pastoralists and Revolutionaries: Hnchakians and Armeno–Kurdish Relations in late Ottoman Eastern Anatolia
   Varak Ketsemanian   107
7. The Hnchakian Revolutionary Party in Aintab: Founders, Ideology and Structure *Ümit Kurt*   132
8. Absolute Monarchy: The Social Democrat Hnchakian Revolutionary Episode in Armenian Musa Dagh during the 1890s
   Vahram L. Shemmassian   148
9. The Hnchakians in South America: Early History *Vartan Matiossian*   172

Section III Ideology

10. Ideology and Reality: Hnchakian Paradoxes at Birth *Gerard J. Libaridian*   193
11. SDHP-ARF: Fraternal Twins or Semi-identical Twins? *Gaïdz Minassian*   205

12 The Istanbul Students' Union of the Social Democrat Hnchakian Party
    and its Periodical *Kaytz* (1911–14) *Yaşar Tolga Cora* 227
13 In the Footsteps of Hidden History: The Roots of Socialism in the
    Ottoman Empire *Kadir Akın* 237

Biographical notes 255
Selected bibliography 259
Index 267

Figures

I.1	Kevork Chekmeyan, a Hnchak *fedayee* from Marash	10
1.1	From left to right, standing, are Gevorg Gharajian, Kristapor Ohanian, and Avetis Nazarbekian. Seated on the central row, from left to right, are Maro Vartanian and Gabriel Kafian. Seated on the floor is Rupen Khan-Azad	30
1.2	From left to right, standing, are Rupen Khan-Azad and Gabriel Kafian. In the central row, from left to right, are Avetis Nazarbekian and Gevorg Gharajian, seated; in the middle of the photo, are Maro Vardanian, and Kristapor Ohanian	31
2.1	Avetis Nazarbekian	44
3.1	Paramaz (Matteos Sarkissian)	61
11.1	Stepan Sabah-Gulian	224
12.1	*Kaytz* June 1911, no. 2	228

Contributors

Toygun Altıntaş is EUME Fellow of the Alexander von Humboldt Foundation at Freie Universität Berlin. He has published book chapters and articles on late Ottoman strategies of rule and minoritization, and Armenian revolutionaries in the Ottoman Empire in various edited volumes and journals.

Kadir Akın is a writer and politician. He is the author of multiple books in Turkish including *The Crisis of Socialism*, *Paramaz the Armenian Revolutionary*, and *Tracing the Hidden History* among others. He is the director of the documentary *Red*, which deals with the life, views and struggles of Paramaz (Matteos Sarkissian), one of the prominent leaders of the Social Democrat Hnchakian Party, who was executed in 1915 along with his nineteen Hunchakian comrades at Beyazıt Square.

Yaşar Tolga Cora is Assistant Professor of Late Ottoman and Turkish History in the Department of History at Boğaziçi University. His work has appeared in many journals including *Journal of the Economic and Social History of the Orient*, *New Perspectives on Turkey* and *International Review of Social History*.

Richard G. Hovannisian was the preeminent historian of Armenia and the Armenian Genocide. He was Professor Emeritus of History and First Holder of the Armenian Educational Foundation Chair in Modern Armenian History at UCLA, the author or contributing editor of thirty-two books, including five volumes on the first Republic of Armenia and five volumes on the Armenian Genocide, together with some 100 scholarly articles. He was a Guggenheim Fellow.

Yeghia (Yeghig) Jerejian is a graduate of the Yerevan State Medical University. He is the author of fifteen books and numerous articles on Armenian and Middle East history. In 2019 he was awarded an honorary doctorate degree in history by Armenia's National Academy of Sciences. He represented the Armenian community of Beirut in Lebanon's Parliament from 1992 to 2009.

Varak Ketsemanian is Lecturer at the American University of Armenia. His articles have appeared in the *Journal of Ottoman and Turkish Studies Association* and the *International Journal of Middle East Studies*, along with many chapters in edited volumes.

Ümit Kurt is Assistant Professor in the School of Humanities, Creative Industries and Social Sciences (History) at the University of Newcastle, New South Wales. He is the author of *The Armenians of Aintab: The Economics of Genocide in an Ottoman Province* (2021).

Gerard J. Libaridian is a retired historian; he has also had a diplomatic career. His most recent published volume is *The Third Republic of Armenia. The Karabakh Conflict* (Yerevan, 2022) in Armenian.

Abel H. Manoukian is currently Scientific Assistant at the Protestant Church in Switzerland and General Secretary of Swiss Council of Religions. He is the author of *Bearing Witness to Humanity: Switzerland's Humanitarian Contribution during the Armenian Genocide in the Ottoman Empire 1894–1923* (2018).

Vartan Matiossian is an independent historian and literary scholar living in New Jersey. He is the author of *The Politics of Naming the Armenian Genocide: Language, History, and 'Medz Yeghern'* (2022).

Gaïdz Minassian holds a doctorate in political science. He teaches international relations at Sciences Po Paris and is a journalist for *Le Monde*. He is the author of several books, including *The Armenian Experience, from Ancient Times to Independence* (2020) and *Les sentiers de la victoire, peut-on encore gagner une guerre?* (2020)

Garabet K. Moumdjian was an independent historian and an Ottomanist. He obtained his PhD from UCLA. His dissertation is titled 'Struggling for a Constitutional Regime: Armenian-Young Turk Relations in the Era of Abdul Hamid II, 1895-1909'.

Vahram L. Shemmassian holds a PhD in History from UCLA. He is Professor and the Director of the Armenian Studies Program at the California State University, Northridge. He is the author of *The Armenians of Musa Dagh: From Obscurity to Genocide Resistance and Fame 1840–1915* (2020), and *The Musa Dagh Armenians: A Socioeconomic and Cultural History 1919–1939* (2015).

Acknowledgements

Half of the articles in this volume were presented at an international conference marking the 125th Anniversary of the foundation of the Social Democrat Hnchakian Party (SDHP). The conference was organized by the Armenian Educational Benevolent Union (AEBU) and Nor Serount Cultural Association (NSCA); and co-sponsored by the Richard Hovannisian, Endowed Chair in Modern Armenian History at UCLA, the Armenian Research Center at the University of Michigan, Dearborn; Woodbury University and the National Association for Armenian Studies and Research (NAASR). It took place on 27 October 2012, at Woodbury College in Burbank, Los Angeles. I would like to thank the conference organizers Harut Der-Tavitian, Vasken Khodanian, Sevak Khatchadorian and Thomas Yeterian for giving me drafts of the articles. Der-Tavitian especially played an important role in the materialization of this project. Special thanks to Vartan Matiossian for thoroughly proofreading the volume and translating Abel Mounkian's and Yeghig Djeredjian's articles from Armenian into English. Thanks to Nazife Kosukoğlu for translating Yaşar Tolga Cora's article from Turkish into English. I benefited a lot from Tara Ballard's feedback on a few articles. Special thanks to Barlow Der Mugrdechian for reading and commenting on the introduction. Thanks to Marc Mamigonian from NAASR for providing me with a few books on the history of SDHP. Thanks to the Department of History at the University of Nebraska-Lincoln (UNL) for its continuous support of my projects. I would like to thank the three anonymous reviewers. Their feedback and constructive criticism were extremely helpful in strengthening the volume. I am indebted to Rory Gormley, the editor of Middle East and Culture of I.B. Tauris, for his encouragement and support of this project. Special thanks to Yasmin Garcha the assistant editor at I.B. Tauris for overseeing the production of the volume. Thanks to the copy editors Louise A. Smith and Vishnu. Special thanks to the project manager Sharmila Mary. The publication of this volume was made possible with a generous donation from Mr. and Mrs. Vasken and Higo Kaltakdjian.

Finally, this project would not have materialized without the unconditional support of my wife Arpi Siyahian and my young daughters Knar and Yeraz Der Martossian. I am indebted to them.

Note on transliteration

Titles of books, periodicals and concepts in Armenian are transliterated according to the Library of Congress Transliteration (LOC) System.

Introduction

The Social Democrat Hnchakian Party in the Course of History

Bedross Der Matossian

The history of the Social Democrat Hnchakian Party (SDHP)[1] is part and parcel of the Armenian revolutionary movement that emerged in the second half of the nineteenth century in response to the deteriorating situation of Armenians in the eastern provinces of the Ottoman Empire.[2] This movement was born outside the Ottoman Empire and, more specifically, in the Caucasus. It was influenced by the regional as well as the global ideological currents and revolutionary movements that emerged in the second half of the nineteenth century, which impacted not only Armenians but also other ethnic groups living in the major empires of the time, such as the Russian, Persian and Austro-Hungarian empires. The ideology behind the Armenian revolutionary movement in general and that of the SDHP in particular is much more complex than what appears in basic history books. It would be impossible to understand the trajectory of the SDHP without also understanding the histories of the Armenakan Organization and the Armenian Revolutionary Federation (ARF). All of these parties were born in the same milieu with the aim of bringing change to their societies and leaving an impact on history while negotiating with socialism, nationalism and populism, among other *isms* of the time. They appeared to have the same objective, namely, to improve the condition of the Armenians of the eastern provinces. But they disagreed on the means of achieving this goal, as well as on their ultimate goals. Did they seek freedom, reform, autonomy, a socialist system or independence? While some of them wanted the complete independence of Armenia, others sought autonomy within the framework of the Ottoman Empire.

This book is the first edited volume in English that addresses the past and the present of the SDHP. It represents the latest scholarship on the history of the party and offers fresh perspectives on the party's different facets – from its inception to the period of the Young Turks, and from the First Republic of Armenia (1918–20) to its activities in the Diaspora. Before presenting the volume, this introduction will provide a historical assessment of the SDHP from the last two decades of the nineteenth century to the end of the twentieth century.

The SDHP and the ARF were not born in a vacuum but were a continuation of the revolutionary movements that emerged right before and after the Russo-Turkish War of 1877–8. Before the birth of the major Armenian parties, minor revolutionary groups existed in Turkish Armenia in cities such as Zeytun, Van and Erzerum. Unlike the later revolutionary parties, these groups did not have grandiose ideologies. For example, the Union of Salvation (*Miyut'iwn i P'rkut'iwn*), founded in Van in 1872, became the first Armenian revolutionary organization established in Turkish Armenia. Their aim was to protect the Armenians of Van from depredations and injustices suffered under the Turkish and Kurdish Aghas. Another example is the Protectors of the Fatherland (*Pashtpan Hayreneats'*), which was formed in 1881 in Erzurum. Its aim was to protect the Armenians of Erzurum from potential attacks by Turks, Kurds and Circassians. When their activities were discovered by the Ottoman authorities, they were arrested and put on trial. In the words of one historian, 'never before had so large a group of men, coming from various ranks of the Armenian population, been placed on trial for political reasons'.[3] The revolutionary activities of these and other societies aimed at defending their Armenian compatriots in the eastern provinces of the empire, in which living conditions had become unbearable due to plundering and persecution. Although these minor groups were short-lived, they played an important role in the emergence of more organized Armenian revolutionary groups, the first of which was the Armenakan Organization.

After the treaties of San Stefano and Berlin of 1878, the second phase of the Armenian revolutionary movement began. This was mainly due to the failure of diplomatic means to remedy the deteriorating situation of Armenians in the eastern provinces. The Russo-Turkish War of 1877–8, which led to a disastrous defeat of the Ottoman troops, ended with the Treaty of San Stefano on 3 March 1878. Armenian hopes rose during this period, as Article 16 of the treaty stipulated that the Russian forces occupying the Armenian-populated provinces in the eastern Ottoman Empire would withdraw contingent on full implementation of reforms:

> As the evacuation of the Russian troops of the territory they occupy in Armenia, and which is to be restored to Turkey, might give rise to conflicts and complications detrimental to the maintenance of good relations between the two countries, the Sublime Porte engages to carry into effect, without further delay, the improvements and reforms demanded by local requirements in the provinces inhabited by the Armenians and to guarantee their security from Kurds and Circassians.[4]

However, because of Great Britain's objections to the terms of this treaty, the Russians were forced to sign a new one, the Treaty of Berlin, on 13 July 1878. Its main aim was to prevent the rising movement of Pan-Slavism and to curtail Russian influence in the region; both Berlin and Vienna were concerned that the Pan-Slavic movement would incite the Slavic nationalities in the Austro-Hungarian Empire. Article 16 was thus altered to Article 61, which also stipulated the removal of all Russian forces from the region that they had occupied after the Russo-Turkish War but did not include an effective enforcement mechanism for the reforms:

> The Sublime Porte undertakes to carry out, without further delay, the improvements and reforms demanded by local requirements in the provinces inhabited by Armenians, and to guarantee their security against the Circassians and Kurds. It

will periodically make known the steps taken to this effect to the powers, who will superintend their application.⁵

Efforts by the Armenian leadership to raise national and international awareness of the Armenian plight in the eastern provinces proved to be in vain. Even with the stipulations of the Berlin Treaty's Article 61, the condition of the Armenians did not improve; on the contrary, depredations by Kurdish and Circassian tribesmen multiplied.⁶ Consequently, a major ideological shift occurred within the Armenian communities of Anatolia and the Armenian Highland in general – and the Armenian intelligentsia in the Caucasus in particular – that led to the emergence of multiple well-organized and sophisticated revolutionary groups. This begs the question: why would the birthplace of revolutionary ideology be the Caucasus and not in the western part of the Ottoman Empire such as Constantinople or Izmir? To understand this, we need to analyse the political and socioeconomic environment in which the Armenians of the Caucasus were living in.

A revolutionary movement cannot exist without a strong intellectual group that moulds and shapes its ideology, as evidenced by the critical role played by the intelligentsia in the revolutionary movements that emerged around the globe in the eighteenth and nineteenth centuries, from the French and the Haitian revolutions to the Serbian and Greek revolutions. In the case of the Armenians, the intelligentsia was formed in two distinct regions. One of them emerged in the western Ottoman Empire, in cities such as Constantinople, whereas the other emerged in the Caucasus. These groups were influenced by different currents. The former group was educated in Western cities such as Paris and Geneva. Their primary aim was to create a more progressive leadership in Asia Minor; they were more moderate and did not believe in the use of violence to improve the situation of Armenians in the eastern provinces. In contrast, the latter group was influenced by Russian political and ideological movements and used violent means to pressure the Ottoman government to implement much-needed reforms.

The Armenian intelligentsia in the Russian Empire took an active interest in the condition of their compatriots in Anatolia.⁷ Intellectual figures such as Khachatur Apovian, Raffi (Hagop Melik Der Hagopian), and Mikael Nalbandian discussed the plight of the Turkish Armenians in their writings and established connections with them. The young Armenian activists and intellectuals in Russia were involved in revolutionary organizations such as *Zemlya i Volya* (Land and Freedom) and *Narodnaya Volya* (People's Will). But as the situation in Turkish Armenia worsened, they shifted their focus to the Armenians of the Ottoman Empire. Figures such as Khrimian Hayrig, with his journal *Artzvi Vaspourakani* (Eagle of Vaspourakan), also influenced Russian-Armenian intellectuals to dedicate themselves to the plight of the Armenians of the eastern provinces. The Armenians of Russia thus shifted their allegiance from the *v Narod* (to the People) movement to *Dēpi Yerkir* (To the Homeland). For Russian-Armenian intellectuals and activists, Western Armenia (*Hayastan*) became the homeland, and the plight of its Armenian inhabitants was their main concern. Members of the intelligentsia were sent to Turkish Armenia to study the situation on the ground.

Armenian intellectuals had first-hand encounters with Russian thought and socialism in St. Petersburg and Moscow. Moscow's Lazarian Institute turned into the intellectual hub for the Armenians of Russia. Many of the Armenian students of Moscow and St. Petersburg became the leaders of the major Armenian revolutionary movements. In addition to the Lazarian Institute, the Nersesian Academy in Tiflis and the Gevorgian Academy in Etchmiadzin also played important roles in preparing a new generation of intelligentsia. Undoubtedly, the Bulgarian revolution of 1876 inspired the modus operandi of the Armenian revolutionaries and intellectuals in the Caucasus. Socialism as an ideology had a tremendous impact on the intelligentsia and on some of the revolutionary groups. The Armenian students of Moscow were imbued with socialist ideologies, which they expressed in their publications.

The radicalization of the Russian Armenians was also motivated by the drastic shift in the Russian government's policies towards them.[8] The Russian *Polozhenie* (Statute) of 1836 acknowledged the institutional autonomy of the Armenian Church and granted it control over education, much like the *millet* system in the Ottoman Empire. With these privileges, Armenians were considered a religious group. Since the state provided physical security and allowed for economic progress, Armenians identified with the Russian state during this period. A Russophile intellectual current also emerged among the Armenians of the Caucasus; for example, Grigor Artsruni, through his newspaper *Mshak* (Tiller), published in Tiflis from 1872 to 1920, aggressively promoted pro-Russian policies among the Armenians.[9] Such groups placed high hopes on the Russian state to save their Christian Armenian brothers in the eastern Ottoman provinces. However, with the assassination of Alexander II in 1881, the conservative flank in Russia rose to power and reversed the liberal policies of their predecessors. Thus, under Russia's last two tsars, Armenians were considered subversive, and their loyalty came under question.[10] As a result of Russification policies, the Viceroy of the Caucasus, Dondukov-Korsakov, ordered the closure of all Armenian parochial schools in 1885. The policy of the Russian state towards the Armenians further deteriorated in 1903, when the government of Nicholas II (1894–1917) seized the Armenian Church properties, leading most Armenians to rally behind the ARF. In Ronald Suny's words, 'For Russians the image of the brother Christian had been effectively replaced by the image of a villainous conspirator who in his fury would undermine both the Ottoman and the Romanov monarchies.'[11] Armenian intellectuals such as Kriastapor Mikaelian (one of the founders of the ARF) protested the confiscation of the properties of the Armenian Church and began printing anti-Tsarist pamphlets.

The anti-Armenian policies strengthened Armenian ethnic boundaries and radicalized the intellectual movement. The result of this was the emergence of multiple groups, chief among which was the Young Armenia Society (*Eritasard Hayastan*), established in Tiflis in 1889 under the leadership of Kriastapor Mikaelian. Its prime objective was to send volunteers to Turkish Armenia to take punitive actions against those who were persecuting Armenians. Within a year the Young Armenia Society, along with other revolutionary groups, became embedded in the Federation of Armenian Revolutionaries (FAR), founded in 1890 in Tiflis.

The roots of the Hnchakian Revolutionary Party go back to the Armenakan Organization (1885–96), established in Van by Mgrdich Portukalian. The government banished Portukalian due to his activities in Van. In 1885 he departed the Ottoman Empire for Marseille, where he began publishing *Armēnia*. The journal aimed to bring international attention to the plight of the Armenians of the eastern provinces, assistance to the Armenians and spread the ideas of the journal and its editor among Armenians.[12] One of the major aims of the Armenakan Organization was to protect the Armenians of the eastern provinces from the depredations inflicted by the Kurds. The party established branches in Trebizond, Bitlis and Moush, among other places.

One of the main founders of the Hnchakian Revolutionary Party, Avetis Nazarbekian, was a frequent contributor to the journal *Armēnia*. A son of a wealthy family, Nazarbekian was born in Tabriz, Iran. He studied at St. Petersburg and the Sorbonne and established close contacts with the Russian socialist Georgi Plekhanov and the Emancipation of Labor group, which was founded in Geneva in 1883. He translated the works of Plekhanov, as well as those of Karl Marx and Friedrich Engels, into Armenian. His fiancée Maro Vardanian was a member of a secret Russian revolutionary group.[13] Due to political difficulties she fled the Russian Empire to Paris, where she met Nazarbekian. In Geneva they met four Russian students – Rupen Khan-Azad, Gabriel Kafian, Nikoli Matinian and Mgrdich Manucharian – with whom they formed the Hnchakian Revolutionary Party.

The situation between Nazarbekian and Portukalian deteriorated when the latter refused to cooperate with the former, and the students decided to act alone.[14] In 1886, only six members remained in the Geneva group when some broke off relations. Those remaining were Nazarbekian and Vardanian (Paris), Kriastapor Ohanian and Gevorg Gharajian (Montpellier) and Khan-Azad and Kafian (Geneva). The group severed their relations with Portukalian through a pamphlet written by Nazarbekian called 'Armenian Eating Chameleon' (*Hayaker K'amelyon*).[15] Furthermore, they decided to publish their own paper, called *Hnch'ak* (Bell) after Alexander Herzen's *Kolokol* (Bell). In the same year, the Geneva students drafted a plan for the organization, which became the programme of the Hnchakian Revolutionary Party.[16] In 1890 the party became known by that name. The seven official founders were Nazarbekian, Vardanian, Khan-Azad, Gharajian, Ohanian, Kafian and Levon Stepanian.

The programme, which was influenced by both Marxism and Russian populism, discussed the necessity of tackling the worsening situation of the Armenians through revolution and the establishment of a new order based on 'economic truth, socialist justice, equality, and freedom'.[17] The programme described the current political as well as economic situation in Turkish Armenia (*T'urk'ats' Hayastan*) as slavish.[18] According to the programme, in order to bring the Armenians out of this miserable situation and put them on the path to a socialist order – which would be the final objective – it was essential 'to achieve in Turkish Armenia a broad democratic political freedom and national independence, which will be the immediate objective'.[19] After the implementation of the *immediate object*, the programme dealt with the *final objective*. This included the formation of a legislative assembly, broad provincial autonomy, extensive communal autonomy, the right of every individual to hold office regardless of background, freedom of speech and press, and universal military service. The programme also addressed economic aims such as progressive taxation, as well as compulsory universal education.[20] These objectives would be reached through revolution, of which Turkish Armenia would be the arena.[21]

The activities were summarized in the following points: *propaganda* (to spread the idea of revolution among people), *agitation* (to raise the fallen spirit of the people and incite them against the enemy), *terror* (to protect the people when they are suffering persecution), *organization* (to create one large organization consisting of many revolutionary societies), *terroristic-martial organization, establishment of a large revolutionary organization among the peasants, establishment of a large revolutionary organization among the workers* and *establishment of martial-rebellious organization both among the workers and the peasants*.[22] The programme argued that the right moment to revolt was when Turkey was engaged in a war.[23]

From its first issue, published in November of 1887,[24] *Hnch'ak* exhorted the Armenians to spread revolutionary activities and called on them to join the party. The newspaper was published in secrecy, and copies were smuggled into the Ottoman Empire and Russia. With its socialist principles, *Hnch'ak* drew the criticism of both the Armenian bourgeoisie and the clergy in both the Ottoman Empire and the Caucasus. Indeed, they despised all the revolutionary groups as a disruption of the status quo. They preferred stability in order to protect their interests and chose to work with the imperial systems.[25] This stance attracted the ire of the revolutionary movement.

The centre of the Hnchaks' organization became Constantinople. They also established branches in the eastern part of the empire in cities such as Tokat, Marsovan, Mersin, Diyarbekir, Arapgir, Amasia, Trebizond, Aintab and Cairo.[26] The party also expanded to Europe, the Caucasus, North and South America and the Balkans.[27] The Hnchaks' activity in Persia was limited, as the situation of Armenians there was better than that of the Ottoman and the Russian Empires, but they were active in cities such as Tabriz, Anzali and Tehran, and played an active role during the Iranian Constitutional Revolution (1905–11).[28]

The Hnchaks' first major event was a demonstration at Kumkapı on 27 July 1890, which aimed at attracting European attention to the plight of the Armenians in the eastern provinces.[29] The demonstration resulted in skirmishes with the police that led to a number of deaths on both sides. Despite its failure of the demonstration, the Hnchaks believed that it succeeded in bringing the attention of the European powers to the plight of the Armenians.[30] Other important events included the placards (*yafta*) incident in Anatolia in 1893,[31] the Sasun rebellion of August 1894 against the nomadic Kurdish tribes and government tax collectors, and the Zeytun rebellion of 1895.[32]

The Hnchaks considered the Sasun rebellion a great triumph that brought European attention to the 'Armenian Question'. It resulted in the 11 May 1895, memorandum sent by Great Britain, Russia, and France to Sultan Abdülhamid II, urging him to implement reforms in the Armenian provinces.[33] However, the unwillingness of the sultan to take any measures led the party to stage the Bab-ı Ali demonstration in Constantinople on 30 September 1895. The Hnchak leadership decided that the demonstration should have a peaceful nature. Garo Sahakian, its leader, was supposed to present a petition to the sultan on behalf of the Armenian population of Constantinople and the six Armenian provinces demanding implementation of civil liberties, the right to bear arms, the rehabilitation of Sasun and an end to Kurdish migration, the recruitment of Armenians to the police and gendarmes, and the territorial redrawing of the six Armenian provinces.³⁴ However, after arriving at the gates of Bab-ı Ali, Sahakian was arrested together with hundreds of demonstrators. Fighting broke out, leading to rioting and bloodshed. The event led the European powers to further pressure the sultan to sign the Armenian Reform Program, which he did on 17 October 1895. Once more, the Hnchaks considered the demonstration a victory.³⁵

The party's largest activity in the Ottoman Empire was the Zeytun rebellion on 12 October 1895.³⁶ The Hnchaks hoped that the rebellion would have a domino effect throughout Cilicia.³⁷ After four months of fierce fighting, the rebellion ended on 1 February 1896, due to the European powers' formulation of peace terms that were accepted by the Porte.³⁸ But like the May Reform Program following the Sasun rebellion, those terms remained mere ink on paper.

As we have seen, a consistent aim of the party was to bring European attention to the Armenian plight in order to trigger a humanitarian intervention. However, such an intervention never took place. Europeans, busy with their own political calculations, were content to sacrifice the Armenians for their national interests.

Another major factor that weakened the party was an internal rift. The primary causes of this rift were disagreements on the issue of socialism and over the tactics pursued by the party. After numerous attempts by the party to bring European attention to the Armenian cause, many members maintained that Europeans had abandoned the Armenian Question due to Hnchak's adoption of socialism. They demanded that the party exclude socialism from its programme and concentrate solely on the independence of Armenia. They also accused Nazarbekian of inciting violence through his articles. This rift resulted in the emergence of pro-Nazarbekian and anti-Nazarbekian factions. While the latter aimed at removing the socialist doctrine from the party, the former backed its inclusion. In 1898 the anti-Nazarbekian faction met in Egypt and formed a new party called the Reformed Hnchakian Party (*Verakazmyal Hnch'akean*).³⁹ The original Hnchakian party maintained its socialist doctrine but abandoned the tactic of public demonstration due to its futility. The tensions between these two factions took an ugly turn when members of both parties began assassinating each other in the United States, London and the Caucasus during and after the Fourth Hnchakian Party Congress, which was held in London in 1901–2.⁴⁰ There is no doubt that the rift weakened the party and led to the rise of the ARF as the dominant Armenian political party.

Socialism and nationalism

As already discussed, the two main objectives of the Hnchak programme were the independence of Turkish Armenia and the establishment of a socialist order, which made them unique among political parties. One can see the strong influence of the Russian Narodnik ideology, such as that put forward by *Narodnaya Volya* (Peoples' Will). This should not come as a surprise, as most of the members were born and educated in Russia and well versed in Russian revolutionary ideology. They were on good terms with Russian Social Democrats G. V. Plekhanov and Vera Zasulich, who were members of *Zemlya i Volya* (Land and Liberty) and *Chornyi Peredel* (Black Partition). In the words of Hagop Turabian (Varaztad) a prominent Hnchak member:

> The founders and the theorists of the Hentchakist Party were all Marxists, who were consequently convinced that the emancipation of the working and producing classes, which form the great majority of mankind, can only be complete when the workers and producers themselves become the owners of all the forces and means of production. The emancipation of the producing classes must, therefore, mean the emancipation of every man and woman, that is to say, the complete social and economic freedom of humanity from the yoke of the capitalist class, which, though it forms the minority, yet oppresses the majority.[41]

The programme of the Hnchakian Revolutionary Party was both socialist and nationalist. As seen earlier, the party believed that through revolution the exploited class would emerge victorious. However, its dedication to socialism not only resulted in the rift within the party but also became an obstacle to uniting with the ARF. The tension between socialism and nationalism that troubled the Armenian revolutionary movement could not be resolved.

Before emerging as the ARF, or Dashnaks, the party was a merger of different revolutionary groups in Russia called the Federation of Armenian Revolutionaries (FAR). It was only in 1892 that the party came to be known as the ARF. While some of the parties of this merger were purely nationalist and aimed solely at the liberation of Turkish Armenia, others believed in socialism as an important component of the FAR; these were the socialist revolutionaries who were influenced by Russian political thought and were followers and members of the Hnchakian Revolutionary Party. The delegates of these different parties met in Tiflis to discuss compromises. In his memoirs, Rupen Khan-Azad says that there were five major issues confronting the delegates. The most important of these were socialism as the objective, the party's official journal and the name of the new party.[42]

The Hnchakians were adamant that socialism should be a primary doctrine of the newly formed Federation. However, while two of the founders of the ARF – Kristapor Mikaelian and Simon Zavarian – shared a commitment to socialism, the same could not be said about the others.[43] In order to satisfy Khan-Azad, they were able to include socialist doctrine in the manifesto of the FAR, but only indirectly. Khan-Azad accepted the compromise, but the Hnchak headquarters in Geneva demanded the direct mention of socialist doctrine. Eventually an agreement was reached whereby the Hnchakian Revolution Party would dissolve itself and become an integral part of the Federation. However, this agreement did not last six months, as former Hnchaks became dissatisfied with their treatment by the Dashnaks.[44] It became evident that the Federation was controlled by an anti-socialist and anti-Nazarbekian group. On 18 May 1891, the Hnchakian Revolutionary Party severed its ties with the FAR.[45]

From the perspective of Hnchaks, socialism was not confined to the Armenians of the Ottoman Empire but included those of Russia and Iran. They firmly believed in a world revolution that would establish a social order on the global level. The party was a member of the second international and participated in the Sixth International Socialist

Congress held in Amsterdam from 14–18 August 1904, where it was represented by Plekhanov, a member of the Russian Socialist Democratic delegation. The Hnchaks took part in other socialist activities prior to the Sixth Congress as well, such as the German Socialist Party convention that took place in Dresden in 1902.

The Hnchaks before and after the Young Turk revolution

Unlike the ARF, the Hnchakian Revolutionary Party maintained a consistent policy towards the Young Turks and their main political party, the CUP (Committee of Union and Progress) in both the pre-and post-Revolutionary periods. Although an informal meeting was initiated in Paris between Stepan Sabah-Gulian, one of the Hnchak leaders, and the Young Turk leader Ahmet Rıza, it went nowhere due to the ideological discrepancies between the parties.[46] The Hnchaks did not trust the Young Turks and did not want to cooperate with them due to their policies. They did not participate in the 1902 Paris Congress of the Ottoman Liberals, nor the Second Congress of Ottoman Opposition Parties in Paris in 1907.

The Hnchaks greeted the Young Turk revolution with great reservation.[47] During the Sixth Congress of the party, which was convened in Constantinople on 12 July 1909, the party decided 'to operate within Turkey on legal grounds, as long as the working people are not robbed of their modern legal rights'.[48] It was during this Congress that the party adopted its new name: the Social Democrat Hnchakian Party (SDHP). They were suspicious about the real intentions of the Young Turks. The Adana Massacres of 1909, during which more than 20,000 Armenians were killed, proved to them that their suspicions were justified.[49] They were very critical of the ARF for signing a cooperation agreement with the Young Turks in the post-massacre period. The Hnchakians cooperated with the Freedom and Accord Party (*Hürriyet ve İtilaf Fırkası*), who were opponents of the CUP.

The SDHP changed its course of operation after the Balkan Wars of 1912–13. The Ottoman Empire lost more than 90 per cent of its possessions in the Balkans, which resulted in a drastic change in the CUP's policy towards Armenians and Greeks. From 1913 until the end of the First World War, the CUP engaged in a radicalized programme of demographic engineering aimed at the homogenization of Anatolia by eliminating its Armenian and Greek inhabitants.

In its Seventh Congress, held in Constanța, Rumania, in 1913, the SDHP decided 'to engage only in illegal activity per its principles, and hence fight a partisan war until more suitable political and economic conditions prevail'.[50] The congress decided to fight the CUP in an attempt to 'completely crush and topple it'.[51] They also adhered to the idea of an 'Autonomous Armenia'. It was probably during this congress that a decision was taken to assassinate the leaders of CUP. A member of the SDHP by the name of Artur Yasian betrayed the party by informing the authorities about this secret decision.[52] Consequently, when the SDHP held its third convention in Constantinople at the beginning of the First World War, all the important leaders of the party were arrested and put in detention on 28 April 1915. On 27 May, twenty-two members were condemned to death, two of whom (Stepan Sabah-Gulian and Varaztad (Hagop

Figure I.1 Kevork Chekmeyan, a Hnchak *fedayee* from Marash (from the private archives of the editor).

Turabian)) were sentenced in absentia. On 15 June 1915, the other twenty were hanged in the Sultan Beyazit Square of Constantinople, including major leaders such as Paramaz, Murat of Bitlis, Aram Achekbashian and Dr. Benne (Torosian).[53] The other prominent Hnchak leader, Hampartsoum Boyajian (Murat), along with all other Armenian intellectuals, was arrested on 24 April 1915 and hanged in Kayseri on 31 July of the same year.

During the Armenian Genocide, the SDHP mounted a resistance in the region of Cilicia and Cappadocia.[54] In addition, they took part in the volunteer movement, maintaining their own regiment. The Armenian Genocide, which led to the annihilation of the Armenian population in the interior of the empire, was a huge blow to the SDHP, as it was to all Armenian parties.

The SDHP played a minimal role in the establishment of the First Republic of Armenia (1918–20). Despite this, the members of the party took part in the Battle of Sardarabad in 1918 defending the Armenian capital of Yerevan from the invading Turkish army. The SDHP cooperated with the ARF during the short-lived Republic. During its Eighth Congress in 1924, the party accepted Soviet Armenia as 'the realization of the goal we have pursued for thirty-eight years', and decided to support the Soviet Republic 'without reservation'.[55] However, cooperation with the Communist International did not yield any results.[56] Hence, like the other traditional parties, the SDHP became a party of the Armenian Diaspora.

Unlike the ARF, which opposed the Armenian SSR, the SDHP remained loyal to the Republic and supported its development. The antagonism between the parties was reflected in the schism in the Armenian Church; while the ARF supported the Cilician See, the SDHP supported that of Etchmiadzin. These tensions, which were also part of the Cold War, sometimes became violent. For example, during the 1958 Lebanese crisis, fighting erupted between the parties that led to the death of a score of members on both sides. However, during the Lebanese Civil War (1975–90) the parties resolved their differences and together defended the Armenian community.

When Armenia became independent in 1991, the SDHP again set foot in the Republic. Yeghia Najarian led the SDHP in Armenia and founded its official organ *Hnch'ak Hayastani*. During the Karabagh Conflict in the 1990s, the SDHP formed two battalions: *Paramaz* and *Jirair-Mourad*. While the latter took part in the Karabagh War, the former took part in defending Zangezur.

* * *

The historiography on the SDHP in English is slim. Its history has always been discussed under the shadow of the ARF and its activities in the Russian, Ottoman and Persian Empires.[57] Besides the recently published book by Abel Manoukian, no academic work exists in English that discusses the history of the party in its totality.[58] Indeed, writing a book on the topic is challenging because – unlike the ARF – the SDHP did not leave behind a major archive. In addition, historians have thus far relied on sources from a single linguistic context, whether it be Armenian, Ottoman or European. However, with the recent development in historiography, new scholars have emerged who are able to use all of these languages and sources in writing the history of the Armenian revolutionary movement.

This volume fills three major gaps that exist within the historiography of the Hnchakian Party: reassessment of the history of the SDHP and its relation to the other revolutionary movements; writing the history of the party from a regional perspective; and an analysis of the ideology of the party in the larger national, regional and global contexts.

So far, the history of the SDHP has been written in the context of Armenian history by relying mostly on Armenian primary sources. By doing so most historians have removed the history of the SDHP from its Russian, Ottoman, Iranian and European milieus that shaped much of the Armenian revolutionary movements in the second half of the nineteenth century. Furthermore, these scholars have followed the same teleological trajectory in writing the history of the party: the birth of the party, its main actors and its major achievements.

The articles in this first section deviate from the traditional way of representing the party and concentrate more on the discussion of critical issues within the historiography such as revisiting the original dates of the foundation of the party; the SDHP's relations with other Armenian revolutionary parties; its role in the other Ottoman opposition groups; and its stance during the First World War.

In the past decade, more scholars of Ottoman and Armenian history have been concentrating on regional and local studies to better understand the ways in which sociopolitical, religious and economic transformations taking place in the empire in the nineteenth century have affected Armenians of the provinces of the empire. For example, a new wave of young scholars began examining the impact of the Tanzimat reforms on the Armenians of the eastern provinces. Even the phase of the Hamidian massacres (1894–96) that has been understudied in the Ottoman/Turkish and Armenian historiographies has begun to attract the attention of young scholars. However, regional and local studies of the Armenian revolutionary movements are still in their infancy. The following volume, by concentrating on a few regions in central and eastern Anatolia and the Diaspora, attempts to fill this gap. Of course, the volume does not cover the activities of the SDHP in all the provinces and the diasporic communities, but the examples covered in this volume demonstrate a more complex picture of the activities of the Armenian revolutionary movements in general and that of the SDHP in particular. The activities of the latter in the eastern provinces were based on local and regional exegesis as well as on the socioeconomic and political transformations in the three empires (Ottoman, Russian and Persian).[59] The articles demonstrate how the activities of revolutionary movements in the region were conditioned by the policies of local, central and international actors. Similarly, the activities of the SDHP in the Armenian Diaspora were contingent on the activities or lack thereof of the other Armenian political or philanthropic organizations. From cooperation with to total opposition to other Armenian organizations, the SDHP navigated through the complex diasporic politics in the post-genocide period in order to mark its stamp on communal affairs ranging from establishing educational institutions to aiding the arriving Armenian refugees.

The last section of the volume addresses the ideological tribulations experienced by the Armenian revolutionary movements. So far most of the studies on their ideology tend to concentrate on the ARF.[60] There is a lacuna in researching the ideological underpinnings of the SDHP in relation to their constituents as well as to other Armenian and non-Armenian political/revolutionary parties. This volume expands on these discussions by analysing the ways in which these parties perceived socialism, Marxism, nationalism, among other ideological currents. Through these studies it becomes evident that the intellectual elite of the SDHP was well versed in the raging ideological currents in Russia and Europe, and tried to adopt them for their goals whether it was through liberating the Armenians of the eastern provinces from the 'Ottoman Yoke' or establish an egalitarian society based on the principles of socialism. However, adopting multiple ideologies at the same time contradicted the vision that these parties were striving to reach. While for some, ideologies seemed to be utopian, for others they were too radical. Others also believed that nationalism and socialism, two opposing ideologies, could be reconciled in order to remedy the condition of the Armenians of the eastern provinces. The ideological factors also demonstrate the wide gap that had existed between the theoreticians/intellectuals/leaders of the party and the agents on the ground who were more realist and had a better understanding of the presiding condition of the Armenians in the eastern provinces. This contradiction gradually became counterproductive, hampering the activities of the party.

Thus, the articles in this volume help us better understand the history of the SDHP not only from an Armenian perspective, but also from Ottoman, Middle Eastern, Russian, Caucasian and European ones. The book is divided into three sections.

Section I deals with the history of the SDHP from its inception to the First Republic of Armenia (1918–20). The first article in this section, by Abel Manoukian, discusses the formative year of the party through an in-depth analysis of a photographic image of the founders. Against the commonly held view that the Hnchakian Revolutionary Party was established in 1887, Manoukian argues that the Hnchakian party as a political group was already formed in 1886 under the name of a 'revolutionary society'. The second article in this section, by Garabet Moumdjian, concerns the relations between the SDHP and the Young Turks in Europe from 1895 to 1909. Moumdjian discusses in detail the ways in which the Hnchaks viewed the Young Turks' nationalist tendencies as a major threat to the future of Armenians in the empire. This was taking place while the SDHP suffered the internal rift that weakened the party. From the beginning, the SDHP was against the idea that Armenians should enter any alliance with the CUP. After the 1908 revolution the SDHP decided to cooperate with the opposition (the Freedom and Accord Party). The third article, by Yeghig Djeredjian, discusses the position of the SDHP in the post-Revolutionary period until the First World War. Through an in-depth analysis of the congresses and the conventions of the party during this period, Djeredjian demonstrates how the deterioration of the internal political situation in the empire and the radicalization of the Young Turks' attitude towards the Armenians resulted in a drastic shift of the SDHP's policy from legal to illegal activism. In shedding light on the atmosphere in 1914, Djeredjian discloses a confidential letter written by Hnchak leader Sabah-Gulian to Paramaz (Matteos Sarkissian), in which the former reveals the activities of Artur Yasian and other spies of the CUP in Cairo who were on a mission to hunt SDHP members down and to topple the Khedive and his government. The letter also discusses the Hnchaks' plans to weaken and overthrow the CUP. In the final article in this section, Richard Hovannisian argues that the SDHP did not play a significant role during the First Armenian Republic (1918–20). The party was highly critical of the government and its policies. Hovannisian demonstrates the SDHP's anti-Bolshevik stance during this period, and how the SDHP collaborated with the ARF against the Bolshevik challenge. However, when Armenia was defeated and came under the control of the Soviet Union, the SDHP accommodated the new Republic.

Section II, entitled Regional and Local Histories, starts with an article by Toygun Altıntaş on the Hnchak pamphleteering in Central Anatolia. By focusing on a particular region, Altıntaş's chapter highlights the local, regional, imperial and international dynamics of the revolutionary organization. The chapter decenters the role and involvement of the central committee in the administration of the Hnchakian Revolutionary Party in Central Anatolia. In addition, it discusses venues used by the Hnchak opposition other than violence. The second article, by Varak Ketsemanian, concentrates on patterns of violence in Sasun in the years 1890–4. Ketsemanian integrates the socioeconomic background in the political and intellectual history of the Armenian revolutionary movement in the last decade of the nineteenth century. He problematizes our understanding of violence as solely a manifestation of nationalism and demonstrates the local context in which violence was shaped and transformed. The third article in this section, by Ümit Kurt, discusses the extensive activities of the Hnchakian Revolutionary Party in the region and the city of Aintab. Through deconstructing the organizational framework of the party, he demonstrates how the party became a force to be reckoned with during the post-Revolutionary period, and how it played an important role in resettling the Armenian refugees after the Armenian Genocide. Furthermore, he demonstrates the strong resistance put on by the Hnchak Revolutionaries against the Kemalist assault. The fourth article in this section, by Vahram Shemmassian, discusses the impact of the SDHP on Musa Dagh. Through detailed research, Shemmassian shows how the party sought to raise the national awareness of the local inhabitants, arm them and prepare them for potential confrontation with the local authorities in order to attract European attention. Shemmassian concentrates on the role of Aghasi (Garabed Tursarkisian), who was sent to Musa Dagh as a regional agent to prepare the ground for armed struggle. The final article in this section, by Vartan Matiossian, discusses the activities of the SDHP in South America in the post-genocide period. Concentrating on the Armenian communities of Argentina, Uruguay and Brazil, he analyses three major fields of activities: institutional work, ideological struggle around Soviet Armenia, and power struggle within the community. He demonstrates how the bipolarity of the Cold War was reflected in the Armenian communities in South America.

Section III deals with different aspects of the SDHP's ideology. The first article, by Gerard Libaridian, analyses three of the major paradoxes relating to the early years of the SDHP. He argues that these paradoxes explain the fissure between the *weltanschauung* of the founders of the party and the significance of that world view to Western Armenian/Eastern Ottoman realities, to the Church and to Marxist ideology. The second article, by Gaïdz Minassian, compares the ideologies of the SDHP and the ARF. His article discusses the forces of attraction and repulsion that linked the formation of both parties in the age of modernity. Minassian demonstrates that the comparative approach to the SDHP and the ARF is not artificial but has been going on since the inception of both parties. He demonstrates how the parties constitute two distinct but parallel itineraries. The third article in this section, by Yaşar Tolga Cora, deals with the newspaper *Kaytz*, which was the organ of the Constantinople Students' Union of the SDHP (*SDHK Polsoy Usanoghakan Miut'iwn*). Through an analysis of the newspaper in its first two years, Cora demonstrates how *Kaytz*, with its strong socialist flavour, developed a new terminology to explain the socialist system. He demonstrates how, using neologisms, *Kaytz* contributed to the development of language in its science articles. In the fourth article, Kadir Akin interrogates the Turkish leftist ideology and decries the absence of the SDHP from the history of the Turkish left. Akin demonstrates how the socialism propagated by the SDHP has been denied not only by mainstream historiography but also in the history of Turkish socialism. Akin implicates here the Turkish left in the uprooting of Armenians from the collective memory of socialism.

The articles in this volume, based on new research, shed light on the history of the SDHP from different perspectives. The articles open the door to more research in the future, with the hope of situating the Hnchakian history in the larger debates around socialism, populism and nationalism. The SDHP was not only an Armenian party but had a global outlook regarding socialism and Marxism. It is the hope of the editor of this volume that the contents will encourage scholars to examine the SDHP more closely, not only from the angle of history but from that of the social sciences.

Notes

1. In 1890 the official name of the organization was the Hnchakian Revolutionary Party. In 1905 the name changed to the Hnchakian Social Democrat Party, and in 1909 the name changed to the current Social Democrat Hnchakian Party (SDHP).
2. For a latest study on the Armenian revolutionary movement in the Ottoman Empire, Russia and Iran, see Houri Berberian, *Roving Revolutionaries: Armenians and the Connected Revolutions in the Russian, Iranian, and Ottoman Worlds* (Berkeley: University of California Press, 2019).
3. Louis Nalbandian, *The Armenian Revolutionary Movement: The Development of Armenian Political Parties Through the Nineteenth Century* (Berkeley: University of California Press, 1963), 89.
4. Gustave Rolin-Jaequemyns, *Armenia, the Armenians, and the Treaties* (London, Manchester: John Heywood, 1891), 34.
5. Jacob Hurewitz, *Diplomacy in the Near and Middle East: A Documentary Record 1535–1956*, vol. I (Princeton: Van Nostrand, 1956), 190.
6. Richard G. Hovannisian, 'The Armenian Question in the Ottoman Empire, 1876–1914', in *The Armenian People from Ancient to Modern Times*, ed. Richard G. Hovannisian, vol. II (New York: St. Martin's Press, 1997), 212.
7. On Armenians of Russia in the nineteenth century, see Stephen Badalyan Riegg, *Russia's Entangled Embrace: The Tsarist Empire and the Armenians, 1801–1914* (Ithaca: Cornell University Press, 2020).
8. On the drastic change of the Russian policy towards the Armenians, see Riegg, *Russia's Entangled Embrace*, 162–98.
9. Ronald Grigor Suny, *Looking Toward Ararat: Armenia in Modern History* (Bloomington: Indiana University Press, 1993), 41.
10. Ibid., 26.
11. Ibid., 46.
12. On the aims and the direction of *Armēnia*, see *Haytararutʻiwn: Armēnia, Hayerēn Lragir* (Announcement: Armenia, Armenian Journal), 18 June 1885, 1–4.
13. Arsen Gidur, *Patmutʻiwn S.D. Hnchʻakean Kusaktsʻutʻean*, vol. I (Beirut: Tparan Shirak, 1962), 29.
14. Rupen Khan-Azad, 'Hay Heghapʻokhakani mě Husheritsʻ', *Hayrenikʻ Amsagir* V, no. 8 (56) (June 1927): 71.
15. Ibid. See also Gidur, *Patmutʻiwn S.D. Hnchʻakean Kusaktsʻutʻean*, vol. I, 30.
16. Rupen Khan-Azad argues that those who drafted the programme represented two currents: *narodnovoltsy* and Marxism. See Khan-Azad, 'Hay Heghapʻokhakani mě Husheritsʻ', *Hayrenikʻ Amsagir* V, no. 8 (57) (27 July 1927): 54.
17. *Hnchʻak*, October–November, 1888, 2. On the platform of the party, see 'Sōtsʻialistakan Dēmokratakan Hnchʻakean Kusaktsʻutʻiwn', in *Tsragir Hnchʻakean Kusaktsʻutʻean*, 3rd ed. (London: Tparan Hnchʻak, 1897). For information about the party, see Anahide Ter Minassian, *Nationalism and Socialism in the Armenian Revolutionary Movement* (Cambridge, MA: Zoryan Institute, 1984); and Anahide Ter Minassian,

'The Role of the Armenian Community in the Foundation and Development of the Socialist Movement in the Ottoman Empire and Turkey, 1876–1923', in *Socialism and Nationalism in the Ottoman Empire 1876–1923*, eds. Mete Tunçay and Erik Jan Zürcher (London: I. B. Tauris, 1994, in association with the International Institute of Social History, Amsterdam), 109–56.
18 Khan-Azad, 'Hay Heghap'okhakani mě Husherits', 55–7.
19 *Hnchʻak*, October–November, 1888, 3.
20 Ibid., 3–4.
21 Ibid., 4.
22 Ibid., 5.
23 Ibid., 4–5. See also Hagop Turabian, 'The Armenian Social-Democratic Hentchakist Party, Part III', *Ararat* 3, no. 37 (July 1916): 35.
24 On the publication of the newspaper see Rupen Khan-Azad, 'Hay Heghap'okhakani mě Husherits', 61.
25 Ter Minassian, *Nationalism and Socialism in the Armenian Revolutionary Movement*, 20.
26 See Houri Berberian, *The Love for Freedom Has No Fatherland: Armenians and the Iranian Constitutional Revolution of 1905-1911* (Boulder: Westview Press, 2001) and Gidur, *Patmutʻiwn S.D. Hnchʻakean Kusaktsʻutʻean*, vol. I, 64–81.
27 For branches of the SDHP in the United States and Canada, See Gidur, *Patmutʻiwn S.D. Hnchʻakean Kusaktsʻutʻean*, vol. II, 9–91. On South America, see Ibid., 220–54. On the Balkans, see Ibid., 255–93.
28 On the Hnchakian activities in Persia and their role in the Constitutional Revolution, see Gidur, *Patmutʻiwn S.D. Hnchʻakean Kusaktsʻutʻean*, vol. I, 396–405.
29 Kumkapı is the district where the Armenian Patriarchate is located. For the Hnchakian Party's pamphlet on the occasion of the Kumkapı demonstration see Gidur, *Patmutʻiwn S.D. Hnchʻakean Kusaktsʻutʻean*, vol. I, 55–7. On the demonstration, see Nalbandian, *The Armenian Revolutionary Movement*, 118–20.
30 *Hnchʻak*, 7 September 1890, no. 7, 1–2.
31 As a result of this event, more than two hundred Armenians were arrested and sent to Angora to be tried. On the Angora trials, see letters and memorandums nos. 97–286, in *Correspondence Relating to the Asiatic Province of Turkey 1892-93*, Turkey No. 3, 1896, presented to both Houses of Parliament by command of Her Majesty, May 1896.
32 See Gidur, *Patmutʻiwn S.D. Hnchʻakean Kusaktsʻutʻean*, vol. I, 135–50. See also Christopher J. Walker, *Armenia: The Survival of a Nation* (New York: St. Martin's Press, 1980), 121–76; Owen Miller, 'Sasun 1894: Mountains, Missionaries and Massacres at the End of the Ottoman Empire' (unpublished PhD dissertation, Columbia University, 2015); and Ronald Grigor Suny, guest ed., 'The Sassoun Massacres', *Armenian Review* 47, no. 1–2 (Summer 2001).
33 See Gidur, *Patmutʻiwn S.D. Hnchʻakean Kusaktsʻutʻean*, vol. I, 151–3. See also France, Ministère des Affaires étrangères, *Affaires arméniennes: projets de réformes dans l'empire ottoman 1839-1897, Documents Diplomatiques* (Paris: Imprimerie Nationale, 1897), 43–56; and Great Britain, Foreign Office, *Blue Book: Turkey. 1896, No. 1* (Correspondence Respecting the Introduction of Reforms in the Armenian Provinces of Asiatic Turkey) (London: Harrison and Sons, 1896), 74–80.
34 For the complete petition, see Gidur, *Patmutʻiwn S.D. Hnchʻakean Kusaktsʻutʻean*, vol. I, 154–6. See also Great Britain, Foreign Office, *Blue Book: Turkey. 1896, No. 2* (Correspondence Relative to the Armenian Question and Reports from Her Majesty's

Consular Officers in Asiatic Turkey) (London: Harrison and Sons, 1896) (Great Britain, Parliament, Sessional Papers, vol. 95, 1896), 30–5.
35 See *Hnch'ak*, 20 October 1895, no. 18, 1–2.
36 See Gidur, *Patmut'iwn S.D. Hnch'akean Kusakts'ut'ean*, vol. I, 160–84.
37 Garabed Aghassi, *Zeïtoun depuis les origins jusqu'à l' insurrection de 1895* (Paris: Édition du Mercure de France, 1897), 261–307.
38 On the terms of the peace agreement, see Gidur, *Patmut'iwn S.D. Hnch'akean Kusakts'ut'ean*, vol. I, 190–2. On the situation in Zeytun, see France, *Ministère des Affaires étrangères, Affaires arméniennes*, 192–95.
39 Manuk G. Djizmedjian, *Patmut'iwn Amerikahay K'aghak'akan Kusakts'ut'eants': 1890-1925* (Fresno: Tpagrut'iwn Nor Ōr-i, 1930), 50–70.
40 Rupen Khan-Azad, 'Hay Heghap'okhakani mě Husherits'', *Hayrenik' Amsagir* VII, no. 7 (76) (February 1929): 100. See also Ter Minassian, *Nationalism and Socialism in the Armenian Revolutionary Movement*, 39.
41 Hagop Turabian, 'The Armenian Social-Democratic Hentchakist Party, Part I', *Ararat* 3, no. 34 (April 1916): 5, 17.
42 Rupen Khan-Azad, 'Hay Heghap'okhakani mě Husherits'', *Hayrenik' Amsagir* V, no. 11 (59) (September 1927): 127–30.
43 Rupen Khan-Azad, 'Hay Heghap'okhakani mě Husherits'', *Hayrenik' Amsagir* VI, no. 3 (63) (January 1928): 115.
44 Rupen Khan-Azad, 'Hay Heghap'okhakani mě Husherits'', *Hayrenik' Amsagir* VI, no. 4 (64) (February 1928): 124–6.
45 *Hnch'ak*, 18 May 1891, no. 6, 8.
46 Gidur, *Patmut'iwn S.D. Hnch'akean Kusakts'ut'ean*, vol. I, 306–14.
47 See Bedross Der Matossian, *Shattered Dreams of Revolution: From Liberty to Violence in the Late Ottoman Empire* (Stanford: Stanford University Press, 2016).
48 Gidur, *Patmut'iwn S.D. Hnch'akean Kusakts'ut'ean*, vol. I, 324.
49 See Bedross Der Matossian, *The Horrors of Adana: Revolution and Violence in the Early Twentieth Century* (Stanford: Stanford University Press, 2022).
50 Gidur, *Patmut'iwn S.D. Hnch'akean Kusakts'ut'ean*, vol. I, 366.
51 Ibid., 367.
52 On Arshavir Sahagian (aka Arthur Yasian), see Gidur, *Patmut'iwn S.D. Hnch'akean Kusakts'ut'ean*, vol. I., 377 9.
53 Gidur, *Patmut'iwn S.D. Hnch'akean Kusakts'ut'ean*, vol. I, 462. See also *K'san Kakhaghanner: Nwēr, 1915 Hunis 2/15in K. Pōlsoy Mēj Kakhaghan Bardzrats'ogh K'san S. D. Hnch'akean Ěnkerneru Hishatakin* (Providence: 'Eritasard Hayastan' Press, 1916).
54 See Gidur, *Patmut'iwn S.D. Hnch'akean Kusakts'ut'ean*, vol. I, 550–69.
55 Ibid., 516.
56 On the relations between the Comintern and the SDHP, see Ibid., 496–503.
57 See for example Berberian, *Roving Revolutionaries*; Berberian, *The Love for Freedom Has No Fatherland*.
58 Abel Manoukian, *The Origins of the Hnchakian Party in Geneva and the Legacy of the Twenty Gallows* (Yerevan: Zangak Publishing House, 2019).
59 See Berberian, *Roving Revolutionaries*.
60 Ibid. See also Dikran Kaligian, *Armenian Organization and Ideology under Ottoman Rule: 1908-1914* (New Brunswick: Transaction Publishers, 2009) and Gaidz F. Minassian and Arsen Avagyan, *Ermeniler ve İttihat ve Terakki: İşbirliğinden Çatışmaya* (İstanbul: Aras Yayıncılık, 2005).

Section I

From Inception to the First Republic of Armenia (1918–20)

The following section deals with some crucial aspects of the history of the formation of the SDHP (Social Democrat Hnchakian Party) and its political activities during the Second Constitutional Period (1908–18) in the Ottoman Empire as well as the First Republic of Armenia (1918–20). The first article by Abel Manoukian challenges the accepted date for the formation of the SDHP, which most historians argue was formed in 1887 in Geneva. In a detailed study, Manoukian demonstrates that the core of the SDHP was established in Geneva in 1886 under the title of 'revolutionary society'. This society took the task of drafting a programme for the party in the same year. He argues that the name Hnchakian Party or the SDHP was a later phenomenon that came after the establishment of the 'revolutionary society'. Furthermore, he maintains that the name Hnchakian entered the vocabulary of the 'revolutionary society' long after the publication of its official organ, *Hnch'ak* (Bell). To support his thesis, Manoukian dwells upon a group picture of the six founding members of the 'revolutionary society' taken in Geneva in 1886. The figures in the picture are the same people who are traditionally considered to be the founders of the SDHP.

The second chapter in this section by Garabed Moumdjian deals with the relation between the SDHP and the Young Turks in exile during the Hamidian period. This phase was crucial for the SDHP as it was struggling on multiple fronts to strengthen its political clout, while at the same time suffering from internal divisions. Moumdjian's article discusses in depth the reluctance of the SDHP to enter into any type of negotiations with the Young Turks headed by Ahmed Rıza. He argues that the SDHP continued its strategy of appealing to the Great Powers to intervene on behalf of the Armenians. He contends that the inability of the Armenian revolutionary parties to establish a unified front in negotiating with the Young Turks would prove to be counterproductive to the interests of the Armenians. While the ARF (Armenian Revolutionary Federation) was not successful in convincing the SDHP to join, it was able to recruit the Reformed (*Verakazmyal*) Hnchaks to participate in the First Congress of the Ottoman Opposition Groups that took place in Paris in 1902. The ARF was aware of the nationalistic tendencies of the Young Turks and approached them cautiously. The Hnchaks on the other hand were adamant not to have any relations with the Young Turks as they did not trust the Committee of Union and Progress (CUP), which constituted the main political party within the Young Turk movement. As Moumdjian demonstrates, they were more inclined to join the faction of Prince Sabahaddin as well as other Ottoman Turkish opposition groups.

This phase of cooperating with the Ottoman opposition is the topic of Yeghig Djeredjian's article. Djeredjian demonstrates how the Hnchaks opted to cooperate with non-dominant Turkish, Kurdish and Arab parties such as the Ottoman Liberal Party (*Osmanlı Ahrar Fırkası*), the Ottoman Socialist Party (*Osmanlı Sosyalist Fırkası*), Nejib Azuri's *Ligue de la Partie Arabe* and Maniasizade Refik Bey's Ottoman Democratic Party (*Osmanli Demokrat Firkasi*), among others. When the Freedom and Accord Party (*Hürriyet ve İtilâf Fırkası*) was founded in November 1911, the SDHP did not think twice and joined the party due to its liberal policies and its policy of administrative decentralization. However, as the Itilaf party was weakened due to the extralegal and extraconstitutional measures taken by the CUP, especially during the Balkan Wars (1912–13), the SDHP now felt the real danger of the CUP. Djeredjian concentrates on a newly found confidential letter from Stepan Sapah-Gulian to Paramaz, which demonstrates the extent that the Armenians as well as the Ottoman opposition feared the CUP. The letter reveals a secret plot by the CUP to assassinate Ottoman opposition figures, including the heads of the SDHP in Cairo. That the Ottoman opposition, as well as the leaders of the SDHP were planning to get rid of the CUP leaders could not be denied. It is important to note here that the SDHP policies were not aimed against the Turks or the Ottoman Empire, rather against the CUP. By cooperating with Turkish opposition figures both in the Ottoman Empire as well as in exile, the SDHP strove to topple the CUP regime. It was in the Seventh Congress of the SDHP in 1913 that the party took the decision of using extralegal methods to wage a struggle against the CUP until more adequate and newer political and economic conditions prevailed. The SDHP's priority now became to overthrow the Ittihad and support the Itilaf party.

The final chapter of this section deals with the policy of the SDHP towards the First Republic of Armenia (1918–20). In his article, Richard Hovannisian argues that the SDHP clearly differed from other opposition groups. It seems that the SDHP realized the great value of Yerevan as the centre of the future Armenian homeland. Despite its disagreement with the ARF, which was in control of the government during the short-lived Republic, the Hnchakians chastised all opposition parties that boycotted the parliamentary elections. They argued that even if the government was controlled by an 'incompetent' party, they should not abandon the state and should support it. Hovannisian demonstrates how an important SDHP leader, Arsen Gidur, was appointed by the ARF-dominated government as its representative for refugee affairs in Cilicia and Mesopotamia. Even when dissention took place among Armenian parties, the SDHP supported the ARF. With the collapse of the newly born Republic due to the Kemalist offensive and the takeover of the Republic of Armenia by Soviet Russia in 1920, the SDHP maintained an anti-Bolshevik stance. Towards the end of his article, Hovannisian argues that the stance of the SDHP in general should be considered exemplary.

1

The History of a Group Picture and the Date of the Formation of the 'Revolutionary Society' of Geneva

Abel Manoukian

The available, contradictory, information about the formation of the Hnchakian Party and its founders makes it plainly clear that there is a dearth of reliable sources on the history of the first Armenian revolutionary party in the last quarter of the nineteenth century. With that said, it is common knowledge that the Hnchakian Party was founded in 1887 in Geneva.[1] Most historiographical books use this date, and party publications such as the thick two-volume work, *History of the S. D. Hnchakian Party 1887–1962*, edited by Arsen Gidur,[2] also recognizes this as its date of foundation.

In my Armenian and English volumes devoted to the history of the formation of the Hnchakian Party,[3] I had also noted 1887 as the date of foundation, although with some reservations, mostly due to the absence of evidence. However, newly discovered data and convincing proof have surfaced to counter the commonly accepted view that the Hnchakian Party was founded in either August[4] or October of 1887.[5]

We all know that, in the 1880s, the conviction of founding a revolutionary organization, essentially aimed at liberating Western Armenia and Western Armenians from Ottoman rule, had gradually taken root in the Armenian student circles of Europe, particularly in Paris, Montpellier, and Geneva. Those ideas were further developed when Mgrdich Portukalian, an educator from Van, took refuge in Marseille after fleeing from Ottoman oppression and persecution, and started publishing his newspaper *Armēnia* in 1885. The free publication of an Armenian paper was cause for great enthusiasm within Armenian student circles, who were imbued with revolutionary ideas and a vision of liberating their homeland. They gathered around *Armēnia* and its authoritative editor.

Searching for the means to achieve this goal, the student circles of Europe fomented the following thoughts:

(a) The necessity of forming a patriotic-revolutionary society, whose members should be ready to go to Western Armenia and develop patriotic and liberation activities.

(b) To achieve this goal, it was believed to be necessary to gather an assembly in a European city, which would be tasked with the creation of a coordinating central body.

Since the end was becoming subsumed into the means and words were not turning into action, Avetis Nazarbekian, writing under the pseudonym Lerents, sent an article entitled 'A Proposal' to *Armēnia* from the Swiss city of Vevey on 10 September 1886.[6] He proposed to create a 'common treasury' that would serve the 'revolutionary work', namely, providing the required funding to further the common goal of liberating the Armenian people, until the proposed assembly could be gathered and the central body formed. Nazarbekian considered *Armēnia*'s editor, Portukalian, the most suitable person to achieve this, and asked him to undertake this important commitment.

Portukalian published Lerents's proposal in the 22 September 1886 issue of *Armēnia*, with an editorial note that the newspaper 'will publish its thoughts in this respect within a few days'.[7] In fact, Portukalian referred to Lerents's proposal in the 9 October 1886 issue, after receiving a donation for the 'revolutionary treasury':

> We received the 10 rubles you sent, of which you want to allocate 5 rubles to the revolutionary treasury that was going to be established at the editorial offices of *Armēnia* according to Mr. Lerents's article 'A Proposal' in the tenth issue of *Armēnia*. The heavy duties of our editorial body do not allow us to commit to that proposed position, especially since we plan to establish a treasury with a different goal, whose plan will be published in brief. Since our editorial body is not connected to any Armenian revolutionary committee and does not want to show any preference toward any of them, in this case it considers more appropriate to send the 5 rubles to the author of that suggestion, Mr. Lerents himself, *for the revolutionary society of Geneva*.[8]

As a matter of fact, Portukalian refused to take Nazarbekian's proposal, arguing that his very busy schedule and his project to establish 'a treasury with a different goal' disallowed his participation. Moreover, he declared that 'the editorial board is not connected [or does not want to be connected] to any Armenian revolutionary committee'.

Portukalian's declaration contains a testimony much more important for this subject, which I would like to highlight: ' [I]n this case it considers more appropriate to send the 5 rubles to the author of that suggestion, Mr. Lerents himself, for the revolutionary society of Geneva'.[9]

This means that either an Armenian 'revolutionary society' had already been formed by October 1886 in Geneva, or that Portukalian was already aware that Nazarbekian and his like-minded followers were gearing towards the formation of a 'revolutionary society'.

Portukalian's refusal to commit to keeping a central revolutionary treasury created strong disillusionment and a feeling of revolt within the Armenian student circles of Geneva, who were already well-inclined towards revolutionary ideas.

An article entitled 'Question to the Noble Armenian Youth', written on 7 October 1886, from Geneva,[10] and signed 'Kafan', made an appeal to the Armenian youth of Europe: 'It is necessary [...] to form a body among us [...] we hope that the Armenian youth living abroad will not regard in vain the grounds of the holy task of liberating their homeland: "unity, unanimity, and fraternity"'.[11]

Interestingly, on 23 October Portukalian declared in *Armēnia*'s response column that the members of the 'revolutionary society' of Geneva had sent a 'Declaration', asking for it to be published in *Armēnia*,[12] but he was unable to do so, since its signature 'Society Members' was unknown to him. He added that he would be ready to publish it once the identity of its authors was disclosed.

In fact, this 'Declaration' was published in the 30 October 1886 issue of *Armēnia*, when Portukalian announced that 'Koran and Kafan immediately let us know from Geneva that they are the representatives of that society who sent us that declaration'.[13]

Koran was Matteos Shahazizian's pseudonym,[14] while Kafan most likely was the pseudonym of Gabriel Kafian (Shemavon) at the time.

In the interest of verifying the actual date of formation of the Hnchakian Party in Geneva, I consider it very useful to quote the abovementioned 'Declaration' almost in its entirety:

> In the sixth issue of this year's *Armēnia*, the Armenian people already read a letter[15] where it is said that the program of our new society should be published in the same newspaper in a short while. Since various individuals and even societies from various places have already asked us not to delay our publication, on this occasion our society considers its duty to give the following response to those respectable individuals and societies expecting the publication of our program in *Armēnia*.
>
> The members of our society, being aware for a long time of the ideas promoted until now in the *Armēnia* newspaper of Marseille and the course it has currently taken, have arrived to the inescapable conclusion that there is not and will not be common ground between our society and the *Armēnia* newspaper. Therefore, our program cannot be published in that newspaper. Our society will soon fulfill the wishes of those individuals and societies that are anxiously waiting for the publication; namely, our society will publish its program, but not on the pages of the newspaper *Armēnia*.[16]

Remarkably, the declaration attests several times to the existence of the 'revolutionary society' in Geneva, which would also be endowed with a programme to be published soon, not in *Armēnia* as previously announced, but in another paper, one that 'the society itself will publish'. Namely, by October 1886, circumstances had brought the 'revolutionary society' of Geneva to the issue of publishing a newspaper of its own.

In October 1886 a 'revolutionary society', although not yet named the Hnchakian Party at that time, had already been formed in Geneva by Avetis Nazarbekian, Maro Vardanian, Rupen Khan-Azad, Gabriel Kafian, Gevorg Gharajian and Kristapor Ohanian.

Although Portukalian published the 'Declaration' of the 'revolutionary society' of Geneva in *Armēnia*, he wrote, in a bitter postscript:

> Yes, gentlemen, you may remain solidly attached to your 'indestructible conviction' that there is not and will not be any common grounds between your 'society' and the *Armēnia* newspaper to hurl insults. And our readers will not have a big loss by not reading anymore the writings of Koran, Kafan, and company in the pages of *Armēnia*.[17]

After this declaration, relations between the 'revolutionary society' of Geneva and *Armēnia* had broken down. That break-up deepened when 'one of the fervent members of Koran, Kafan and company'[18] addressed a letter to *Armēnia*[19] – most likely authored by 'red revolutionary'[20] Avetis Nazarbekian – in a strong critique against Portukalian, and then, in November 1886, he published in Geneva a pamphlet entitled 'Armenian-Eating Chameleon' against Portukalian with a text equivalent to eight full columns in *Armēnia*.[21] Portukalian bitterly referred to the pamphlet, outlining its contents, in the 1 December 1886 issue.[22] Thus, nine young Armenians from Geneva:

> In an eight-column piece try to affirm that we are not revolutionaries, that we even fear the name of the revolution, that we are egoists, etc., and the proofs that you bring for all that is just that we did not accept Mr. Lerents' offer of the revolutionary treasury and we later undertook the foundation of the 'Union of Children of Armenia,' because as true revolutionaries we would remain away from these peaceful, progressive works (…) you who call us pseudo-revolutionary, revolution-fearing, etcetera.[23]

It is most unfortunate that Portukalian refused to publish 'Armenian-Eating Chameleon' in *Armēnia*, as he stated:

> We do not have room for your piece in *Armēnia*, not because it is written against the editorial body of *Armēnia*, but because we cannot sacrifice the precious pages of *Armēnia* to such a childish article. And we will keep the article as memento and evidence of the spirit of the nine signatory gentlemen who have proffered such insults against the editorial body of *Armēnia*.[24]

Despite my efforts, it has been impossible thus far to find a copy of 'Armenian-Eating Chameleon', which would have allowed to not only learn about its contents, but also to confirm the names of the nine members of the 'revolutionary society' of Geneva who had signed the pamphlet.

Fortunately, I am able to give these names, based on Rupen Khan-Azad's memoir serially published in *Hayrenik*ʻ monthly.[25] These names include Avetis Nazarbekian, Maro Vardanian, Rupen Khan-Azad, Gabriel Kafian, Gevorg Gharajian, Kristapor Ohanian, Matteos Shahazizian, Poghos Afrikian and Mgrdich Manucharian.

The abovementioned list is confirmed through another testimony by the same author, included in a publication devoted to the fortieth anniversary of the Hnchakian

Party (Paris, 1930). Khan-Azad wrote this memoir in May 1927 in Tabriz. It was more succinct than the other, which was published in 1927–8 in *Hayrenik'*:

> Kafian, whose energy was inexhaustible, in just half hour decided to personally go to Montpellier, get acquainted and talk with the local Armenian students (…). Barely a week later, Kafian returned bringing most of the Armenian students of Montpellier: Matteos Shahazizian (…), Gevorg Gharajian, Kristapor Ohanian, and Poghos Afrikian. (…) Being *nine people* gathered in Geneva, we decided to not wait for any general assembly, whose realization was impossible without a newspaper, and to found for ourselves the desired revolutionary society, prepare its program, and then call others to join us.[26]

Gabriel Kafian's spontaneous and quick departure to Montpellier, as well as his return to Geneva with the abovementioned students should be dated October 1886, since, as has been noted before, the 'Declaration' sent to *Armēnia* for publication on behalf of the members of the 'revolutionary society' of Geneva bears the date 30 October 1886, as well as the signatures of Koran (Matteos Shahazizian) and Kafan (G. Kafian).

After going to Montpellier, Gabriel Kafian also went to Marseille to persuade Portukalian to join their revolutionary activities. However, his efforts in this regard were fruitless.[27]

With reference to the formation of the 'revolutionary society' of Geneva and the later Hnchakian Party, I should mention that Gevorg Gharajian's various publications, starting in 1907, aimed at denying his membership in this group of founders:

> After definitively parting ways with the group in July 1887, I did not have any business with any of its members; I did not write any word in the newspaper *Hnch'ak* after its publication or in any other Hnchakian publication; I have never had any organizational and ideological relation with the Hnchakian Party, I have never carried out any Hnchakian party work or have any dealings with this or that Hnchakian organization or individuals; I have never held the Hnchakian 'socialist' worldview.[28]

In relation to my topic, I am naturally interested in the period prior to July 1887, namely, the period of formation of the 'revolutionary society' of Geneva, during which Gharajian, despite his many rejections, was undoubtedly part of the group of founders and brought his undeniable share to the organizing activities.

Returning to the issue of the students from the University of Montpellier who arrived in Geneva with Gabriel Kafian, Gharajian claimed:

> My acquaintance and relation with the abovementioned members of the group was only random and very brief. In the fall of 1886, when moving to Switzerland from the French city of Montpellier, G. Kafian accompanied me to Geneva. Supposedly based on the information provided by the latter, Khan Azad writes that a wagon full of students had come to Geneva from Montpellier with Kafian. We were just two people. Does two people, one of which was Kafian himself, mean a wagon full of students? (…)

After us, two other students came to Geneva from Montpellier: Poghos Afrikian and Matteos Shahazizian.[29]

This detail, indeed, adds nothing essential to our subject, since Gharajian does not mention Kristapor Ohanian at all. The 'later' arrival in Geneva of the other two does not contradict the formation of the 'revolutionary society' in October 1886, since, as we saw above, the 'Declaration' sent to *Armēnia* on behalf of the '[revolutionary] society members' bears the date 23 October 1886.

Sometime later, the last three names, Matteos Shahazizian,[30] Poghos Afrikian[31] and Mgrdich Manucharian,[32] left the 'revolutionary society',[33] but within the period of publication for the abovementioned 'Declaration' in *Armēnia* and the signature of the pamphlet 'Armenian-Eating Chameleon' against Portukalian (namely, between October and November 1886), they were already members of a 'revolutionary society' that formed in Geneva.

It has already been observed that the 'revolutionary society' of Geneva undertook the task of developing its programme in October 1886 and also decided to publish its tenets and efforts through a printing house and newspaper founded or directly owned by the 'revolutionary society' and not dependent on a foreign printing house or periodical. To that end, it was necessary to ensure financial backing. Besides contributing a small amount from their meagre pockets,[34] they organized a 'Caucasian Night' (*Soirée caucasienne*) on 22 December 1886 at the Schiess beerhouse in Geneva.[35] The entire income, along with the amount they had personally set aside, was allocated to the acquisition of a printing house and the publication of a paper. As a matter of fact, they asked the Mekhitarist Congregation of Vienna[36] for the provision of Armenian typefaces. Unfortunately, their acquisition was delayed until the summer of 1887. In the meantime, during the period of tension with Portukalian and afterwards, namely, in October 1886, the designated committee (Avetis Nazarbekian, Maro Vardanian and Gevorg Gharajian) had to undertake the preparations for the programme as desired by the 'revolutionary society'.

The following details provided by Rupen Khan-Azad are important in this regard:

> After we severed our relations with *Armēnia*, we decided not to wait for the gathering of the abovementioned general assembly, but to prepare a program for the revolutionary society, create the core of the society, and then make an appeal to the youth to join us. We elected a committee from our midst to prepare the program: Miss M. Vardanian, A. Nazarbek, and G. Gharajian.
>
> To understand accurately the program and the spirit of that first Armenian revolutionary society it is necessary to take the following circumstances into account.
>
> First, the group of founders of the Armenian revolutionary society were all Russian Armenians. It means that we were totally under the influence of Russian revolutionary currents. And at the time, in 1886, there were two main currents among the Russian revolutionaries that fought each other bitterly: the 'Narodovoltsy' and the 'Marxists.'[37]

In this context, it is obvious that the preparatory work for a 'revolutionary society' programme had been undertaken in 1886. However, the author of the memoir also writes elsewhere:

> This was the program that the committee elected by us, the group of students in Geneva, had compiled, worked out, and presented, and we accepted and approved almost without debate and with great excitement. *Exactly forty years have passed since that day* (…).[38]

If we take into account that this paragraph of Rupen Khan-Azad's memoir was published in *Hayrenik'* monthly in 1927, the day in question, forty years before, would have corresponded to 1887.

Unfortunately, this programme has no date of preparation or approval. Therefore, we will accept the version that the 'revolutionary society' started preparing the programme in October 1886 and that it was approved during the first half of 1887.

This version was later confirmed during the polemics regarding the formation of the Hnchakian Party that developed between Gevorg Gharajian and Rupen Khan-Azad. The latter, reacting to Gharajian's denial in the newspaper *Erkri Dzaynĕ* of Tiflis, wrote in 1907: 'We could not avoid thinking about that, since we were preparing the party program together for months'.[39]

In his flat-out, but contradictory denials of any relationship with the Hnchakian Party, Gevorg Gharajian also rejected any participation and contribution to the committee elected to prepare the 'revolutionary society' of Geneva programme. As previously mentioned, in 1907, first with a letter published in the newspaper *Erkri Dzaynĕ*,[40] and later with a lengthy piece of writing entitled 'My Response to Khan Azad',[41] Gharajian protested against his statement. Later, as was also noted previously, Gharajian published a booklet entitled 'The Tales of Rupen Khan-Azad', which revolved almost entirely around refuting everything that Khan-Azad had written about him in the memoir published in *Hayrenik'* (1927–8). Particularly in reference to the abovementioned programme, he claimed:

> We have to suppose that if such a committee ever existed, where Khan Azad places me as member, it should have been elected in late 1886 or during the first semester of 1887, because in the summer of this year (in July) I had completely broken off from the group. In that period, I had not seen 'the group members working out the party program' for months; I have never heard the election or existence of a committee to prepare a program (…). It is not unlikely that the Nazarbekian spouses at the time and later had retreated into their office and made efforts to prepare such programs by themselves, and the importance of my participation in them has been expressed as desire in the imagination of Khan Azad or perhaps some other member of the group, but I categorically and publicly declare that I have never been a member of the Hnchakian program committee; I have never participated in the tasks to prepare the program of the Hnchakian Party.[42]

Of course, Gharajian had strong psychological and political reasons for such robust denials. Shortly after leaving the 'revolutionary society' of Geneva, he published a slanderous article against the university students of the same city in *Mshak*,⁴³ which was followed, naturally, by a rejoinder written from Geneva,⁴⁴ which bore the signature 'A Group of Students', but was most likely authored by Rupen Khan-Azad. Gharajian's defamatory writing denoted his deep antipathy towards his former revolutionary comrades from Geneva. Other than that, he later joined the ranks of the Russian Social Democratic Labor Party (RSDLP) and then took positions of leadership in the foreign affairs department of the Soviet government, which was reason enough to distance himself from past relationships that could endanger or overshadow him. In any case, as long as we lack other historical testimonies that could shed light on the contradictory data of both sides (Gharajian and Khan-Azad) regarding the development of the programme in question, we have to leave the issue open for further investigation.

Notwithstanding this, as it is known, the programme was published in both the October and November 1888 issues (numbers 11 and 12) of *Hnch'ak*. Neither the title nor the contents of the programme have any mention of the 'Hnchakian Party'. It only refers to the activities of the *Hnch'ak* group, for which the programme served as a guideline.

The 'Hnchakian Party' and then the 'Social Democrat Hnchakian Party' identity is a much later phenomenon that has no relation with the early formative period (1886–90). History has recorded that the name 'Hnchakian Revolutionary Party' was officially adopted in 1890,⁴⁵ becoming the 'Hnchakian Social Democrat Party' in 1905 and 'Social Democrat Hnchakian Party' in 1909, a partisan and political identity that has existed to this day.

In its editorials and analytical articles, *Hnch'ak* often refers 'to the issue of organization of the Armenian revolutionary party' and, as I noted before, speaks on behalf of the *Hnch'ak* group. However, it directly uses the term 'Hnchakian' for the first time in September 1889, in the description of the First Conference of the Second International (Paris, 14–21 July 1889), where noted Russian revolutionary and *narodnik* theoretician Pyotr Lavrovich Lavrov also represented the Armenian revolutionaries: 'Russian famous socialist revolutionary and scholar P. L. Lavrov was delegate on behalf of the Armenian socialist revolutionaries (*Hnchakian group*).'⁴⁶

Later, in the same issue, *Hnch'ak* replied to A. Siuni's series entitled 'Socialism in the Armenian Newspaper', published in several issues of *Armēnia* in 1889,⁴⁷ and again used, this time uppercased, the term 'Hnchakian group'.⁴⁸ The name 'Hnchakian Party', however, appears for the first time in the pages of *Hnch'ak* in March 1890, at the end of an article entitled 'A Response', which was once again directed against *Armēnia*: 'They should not rush to utter phrases about the Armenian popular work; the future will indeed show them how beneficial the *Hnchakian Party* is. *Qui vivra, verra*.'⁴⁹

During its eight years of existence, from November 1887 until 31 July 1895, *Hnch'ak* only bore its name on its masthead as an identity. Beginning in August 1895, it added a new subtitle, the '*Central Organ of the Hnchakian Party*'.⁵⁰

After organizing the 'Caucasian Night', ordering the Armenian typefaces from the Mekhitarist Congregation of Vienna, and, possibly, preparing the programme of the 'revolutionary society' of Geneva, Avetis Nazarbekian and Maro Vardanian published an appeal to join the 'revolutionary society' addressed 'To Sisters and Brothers!'⁵¹ and sent it to the Armenian student circles of Europe. 'To Sisters and Brothers' was a

Russian *Narodnik*-style call from the 1870s to the 1880s adopted by the coauthors of the appeal, still under *Narodnik* influence. Unfortunately, the appeal had no echoes and the members of the 'revolutionary society' of Geneva – in fact, the six founding members – continued to pursue their goals independently.

Indeed, it would have been impossible to undertake the preparation of a programme and the task of publishing a paper if the 'revolutionary society' of Geneva had not already been previously formed, at least from October 1886, by Avetis Nazarbekian, Maro Vardanian, Rupen Khan-Azad, Gabriel Kafian, Gevorg Gharajian and Kristapor Ohanian.

Usually, studies on the history of the Hnchakian Party utilize the information contained in the abovementioned memoir of Rupen Khan-Azad, one of the noted founders of the party, published in the monthly *Hayrenik'* starting in June 1927. However, it is noteworthy that more than forty years had passed since the formation of the 'revolutionary society' of Geneva and, naturally, Khan-Azad might have forgotten, or considered superfluous, the mention of some specific details. Fortunately, the same author recorded his recollections related to the Hnchakian Party in several publications.[52] One of the most important publications was the article in Russian, 'How the "Hnchakian" Party Was Formed?'[53] subtitled 'Memoirs', which appeared in the newspaper *Armyansky Vestnik* in Moscow in 1916.[54] Here, Khan-Azad reported that the Armenian students of Geneva 'decided to operate separately from Portukalian. After long debates, the grounds for the new party (i.e. the "revolutionary society") were finally set forth. A group comprised of six people was formed, which became the core of the future organization'.[55]

This article provides another relevant piece of information related to our subject: it states that 'after preparing the program' of the 'revolutionary society', 'that group started thinking about having its own periodical'.[56] This important testimony shows that the 'revolutionary society' of Geneva had already prepared its action plan before even publishing *Hnch'ak*. The existence of a programme is an essential indication of the activities of an already formed organization. As a matter of fact, Khan-Azad reported that 'after establishing and approving the program submitted by the committee, our revolutionary society was already considered formed. Its members were Miss M. Vardanian, A. Nazarbekian, G. Gharajian, G. Kafian, K. Ohanian, and the author of these lines [i.e. R. Khan-Azad]'.[57]

Besides, while the group picture of the so-called 'seven founders' has often been taken into account in determining the date of foundation of the Hnchakian Party, it is remarkable that Rupen Khan-Azad attached another historical picture to his article of 1916, directly related to the sources of the party's foundation. The latter depicts the six founding members of the 'revolutionary society' and, by a wonderful strike of good fortune, the names of each person, unknown to many, are mentioned one by one. Thus, on the upper row, from left to right (standing), Kristapor Ohanian and Avetis Nazarbekian; on the middle row, from left to right, Gevorg Gharajian, Maro Vardanian and Gabriel Kafian; on the lower row, reclined, Rupen Khan-Azad.

I would like to show that the photo has a formal character and may have been taken on the founding of the 'revolutionary society' of Geneva. Moreover, it may have been the result of a core motivation, which I will substantiate later.

Figure 1.1 From left to right, standing, are Gevorg Gharajian, Kristapor Ohanian and Avetis Nazarbekian. Seated on the central row, from left to right, are Maro Vartanian and Gabriel Kafian. Seated on the floor is Rupen Khan-Azad. Source: National Library of Armenia.

The group picture of the so-called 'seven founders' of the Hnchakian Party shows an aesthetic of formality and also demonstrates a deliberate intent. The external elements of the photograph, i.e. the clothing and the gesture of the individuals, make clear that it is not a random picture, but that it was taken on or for a special occasion.

Initially, I leaned towards the idea that the pictures belong to different dates, because one of them has six people, and the other seven. However, their careful comparison yields the following details:

a) The photographs were taken at the same studio in Geneva;
b) They have the same background, which depicts the same tower of a castle;
c) Except for a few insignificant differences – a change in the places and positions of the people included in the photograph, plus the walking stick of Rupen Khan-Azad – the founding members of the 'revolutionary society' of Geneva appear with the same formal clothes.

In consequence, it can be said that these facts prove that both pictures are not from different times but were taken in the same place and on the same day.

Let us first verify the identity of the people included in the picture and then the time, which is related to the mandatory presence of the founders in full on the same day and in the same place.

Figure 1.2 From left to right, standing, are Rupen Khan-Azad and Gabriel Kafian. In the central row, from left to right, are Avetis Nazarbekian and Gevorg Gharajian, seated; in the middle of the photo, are Maro Vardanian and Kristapor Ohanian. Source: Arsen Gidur, *Patmutʻiwn S.D. Hnchʻakean Kusaktsʻutʻean, 1887–1962*, vol. I (Beirut: Shirag Press, 1962), 30.

From left to right, standing, are Rupen Khan-Azad and Gabriel Kafian. In the central row, from left to right, are Avetis Nazarbekian and Gevorg Gharajian, seated; in the middle of the photo, are Maro Vardanian, seated, and on the right, also seated, Kristapor Ohanian. The main difference here is the presence of a seventh individual. Who is the seventh person half seated behind a 'rock' on the left side of the so-called photograph of the 'seven founders'? Why is he absent from the first picture?

Many authors who have referred to the history of the formation of the Hnchakian Party, including party members, have often come to wrong conclusions, based on this photograph of the 'seven founders'. Thus, later authors have generalized a historical inaccuracy without further inquiry and passed it down as received knowledge, helping convert it into a symbol decorating the walls of Hnchakian clubs as an expression of identity. In fact, it is pertinent to ask when the picture of the founders of the Hnchakian Party was taken and who that unknown individual could be.

With this in mind, the date so far accepted for the foundation of the Hnchakian Party, August 1887, does not correspond to historical reality. Rupen Khan-Azad is very clear in his memoirs:

The typefaces that we had ordered from Vienna came late, in the summer of 1887. Two of our comrades had already left Geneva: Kafian had gone to Leipzig to study pedagogy, while Ohanian had traveled to his hometown Shushi with the aim of returning in the fall.[58]

We saw previously that Gabriel Kafian, expelled from the canton of Geneva, was forced to leave the city on 27 April 1887. Similarly, Kristapor Ohanian was not in Geneva during the summer of 1887. Moreover, the other relevant founding member of the Hnchakian Party, Gevorg Gharajian, was no longer with the group, according to his repeated assertions, because he had left the 'revolutionary society' of Geneva for good by July 1887.[59] Altogether, the abovementioned facts make the generally accepted date of foundation of August 1887 improbable, because it would have been impossible to realize the foundation of the party in the absence of three founding members, as well as to have the picture with the 'seven founders'.

The chain of events confirms that Gabriel Kafian was absent from Geneva between 27 April 1887 – the date of his involuntary leave – and 2 April 1889. This also helps elucidate the approximate date of the photographs of the 'founders' of the 'revolutionary society' of Geneva or the later Hnchakian Party, which should have happened in the first quarter of 1887, in any case, before 27 April. As a matter of fact, it is not completely unlikely that one of the main reasons for those two group pictures being taken, one with six and another with seven people, may have been Gabriel Kafian's impending departure from Geneva.

The descriptions presented so far attest that the founding members of the 'revolutionary society' of Geneva were just six Armenian students of Russian citizenship. Already in 1907, Rupen Khan-Azad had corrected one Hrahat's omission and added that 'the founders of the Hnchakian Party were not five, but six people'.[60] It is obvious that he referred to the 'revolutionary society' of Geneva, according to the group picture of the six founders, namely, Maro Vardanian, Avetis Nazarbekian, Gevorg Gharajian, Gabriel Kafian, Kristapor Ohanian and Rupen Khan-Azad.

Before Gabriel Kafian left Geneva for Leipzig, they wanted to reaffirm, or in other words, 'immortalize' their work and their mission of national liberation, which had already taken shape in October 1886 in Geneva with a group picture. The other, so-called 'seven founders' picture, which has become the source of a huge misunderstanding in Hnchakian literature, resulted from the chance presence of a seventh person who bore no relation at all with the 'revolutionary society' of Geneva, in other words, with the formation of the Hnchakian Party or with its activities in general.

At long last, who is the mysterious unknown person in that group picture of the founders? The convincing response comes from Gevorg Gharajian in his abovementioned booklet 'The Tales of Rupen Khan-Azad'. While denying that he was a member of the group of Hnchakian founders, he countered his opponent's objection with the following remark:

> You are similar to that pitiful Hnchakian, who during a private conversation, when I responded in the negative to his question whether I had been Hnchakian or not, he exclaimed: 'How come? Haven't you been Hnchakian and a founder of the Hnchakian Party, since I have seen you pictured in a group photograph along with the founders of the Hnchakian Party? 'Thus, in your opinion,' I respond

to him, 'a poor Russian student called *Kazitski*, who frequented the Nazarbekian spouses, was also a Hnchakian and a founder of the Hnchakian Party because he was photographed once along with all the members of the Geneva group.[61]

Thus, the person appearing at Maro Vardanian's side in a semi-reclined position in the group picture of the 'seven founders' is not another Armenian revolutionary, but a Russian student called Kazitski. Like many Russian students and anti-Czarist exiles in Geneva, he was one of the reliable acquaintances of the national and revolutionary activists, who accompanied the group of founders that day. This is the reason for the existence of two pictures taken on the same day and in the same place. The sextet of founders appears in one of them, alone, and appears with Kazitski in the other, perhaps by chance or friendship.

Conclusion

The name does not condition the existence of an unnamed phenomenon, object or even person. Parents often spend days and weeks to give their preferred name to their newly born child, but that does not mean that the child had not already been born or that it does not exist. It is true that the name characterizes a phenomenon or object already existent and can identify a person, but, nevertheless, the name itself does not condition the fact of their existence. The future Hnchakian Party was a political group that had already been formed in 1886 under the name of a 'revolutionary society'. In particular, the reliable details communicated by Rupen Khan-Azad in his series of articles 'From the Memories of an Armenian Revolutionary' attest to that. He argues in response to Gevorg Gharajian's denials of having ever been a member of the Hnchakian Party in the following terms:

> I had the opportunity to narrate the story of the foundation of the Hnchakian Party a couple of times, and every time G. Gharajian has considered his sacred duty to forcefully protest against my accounts, claiming that he was never among the founders of the Hnchakian Party.
>
> If he corrected my accounts, saying that at the time of the program I quoted above, our society had no name and the 'Hnchakian Party' did not exist yet, I would have nothing to argue, indeed. However, when he rejects and denies to having been our comrade, his participation in the preparation of the program of our *revolutionary society* [in Geneva], and even the fact of writing an article for the first issue of *Hnch'ak,* I cannot understand and pardon that.[62]

In fact, the absence of the name 'Hnchakian Party' – an identity that was adopted at a later time – does not contradict at all the existence in Geneva of a 'revolutionary society' that had already been formed in 1886, which became the foundational core for the future 'Hnchakian Party'. The name 'Hnchakian', in practical terms, became current long after the initial publication of *Hnch'ak*, as it was noted, and before becoming a particular political identity. What happened in 1890, as a matter of fact, was reflective of a change in name and not the foundation of a new political organization. The overwhelming majority of the founding members remained the same people, and the political programme was literally almost identical to what had been introduced in the October–November 1888 issue of *Hnch'ak*.

The six founding members of the 'revolutionary society' of Geneva undertook the preparation of their political-revolutionary programme in the last quarter of 1886.[63] After a long period of discussion and the introduction of various modifications and improvements, the committee dedicated to elaborating upon the programme (the Nazarbekian couple and Gevorg Gharajian) submitted the final draft to the other members of the 'revolutionary society' and had it approved in the first quarter of 1887.

Thus, the 'revolutionary society' was formed in October 1886 in Geneva. Its founding members included just six Russian Armenian students: Avetis Nazarbekian, Maro Vardanian-Nazarbekian, Rupen Khan-Azad, Gabriel Kafian, Gevorg Gharajian and Kristapor Ohanian. They left us with their official group photographs of six and seven people. As a matter of fact, the seventh person in the photograph was Kazitski, one of the many Russian students attending the University of Geneva, who had absolutely no relation to either the foundational history of the Hnchakian Party or with its six founding members and their work. His presence in the group picture is either the result of friendship or chance. The six-member group of founders accomplished the approval of its programme for the 'revolutionary society' in the first quarter of 1887, and this was considered the date of foundation of the Hnchakian Party.[64] The 'Hnchak Group', then the 'Hnchakian Group', and, finally, the 'Hnchakian Party', began its public activities in November 1887 with the publication of *Hnch'ak*.

Notes

1   See A. G. Hovhannisyan, 'Hnch'akeanneri Kazmaworman Gaghap'arakan Armatnerĕ', *Patma-Banasirakan Handes* 2 (1968): 19; M. G. Nersisyan, 'Hay Azadagrakan Sharzhumĕ ew Hnch'akeannerĕ 1880-1990-akan Twakannerin (Hnch'akean Kusakts'ut'ean Himnatrman 100-ameakin Aṛt'iw)', *Patma-Banasirakan Handes* 3 (1987): 25; Gegham Hovhannisyan, *Hnch'akean Kusakts'ut'ean Patmut'iwn (1887-1915 tt.)* (Yerevan: Patmut'ean Institut, 2012), 3; A. Hambaryan, G. Hovhannisyan, 'Hnch'akean Kusakts'ut'iwn', in *Hayots' Patmut'iwn*, vol. 3, book 1 (Yerevan: Zangak-97, 2010), 419–98.

2   Arsen Gidur, *Patmut'iwn S.D. Hnch'akean Kusakts'ut'ean, 1887-1962*, vol. I (Beirut: Shirag Press, 1962), 29–31.

3   Abel Manoukian, *Hayrenik'i Azadagrut'ean Banakin Hamozwatz Zinwornerĕ* (Beirut: Araz Printing Press, 2014), 13; Manoukian, *The Origins of the Hnchakian Party in Geneva and the Legacy of the Twenty Gallows* (Yerevan: Zangak Publishing House, 2019), 13.

4   See Louise Nalbandian, *The Armenian Revolutionary Movement: The Development of Armenian Political Parties through the Nineteenth Century* (Berkeley: University of California Press, 1963), 104.

5   See Rupen Berberian, 'Erku Dareri Shemk'in', *Hayrenik' Amsagir*, February 1939, 69.
6   *Armēnia*, 22 September 1886.
7   Ibid.
8   *Armēnia,* 9 October 1886, 3 (emphasis added).
9   Ibid.
10 *Armēnia,* 20 October, 1886, 2.
11 Ibid.
12 *Armēnia,* 23 October, 1886, 3.
13 *Armēnia,* 30 October, 1886, 2.
14 See Rupen Khan-Azad, 'Hay Heghap'okhakani Mě Husherits'', *Hayrenik' Amsagir*, June 1927, 69.
15 This letter bearing the signature Koran (Matteos Shahazizian) and entitled 'Monpeliayi Usanoghakan Akumbě Hay Zhoghvrdi Aṛaj' (The Student 'Club' of Montpellier before the Armenian People) was sent to the editorial board on September 8, 1886. This makes clear that Matteos Shahazizian, Poghos Afrikian, and Kristapor Ohanian were still in Montpellier in September 1886. See the letter in *Armēnia,* 8 September 1886, 2.
16 See *Armēnia,* 30 October 1886, 2.
17 Ibid., 3.
18 *Armēnia,* 3 November 1886, 1.
19 Ibid.
20 Ibid.
21 See Khan-Azad, 'Hay Heghap'okhakani', June 1927, 71.
22 *Armēnia,* 1 December 1886, 3.
23 Ibid.
24 Ibid. Portukalian felt so deeply insulted that at the same time he refused to publish a poem by Lerents: 'We have returned your poem "Masis" to you. We do not have room for your poems in *Armēnia*' (Ibid., 3).
25 See Khan-Azad, 'Hay Heghap'okhakani', June 1927, 60–72; July 1927, 52–63; August 1927, 56–72; September 1927, 124–38; October 1927, 122–9; November 1927, 122–35; December 1927, 112–24; January 1928, 114–28; February 1928, 123–35; March 1928, 102–14; April 1928, 126–41; May 1928, 147–60; June 1928, 134–48; July 1928, 131–43; August 1928, 136–42; September 1928, 146–56; October 1928, 149–57; November 1928, 146–55; December 1928, 91–100; January 1929, 117–25; February 1929, 99–108; March 1929, 102–14; April 1929, 107–15; May 1929, 147–60.
26 Rupen Khan-Azad, 'Inchpēs Kazmuets' Hnch'akean Kusakts'ut'iwně', in *Hushardzan Nuiruatz Sots'ial-Demokrat Hnch'akean Kusakts'ut'ean* (Paris: H. Turabian 1930), 35.
27 Ibid.
28 G. Gharajian (S. T. Arkomet), *Rubēn Khan Azadi Hēk'iat'nerě* (Tiflis: n.p., 1928), 18–19.
29 Ibid., 6–7.
30 Rupen Khan-Azad writes about Matteos Shahazizian that 'barely a year later, Shahazizian took his own life; he cut his throat with a razor blade' (Khan-Azad, 'Hay Heghap'okhakani', June 1927, 71.
31 Poghos Afrikian pursued the study of medicine first at the University of Geneva (1890-1891) and then at the University of Lausanne, where he continued his studies in 1891-1892.
32 Mkrtich Manucharian studied law at the University of Geneva. In this respect, we find the following information in *Armēnia*: 'In the same [Armenie] ship traveled Mr.

Manuchariants, one of the Armenian students of Geneva, who has studied law in Geneva' (*Armēnia*, 4 December 1888, 3).
33 Khan-Azad, 'Hay Heghap'okhakani', June 1927, 70–1.
34 See Ibid., 'Hay Heghap'okhakani', July 1927, 53.
35 About the 'Caucasian Night', see *Journal de Genève*, 24 December 1886; Khan-Azad, 'Hay Heghap'okhakani', July 1927, 53. Interestingly, the memoir mentions the names of his comrades with the duties they had taken upon themselves for the event (Maro Vardanian, Gabriel Kafian, Gevorg Gharajian, and Rupen Khan-Azad). Avetis Nazarbekian and Kristapor Ohanian are not mentioned here, even though it was logical that they would have participated.
36 Rupen Khan-Azad does not clearly mention whether the Armenian typefaces were received from the Mekhitarist Congregation of Venice or Vienna. In her memoir, Maro Vardanian directly attests that the typefaces were received from Vienna, while Gharajian writes Venice.
37 See Khan-Azad, 'Hay Heghap'okhakani', July 1927, 53–4.
38 Ibid., 57.
39 *Erkri Dzaynĕ*, 25 November 1907, 14–15.
40 *Erkri Dzaynĕ*, 11 November 1907, 15–16.
41 *Erkri Dzaynĕ*, 20 January 1908, 4–16; *Erkri Dzaynĕ*, 27 January 1908, 14–15; *Erkri Dzaynĕ*, 3 February 1908, 14–15.
42 Gharajian, *Rubēn Khan Azadi Hēk'iat'nerĕ*, 15.
43 *Mshak*, 18 August 1888, 2–3.
44 *Mshak*, 15 September, 1888, 2–3.
45 "The party of Hnchaks, founded in Geneva in August 1887, did not have an official name until 1890, when it became known as the 'Hnchakian Revolutionary Party'. See Nalbandian, *The Armenian Revolutionary Movement*, 115.
46 *Hnch'ak*, September, 1889, 13.
47 *Armēnia*, 18, 21, 23, and 28 September 1889.
48 *Hnch'ak*, September, 1889, 17.
49 *Hnch'ak*, March 1890, 14 (emphasis added).
50 *Hnch'ak*, August 1895.
51 See Maro Nazarbek, *Husher* (Memoirs), National Archives of Armenia, fund 1456, catalog 2, file 27; Khan-Azad, 'Hay Heghap'okhakani', July 1927, 59. Unfortunately, the appeal has not reached us, and I was unable to find it despite long searches.
52 Rupen Khan-Azad published his memoirs in subsequent numbers of the weekly *Zang* of Tabriz (Iran) in 1922. Unfortunately, only the issue of February 4, 1922, has been available. The title of the memoir was 'A Page of Our Modern History: How Was the Hnchakian Party Organized?' It seems that Khan-Azad reprinted this memoir almost literally in the *Hayrenik'* monthly with the title of 'From the Memoirs of an Armenian Revolutionary'.
53 See *Armyansky Vestnik*, no. 44, 1916, 5–7. I am indebted to Yeghig Djerejian, Honorary Doctor of the National Academy of Sciences of Armenia, who brought this article to my attention.
54 Ibid.
55 Ibid.
56 Ibid.
57 Khan-Azad, 'Hay Heghap'okhakani', July 1927, 58.
58 Ibid., 60.
59 See *Erkri Dzaynĕ*, 11 November 1907, 15–16; *Erkri Dzaynĕ*, 20 January 1908, 15; Gevorg Gharajian (S. T. Arkomet), *Ants'eali Hishoghut'iwnnerits'* (Tiflis: Mamul, 1918), 46; Gharajian, *Ṛubēn Khan Azadi Hēk'iat'nerĕ*, 13.

60 *Erkri Dzaynĕ*, 25 November 1907, 14.
61 Gharajian, *Ṛubēn Khan Azadi Hēk'iat'nerĕ*, 17.
62 Khan-Azad, 'Hay Heghap'okhakani', July 1927, 60–1.
63 In this connection, Louise Nalbandian wrote: 'In the latter part of 1886 the six Geneva students chose a committee of three, consisting of Mariam Vardanian, Avetis Nazarbekian, and Gevorg Gharadjian, to draft the plan for the future organization. The plan [...] later became the program of the Hnchakian Revolutionary Party'. See Nalbandian, *The Armenian Revolutionary Movement,* 108.
64 In his memoirs, Rupen Berberian also confirms what was said above: 'The Armenian revolutionary party founded in Geneva in 1886 took form in 1887 under the name "Hnchakian Revolutionary Party" and published the first issue of *Hnch'ak*'. Rupen Berberian, 'Patrank'neri Shrjanits', *Vēm,* January 1938, 24. Of course, there is a generalization of the name of the party in what Berberian says. The denomination of the party is a later phenomenon, as the outcome of my study shows.

2

The Hnchakian 'nay' to Young Turk Overtures, 1895–1908

Garabet K. Moumdjian (†)

The process of dealing with the historiography of the Social Democrat Hnchakian Party (SDHP, Hnchak, Hnchakists) is a daunting task since the party has not kept a repository for its archives to be utilized for such purposes. One way to remedy this is to use other primary sources such as the party's official organ, *Hnch'ak*, and other secondary sources, such as other party publications and memoirs of seasoned and responsible party members who were knowledgeable eyewitnesses to what they narrated. One source, which is extremely important in this regard, is Arsen Gidur and his two-volume *History of the Hnchakian Party*.[1]

This chapter will mainly deal with the history of the relations between the Hnchakian party and the émigré Young Turk organizations in Europe during the period between 1895 and 1909. It was during this period that the party was consumed with internal strife due to ideological differences. This strife began to surface immediately after the suppression of the first Armenian uprising in Sasun by the Ottoman Fourth Army and the Kurdish Hamidiye Light Cavalry Regiments.[2] That such divisions within the leadership of the SDHP would occur was to be expected. In fact, anecdotal tendencies that questioned Western Armenian objectives vis-à-vis what Eastern Armenians wished to accomplish within the Armenian-inhabited provinces of the Ottoman Empire were increasingly confirmed in archival materials published during the last decade. In other words, the archival records of the ARF, for example, demonstrate that genuine revolutionary and socialist ideas entered the Ottoman Empire via Eastern Armenian agents.[3]

In addition to the ideological strife, this chapter will also discuss SDHP relations vis-à-vis the Young Turks. Unlike the case of the Dashnaks, the Hnchaks remained aloof, if not totally disinterested and even against establishing any contacts with the Young Turk émigré communities in Europe who also aimed at toppling the regime of Abdülhamid II and reestablishing the constitutional regime that the latter had suspended due to the Russo-Turkish War of 1877–8.

Formation and Disintegration

The SDHP was the first full-blown Armenian revolutionary and political party that adhered to an adapted Marxist ideology. The party's mission envisaged a two-step programme of action: to establish a free and independent Armenia and to strive for the creation of a social-democratic state structure for the fledgling republic.[4] The SDHP masterminded, executed and blundered the implementation of the disastrous 1894 Sasun rebellion, which cost it dearly. Internal disagreements between Western and Eastern Armenian leaders caused a rift leading to a split into two distinct factions.[5] As it turned out, Western Armenian Hnchak leaders yearned for a party with nationalist tendencies vis-à-vis the liberation of Western Armenia, while their Eastern counterparts remained unyielding on the tenets of their Marxist ideology. The polarization continued until 1905 when the party's General Meeting in Paris tried to amalgamate competing ideological doctrines. Divergent thinking continued and the party's Vienna General Meeting witnessed a final internal rupture; those advocating nationalist tendencies separated and formed the Reformed Hnchakian party (*Verakazmyal Hnch'akean Kusakts'ut'iwn*), while the supporters of social democracy continued with the party's old name. After the abortive 1894 Sasun rebellion, the party concentrated its efforts on Cilicia and the Ottoman capital, Constantinople.[6]

The First Sasun Uprising and the 'May Reform Project'

On the first day of August 1894, the mountainous Armenian region of Sasun in the province of Bitlis was swarmed by regular Ottoman troops and Hamidiye regiments. The official reason given by the Ottoman government for the initial military concentration and the subsequent attacks against the villages was that the raids were organized to crush an alleged uprising against the government.[7] Official sources referred to frequent raids organized by bands of Armenian *fedayees* (freedom fighters) against the government in Sasun, as well as in the Mush district, thereby endangering the peace and tranquillity of the whole region.[8] Executing such punitive measures for the reasons given was an exaggeration. The Armenian *fedayees* were few in number and tried to exact some punishment upon Kurdish bandits to warn them away from attacking and looting Armenian villages. The Ottoman government used this pretext to present the events in a different perspective in order to legitimize its actions.

In this case, the military offensive left more than 3,000 dead, as thousands of refugees saw their homes and villages methodically demolished. 'For three weeks in the late summer of 1894 the district of Sasun in the province of Bitlis became the scene of horrors which recalled those of Batak', wrote a leading historian. 'The Kurds', he continued, were 'aided by Turkish troops, under the command of Zeki Pasha, [who] destroyed 24 villages, and butchered, with the most revolting cruelty, every Armenian whom they could find. Zeki was decorated for his services'.[9] As if the massacres were not sufficient, Ottoman authorities initiated a full-fledged deportation policy that affected a considerable part of the Armenian population, many of whom were expelled to distant locations. Undoubtedly, this was a step in a scheme to alter the very ethnic composition of the area. In the words of Avedis Nakashian, an Armenian physician from Urfa and an eyewitness to the destitute conditions of deported Armenians when they arrived in the city, conditions were appalling. He opined:

> The exiles . . . arrived at Urfa. It was like a caravan of death. I shall never forget those tattered, pain-wracked victims, their staring eyes filled with horror, their gaunt faces. Women [were] clinging to their starving babies, little children with bleeding feet, men, women, and children who had been slashed with swords or beaten from head to foot. Had anything in history ever compared to it? I wondered, and I doubted if it had. Tears streamed down their faces, prayers were on their lips, and when they learned that they would be safe in Urfa, they fell upon their knees and gave thanks to the God they worshiped so devoutly.[10]

Eyewitness reports revealed that the participation of the Hamidiye Regiments gave much cause for alarm since their ranks were formed largely by recruits from poorer Kurdish tribal horsemen – thieves and brigands to be more precise – for the sole purpose of pillaging and terrorizing Armenians. Thus, many believed that they were a potent instrument in the hands of both the central as well as local Ottoman authorities, determined to rid the region of its Armenian inhabitants.[11]

On 23 January 1895, a commission of inquiry visited the devastated area whose formation was triggered by reports of ongoing atrocities received by the British, French and Russian ambassadors in Constantinople and forwarded to their respective governments.[12] The findings of this commission raised serious doubts about the Porte's official explanation that it was responding to a 'popular uprising'. Instead, commissioners viewed the military campaign as one organized by army units against a peaceful and defenceless population. Moreover, Armenian revolutionary fighters' raids were not considered sufficient reason to permit such a punitive collective punishment.[13] Parenthetically, several Ottoman members of the delegation that accompanied the commissioners on their journey were outraged that as soon as the official party reached the area of the so-called Armenian insurgency, European members conducted their own independent investigations.[14] This was unusual, to say the least, but also indicative of the mistrust then permeating Ottoman ties with leading European powers.

The foreign officials were livid with what they observed and were particularly offended by Ottoman intrigues to advance a major diplomatic initiative. Ambassadors representing the three powers that were in a state of conflict over the Balkans confronted the sultan on 11 May 1895, with a Memorandum and Project of Reforms for the Eastern Provinces of Asia Minor. Carefully vetted by the governments of Great Britain, France and Russia, the document intended to punish Constantinople for its inaction and hold the Porte accountable for past treaty breaches.[15] Referred to as the May Reform Project,[16] the memorandum contained twelve major reform issues, along with lengthy explanations regarding each.[17] In summary, the document addressed:

1. Decreasing the number of provinces;
2. Appointing suitable governors consistent with the needs of the different provinces;

3. Granting amnesty to Armenian political prisoners;
4. Providing the means for the return of Armenian refugees to their regions;
5. Appointing a permanent Control Commission in Constantinople;
6. Assigning a mobile commission to oversee implementation of reforms in the provinces;
7. Securing reparations to Armenians in Sasun, Talori [Dalvorig] and other areas where massacres occurred;
8. Establishing laws to reduce instances of forced religion conversions, and
9. Adopting measures to sustain Armenians' rights and privileges.

As customary diplomatic maneuverings were underway to refute these imposed conditions, events took on a dramatic turn at the end of September 1895, which complicated matters. On 30 September, the Hnchaks organized a demonstration of thousands of Armenians in front of the Sublime Porte. Unabashedly, the demonstrators demanded the application of the May Reform Project, which was perceived as a provocation.[18] In response, Ottoman authorities retaliated by clamping down on the demonstrators and encouraging a series of massacres in Constantinople and various provinces.[19]

These actions did not go unnoticed by frustrated European representatives. Most concluded that the sultan was reluctant to implement the reforms they demanded, and infuriated by the new round of massacres, they decided to display their power in Constantinople. Vessels of the British and French fleets engaged in a naval demonstration in October 1895 to intimidate Sultan Adülhamid II. This 'show of force' introduced no tangible results and failed to alter conditions, as far as Armenian reforms were concerned.[20]

A commentary in *Hnch'ak*, the official organ of the Hnchakian party published in London, described how the Armenian Patriarch Matteos Izmirlian's resignation was perceived in some Armenian circles:

> Izmirlian's predecessor, Patriarch Ashekian, who was elected in 1891, was obliged to cleanse the [Armenian patriarchate's] National Council of people with real nationalistic feelings and to appoint others who were willing to become instruments in the hands of the likes of Nurian and Maksud pashas. However, when Izmirlian was elected in 1894, things changed. Europe's eyes were on the Armenian Question and the likes of Nurian and Maksud pashas suddenly disappeared from the scene. This time, however, it was the likes of Apraham Kara-Kehyayan Pasha, who entered intra-Armenian politics at a very old age as a crony of Nurian and his faction. He was to bring shame and dishonor upon the name of his noble family. It was telegrammed to the *Times* [in London] that the Sultan had promised 10,000 gold coins to this traitor, if he secured Izmirlian's resignation.[21]

Ottoman and Armenian records confirm that the first contact with the hitherto politically marginal Young Turk movement transpired on the occasion of the aforementioned Bab-ı Ali demonstration of 30 September 1895, organized by the Hnchakian party. After the demonstration, a leaflet signed by the Committee of

Union and Progress (CUP) criticized the gathering as a separatist activity, exhorting the populace to protect the country.[22] Despite the negative tone of the Constantinople branch of the CUP towards the Armenian revolutionary agitation, early Young Turk leaders such as Izzet Bey in Egypt were eager to establish bridges. In the words of one leading Turkish historian:

> At the peak of the Armenian Crisis [1895], the lawyer Izzet Bey, nicknamed 'Persian Izzet,' was also apprehended [in Egypt]. He had written and disseminated a manifesto inviting Armenians to join in common action, which the Armenians welcomed. He then sent a letter to Lord Salisbury calling for the latter's intervention in the [Armenian] crisis.[23]

While several Turkish politicians forged ties with Armenian leaders, the initiator of the genuine cooperation that emerged between Armenian revolutionary committees in Europe and Young Turk representatives in Constantinople was Mizanci Murad Bey, a proponent of a palace *coup d'état*, as it was envisioned by the so-called Palace Party, comprised of Ottoman officials who were advocates of change themselves.[24] Murad Bey published a much-noticed editorial addressed to the Armenian committees in his newspaper, *Mizan* (Balance). The column invited Armenian organizations to work with the Young Turks, considering them partners in building a new country, a common fatherland no less. In Murad Bey's own words, the call to Armenians was striking:

> O our Armenian Compatriots! O the committees of [the] nation [within the fatherland] and abroad! We are addressing this invitation to you on behalf of the Ottoman Committee of Union and Progress. Let's devote our efforts to the future by forgetting the past. Let us unite to rescue the fatherland from the calamity to which it is being subjected.[25]

Given its tone as well as the rarity of such appeals, *Hnch'ak* welcomed Murad Bey's appeal, hoping that together they could topple the regime of Abdülhamid. *Hnch'ak*, however, did criticize the Young Turk leader for hinting that the 1894 massacres in Sasun were the result of Armenian revolutionary activists who had planted the seeds of hatred towards Turks in Armenian minds. The editorial stressed that Armenians did not hate the Turkish people and that their objections rested with the sultan and his tyranny.[26]

The Hnchakian division

The Hnchakian party eventually encountered an internal division. Stricken by personality conflicts, the party split into two rival groups: the Hnchakian center in London and the Reformed (*Verakazmyal*) faction in Constantinople under the leadership of Arpiar Arpiarian.[27] The division weakened the party, leaving the revolutionary field wide open for the ARF.

The schism within the Hnchakian party started in 1896 when nationalist elements of the party rejected aggressive socialist policies favoured by Hnchakian leaders living in London. This issue, which was to afflict the ARF as well after 1903 (see as follows), was due to the influence of Eastern Armenian university students – the founders, including Avetis Nazarbekian, Mariam (Maro) Vardanian-Nazarbekian, Rupen Khan-Azat and others – whose Marxist-Socialist ideological preferences advocated the politics of class struggle against tsarist tyranny in the Caucasus. This was in utter contrast to the Ottoman milieu, where the Armenian revolution strove to achieve reforms and local autonomy. Leaders of the Verakazmyal faction, such as Arpiar Arpiarian, Mihran Damadian and Mihran Sevasly, among others, wanted the party to engage solely in the national liberation struggle of Western Armenians. When Nazarbekian and his cohort remained adamant towards their ideological programme, the nationalists called for a general meeting in Alexandria, Egypt, where, in 1896, they adopted a totally nationalistic anti-socialist programme.

To mitigate his perceived threats, the sultan opened a communication line with the leaders of Armenian revolutionary organizations through Herafion Nivlinsky.[28] Little is known about this envoy, although it is assumed that he met with members of the Anglo-Armenian Committee in London to gauge their interests. Still, Nivlinsky's meeting with the Hnchakian party, as reported in the Paris-based *New York Herald*, could not be verified.[29] *Hnch'ak* denied that such a person contacted their headquarters in London for the purpose of negotiating the issue of Armenian reforms in the Ottoman Empire. British newspapers that reported the envoy's meetings with Armenian committees first in London and later in Paris – apparently through the efforts of the Ottoman embassies in both European capitals – later rescinded their previous reports.[30] No concrete evidence was ever found to buttress the wild claims to the contrary. Some concluded that the Nivlinsky episode, and the sultan's tactics to misinform European public opinion, highlighted the sultan's mindset as a full-fledged tyrant. *Hnch'ak* opined: 'O You prosecutor, Criminal Sultan... Now that you are fallen into the trap [coup attempt of September 1896] you are trying to escape with your skin. As long as there is breath in us, we will continue to struggle against you and to crush your regime, O miserable fox.'[31]

A letter sent by the ARF, obliged the Hnchakian party to clarify its own positions on several pertinent questions. In response to the manifesto, for example, a letter bearing the signature of the Hnchakian party was delivered to various embassies, wherein the party disengaged itself from the ARF manifesto in question. The Hnchakians explained that they had no Central Committee in the capital. They thus concluded that they did not share most of the ideas expressed in the proposal, which was not particularly surprising given the competing interests between the two groups.[32] Furthermore, they disagreed on a sensitive point, namely the alleged ineffectiveness of European endeavours vis-à-vis Armenian reforms.[33] This particular difference was the result of lofty promises made to Hnchakian party members by European acquaintances, many of whom were eager to reinforce the notion that these Armenians could be a viable force to the British government's aims. In December 1897, the Central Committee of the Hnchakian party in London informed Ambassador Currie that the party had just concluded its General Congress in the British capital and had elected a new central committee representing all of its members.[34]

Figure 2.1 Avetis Nazarbekian. Source: Gidur, *Patmut'iwn S.D. Hnch'akean Kusakts'ut'ean, 1887-1962*, vol. I, 63.

If anything, the move reflected the effects of the split within the organization, rather than any political relevance for the motherland. The claim that 'a central committee, representing all party members', had been elected was simply an attempt to undermine the legitimacy of any other Hnchakian faction vis-à-vis British authorities. Clearly the London group feared that the Constantinople-based Reformed faction would fill the political vacuum, which was an indication of the party's disorganized state.

To garner further recognition, the Hnchakian letter drew the British Embassy's attention to information that the Turks were still massacring Armenians, especially in Cilicia. Clearly, Ambassador Currie and his staff in Constantinople were aware that Armenians were in danger, although the communication emphasized that 'events in Hajin [we]re a good example of this [threat]'. It pointed to French reluctance to intervene and asked London to 'interfere on behalf of Cilician Armenians'.[35] Thus, the Hnchakian party continued its strategy of appeals to the Great Powers regarding perhaps its only stronghold in the empire, Cilicia, just as before the internal split that damaged the party's credibility.

In the annals of major developments that marked the year 1897, and which were dutifully noted by Şükrü Hanioğlu, were the arrests of several prominent Armenian operatives who played critical roles with the CUP. In February 1897, Ottoman intelligence agents intercepted a secret message that was sent from Paris to Erzerum by the Dashnaktsutiun Committee. In this message the Dashnaktsutiun Committee stated that its purpose was completely different from that of the CUP. However, they were continuing their contacts with Murad Bey [Mizanci]. They requested that their Erzerum branch have closer contact with banished officers who were also CUP members.³⁶ After further investigation by the government, it was discovered that Setrak Pastermajian, a member of the local Dashnaktsutiun branch, distributed the money sent from Europe to the Young Turks in Erzerum. He was arrested, but the local Russian Consul intervened and he was released.³⁷ Moreover, when the government learned that Young Turk cells had been formed in Mersin and Adana [in Cilicia] it arrested their members. There were four Armenians in the Mersin branch: Garabet Kilimjian, Murad Tekeyan, a second Murad whose last name is not given and Setrak [no family names furnished either], as well as three in the Adana branch: Khatchig Babaian, a doctor named Boghos and a pharmacist named Garabed [again no last names furnished].³⁸ Ottoman officials presented these Armenians as members of the Young Turk organization in Mersin and Adana. While some Armenians may well have been members of Young Turk committees, it was more likely that they were Reformed Hnchakians, as the faction operated mainly through Cilicia during this period.³⁹ Moreover, credible sources indicated that the second Murad, whose family name was not given in the documents cited by Hanioğlu, was no other than Hampartsoum Boyajian (Murad), the famous Hnchak leader who was in Cilicia at the time.⁴⁰ A March 1898 letter from the Hnchak Center in London to Patriarch Maghakia Ormanian inquired about Murad's imprisonment and sought the clergyman's assistance to secure his release.⁴¹ This correspondence was also important because it contained a direct threat to Ormanian, which was somewhat odd. According to the dispatch:

> The Hnchakian party had thus far acted diplomatically so that it would not create hurdles between you and the government . . . However, in the face of such blatant misrule we indicate that if our letter remains unanswered, we will restart our activities after March.
>
> You know, dear patriarch, that in such a situation you are in, not only your but even the patriarchate's board's honor will be questioned by the population. We know that you do not want something like that to happen.⁴²

How Patriarch Ormanian responded is unknown but on 6 January 1898, he informed Ambassador Currie that he had submitted a new *takrir* to the sultan with sixteen points, in which he proposed to bring some sort of relief and normalcy to Armenians in the interior. Twelve of the more relevant measures presented to the Porte sought:

1. Permission to collect funds for orphans;
2. Consent for merchants to travel;
3. Temporary remission of the military tax;
4. Authorization for Armenians with claims against the government to return to their homes;
5. Return of Armenians government employees to their duties;
6. Admission of Armenian students to government schools;
7. Allowing Armenians exiled to provinces to return to Constantinople;
8. Acquiescence for patriarchal delegates to assume positions throughout the provinces;

9. Approval to reopen parochial schools;
10. Exemptions for church properties from taxes;
11. Cessation of conversions [to Islam]; and,
12. Endorsement to print patriarchal press releases without censorship.[43]

Ormanian's report drew a dark picture of the conditions Ottoman Armenians endured as his suggestions were nothing short of an incriminating summary of the Sublime Porte's failure to provide even minimal civil and human rights to its Armenian citizens. Moreover, Ormanian's *takrir* left no room for doubt that the Armenian community as such was facing grave dangers and was literally on the verge of institutional destruction. In view of the pending reform programmes, Ormanian's report constituted an urgent appeal to the Great Powers to follow through on their political promises by urging the Ottoman government to implement sorely needed modifications that could improve living conditions for its Armenian citizens. The patriarch's initiatives were to no avail. In March 1898, Ormanian called upon Currie once again to share with him the sultan's decision to issue a decree (*irade*) regarding his *takrir*. The decree remained worthless since the document could not guarantee the execution of any reforms formulated in the appeal.[44]

First contacts with Young Turks

In November 1898, an informant claimed that a 'Constantinople agent' wished to establish contact with ARF leaders. He thus inquired whether the ARF would send someone to meet with this 'gentleman' in Lausanne. It turned out that this gentleman was none other than Kevork Bulbul (Bulbulian). Apparently, when his efforts failed in Paris, the enterprising Bulbul travelled to Lausanne to try his luck there. During his travels, Bulbul evidently met several Hnchakists and persuaded them that he was on official business as an envoy of the Ottoman government.[45] *Drōshak*, the official organ of the ARF, relished the entertaining story and published all that was known regarding the whole affair. It reported that this 'gentleman' was a close friend of the governor of Pera, Enver Bey, who masterminded the Armenian massacres in the capital after the seizure of the Ottoman Bank. The ARF organ further denounced Bulbul and exposed him as a spy, alleging that he carried police credentials from Galata Palace (Constantinople police headquarters). That Bulbul's task was likely to gather information about Armenian revolutionaries and revolutionary cells in Europe and the Ottoman capital was entirely plausible.[46]

A month and a half later, the Hnchak Center in London drafted a letter to German Kaiser Wilhelm II on his visit to Constantinople. The eloquent communication chronicled for the monarch the conditions that befell Armenians and reacquainted him with details included in the Treaty of Berlin concerning the question of Armenian reforms. Wilhelm II was explicitly told that the pact was endorsed by all European powers and underlined that since the signing of the treaty in 1878 some 300,000 Armenians had lost their lives.[47] Naturally, the Kaiser was solicited not only to uphold the Berlin concordat but also to use the opportunity of his visit to press the Sublime Porte for action. For their part, Armenian committees in Europe remained adamant in their demand to implement belated reforms, aware that these were issues of survival.

Towards a First Congress of anti-Hamidian groups

This fact being unknown to Armenian revolutionaries, Prince Sebaheddin advocated a major congress and funded the printing of various appeals in Young Turk journals for the long-awaited gathering of Ottoman dissidents.[48] The Young Turks, in particular, wrote to persuade Armenian organizations to take part in such a congress. In one such appeal, they went straight to the point, calling for the adoption of a courageous position:

> After the demise of this scourge to humanity, Sultan Abdülhamid [II], will Turks, Kurds, and Armenians embrace each other as the citizens of one country? They will understand that the enmity is the result of the policies of this one man. We reiterate our enemy is one and so is our future and goals. We must work together so that all Ottoman subjects are free under the rule of a fundamental law.[49]

Appeals to vital Armenian revolutionary societies continued in other arenas, too. Both sons of Damad Mahmud Pasha and Ismail Kemal privately met with ARF and Hnchakian representatives to iron out some of their differences. The ARF representatives gave their word to participate only after they were assured that the organizers were willing to accept Article 61 of the Treaty of Berlin regarding Armenian reforms, as well as the 11 May 1895 Memorandum of the Armenian Reform Project together with the British Appendix attached to it. The Hnchakian center in London put forth even more stringent proposals. Regardless, Sabaheddin knew well that it was going to be hard to persuade the Young Turk leader, Ahmed Rıza and his cohorts, given existing sensitivities to Article 16 of the 1878 Treaty, and the subsequent, watered-down Article 61 of the Treaty of Berlin.[50] According to *Hnch'ak*:

> The world acknowledges the Armenian issue, and it is documented in the 61st [A]rticle of the Berlin Convention . . . . There also are the May 1895 reforms set forth by European powers and accepted by the sultan and not yet implemented. These could be achieved by keeping the Ottoman state as one unit with internal autonomy for minorities. If the Young Turks agree to these [terms], then we can work together . . . .. We have thus far considered that there is a united party of Young Turks. Now we know that there is no such thing. There are factions and then there are personalities each with their own agenda. How can one work with such a 'group'?[51]

It was initially decided that the conference would convene on 15 January 1902, but the Armenian delegations' hesitation made this impossible.[52] Organizers had sent invitations to the Reformed Hnchakian party, *Drōshak*, the central organ of the ARF, and the editorial board of *Hnch'ak*. Both Hnchak and Dashnak delegates considered it prudent to meet before the conference and to maintain a united stance throughout the conference.[53]

There were two important reasons for the Armenian hesitation. The first was the absence of internal unity within the Armenian camp in attending the conference. The Hnchakian center in London was totally against participating. Thus, the Armenian delegation was eventually formed and headed by ARF member Avetis Aharonian.[54] Several Armenian leaders in Paris were invited, though only Minas Cheraz and Garabed Basmajian agreed to be present. Both announced during the congress that they represented no Armenian political party and that they were going to uphold what the Armenian delegation decided. Their presence was thus perceived as being partisan.[55]

The Armenian representatives, seeing that there were no real intentions for further negotiations on Ahmed Rıza's side, left the conference in protest.[56] With that said, however, even the Reformed Hnchaks, whose members had answered Sabaheddin's invitation to attend the congress, shared sobering news with the Young Turks by positing the following:

> If today's Young Turks really want to change their country towards the better, they still have time. Our reformist ideas are not dissimilar to theirs. Their only problem is that they are evolutionists rather than revolutionists, which is necessary in Turkey's case. Things have to change soon for Armenia, since it is Armenians who are dying. They [the Young Turks] have to accept the fact that Turkey is a heterogeneous rather than a homogeneous entity. All minorities should have rights but must also work for the one fatherland.[57]

It is critical to emphasize that Hnchakists did not consider the work of the congress a victory to be celebrated. On the contrary, *Hnch'ak* summed up this pessimistic feeling when it declared:

> The congress was a total failure. The idea of being able to work with the Young Turks is not valid anymore. All utopian thinking can be discarded. It is now clear that it is impossible to work with them [Young Turks] against the old regime. We are happy that the Hnchaks said this a priori, while the Armenian participants of the Congress [ARF and the Reformed Hnchakian party] assumed the same stance a posteriori by leaving the congress in protest. There was no other way. This was expected.[58]

Simply stated, and unequivocally, this was a clear conclusion. Whether anything could be done to salvage discussions and negotiations was difficult to determine. As time would tell, this was explicitly so for the Hnchakians for whom the whole affair of sitting down to negotiate with the Young Turks was a futile debacle at best. What was abundantly clear was the gap that existed among delegates on conditions that Armenians confronted in the eastern provinces of the Ottoman Empire and why it was so urgent to address them was not at the centre of the issue at hand.

Moreover, in October 1900, the Ottoman government provided information to the British regarding alleged smuggling of weapons between Cyprus and Cilicia.[59] This was a serious matter since Cyprus was under British rule and Cilicia was known to harbour Armenian revolutionaries [Hnchakian] as well as CUP agitators.[60] Furthermore, there were fears of new massacres in Diyarbakir, which were reported in Western newspapers.[61] Such reportage of Armenian massacres left their marks in British society, even if a report published in the *Times* of Armenians burned alive, according to Francis Richard Maunsell, the British military attaché at the Constantinople Embassy at the time, was apparently unfounded. Maunsell stressed the author had 'no reliable sources, not even rumors concerning the alleged event were abound', which could not be verified.[62]

A temporary Hnchakian reconciliation?

Significant faux pas were not the only stumbling blocks that confronted Turks and Armenians at this time. The Hnchakian party too preferred not to respond positively to Sabaheddin's invitations to participate in the congress. As stated earlier, the Reformed Hnchakian party managed to send a representative to the congress, who hinted at a possible reconciliation. Indeed, soon after news of the congress spread, the Hnchakian leadership in London announced that the two factions reconciled differences and were finally united after arduous deliberations.[63]

In April 1902, London leaders informed readers through *Hnch'ak* that party unity was achieved. The presidency of the Hnchakian General Congress wrote to inform the ARF that communication between the two parties could resume as soon as the congress elected a new central committee, but this too was not deemed entirely persuasive by ARF leaders.[64]

ARF leaders in Geneva apparently were not ready to resume cooperation with the Hnchaks. *Drōshak* published a scathing editorial, which concluded that Hnchaks were not yet ready for, or did not want the unification of all revolutionary forces. Moreover, the rift within the Hnchakian party was not solved as announced, given that two organs were published, both in London, one in Western and the other in Eastern Armenian. *Drōshak* stated that its caution stemmed from the implication – about which rumours were circulating within the Armenian communities – that Hnchak leaders had pocketed around 100,000 French Francs for their personal uses.[65]

Though encouraged by all these groups, Behaeddin Şakir, one of the CUP leaders, still relied on his Armenian contact, Diran Kelekian, to obtain a sorely needed alliance with Armenian committees, especially the ARF.[66] In turn, this meant that he would face Rıza's wrath, whose anti-Armenian sentiments were well-known. At this juncture, Şakir had a wild card to play in the person of Ahmed Jelaleddin Pasha, the former chief of Ottoman intelligence, who had joined the Young Turk cause in Paris. To be sure, Şakir cultivated Jelaleddin since his days in Constantinople, and he finally persuaded the pasha to become the de facto financier of the movement. This gave Şakir the upper hand in dealing with Rıza. Moreover, Kelekian coached Şakir on critical ideas about starting a new organization or possibly taking control of an existing one. Jelaleddin

Pasha, however, insisted on the inclusion of the ARF and the Hnchakian party in the new organization. He further demanded that Rıza must be demoted to the status of a regular member with no leadership responsibilities. It was clear that Jelaleddin Pasha was not only positioning himself to assume full authority over the new organization but also wished to appoint Şakir as second in command. Of course, the ambitious Şakir was not ready to be taken advantage of in such a manner. The friction between the two ambitious men led to the demise of Şakir's plan for a quick and unequivocal assumption of power within the émigré Young Turk movement in Paris. The ever-cautious Şakir, however, was still able to manoeuvre and scheme until he assumed the leadership of the existing coalition.

The Second Congress of anti-Hamidian forces

One of the key decisions emanating from the ARF Western Bureau in October 1907 motivated members of the party's negotiating team to 'consider negotiations with Ahmed Rıza as consumed and depleted'. According to the record, the ARF pledged to 'continue negotiations with all elements [unhappy with] Ottoman rule, and to entice all to join forces'. The ARF further proposed to hold an initial meeting with the Armenakans and Hnchakians.[67]

At the beginning of November 1907, the Western Bureau dispatched Aknuni (Khachatur Malumian) to Paris where he was tasked to oversee preparations for the Second Congress of Ottoman Dissidents. He was further mandated to approach the Armenakans and the two Hnchakian factions to present a unified Armenian front during upcoming deliberations.[68]

Although the ARF invited Armenian parties to attend in a united front, this did not happen. The Reformed Hnchakians proposed Arshag Chobanian as their delegate though the latter declined on the grounds that he was not a party member.[69] The only other Armenian delegate was Hovsep Sarafian, who represented the journal *Armēnia*, the organ of the Armenakan Party.[70]

Conclusion

To say that the ultra-nationalistic tendencies of some Young Turk leaders, including those promoted by Ahmed Rıza and later Behaeddin Şakir, shaped Hnchakian views vis-à-vis the Young Turk movement in general would be an understatement. Indeed, the Hnchakians were extremely aware of these leaders' ultra-nationalist ideologies and the competition among factions within the Young Turk émigré societies in Europe. Thus, Hnchakists saw no prospect of working with those that espoused nationalistic tendencies and preferred to work with Sabaheddin's party.[71] During the parliamentary elections in late 1908 and thereafter, they joined forces with Prince Sabaheddin, whose faction became the leading opposition group on account of its union with Ottoman Greeks and some other minority groups. Stepan Sabah-Gulian, a leading figure within the SDHP, declared his and his party's opposition to the CUP and urged other

Armenian political parties (i.e. the ARF, Ramkavars and the Reformed Hnchakians) to coalesce with Sabaheddin and his party and to constitute an opposition to the CUP.

Had the SDHP, which had, since its formation, adhered to a centralized structure, decided to coalesce with Sabaheddin, the champion of the decentralization (*Adem-i Markaziyyet*) movement for the future political and administrative system of the Ottoman Empire, this system would have benefited the minorities well in the locales they lived in. On the other hand, however, it is flabbergasting to say the least that a party like the ARF, which steadfastly worked as a decentralized structure and bore the fruits of such an endeavour through the creation of robust local bodies within three empires (Ottoman, Russian, Iran), would hastily join in with the centralist Young Turks.

Regardless, after the 1908 revolution, Constantinople and the Ottoman territories became the new centre of gravity not only for the ARF but also for the Hnchakian party, as most of their cadres fleeing the oppressive 'Russian Winter' found refuge in Constantinople. This was an ironic development, since the roles were now reversed, and the Ottoman Empire became a free haven for Armenian revolutionaries.

Although Armenian political and revolutionary parties welcomed European intervention for the betterment of Armenian life in the Ottoman Empire, one must also remember that both the ARF and the Hnchakian party leaned towards leftist, socialist ideologies that meant, if anything, that both parties were somehow cognizant of Western imperialist motives vis-à-vis the Ottoman Empire.[72]

Moreover, the years 1909 to 1915 saw no Armenian revolutionary agitation as was the case during the reign of Abdülhamid II, and confirmed that the Armenian parties truly believed in the new constitutional system and worked in earnest to maintain it. In fact, the Armenian organizations openly declared their devotion to the newly established constitutional regime and ceased to pursue any armed struggle, since they were now recognized as legal political entities.[73]

Notes

1 Arsen Gidur, *Patmut'iwn S.D. Hnch'akean Kusakts'ut'ean*, vols. I and II (Beirut: Shirag Press, 1962–3).
2 In fact, the idea of the formation of the Hamidiye regiments came from Zeki Pasha, who persuaded the sultan that such a paramilitary force would be instrumental in defending the porous eastern border with Russia, which was in the habit of utilizing Cossack regiments for the same purpose.
3 Yervant Pambukian (ed.), *Niwt'er H.H. Dashnakts'ut'ean Patmut'ean*, vol. V (Beirut: ARF Publications, 2007), 355–66. The document is part of the Armenian Revolutionary Federation (ARF) Archives that are housed at the Hairenik Building in Watertown, Massachusetts. Thirteen volumes of the Archives are thus far printed under the title *Niwt'er H.H. Dashnakts'ut'ean Patmut'ean Hamar*. The first four volumes of the series, which will henceforth be presented as *Niwt'er*, were published under the editorship of Hrach Dasnabedian, while volume V through XIII have been published by Yervant Pambukian. A word regarding the difference in editorship is in

place. At the time Dasnabedian edited volumes I through IV, the archival material was not yet classified. Hence, the reference to these documents is done through the page number(s) in the printed volumes (I-IV). With volume V onwards, Pambukian uses a reference system that was implemented in the 1980s, whereby each document now had a separate archival referral number attached to it as well as the page number of the volume where it appears.

4 *Tzragir Hnch'akean Kusakts'ut'ean*, second edn. abridged (London, 1897).
5 Hrach Dasnabedian, *Patmut'iwn Hay Heghap'okhakan Sharzhman ew Hay Heghap'okhakan Dashnakts'ut'ean* (Beirut: Hamazkayin, 1988), 68–76. The problems within the Hnchakian party were the result of acute differences between the Western and Eastern Armenian leaders. While the Nazarbekian couple (founding members of the party) and Rupen Khan-Azat insisted on continuing the centralized form of governance of the party (i.e. all decisions to be dictated from the centre) and abiding by leftist, revolutionary ideology and zeal in the eastern provinces, Western Armenian Hnchak leaders such as Mihran Damadian and Mihran Sevasly stressed the nationalist character of a popular unrest, preparedness, and 'education' of the villagers. This was akin to the differences that surfaced within the ARF – such as those between Hrair Tzhokhk and his Eastern Armenian counterparts in Sasun after 1904.
6 The Zeytun rebellion of 1895 was in conjunction with the Sasun rebellion of 1894. Both acts led to further Armenian bloodshed throughout 1895 and 1896.
7 BOA, 255-97-39, Yıldız Esas Evrakı, 255-97-39, *4cu ordunun muşiri Zeki Paşa Talori ve havalisine teftiş ederek Muşa döndüğü, Askeri hareket, 1894* (Zeki Pasha, the commander of the Fourth Army, returning to Mush after inspection in Talori and its environs, Military Action, 1894).
8 William Miller, *The Ottoman Empire and its Successors 1801-1927* (London: Frank Cass, 1966), 429. Sasun is located in the Province of Bitlis; See also Avetis Papazian, *Zhamanakagrut'iwn Haykakan Harts'i ew Metz Egherně* (Yerevan: National Academy of Sciences, 2000), 7; *Fedayee*, from the Arabic *fida'i*, literally means a person who is ready to sacrifice his/her life for a cause. *Hayduk* was adopted by Armenians from the Serbian/Macedonian language. It was an appellation that referred to their freedom fighters. It was intermittently used in Armenian to mean freedom fighter. The adoption of this name shows the affinity that the Armenian revolutionary movement had with its counterparts in the Balkans (Serbs, Bulgars, Macedonians, etc.)
9 Papazian, *Zhamanakarut'iwn*, 429. See also Louise Nalbandian, *The Armenian Revolutionary Movement: The Development of Armenian Political Parties Throughout the Nineteenth Century* (Berkeley: University of California Press, 1963), 120–2. According to Nalbandian, the 'uprising' was organized by Murad (Hampartsoum Boyajian), a devoted member of the Hnchakian party, who came to Sasun at the beginning of 1894. Mihran Damadian, another Hnchakist leader at the time, was also instrumental in the organization of self-defence battles during the turmoil. See also Stephen Duguid, 'The Politics of Unity: Hamidian Policy in Eastern Anatolia', *Middle Eastern Studies* 9, no. 2 (1973): 151. On the other hand, Duguid plays down the role of the central authorities. He asserts that the government stepped aside, and the Kurds went ahead in committing the atrocities.
10 Avedis Nakashian, *A Man Who Found a Country* (New York: Crowell, 1940), 135.
11 Nalbandian, *The Armenian Revolutionary Movement*, 161. See also Janet Klein, *Power in the Periphery: The Hamidiye Light Cavalry and the Struggle over Ottoman Kurdistan, 1890-1914* (Stanford: Stanford University Press, 2016). Klein's book is the latest

revisionist history of the Kurdish Hamidiye regiments and discusses the particularities of the points I try to raise in this chapter.
12 Miller, *The Ottoman Empire*, 429. According to Miller, the commission was appointed by the Ottoman government on the insistence of Great Britain, which demanded that British, French, and Russian delegates accompany it. See also BOA, 1552-66-10, Yıldız Esas Evrakı. Nalbandian, *The Armenian Revolutionary Movement*, 122.
13 Miller, *The Ottoman Empire*, 429. According to Miller, 'the commission officially designed as intended "to inquire into the criminal conduct of Armenian brigands" [i.e., fedayee bands], conducted its proceedings with the partiality which might have been expected from this statement of its object, and proved as dilatory as most Turkish institutions'.
14 BOA, 1552-66-10, Yıldız Esas Evrakı.
15 F.O.424.182.182. See also J[on] Kirakosian, *Hayastaně Mijazgayin Divanagitut'ean ew Sovetakan Artak'in K'aghak'akanut'ean P'astat'ght'erum* (Yerevan: Hayastan Publishing, 1972), 130–47. The book is a compilation of Russian archival documents relevant to the period 1828–1923.
16 Supplement to F.O.424.182.182. The supplement is the main body of the reforms project. It consists of fourteen one-column pages. The original is in French.
17 Kirakosian, *Hayastaně*, 130.
18 BOA, 131-94-60, Yıldız Esas Evrakı. See also Miller, *The Ottoman Empire*, 429; Avetis Papazian, *Haykakan Harts'ě ew Mets Egherně* (Los Angeles, 1997), 7.
19 Arman Kirakosian, *Britanakan Divanagitut'iwně ew Arewmtahayeri Khndiṛě: 1830-1914* (Yerevan: Gitutyun Publishing, 1999), 346. Arman Kirakosian's book is an important source, based primarily on British governmental documents. See also Miller, *The Ottoman Empire*, 429. In Miller's own words, 'the cathedral at Urfa, the Edessa of the Crusaders, was the scene of a human holocaust, in which 3000 persons perished'.
20 France, Affaires Étrangères–CP-T, 524, October 1895, 114–18. Cited also in M. Şükrü Hanioğlu, *The Young Turks in Opposition* (New York and Oxford: Oxford University Press, 1995), 43.
21 *Hnch'ak*, 2 April 1896. The passage from *Hnch'ak* clarifies why Abraham Kara-Kehia[ian] Pasha met with Ambassador Currie, and under what circumstances did the latter receive the unsigned letter demanding Izmirlian's resignation.
22 Ibrahim Temo, *İttihad ve Terakki Cemiyetinin Teşekkülü ve Hidematı Vataniye ve İnkılâbı Millîye Dair Hatıratım* (Mejidiye, Romania: n. p., 1939), 48–9.
23 Diran Kelekian, 'La Turquie et Son Souverain', *The Nineteenth Century* 40, no. 237 (November 1896): 696. Kelekian would later appear as a comrade and an important aid to Dr. Behaeddin Şakir, when the latter assumed the leadership of the Young Turk Movement in Europe in 1906.
24 The Ottoman Turkish adjective *Mizanci*, literally meaning 'from the Balance', was in reference to the periodical *Mizan*, which Murad Bey published first in Egypt and then in France.
25 *Mizan*, no. 162, 6 December 1895, 2384. Cited also in Hanioğlu, *The Young Turks*, 280.
26 *Hnch'ak*, 29 February 1896, vol. 9, no. 4, 1–3.
27 *Hnch'ak*, 10 March 1897, vol. 10, no. 10, 1.
28 Almost nothing is known about Herafion Nivlinsky. It is plausible that the character was a creation of the Paris-based Ottoman Ambassador, Munir Bey, who during these times was heavily involved in gathering intelligence about Young Turk and Armenian revolutionary cadres in Europe.

29 *Hnch'ak*, 31 May 1896, vol. 9, no. 11 According to the same newspaper, which in *Hnch'ak*'s opinion was a Turcophile publication, Nivlinsky had approached the Anglo-Armenian Committee and asked its executive board to write a special letter to the sultan asking him to implement reforms in the empire out of his goodwill. The news appeared in other British newspapers too. However, after *Hnch'ak*'s clarification, the newspapers retracted their previous coverage by stating: 'Although the Sultan's representative had met with the Anglo-Armenian Committee, the latter, however, had not written any letters to the Sultan.'
30 *Hnch'ak*, 21 June 1896, vol. 9, no. 13.
31 *Hnch'ak*, 25 October 1896, vol. 9, no. 19.
32 F.O. 424.192.97. This is yet another proof that the manifesto in question was that of the ARF.
33 Ibid.
34 F.O. 424.195.16. [In French, dated 18 December.]
35 Ibid.
36 BOA, BBA-YEE, 36/2470-3/147/36. Governor Rauf Bey to the chamberlain's office (9 February 1897, and 1 April 1897), no. 76.
37 BOA, Mehmed Kamil Bey to Governor Rauf Bey (10 March 1897), No. 72. Also, communication from the latter to the former (30 March 1897), no. 74.
38 Hanioğlu, *The Young Turks*, 120. The sources are BOA, BBA-YEE, 36/2470-18/147/XVI, Ali Muhsin Bey to the chamberlain's office (10 September 1898), no. 147, *Haleb ve Adana Kumandan Vekaletine Mahsus Defterdir* (Special Registry for the Aleppo and Adana Command Center). See also Tahsin Bey to commander of Aleppo and Adana (23 August 1898), no. 140, *Haleb ve Adana Kumandan Vekaletine Mahsus Defterdir*, BBA-YEE, 36/2470-18/147/XVI.
39 *Hayrenikʻ Amsagir*, May 1938, no. 7, 141–7. The article contains a series of letters pertaining to the negotiations. One letter, addressed to Patriarch Ormanian from the Hnchak center in London and dated 25 March 1898, is interesting, since it speaks about the Armenians apprehended in Cilicia.
40 *Hayrenikʻ Amsagir*, May 1938, no. 7, 141–7.
41 Ibid.
42 Ibid.
43 F.O. 424.195.8.
44 F.O. 424.195.72.
45 *Drōshak*, June 1898, no. 6 (97), 90–2.
46 Ibid.
47 F.O. 424.197.58. and enclosure 58. On Wilhelm II's visit to the Ottoman Empire, see Nazaret Naltchajian, 'Kaiser Wilhelm II's Visits to the Ottoman Empire: Rationale, Reactions and the Meaning of Images', *Armenian Review*, no. 42 (1989): 47–78.
48 Hanioğlu, *The Young Turks*, 173.
49 Ibid.
50 *Drōshak*, February 1902, no. 2 (122), 23–6; Hanioğlu, *The Young Turks*, 182.
51 *Hnch'ak*, 30 March 1901, vol. 14, no. 3, 2–5.
52 Hanioğlu, *The Young Turks*, 176.
53 *Drōshak*, February 1902, no. 2 (122), 23–6.
54 Ibid.
55 Hanioğlu, *The Young Turks*, 182. Hanioğlu states that Cheraz was the editor of *Armenia*. In fact, *Armēnia*'s editor was Mgrdich Portukalian, who was exiled from Van, where he was a teacher, because of his political agitation. Portukalian settled

in Marseille where he published *Armēnia*, which became the de facto organ of the Armenakan Party, founded by his students in Van. See also Nalbandian, *The Armenian Revolutionary Movement*, 90–103. In 1921, the remnants of the Armenakans and Reformed Hnchaks later coalesced with others and founded the Ramkavar Party. Hanioğlu contradicts himself when he later mentions that other, non-partisan prominent Armenians such as [Arshag] Chobanian Effendi and Sisian Effendi also participated in the conference. Hanioğlu, *The Young Turks*, 348; Mikayel Varandian, *H.H.Dashnakts'ut'ean Patmut'iwn*, vol. 1 (Paris: Imp. de Navarre, 1932), 2–3.
56 Ibid.
57 *Hnch'ak*, 10 February 1901, vol. 14, no. 2, 2–5.
58 *Hnch'ak*, 1 May 1902, vol. 15, no. 2, 2–5.
59 F.O.424.200. no. 114. Sanderson to Colonial Office, Foreign Office, 4 October 1900.
60 Ibid.
61 F.O.424.200. no.134. Jones to de Bunsen, Kharput, 17 October 1900, no. 41 enclosure in de Bunsen to Salisbury, Constantinople, 30 October 1900, No. 373.
62 F.O.424.200. no.151. Maunsell to de Bunsen, Van, 10 November, no. 44 enclosure in De Bunsen to Lansdowne, Constantinople, 28 November 1900, no. 418.
63 *Hnch'ak*, 1 April 1902, no. 15, vol. 1, 1–4.
64 Drōshak, April 1902, no. 24 (124), 1–3.
65 *Drōshak*, May 1903, no. 5 (136), 72–4.
66 Dr. Behaeddin Şakir was one of the leaders of the Young Turk movement who had arrived in Paris to conduct negotiations and to strive for meaningful and smooth dialogue between different anti-Hamidian factions to create a united Ottoman opposition. Şakir would later become the administrative director of the Ottoman paramilitary organization, *Teshkilat-i Mahsusa*, which played a crucial role in the implementation of the Armenian Genocide. Dikran Kelekian (also known as Diran Kelekian), was an Ottoman Armenian writer. He had been the editor of *Cihan* (The World) since 1883 and that of *Sabah* [Morning] newspapers as of 1908. He had studied at the French Academy of Sciences in Marseille, then become a lecturer at the Ottoman University of Istanbul. He also worked as a correspondent for the *Daily Mail* and *Presse Associée*. He also published journalistic works in Turkish using Armenian letters and compiled a French–Turkish dictionary. For more information regarding Kelekian and his role vis-à-vis Şakir's organizational research, see Christopher J. Walker, *Armenia: The Survival of a Nation* (New York: St. Martin's Press, 1980), 427. See also Friedrich Schrader, 'Politisches Leben in der Türkei', *Die Neue Zeit* 37, no. 2 (1919): 463.
67 *Niwt'er H.H. Dashnakts'ut'ean Patmut'ean Hamar,* vol. VII, 37.
68 Ibid., 43.
69 ARF Archives, Document 1715a-1, *Niwt'er H.H. Dashnakts'ut'ean Patmut'ean Hamar*, vol. VI, 223. Chobanian informed the ARF Western Bureau about not attending the congress through a letter dated December 6, 1907.
70 ARF Archives, Document 872 a-9, *Niwt'er H.H. Dashnakts'ut'ean Patmut'ean Hamar* vol. VI, 229. Letter from Mgrdich Portukalian to Aknuni, dated 10 December 1907.
71 *Hnch'ak*, 15 December 1900, vol. 13, no. 7; *Hnch'ak*, 10 January 1901, vol. 14, no. 1; *Hnch'ak*, 10 February 1901, vol. 14, no. 2; *Hnch'ak*, 30 March 1901, vol. 14, no. 3.
72 International Socialist Congress, *Rapport présenté au Congrès socialiste international de Copenhague par le parti arménien "Daschnaktzoutioun". Turquie-Caucase - Perse* (Geneva: Droshak, 1910), 12.
73 Murat Koptaş, 'Armenian Political Thinking in the Second Constitutional Period: The Case of Krikor Zohrab' (Master's thesis, Boğaziçi University, 2005), 4.

3

A Newly Discovered Letter of Sabah-Gulian to Paramaz[1]

Yeghig Jerejian

The Young Turk Revolution of July 1908 put an end to the thirty-year tyranny of Sultan Abdülhamid II in the Ottoman Empire. The Committee of Union and Progress (CUP, also known as *Ittihad ve Terakki Cemiyeti*), born and formed in exile, came to power, and the Constitution proclaimed by the sultan in 1876 and suspended in 1878 was restored. This constitutional revolution was received with unanimous enthusiasm, particularly by Armenians.

In this enthusiastic atmosphere, the chairman of the Social Democrat Hnchakian Party (SDHP) and editor of its organ *Hnch'ak*, Stepan Sabah-Gulian,[2] wrote:

> With the rule of the Union and Progress Party that speaks on behalf of 'Young Turkey,' Turkish nationalism enters the active political arena and assumes the role of leader (…) It will give as much freedom to the dominated peoples as its nationalist principles allow; namely, the national development of the component peoples will enter within the circle to be established by Turkish nationalism.[3]

On this occasion, circular no. 14 of the SDHP Central Commission, whose language undoubtedly belonged to Sabah-Gulian's pen, found that, with the restoration of the Constitution,

> our series of considerations, on whose basis we strived for independence, separation from the ruling tyranny, do not have the right to exist anymore. With the overthrow of the absolutist monarchy, we find ourselves with a Turkey endowed with a narrow constitution; therefore, from now on, we will work to realize a democratic constitution for the whole of Turkey and autonomy for the component nationalities.

Regarding this new aim, the circular suggested:

> To reach our goal, we will strive to come to an agreement with all elements of the opposition—Armenian, Turkish, Arab, Kurdish, Bulgarian, etc.—that are close

to us with their programs. The Turkish Committee of Union and Progress is the governing party in Turkey and absolutely antagonistic to us. The party of Prince Sabaheddin, however, is close to our views in a known degree with its program and demands. More than ever, it is necessary to be in agreement with all elements of the opposition without delay.[4]

In the following years, the SDHP deepened its opposition to the Ittihad. The basic agenda of the Sixth Convention of the SDHP, opened on 12 July 1909, in Constantinople, was to establish the position and programme of action within a constitutional Turkey. The majority adopted the view of becoming a legalized party and continuing the struggle against the Ittihadist government using lawful methods (political, propagandistic and electoral), 'as long as those legal rights have not been taken from the working people'. Afterwards, the Convention concluded:

Taking into account that the Turkish nationalists and the political activists of that nationalism [i.e. the Ittihadist] are conscientiously striving to denationalize the nationalities existing in Turkey and merge them within the Turkish nationalism under the general name of OTTOMAN, OTTOMAN NATIONALITY, the Sixth General Delegate Assembly of the Social Democrat Hnchakian Party rejects categorically that idea of nationalization and resolves to struggle until the end against that orientation, accepting the inviolability of the historical-individual existence of nations and the right to their unrestrained and free development and self-determination.[5]

At its turn, *Hnch'ak* wrote:
The assembly, standing on the direction of class warfare, according to Social Democratic principles, analyzed this and highlighted again the urgent need of the fast realization of the consensus of nations, recognizing as condition THE NEED OF THE RIGHT OF HISTORICAL-INDIVIDUAL EXISTENCE OF NATIONS, rejecting on one hand SEPARATIST ideas and on the other, THE RULE AND HEGEMONY OF ANY NATION OVER THE OTHER.[6]

In the following years, the SDHP agenda included, as one important item, finding allies in opposition to the Ittihad authorities. In this regard these attempts had some success. Terms of cooperation were established with the current opposition[7] led by Prince Sabaheddin,[8] which operated almost monolithically with the Ottoman Liberal Party (*Osmanlı Ahrar Fırkası*). Friendly relations, initiated in Paris, continued with the current Kurdish opposition led by Bedir Bey Bedirkhan[9] and the *Ligue de la Partie Arabe* of Arab-Christian Nejib Azuri.[10] Cooperation was also established with the newly-created Ottoman Socialist Party[11] (*Osmanlı Sosyalist Fırkası*), as well as the multiethnic (Turks, Albanians, Circassians, Arabs) Ottoman Democratic Party (*Osmanlı Demokrat Fırkası*)[12] of Maniasizade Refik Bey.[13] Secret meetings were held in his residence with Albanian Ibrahim Temo, one of the founders of the CUP in 1889, along with students of the School of Medicine of Constantinople.[14] Relations with the Workers Federation of Salonica ('Clubistes', WFS) had a positive outcome in September 1912, when the Second Representative Assembly of the SDHP of Turkey approved a cooperation agreement between the SDHP and the WFS[15] in the presence of one of its leaders, the MP Dimitar Vlahov.[16] The SDHP was also a member of the Assembly of Ottoman and Balkan Socialist Parties, led by Romanian Christian Rakovsky.[17] For the Hnchakians in particular, these opposition movements were sparks of hope that the Ottoman Empire would adopt a more acceptable internal policy towards its non-Turkish minorities. The SDHP, which was in opposition to the Ittihad party from its time abroad, clearly fought against it in order to impede the execution of its Turkish programme. Its rapprochement to Ahrar and then to the Itilaf did not pursue any other purpose than to fight against Young Turkish chauvinism.[18] These parties and groups were small political forces and not serious competition for the Ittihad; however, in Sabah-Gulian's reasoning, 'even the splinter was a force for us when it bristled against the Ittihad'.[19]

A serious contending force to the Ittihad appeared with the birth of the Freedom and Accord Party (*Hürriyet ve İtilâf Fırkası*) in November 1911. The Itilaf was not only a competitor, but it had a more liberal electoral programme. It shared many of the demands asked for by the various ethnicities and also advocated for administrative decentralization.[20] Naturally, a cooperation sprang up between the SDHP and the Itilaf, becoming an electoral alliance on 7 February 1912, on the eve of the parliamentary elections:[21] 'The Hnchakian Party saw that the danger threatening Western Armenians came from the Ittihad and undertook a consistent development of the idea of creating a bloc with the Itilaf'.[22] The other political parties active in Armenian life, the Armenian National Assembly, the liberal branch as well as the ARF, and the assembly formed by the Armenian Apostolic as well as Protestant communities preferred to participate in the elections on the electoral list of the Ittihad.

The parliamentary elections of 1912 were held in an atmosphere of extreme violence and fraud and are remembered in history as the 'Election of Clubs'.[23] The Ittihad obtained more than 95 per cent of the votes, which was completely at odds with reality. The wave of discontent that followed took on a new momentum. In July a group of rebel officers headed by Colonel Sadık Bey[24] and called *Halâskâr Zâbitân Gurubu* (Savior Officers Group), which was de facto the military wing of the Itilaf,[25] demanded the dissolution of the Chamber of Deputies, threatening radical measures otherwise. On 17 July the Ittihadist government of Prime Minister Said Pasha[26] resigned two days after receiving the results of a confidence vote from almost the entire Parliament.[27] The Sultan appointed Ahmed Mukhtar Pasha[28] as new Prime Minister, who formed a new cabinet with ministers from the opposition. On 30 July the anti-Ittihad government received a vote of confidence from the Ittihadist Chamber of Deputies.[29] The new Prime Minister read the sultan's decree dissolving the Chamber of Deputies and power was transferred, constitutionally, into the hands of the Itilaf and the opposition.

On 13 January 1913, the Ittihad took power back with a well-organized *coup d'état*. A group of officers headed by Enver Pasha entered the Sublime Porte and murdered the Minister of War, Nazım Pasha.[30] Under the force of death threats, Mahmut Şevket Pasha was appointed as Prime Minister and soon approved by the sultan.[31] Power went to the Ittihad triumvirate of Enver, Talat and Cemal: 'The Red Triumvirate began leading the country in the image of the Red Sultan Hamid'.[32]

During these events, Sabah-Gulian was in Paris. He had already shaped his solid conviction, which he expressed in the press:

> Once and for all, the following must be bore in mind as an indisputable truth. Turkish Nationalism, which manages today the government of the country, will mercilessly massacre the Armenians [sic] as a **historical necessity**, without hesitation, when the tiniest **window of opportunity**[33] appears and it is convinced that its action will be easily digested. And this time [it will be] more implacable [sic] than in 1895–1896, more terrible than the Crime [*Eghern*] of Adana.[34]

When could that 'window of opportunity' arise? Sabah-Gulian found that a world war – a 'general war' or an 'all-European war' in his words – was close, 'in which the victorious will not be different from the defeated, because the whole of Europe, civilization, humanity, would be the victim in the last count'.[35] He had no doubts that in such a case, the Ittihad would adopt a pro-German position, and the Itilaf a pro-British position.[36] As a matter of fact, this opposition was the outside factor in the bloody struggle for power.

After this, Sabah-Gulian concluded:

> I traveled three times to Armenia Minor.[37] My last trip brought me to the ultimate conclusion that *either we will kill the Ittihad or the Ittihad will kill us*. What I saw, my impressions, the facts, the expressed aspirations and trends did not leave any doubt that the Ittihad, sooner or later, will undertake its policy of erasing the Armenians [sic] at any price. Therefore, not only there was the need to get ready, but the killing [sic] of the Ittihad had to be the first and immediate aspiration for the Armenian revolutionary activist who understood the spirit and requirement of the times.[38]

Two circumstances restrained Sabah-Gulian from turning his convictions into action. First, Western Armenian national-political thinking was still far away from the idea of undertaking 'the killing of the Ittihad'[39] and contented itself with the programme of reforms in those provinces inhabited by Armenians. Second, the resolutions of the Sixth Convention of the SDHP had established that the party would adopt a lawful course of action to continue the struggle against the 'representatives of Turkish nationalism' who strived to merge national identities by legal means, 'as long as those legal rights have been wrested from the hands of the working people'.[40] It was clear for Sabah-Gulian that 'those legal rights' had already been taken away from the people with the advent of the Ittihadist 'red triumvirate'. Moreover, the ideological struggle against Ottomanism, in which Sabah-Gulian himself had 'ripped his throat' and 'spilled ink', had become anachronistic. The physical existence of the Armenian people was at stake. For that reason, the only way to fight against the imminent danger was to return to revolutionary and unlawful methods. This decisive, even crucial, resolution was the sole prerogative of the party convention.

Sabah-Gulian departed for Romania and then Bulgaria in May 1913 to deal with organizational, political and propagandistic issues of the forthcoming Seventh

Convention. The convention was postponed due to the Second Balkan War, and his movements from town to town were hampered.⁴¹ In the meantime, on 11 June 1913, the Itilaf organized a countercoup in Constantinople. Prime Minister Şevket Pasha was killed, but the coup failed. The Ittihad moved very swiftly and brutally. Opposition members were arrested in great numbers and twelve of them were hanged in Sultan Bayazid's Square. Other opposition activists, including Sadık Bey, Şerif Paha,⁴² Sabaheddin, Ismail Hakkı, among others, fled abroad to Paris, Cairo and Athens. The opposition cells active in the army then went underground.

In the same year, after returning to Paris, Sabah-Gulian had meetings with Şerif Pasha, who was exiled there, and, despite the grave consequences of the failed *coup d'état*, they clung to the idea of overthrowing the Ittihad government through conspiratorial means. He also understood that Cairo-based Sadık was the organizing mind of the Itilaf abroad and intended to meet him. Sabah-Gulian, who had been a declared enemy of the Ittihad since 1895 and developed a fierce propaganda against it, saw the success of the Itilaf conspiracy plan as the only practical means of eliminating the danger of the 'red triumvirate' that threatened the Armenian people.

The Seventh Convention of the SDHP opened in the Romanian city of Constanţa on 7 September 1913. It evaluated the four-year government of the Ittihad and made the following resolutions:

> Being clear that the entire Ottoman state body and its state understanding are definitely directed toward merging, exterminating [sic] the composing nationalities, and the 'ruling nation' has been unable until now to originate a New State;

> Taking into account that an OLIGARCHY, whose leading force is the *Ittihad ve Terakkı* Party, rules in Turkey;

> Being certain that the basic principles of that Party are to keep Turkish bureaucracy and not allow a New State to develop, and its apparent intent is to merge, to exterminate if needed, and to massacre [sic] the component nationalities;

> Considering indisputable that the Ruling Class handling power executes its Armenian-destroying policy systematically and implacably;

> Seeing that, due to the internal policy being executed and predominating, the Armenian people are on the threshold of ruin and destruction;

> Convinced that a political party such as the Social Democrat Hnchakian Party cannot pursue the realization of its principles and push aside the deadly sword [sic] hanging over the head of the Armenian Nation by just standing on LAWFUL grounds;

> The Seventh General Representative Assembly of the Social Democrat Hnchakian Party resolved, by unanimous vote except one against, on behalf of proletarian interests, Human and National inviolable rights, to stand on UNLAWFUL ground from now on and wage its Party Struggle until more adequate and new political and economic conditions have developed.⁴³

The convention adopted the principle of 'autonomous Armenia' as a political demand.[44]

Straight after the closure of the convention, a secret meeting was held to implement the *non-lawful* resolutions with the participation of P. Varaztad,[45] Sabah-Gulian, Dr. Benne,[46] Sarkis Sarkisian[47] and S. Vahakn.[48] These resolutions of the closed-door session remained in strict secrecy and were not even communicated to the delegates.[49] The meeting discussed the conspiratorial plan of the Itilaf and the issue of participating in the said plan. A body was formed to pursue the plan, integrated by Dr. Benne, S. Vahakn, Rupen Garabedian[50] and Paramaz, who did not participate in the Convention and, therefore, was not present in the 'secret meeting'.

In the meantime, Arshavir Sahagian, delegate from Cairo and Alexandria – the future infamous traitor Artur Yasian – arrived at the meeting place. He got acquainted with the resolutions of the convention and agreed with them. Nothing in the minutes, which recorded the resolution to take the party into clandestineness, deserved the characterization of betrayal. The resolution was no secret, as it had been mentioned in the final declaration of the Convention and the internal circular, and it would be published in *Hnch'ak*.[51] P. Varaztad insisted that Yasian was not informed of the secret meeting.[52] However, the latter conjectured, on the basis of the minutes and conversations with delegates, that the driving force behind the 'unlawful' activities was Sabah-Gulian, whose next stop would be Egypt.[53] Going from Constanța to Constantinople, Yasian passed his knowledge and his conjectures to the Ottoman secret police, who started searching for Sabah-Gulian, especially in the ships arriving in Constantinople from Europe. Sabah-Gulian's comrades from Romania alerted him; and, meanwhile, he

Figure 3.1 Paramaz (Matteos Sarkissian). Source: Social Democrat Hnchakian Party Archives.

wrote letters to Paramaz, who was in Van, 'underscoring in the most imperative terms that it was absolutely necessary that he left as soon as possible'.[54]

On 6 December, Sabah-Gulian departed from the Italian city of Trieste to Alexandria in a ship that did not make a stopover in Constantinople. He learned from the comrades sent to welcome him on the same day that Azmi Bey, the head of the Ottoman secret police, had arrived in Alexandria and met Artur Yasian. There were secret policemen everywhere on the look-out, probably to kill him. He found shelter in a safe place and sent word to the comrades in contact with him and to his wife not to maintain correspondence until he was able to provide a new address.

A short time later, Paramaz arrived in Paris and was naturally upset that Sabah-Gulian, who had been calling him to Paris with 'incessant letters',[55] was not there. He wrote a letter to him, to which Sabah-Gulian was only able to answer on 3 March 1914. This response has remained unnoticed in the Hnchakian Archive, and we publish it below for the first time. Only the first eight pages, where Sabah-Gulian explains the reasons for not being in Paris and for delaying his return from Cairo, have reached us. He was forced to speak about details that he had not addressed in other circumstances and have remained, thus far, a historical secret.

Cairo, March 3, 1914

Dear Paramaz,
I received your letter, as well as your two telegrams. I kept silent for too long, and it seems that it would be upsetting, but there was no other way. It was necessary to clarify the issues and put them into their due course in order for me to know what to do and what to write. I had telegraphed that 'stop the letter, I am coming.' Why that? Let me tell you in brief. You are aware of the miserable Yasian's treason. When Azmi Bey returned to Constantinople lately, he was particularly active. Egypt was filled with packs of spies and killers, well-organized and sent by the Central Committee of the Ittihad with certain goals. I had left that brat in his former house and bribed his lover to watch over him and keep me informed, which she did, even though not as much as I wanted. But nevertheless, I received some information. The lamentable thing is that the miserable [man] had other Armenian, Greek, Arab spies, even women at his disposal; they had spread the network of their organization everywhere. The encounters happened at the home of that miserable and out of town, at the Turkish commissariat, at private homes. I learned that they had received important instructions from Azmi Bey. Araxi, the lover of that miserable, confessed that Artur would flee tomorrow, fully disguised. Why? Because it had been arranged that they would shoot Sadık Bey and me, so after making arrangements he wanted to save himself. They had reported that special emissaries arrived from Constantinople had prepared a printed list. I made all promises to the girl so she started a trial of honor against the scoundrel, but she did not agree. Attorney Asadourian,[56] Sadık Bey, Birtev Teffik Bey, etc.,[57] along with me decided that Sadık Bey [would] deliver a written complaint to the police, not only to prevent the scoundrel from leaving, at least temporarily until the circulars with his picture reach their addressees, but to have the house searched and the correspondence confiscated. In the end, after not finding another legal means, thanks to attorney Asadourian's work on the side, six or seven of our comrades complained to the police [about Yasian] as swindler and fraudster, and somehow we made it work. We had

the house searched. He was totally disguised (he was going to escape half hour later), unrecognizable. Thirty bottles of poison, from the one acting at once *to the one* continuing for 1–2 months, *poisoned dagger, poisoned needles and pins, various instruments to make sleep and inject. It was a full depot. They arrested the scoundrel. The whole world, from Constantinople to Cairo, was turned upside down. Hadn't Azmi Bey come to Alexandria with his terrorists before going to Paris?*[58] *Hadn't he had an interview here* with the Khedive, *with the Turkish high commissar having a share of the job? Isn't Said Halim*[59] *(Prime Minister) [an] Egyptian and close relative of the Khedive (the son of his maternal uncle)? Then, fearful that the scoundrel would confess everything, they released him from prison on the basis of telegrams from Constantinople and put him under police surveillance. I will say that the scoundrel confessed being an official spy and said that he had taken Sadık Pasha and the Hnchakians under surveillance. On the fourth day, we learned that they wanted to close the case. We even published the telegram, by which the local Turkish high commissar called Artur to Alexandria, to Hotel Savoia, the day of Azmi's arrival, where the Khedive came on that day and time and conceded an audience to him. The Prime Minister, the Minister of Justice, and the Khedive were directly embarrassed by a trap in which they had inadvertently fallen... In the end, after releasing the scoundrel under surveillance, four or five days ago they said that he fled. But the chapter has already disseminated 2 classes of pictures of the scoundrel and a brief circular everywhere.*[60] *He will be recognized wherever he goes. I have also written everywhere. We have sent them to the Allies [the representatives of France and Great Britain. Y. J.]. In those days, the Ottoman high commissar demanded, on behalf of his government, that* our homes *be searched, on the grounds that we are conspiring against the Ottoman state and the life of its higher officials. All comrades took necessary precautions. I did not leave any trace; I did not leave any piece of paper with me. Even our postmaster became a suspect. Since there was no time to write a letter and make Varaztad aware, I telegraphed that he* stop the letters *and that I am coming. In the end, Lord Kitchener,*[61] *who is a weak man, came. Sadık Bey was ingenious and disclosed* a great secret, *that is, the Ittihad—according to a resolution—wants to overthrow the current Khedive and put Said Halim as Khedive, and to that effect they are preparing a* fatwa *on the basis that the father of the current Khedive took his position of Khedive through* bribe *and not legally, since according to age and heritage, the right of Khedive belonged to Said Halim's father. Therefore, they wanted to declare the Khedive a usurper according to Quranic law.*[62] *On that basis, the Khedive changed his side and, after having demanded from Sadık Bey to leave the country the day before, now asked him to stay without any problem. In that way, we neutralized that blow.*

The Sherif of Mecca's son was going to come here to go to Constantinople as member of the Parliament.[63] *Sadık Bey asked me especially to stay and prevent him from going. The man came and became totally convinced; not only he does not want to go to Constantinople, but he is trying to forbid all* genuine Arab *representatives from going, even if they elect [even if they were elected? Y. J.]. Since he is the son of the most influential person in the Muslim world, he convinced his father, and today the Sherif of Mecca has become the head of the opposition and is ready for all sacrifices. This impacted on the* Khedive, *who is now on a direct anti-Ittihad line and ready for sacrifice.*[64]

Sixteen *thousand armed Arabs from Basra are waiting for a signal,*[65] *and these have released a very good declaration that I will translate and send to* Eritassard Hayastan.[66]

They come in groups from different zones of Turkey to see Sadık Bey and ask for his advice. An army of discontents from everywhere is being formed, especially from Turkish, Arab, and Syrian elements.[67] *They are all convinced that the spirit leading the Ittihad is German diplomacy, and the destruction of Turkey is Germany's gain. I don't enter into this here to avoid making it too long. We had first decided to come to Paris with Sadık Bey. But* today *the situation has changed. Since the Arabs and the discontented have started moving, that cannot happen without Sadık Bey's presence on the stage. Storrs,*[68] *the local British representative (we met two days ago), gave us total assurances, and they promised him here to pay the travel expense. Sadık Bey called Ismail Bey with a telegram; I said, I will write a letter, if he does not come or gets delayed, meet him (at Sherif Pasha's) and ask why he did not come, or when he will depart and come back. And if he is already on the road, then* send me a telegram, so I have you sent travel expenses for second class. Ismail Bey is quite influential in Turkish circles; his appearance may generate more enthusiasm, especially since he has an enterprising spirit. Your coming is again necessary, because the general movement and activities will be planned, whose stage will mainly be Constantinople, Izmir, Izmit, Bursa, Damascus, and Arabia (Mesopotamia, Basra).*

I have said from the first day that we can help, but we do not have money, they will take care of the finances, as they promised. So, whatever we conclude, we will submit our financial requirement-list appropriately. It is absolutely needed that you come, especially when Ismail Bey comes.

I was going to come, but my coming would not have solved the issue, since both Sadık Bey and the others, especially the Sheikh's son and other leaders would be unable to come.

It is obvious that the Armenian Question had a total fiasco, and the Sisyphean work has to begin anew,[69] *and if we cannot do anything else, to erase the existence of the [one word illegible] Ittihad, to overthrow it, to weaken it will ease greatly our ability to achieve our future. We cannot live without Autonomous Armenia, the danger is always present. After so much blood, so much effort, Armenia was divided into two parts,*[70] *which means that the door of* occupation *moved a step forward. Could [we] have ended the question in that way if the Armenian parties had weakened the Ittihad until now? The stupid Federation* (Dashnaktsutiun) *strengthened the Ittihad for 4–5 years, became a toy in its hands, and then got kicked. The Hnchakian Party saw that risk from the beginning (already since 1894) and did not forget to direct its arrows at the Ittihad.*

I want that the three of us[71] *first come together too, but you were late, and the course of the activities is falling down; if I come, but without money, we will look to each other in Paris and the work started here will be endangered. I have taken upon the* Cilician job;[72] *there is a good spirit of rebellion there, especially now. What can we do? Two or three people cannot do everything. If the comrades do not come to help, what can we do? We were embarrassed; let's put some grounds, create stability, and start* Hnch'ak, *and not let's publish one or two issues and then say, 'It can't happen for lack of money.'*

What are our roles and our work going to be? True, the three of us should be together to think, but I do not think that there is no consensus among the three of us about principle and activity. If it remains to them, in one or two years later it will be very hard, if not impossible to overthrow the Ittihad. To overthrow the Ittihad, to weaken and to rout it will be the greatest legacy that the Hnchakians will offer to socialism and to the Armenian nation from the viewpoint of the future. That enormously dangerous party that embodies Pan-Turkism, Pan-Islamism, and nationalism will be the most dangerous in the future from the viewpoint of our *future. The European conflicting interests, seemingly, regard its existence suitable, at least temporarily, to them. It is necessary to give the blow as long as it is weak. The Hnchakians, as they did from day one, must be the first to unify those dispersed foreign forces*[73] *and orient them toward a certain direction. They do have that trust in* [us]. *If Sadık Bey leaves immediately, the Sherif of Mecca, his son, the Arab deputies, that local circle that will give huge material assistance, all them may not only hesitate, but fail to show the necessary bravery and speed. Aren't they children of the Orient? They all believe and follow Sadık Bey like a banner, because he is an honest, noble, and enormously disinterested man. Sherif Pasha does not generate activity, and neither [do] the discontented elements trust him entirely. They all have the unwavering conviction that Turkey will fall and the Ittihad is accelerating and making unavoidable that fall with its internal and external policy. If Turkey is saved, the only hope will be through the execution of the broad Itilaf program. They have hope anyway, and that is not strange, but [reflective of] the psychology of the historical moment.*

The Armenian Question – 'the mountain gave birth to a tiny mouse';[74] *it could not be otherwise. What to do? Either conservatism of rayah or energetic activity; there can be no word about the former, regardless of whether that is the desire of the Mourads,*[75] *the Achikbashians,*[76] *those* mental eunuchs.[77] *We have nothing to do with the mentality of* rayah, *it is dead from the start, with its masters and students.*

Now, there is a project for a general movement in broad strokes, which will be continuing until the radical overthrow of the Ittihadist government and party. There is the need for a general consultation on that. That consultation should happen either here or in Paris. The question of coming to Paris does not work with Sadık Bey and me coming. In our absence, the local work, which we have created with so many hardships, may be endangered, and besides, we cannot bring everyone with us. Today Sadık Bey sent a telegram to Paris, to Ismail Bey *(from Kumuljina), to [come] here.*

I said that the issue does not end just with my experience; on our side, besides me, it is necessary for my comrade Paramaz to be here and participate in the preparation of the plans. They accepted with joy and...[78]

Unfortunately, the rest of the letter, which could also contain details still unknown to us, remains unlocatable. From recently discovered additional archival materials, we have learned that Sabah-Gulian departed for Paris via Marseille on 28 March.[79] He presented the details of the plan to his colleagues of the Centre. Regarding the SDHP share, Paramaz took charge of the Constantinople section of the plan. Sabah-Gulian returned to Cairo with Paramaz in mid-April; Paramaz participated and headed the meeting of the SDHP Cairo Commission.[80] They continued the preparation of the plan with Sadık, while enrolling experienced comrades who were able to execute it.[81] About a month later, Paramaz arrived in Constantinople via Trieste and Constanța.

On the evening of 17 July, Paramaz was one of the first Hnchakian activists to be arrested in the raid initiated in Constantinople.

Notes

1 Paramaz (Matteos Sarkissian) (1863, Meghri – 15 June 1915, hanged in Constantinople). He attended the Gevorgian Seminary of Etchmiadzin (1878–93) and worked as a teacher in Nakhichevan and Ardabil (Persia) (1884–95). He participated in the transport of weapons and *fedayee* groups to Western Armenia from Salmast (Persia) in 1895–6. He headed a group transporting weapons, which arrived in Van in 1897. His mission was to replace the late Mardig (Martiros Sarukhanian). He was arrested and in 1898 gave his famous defense speech before the court of Van. In 1903 he organized popular resistance in the Armenian centers of Transcaucasia against the decision of the Tsarist government to confiscate the properties of the Armenian Church. In this occasion, he organized an assassination attempt against Prince Grigoriy Golitsyn, the viceroy of Transcaucasia, who had conceived the decision. In 1905–6 he led the Hnchakian groups that participated in the Armeno-Tatar clashes. He was arrested in Shushi in 1906 along with several collaborators and sentenced to one year of prison by a tribunal in Tiflis (1907). He participated as a delegate in the Sixth Convention of the SDHP in Constantinople. He carried out anti-Ittihadist propaganda in Diyarbekir, Kharpert, Van, and other areas. He participated in the planning of the forceful removal of the Ittihadist triumvirate in Paris and Cairo, leading the activities of the SDHP in Constantinople to that regard. He contributed to *Hnch'ak, Mshak, Nor Ashkharh*, and *Arewelk'*, and authored numerous plays.

2 Stepan Sabah-Gulian (Stepanos Ter Danielian) (1861, Jahuk village (Nakhichevan) – New Jersey, 1928). After graduating from the Nersesian Lyceum in Tiflis, he taught in Nakhichevan, the diocesan school of Yerevan, the seminary of the monastery of St. Garabed in Mush, and the convent of Sts. James (Jerusalem). He graduated from the École Libre des Sciences Politiques of Paris in 1894 and founded the Armenian Students Union, which actively promoted the Armenian Question to the French public opinion. The SDHP advisory meeting of 1899 in Rostov-on-the-Don elected him as member of the SDHP Central Commission. He was elected chairman of the Central Commission at the three SDHP conventions (Paris, 1905; Constantinople, 1909; Constanța, 1913). In 1919 the SDHP Central Commission designated him as plenipotentiary activist for the United States and Europe. He was the editor of *Hnch'ak* in London (1901–3) and Paris (1906–12). He lived in Constantinople (1908–12), Cairo (1913–16), and after 1917, the United States. He founded and edited the newspapers *Ashkharh* (Roustchouk, 1898), *Eritasard Hayastan* (Boston, 1903–5 and 1917–24), *Nor Ashkharh* (Constantinople, 1912), *Ink'nawar Hayastan* (Bucharest, 1916), and contributed to *Meghu Hayastani* (Tiflis, 1880–4), *Nor Dar* (Tiflis, 1895–6), *Arew* (Alexandria, 1915–16), *Kṛan* (Chicago, 1919–20), and others. He wrote several books of ideological and political contents in Armenian: *Pataskhanatunerě* (Providence: Eritasard Hayastan Press, 1916); *Ewropayi K'aghak'akan Drut'iwně Berlini Dashnadrut'iwnits' Hetoy* (Ruschuk, 1898); *Sots'ializm ew Hayrenik'*, A. Prak (Providence: Eritasard Hayastan Press, 1907); *Eritasard T'urk'ia* (Paris: [n.p.]1908); *Herder ew Ir K'aghak'akan Hayeatsk'neré* (K. Polis: D. Doghramajian Press, 1909); *Ink'nawar Hayastan* (Cairo: Z. Biberian Press, 1915); *P'ok'r Hayk'i Hishatakner* (Chicago: Eritasard Hayastan Press, 1917); *Armenak ew Abraham* (Chicago: Eritasard Hayastan Press. 1917); *Baṛeri ew Ezreri Pats'atrut'iwnner* (Boston: SDHP Press, 1927).

3 *Hnch'ak*, June–July 1908. The article is unsigned, but we have grounds to confidently identify Sabah-Gulian as the author.

4　National Archives of Armenia, fund 1456, catalog 1, file 147, 'Circular No. 14 of the SDHP Central Commission, Paris, August 19, 1908.'
5　Idem. The upper-case letters appear in the original.
6　*Hnch'ak,* August-September 1910. The upper-case letters appear in the original.
7　Arsen Avagyan and Gaïdz F. Minassian, *Ermeniler ve Ittihat ve Terakki* (Istanbul: Aras Yayincilik, 2005), 40. See also Sabah-Gulian, *Pataskhanatunerĕ,* 287.
8　Prince Sabaheddin (1877–1948) was the son of Damad Mahmoud Pasha, a well-known politician from Sultan Abdülhamid's period. He was exiled in Paris with his father and brother Lutfullah in 1899. After the death of his father (1903), he founded the League for Private Initiative and Administrative Decentralization (*Teşebbüs-i Şahsî ve Tevsi-i Mezuniyet*), which forged an alliance at the second Congress of Ottoman Opposition (Paris, 1907) with the Committee of Union and Progress and the Armenian Revolutionary Federation (ARF) on the grounds of an all-state program. After the Young Turk Revolution of 1908, he maintained his liberal outlook and opposed the Ittihad, but did not pursue any party activity. After the failed Itilaf *coup d'état* (1913), he spent the rest of his life in Europe.
9　Sabah-Gulian, *Pataskhanatunerĕ,* 275.
10　The relation of comradeship between Najib Azuri, founder of *Ligue de la Partie Arabe* (Paris, 1904), and Sabah-Gulian began in those days. One of its expressions was the publication of Sabah Gulian's programmatic article 'La Tyrannie Turque et les Jeunes-Turcs', in N. Azuri's *L'Indépendance Arabe* (February–March 1908), No. 11–12. The Armenian original appeared in *Hnch'ak* in January 1908. The translator of the article was Serge d'Herminy, the pseudonym of M. S. David-Beg (Mardiros Sarkissian).
11　*Eridasart Hayastan,* 17 August 1918.
12　Sabah-Gulian, *Pataskhanatunerĕ,* 278 and 285.
13　Manyasizade Refik Bey (1853-1909) was a professor of law. As collaborator of Midhat Pasha, author of the Young Turk Revolution, he was also exiled. He became an Ittihad member but grew disillusioned. He was a Parliament member representing Constantinople and has been depicted as fair-minded and of liberal thought.
14　Sabah-Gulian, *Pataskhanatunerĕ,* 285.
15　*Nor Ashkharh,* 13/26 September 1912.
16　Dimitar Vlahov (1874-1954) was a political activist of Macedonian origin. He started his political activities in Bulgaria, becoming a member of the Inner Macedonian Revolutionary Organization (IMRO). He severed his links with it and founded the National Federal Party. He later joined the SAF. He was a Parliament member in 1909–12, elected on the list of the CUP like all Armenian MPs. He cooperated with the Armenian deputies in the parliament, especially on labor issues.
17　*Kohak,* 5/18 September 1912. See also Paul Dumont, 'A Jewish, Socialist and Ottoman Organization: The Worker's Federation of Salonica', in *Socialism and Nationalism in the Ottoman Empire 1876-1923,* eds. Mete Tuncay and Eric Zurcher (London: British Academic Press & International Institute of Social History, 1994), 72–3, 183. Cristien Rakovski (1873-1941) was an internationalist revolutionary born in Romania with Bulgarian citizenship. Since 1905 he was one of the leaders of the Romanian Social Democratic Party. In 1917 he participated in the Russian Revolution in Odessa and St. Petersburg and joined the Bolshevik Party. He managed political, state, and diplomatic positions in the Soviet Union and the Communist Party. He criticized Stalin's policies publicly and was arrested three times. He died in prison.

18 Raymond Kévorkian, *The Armenian Genocide: A Complete History* (London and New York: I.B. Tauris, 2011), 70. After the Balkan Wars, when the peninsula was separated from the Ottoman Empire, the issue of cooperation with the local Socialist parties became history.
19 Sabah-Gulian, *Pataskhanatunerě*, 288.
20 *Nor Ashkharh*, 7/20 March 1912. See also Dikran Kaligian, 'The Armenian Revolutionary Federation under Ottoman Constitutional Rule' (Ph.D. diss., Boston College, 2003), 191.
21 *Rahvira*, 8/12 February 1912. In the beginning of 1912, the newspaper *Biwzandion* was closed by the government and published for fifteen days with the name *Rahvira*.
22 Meri Kochar, *Armyano-turetskie obshestvenno-politicheskie otnosheniia i Armyanskii vopros* (Yerevan: Yerevan State University Press, 1988), 180.
23 Erik Zürcher, *Turkey: A Modern History* (London: I.B. Tauris, 1994), 107-8.
24 Mehmed Sadık (1860-1940) was a colonel who graduated from the Officers' Lyceum. He served in the province of Monastir during the Constitutional revolution and headed the local Ittihad chapter. After the Constitution, he founded the *Hizb-i Cedid* (New Party), which joined the *Hürriyet ve Itilaf* opposition party. After the war, he was not allowed entry to Turkey on charges of having cooperated with the enemy.
25 Feroz Ahmad, *The Young Turks: The Committee of Union and Progress in Turkish Politics, 1908-1914* (Oxford: Oxford University Press, 1969), 110.
26 Mehmed Said Pasha (1838-1914) formed part of the political high class from his young age in his birthplace Erzerum. He became Prime Minister seven times during Abdul Hamid II's reign.
27 Ahmad, *The Young Turks*, 110.
28 Gazi Ahmed Muhtar Pasha (1839-1918) was well-regarded for his success in the military career. He earned the title of *Gazi* during the Russo-Turkish War of 1877-8. He was general governor of Egypt (1885-1906) and President of the Senate in 1911. The opposition brought him to power as Prime Minister in order to exploit his authority as a senior politician.
29 To explain this uncommon phenomenon, the Ittihadist newspapers wrote that it was not a vote of confidence to the government, but an expression of civic consciousness to avoid leaving the country in a grave situation. See *Azatamart*, 1 August 1912.
30 Huseyin Nazım Pasha (1848–1913) received his higher military in France after graduation from the Officers' School. During the Constitutional movement, he cooperated with the Young Turks as commander of the Second Army in Edirne. He was governor of Baghdad (1910–11) and earned respect from the Arab population. His spirit of military discipline and his reformist zeal put him at odds with the unlawful measures of the Ittihad.
31 Mahmud Şevket Pasha (1874–1957) was born in Basra and graduated from the School of Officers. He was designated governor of Kosovo. He lived in Germany for nine years. During the counterrevolution of 1909, he restrained the rebel forces in Constantinople as commander of the Third Army (Liberation Army). He earned, during those years, the reputation of being 'the strongest man of Turkey'.
32 André Mandelstam, *Eritasard T'urk'erě: Paterazmēn Aṛaj* (Constantinople: H. Asadurian and Sons Press, 1919), 93–4.
33 This and all bold underlining in the text are from the original.
34 *Hnch'ak*, March 1913.
35 *Hnch'ak*, January 1913. See also *Nor Ashkharh*, 6/19 September 1912.

36 *Nor Ashkharh,* 11/24 April 1912.
37 In 1911-1912 Sabah-Gulian made three tours to cultivate or establish anti-Ittihadist propaganda through the coast of the Black Sea and the areas of Armenia Minor (Samsun, Ordu, Amasia, Marsovan, Sebastia, Tokat, Everek-Fenese, Caesarea, Tomarza, etcetera).
38 Sabah-Gulian, *P'ok'r Hayk'i Hishatakner* (Beirut: Ararat, 1957), 431. The bold characters appear in the original.
39 Later, Zaven Yeghiayan, the Armenian Patriarch of Constantinople, made an interesting confession in this regard: 'When they were about to arrest a series of revolutionaries in mid-1914, we were interested to know the motive. When we became aware of the conspiracy attempt against Talat's person, from the political parties to the national council, including me, criticized the arrested Hnchakians, because we were all convinced that Talat loved the Armenians and received me and the people from the [national] council with an always smiling face. Those Twenty had said: "That smile is fake". Time proved that the hanged ones had understood it most accurately among all of us' (*Eritasard Hayastan,* 23 July 1919, reprinted from *Jamanak*).
40 Hnchakian Archive, 'The Main Decisions of the Sixth Representative Assembly of the SDHP'.
41 Hnchakian Archive, 'Letter of Sabah-Gulian to Varaztad, Sofia, June 28, 1913'.
42 Şerif Pasha (1865–1944), an Ottoman diplomat of Kurdish origin. He was the son of Prime Minister Said Pasha and brother-in-law of Prime Minister Said Halim Pasha. He was Ottoman ambassador in Sweden. In 1911 he resigned from the Ittihad and joined the Itilaf. He published the opposition newspaper *Mechroutiet*, which he continued in Paris, where he took refuge after the failed *coup d'état* of 1913. He founded the *İslahat-ı Esasiye-i Osmaniye Fırkası* (Ottoman Radical Reform Party). The Ittihad organized a failed assassination attempt against him in January 1914 in Paris. He forcefully condemned the leadership of the Ittihad in the *Journal de Geneve* (September 1915) for the crime of 'exterminating the Armenians'. He founded the Kurdish *Hoybun* organization. In 1919 he signed an agreement with Boghos Nubar Pasha to jointly promote the ideas of independent Armenia and independent Kurdistan in diplomatic circles.
43 Hnchakian Archive, 'Resolutions of the Seventh General Representative Assembly of the SDHP. Constanța, September 7, 1913'.
44 Idem. Under the title 'General and Partial Reforms – Autonomous Armenia', the Seventh Convention resolved:

'Considering that the all-state promises of general and partial reforms of the Turkish government, as well as the Ittihad party are just diplomatic tricks to win time and paralyze internal agitations; Being historically determined that the Leading Class of Turkey has always engaged in such games when the ISSUE of any of the component nationalities has taken threatening proportions; Seeing the conflicts of the European capitalist states and their venal actions in the Eastern Question; On the basis of the right of self-determination of Nations and the foreign origin of the nations in the body of Turkey with different cultural grades; It resolves: To defend the idea of Autonomous Armenia as the only means for the tolerant, peaceful, and unmolested development and progress of Armenians and others living in Armenia; Convinced that this is the necessary condition by which the Armenian nation can ensure their national individual existence against internal and external harassment; And because the historical inability and unwillingness of the Turkish ruling nation and their leading classes is now indisputable, as well as the relations and political ambitions of external forces: to defend THE IDEA OF AUTONOMOUS ARMENIA WITH EUROPEAN CONTROL.

45   P. Varaztad (Hagop Turabian), Western Armenian Hnchakian activist. He was a member of the SDHP Central Commission through the Sixth and Seventh Conventions. He edited *Hnch'ak* in 1913-1915 and contributed to other periodical publications. He maintained relations with the diplomatic and press circles of Egypt during World War I. Later, he carried out party activities in the United States and France. As the owner of a printing house, he published books related to the Armenian Cause and the Armenian Genocide.

46   Dr. Benne (Bedros Torosian, 1887, village of Huseinig in Kharpert – 15 June 1915, hanged in Constantinople). He received his education at the Euphrates College and then graduated from the American University of Beirut, where he founded the Hnchakian Student Union. He visited the United States and Canada, pursuing party activities, and served as delegate to the National Assembly representing Kharpert.

47   He was the secretary of the congress sessions and a delegate from Constanța.

48   S[epasdatsi] Vahakn (Krikor Nalbandian, 1872 Sepastia – 1953 Yerevan). He participated in the demonstrations of Kumkapı (1890) and Bab Ali (1895), terrorist actions, and the occupation of the Ottoman Bank (1896), where he was gravely wounded. In 1903 he organized popular demonstrations against the confiscations of the properties of the Armenian Church. In 1905 he participated in the Armeno-Tatar clashes and defended the monastery of Etchmiadzin with his group. After the Young Turk Revolution, he was active in Sepastia and Diyarbekir. After the congress of Constanța, he returned to Constantinople and then to Van to help provide weapons. He was sought by the authorities and forced to cross the road to Persia by foot. In 1915-1917 he participated as a combatant in Van, Bitlis, Erznka, and Erzerum. In 1918 he participated in the self-defense of Baku headed by Stepan Shahumian. In 1919 he participated in the task of punishing those Armenians who had become Turkish agents during the days of the genocide. He led the Hnchakian volunteer battalion that departed from the U.S. to Cilicia in 1920. He was actively involved in partisan work in different communities of the Diaspora between 1921 and 1938, including the organization of the first assembly of delegates of the SDHP in Lebanon (April 1929) through his efforts. He participated as delegate in the ninth congress of the SDHP in Marseille. In 1948, he repatriated to Armenia.

49   *Zang*, 17 February 1934.

50   Rupen Garabedian (Hagop Boyajian) (Chemeshgadzak, 1874 – June 15, 1915, hanged in Constantinople). He arrived in London in 1895 with a group of volunteers from the United States who were headed to Zeytun. He assisted in the publication of *Hnch'ak*. He executed party assignments between 1900-1908 in Bulgaria, Odessa, and Egypt. He was a deputy to the National Assembly from Chemeshgadzak.

51   *Hnch'ak*, May 1914.

52   *Zang*, 17 February 1934.

53   Hnchakian Archive, 'Letter of Artur Yasian to the Cairo Commission of the SDHP, Constanța, September 22, 1913'. At the end of the letter, A. Yasian's post scriptum attracted our attention. 'I must not forget to say, comrades, that public meetings should be organized as soon as Sabah arrives. Theater, etc. is needed for that; so, your foremost duty is to achieve the theatrical representation if you want to keep the party in high place and the plans do not go into waste. The comrade will remain just for 20-30 days. Afterwards, he will leave elsewhere. Comrades, encourage the theater.

Provide many at any cost and sacrifice; here is where you will show your gesture of revolutionaries, of which I am already sure'. These statements require us to ask: How was the theatrical representation connected to Sabah-Gulian's worries? What was the connection between the theatrical representation of an amateur group and 'the huge plans of the party' and the revolutionary devotion of the comrades? Was that an attempt to learn from Sabah Gulian's presence at that given day and hour and in that given place?

54 Hnchakian Archive, 'Letter of Sabah Gulian to Varaztad, Constanța, October 15/28'.
55 National Archives of Armenia, fond 1456, catalogue 1, file 179, No. 41-47, 'Sabah-Gulian's letter to an unknown comrade (supposedly Sirvart [Yeghia Krikorian]), Heliopolis, April 6/9, 1915'.
56 Hagop Asadurian (Ardzruni), lawyer. He participated in the liberation movements of the 1890s in Armenia Minor.
57 In his book *Pataskhanatunerě*, Sabah-Gulian notes that Nejib Azuri also gave valuable assistance to solve this perilous situation in Cairo.
58 It is very likely that Azmi Bey's departure to Paris was related to the murder attempt organized against Şerif Pasha.
59 Mehmed Said Halim Pasha (1863–1921) was an offspring of the princely family of Egypt. He was a member of the *Şurayi Devlet* (State Council) in 1888 and Senator after the Constitution. He was also the President of the State Council in 1912, Grand Vizier (1913–17), and Minister of Foreign Affairs (1913–15). He was exiled by the allies to Malta in 1919 and assassinated by Arshavir Shiragian in Rome.
60 National Archives of Armenia, fund 1456, catalogue 1, case 178, number 2, 'The Declaration of the Cairo commission of the SDHP about Arshavir Sahagian being a Turkish spy, with his picture and mention of his pseudonyms'.
61 Lord Kitchener, British commander who conquered the Sudan and military governor of Egypt and Sudan (1911–14).
62 Sabah-Gulian was well versed in Egyptian modern political history. He had published a serious study ('Egiptos', *Nor Dar*, 4, 6, 10 and 11 April 1896), where he explained the circumstances of the origin of the function of Khedive, including the hereditary nature of its transmission; the legal form of the relation Khedive-Sultan; the different components of the Egyptian population (*fellah*s, Circassians of the Ottoman army, remnants of Mamluks, etc.); the economic ups and downs of Egypt; the military and economic interests of France and England, etc. At the beginning of the study, Sabah-Gulian wrote: 'It is more important for us to get acquainted with the broad lines of the contemporary history of Egypt [...] because the factors also operating in that country [he refers to the Ottoman Empire, England, and France. Y. J.] have been the same as in Armenia in a more or less fluid course'. The circumstances made Sabah-Gulian the one who benefited most from his own advice.
63 The Sherif of Mecca was Emir Hussein bin Ali, officially the governor of the province of Hejaz (now Saudi Arabia). He was a descendant of Prophet Muhammad and enjoyed great authority among the Arab tribes. He led the Arab rebel movements and was in contact with the British in that regard. During the Armenian Genocide, Sherif Hussein proclaimed the Armenian people as *Ahl al-Dhimma* (people of the Book). He personally showed his benevolent stance toward the Armenian refugees on many occasions. The elder son of the Sherif of Mecca, Sherif Faysal, headed one of the three Arab rebel armies and occupied Damascus in 1918. After the war, he was proclaimed king of Syria and Iraq. In March-April 1914 he was elected to the third Chamber of Deputies. Taking into account the relations of the Ottoman opposition with Sherif

Faysal, Hasan Kayali writes: 'Some pro-British decentralist opponents of the CUP who had been forced to leave the empire to settle in Europe also declared their support for Sherif Hussein'. Hasan Kayali, *Arabs and Young Turks: Ottomanism, Arabism, and Islamism in the Ottoman Empire, 1908-1918* (Berkeley: University of California Press, 1997), 198.

64   Khedive Abbas Hilmi II Pasha had nationalist tendencies and was not amenable to British rule. From this viewpoint, he was more pro-Ottoman. He became politically vacillating when the pro-British and anti-Ottoman Sherif of Mecca took the helm of the Arab liberation movement. Sabah-Gulian's remark is about this period. In the end, the khedive posited himself in favour of the Ottoman Empire. As a result, he settled in Constantinople, where he was the target of a failed assassination attempt in July 1914. After the empire joined the alliance with Germany and Austria-Hungary, in December 1914, England eliminated the position of khedive and proclaimed Huseyin Kamil the Sultan of Egypt. Abbas Hilmi led the Ottoman attack on the British positions of the Suez Canal in January-February 1915, which ended in Ottoman defeat. This also had a stimulating effect on the Arab rebel forces.

65   Later, on October 14, 1915, Turkish officer Rifat Efendi, who served in Egypt, aiming at covering the reality and the causes of the Armenian Genocide, in an interview granted to the Danish *Extrabladet* newspaper 'that is reprinted by the entire German press', spoke about a 'conspiracy that includes the entire Armenian people' threatening the existence of Turkey whose goal was to deliver Constantinople to the Allies. According to him, the participants in this conspiracy 'considered the greatest in the history of Turkey', including Abdul Kadir, the head of the rebellion in Arabia, were arrested and 21 of them hanged in Constantinople, while a hundred people were condemned to forced labor. Johannes Lepsius, *Rapport secret sur les Massacres d'Arménie* (Beirut: Hamaskaine, 1968), 203-4.

66   The leaflet released by the General Center of Basra of the Fatherland Reform Party was published in the biweekly *Ink'navar Hayastan*, edited by Sabah-Gulian in Bucharest (24 April, 1, 8, 15, and 22, May 1916). The leaflet charged the Ittihad leadership, according to Islamic principles, with all sorts of unlawful and infamous actions. According to Sabah-Gulian, in March 1914, the leaflet 'was translated into Turkish following our observation and disseminated in great number amid the Turkish population in Anatolia proper (Konia, Brusa, etc.), especially the military'.

67   Midhat, one of the collaborators of Sherif Pasha in Paris, spied on the relations of the Ottoman opposition with the Arab rebels, as well as on their relations with Lord Kitchener and Greek Prime Minister Venizelos. He reported to the Ottoman secret police about the contents of the letters exchanged by Sadık Bey and Sherif Pasha between July 1913 and July 1914, which show that 'Hnchakian Sabahgulian from Egypt had entered in this conspiracy through deputy Sadik' (Lepsius, *Rapport secret*, 206).

68   Ronald Storrs (1881-1955), official in the British Foreign and Colonial Office and Oriental Secretary in Cairo, who coordinated tasks with Arab rebels.

69   Sisyphus was a mythological king of Corinth who cheated death twice and Zeus punished him by forcing him to roll an immense and heavy boulder up a hill. Every time that he neared the top, the boulder rolled down. He had to repeat this action for eternity. When comparing the pursuit of the Armenian Question to a Sisyphean task, Sabah-Gulian takes into account the program of reforms in and for the provinces inhabited by Armenians, after which, that pursuit would return to its departure point.

70 According to the project of reforms, the six Armenian provinces were divided into two administrative areas.
71 The Central Commission of the SDHP was formed by three members: Sabah-Gulian, Paramaz, and P. Varazdat.
72 The plan to arm the Armenians of Cilicia (see also footnote 83).
73 He refers to the Turkish, Arabic, Kurdish, and Albanian opposition.
74 The reference is again to the project of reforms in the provinces inhabited by Armenians.
75 Murad the Great (Hampartsoum Boyajian, Hajin, 1860 – Kayseri, hanged in July 1915) was studying at the Medical School in Constantinople in 1885, where he founded the Armenian Revolutionary with a group of friends. In 1890 Murad and the members of the Society joined the Hnchakian Party in full. In the same year, he led the well-known demonstration of Kumkapı. He fled abroad and lived in Geneva and Athens. He returned to Sasun in 1892. He crossed the Russo-Ottoman border on foot and reached Tiflis. He led the first rebellion of Sasun in 1893-1894. He was arrested and exiled to the prison of the city of Fizan in Tripolitania. He was elected member of the Central Commission by the sixth Convention of the SDHP in 1905, when he was still in exile. Carrying out an escape of legendary proportions, in 1906 he arrived in Paris and joined his colleagues of the Center. In the same year, he made an appeal to the Armenian revolutionary parties to have a conference and establish unified action. In 1907 he visited the Armenian communities of Egypt, Canada, and the United States, enjoying a warm reception everywhere. He was elected deputy to the Ottoman Parliament from the province of Cilicia (Kozan) (1908–12) and was deputy to the National Assembly from 1908–15. In 1914 he was a member of the Committee of Reforms for the Armenian provinces, formed under the auspices of the Armenian Patriarch. In 1915 he was exiled to Ayash with other Armenian intellectuals. He was separated from the other exiles and taken to the prison of Caesarea, where he was subjected to inenarrable tortures.
76 Aram (Krikor) Achikbashian (Arabkir, 1867 – Constantinople, hanged on June 15, 1915) was a student at the School of Law of Constantinople in 1886. He joined the Revolutionary Society and was one of the organizers of the demonstration of Kumkapı in 1890. In 1893 he was the organizer and coordinator of the groups of *fedayees* in Armenia Minor. In 1895 he headed the self-defense of Shabin Karahisar. He led the activities of transportation of weapons to Armenia Minor until 1906. He was a member of the Central Commission in the third (London, 1903) and fifth (Paris, 1905) conventions. He moved to Paris in 1905, and after the Young Turk Revolution, he lived at times in Paris and in Constantinople, where he was a deputy to the National Assembly. He was arrested in 1914 under the suspicion of an assassination attempt against A. Yasian.
77 In fact, the decision of 'unlawfulness' taken by the Convention at a crucial moment for the Armenian people was not considered to be very responsible. As it happens in such cases, the exchange of different viewpoints was natural. Not only were Murad and A. Achikbashian worried about these decisions, but other people who had gone through the trials of jail and exile in liberation struggles, like Harutiun Jangulian, Hagop Ardzruni (Avedisian), Sako (Aghamirzian), and others, were not enthusiastic either. In our opinion, Sabah-Gulian's characterizations about his comrades were exaggerated and unfair.
78 Hnchakian Archive, Letter of Sabah Gulian to Paramaz, Heliopolis, 3 March 1914.
79 Museum of History of Armenia, Fund of New History, department book 1369/17, Letter of Armenag Garabedian to Zareh Kochian, Alexandria, 18 March 1914. A.

Garabedian and Z. Kochian were two Hnchakian young men who had been related to the activities of transporting weapons from the Greek port of Piraeus to Alexandria headed by Mihran Damadian. They exchanged correspondence with each other, as well as with M. Damadian. Sabah-Gulian's reference to the 'Cilician job' is related to this attempt, which later had other phases.
80 Hnchakian Archive, Register book of the sessions of the SDHP Committee of Cairo, session IV, 19 April/2 May, 12.
81 Sabah-Gulian, *Armenak ew Abraham*, 21.

4

The Social Democrat Hnchakian Party and the First Republic of Armenia (1918–20/21)

Richard G. Hovannisian (†)

The Social Democrat Hnchakian Party (SDHP) did not play a significant role in the First Armenian Republic (1918–1920/21), especially as most of its members at that time were Western Armenians, scattered the world over, with strongholds in the Balkans and in Cilicia. Yet the position of the SDHP vis-à-vis the Armenian Republic may be regarded as being sound and correct. A bitter rival of the *Hay Heghap'okhakan Dashnaktsut'iwn* (Armenian Revolutionary Federation; ARF) and vying to attract much of same elements of society – intellectuals, labourers, freedom fighters – the SDHP clearly differed from other opposition groups.

By the early twentieth century, the fractured Hnchakian movement was overshadowed in the Caucasus by the ARF, which became an active participant in nearly every regional administrative body prior to and during the First World War, the Russian revolutions of 1917, and the short-lived Transcaucasian Federative Republic that preceded the declaration of Armenian independence in May 1918.[1] Many Russian Armenian Hnchakians in Baku, Tiflis and the North Caucasus had by then shifted their allegiance to the more radical and internationalist Menshevik or Bolshevik Marxist Social Democratic factions. Only a small group of veteran intellectuals, together with a number of Western Armenian refugees, remained loyal to the SDHP, nonetheless managing for a time to publish the weekly newspaper *Gortsavor* (Worker) in Tiflis.[2]

Yet there was a sharp contrast between the positions of the SDHP and those opposition elements made up almost exclusively of Western Armenians (Sahmanadir Ramkavar/Constitutional Democrat; Verakazmyal/Reformed Hnchakian; AGBU/ Armenian General Benevolent Union, among others), who clustered around Boghos Nubar and his Armenian National Delegation in Paris. While those groups had difficulty accepting what they referred to as the 'Araratian republic', especially because their perceived 'real' Armenia lay to the west in the Ottoman Empire, the SDHP from the outset recognized the symbolic and judicial importance of Yerevan as the nucleus of a future united, independent Armenian state. The SD Hnchakians, after the schism with the Verakazmyal Hnchakians at the turn of the century, were now much less affected by the Russian Armenian-Turkish Armenian, *Arevelahay-Arevmtahay* dichotomy. They were acerbic and sarcastic when it came to the ARF leadership heading the

Armenian government, men whom they referred to as 'schoolmasters', but they sharply differentiated between the temporary political dominance of any single element, on the one hand, and the permanence of the state and the primacy of defending its sovereignty, on the other. Party intellectual Stepan Sabah-Gulian in particular repeatedly stressed this approach in his prolific writings.[3] When the Zhoghovrdakan (Democratic) party, which was the Caucasian equivalent of the Western Armenian Sahmanadir Ramkavar party and made up largely of highly educated, experienced professionals, boycotted the first national elections for the Armenian Parliament in the summer of 1919, the SDHP deplored this tactic.

The following, I believe, is a fair reflection of the Hnchakian position, as portrayed in this author's multivolume study, *The Republic of Armenia*:

> The Hnchakian attitude toward the Armenian republic was clear-cut. Without sparing the Dashnaktsutiun for its pseudo-socialism, courtship of the Armenian bourgeoisie, and pretensions to leadership in national affairs, the Hnchakian press castigated all parties that boycotted the parliamentary elections, Populist [Zhoghovrdakan] opportunism in first honeymooning with the Dashnaktsutiun [in a coalition government] and then embracing the reactionary elements around Boghos Nubar and the hard-headed intellectuals who were unable to distinguish between state and government, that is, the permanency of the one and the transitory nature of the other. If the government was controlled by an incompetent clique, the state should not be abandoned or undermined but rather aided by the providing of new leadership. No longer could there be Turkish or Russian Armenians, two separate delegations at Paris, or divisive arguments about the historic importance of any one region. There was only one nation and one struggle. The Armenian republic was the Piedmont that would give rise to a free, united, and independent people. The Hnchaks did obeisance to the distant goal of international socialism and demanded radical socioeconomic reforms once Armenia had been united within secure borders, but these gestures were overshadowed by their intense manifestations of specifism [that is, the Armenian road to socialism had special issues that had to be taken into consideration] and nationalism.[4]

Throughout the period of the First Republic, the Hnchakian press remained critical of the self-serving West. In the summer of 1919, for example, when an investigative mission led by Major General James G. Harbord travelled through Asia Minor and Armenia to collect information that would be useful in determining whether the United States should assume a protectorate or mandate for Armenia and, if yes, to be helpful to the mandatory administration by providing it with detailed data on the region, the Hnchakian newspapers noted with stinging sarcasm that economic gain was the moving force in American foreign policy. Seeking profitable world markets, the Americans had discovered Armenia's natural resources and ample potential for foreign investments, but they also wanted to impose the unacceptable scheme of combining Armenia with Asia Minor (Anatolia) and the rest of Transcaucasia (Georgia and Azerbaijan) into a single territorial and economic unit in order to turn an immediate profit. The United States, it was predicted, would probably attempt to attain economic dominance in the region without incurring military or political obligations relating to Armenia by hiding behind the Monroe Doctrine, while at the same time pushing for application of the open-door principle as a way to reap huge economic benefits.[5]

When in the summer of 1919, a subcommittee of the US Senate Foreign Relations Committee held hearings on extending recognition and assistance to the Republic of Armenia, three representatives of the Armenian National Union of America (organized in the United States in 1917 during the First World War and headed by Reformed/Verakazmyal Hnchakian Mihran Sevasly, with the active participation of the Sahmanadir Ramkavar party, Apostolic and Evangelical churches and the AGBU) performed miserably, as they were drawn into snares set by senators vehemently opposed to any American commitment in Armenia.[6] Now, the SDHP press joined that of the Dashnaktsutiun in berating these inept spokesmen for their 'courageous feats' in perpetuating the image and stereotype of helpless Armenians rather than of a freedom-loving people who could defend itself if only provided with arms, financial aid and military advisers. They demanded that henceforth plenipotentiaries of the Armenian government, who would be far more adept in dealing with politically loaded critical questions, should represent the Armenian case in Washington D.C. and everywhere else.[7]

During the fall of 1919, negotiations took place in Yerevan between the Western Armenian National Delegation associated with Boghos Nubar and the Armenian government to create a single cabinet, legislature and peace delegation of the Republic. The envoys of the National Delegation (Vahan Tekeyan and Nshan Der Stepanian), whose charge it was to advance the interests of the Western Armenians, oddly invited a prominent Caucasian Armenian Zhoghovrdakan leader, Samson Harutiunian, to join them, adding to the partisan nature of the mission. Facing them, representing the Armenian government, were equally partisan stalwarts of the Dashnaktsutiun. After protracted negotiations, matters came to an impasse over equations of how many Eastern and Western Armenians and how many Dashnaktsakans and non-Dashnaktsakans would be allocated places in these bodies.[8] In their commentaries, Hnchakian newspapers reflected that this outcome should not have been unforeseen, because the negotiations had been entrusted to '*Dashnakts'akan varzhapetner ew burzhuakan pahpanoghakanner*' (Dashnak schoolmasters and bourgeois conservatives) obsessed with the number of positions they would secure for themselves. And why had Boghos Nubar's delegation, which claimed to represent all Western Armenians, excluded Hnchakians and Verakazmyal Hnchakians from the mission to Yerevan, while adding a Russian Armenian bourgeois Zhoghovrdakan leader? Such mutual partisanship was entirely unacceptable.[9]

Despite such criticism, at least one prominent Hnchakian served in the Republic's fledgling diplomatic corps. In June 1919, the Armenian government appointed Arsen Gidur (Kitur) as its representative for refugee affairs in Cilicia and Mesopotamia, granting him full authority to study the situation of the wartime deportees, assist in meeting their needs and arrange for their return home or else transfer to Armenia. Prime Minister Alexander Khatisian requested that the Allied civil and military authorities extend their support to Gidur, who set out from Constantinople to Baghdad with very limited funds for relief. Many of the Armenian refugees in Mesopotamia were natives of the province of Van who had retreated southward to escape from the Turkish armies. More than 15,000 Armenians and Assyrians were concentrated in a refugee tent city at Bakuba. They were assisted somewhat by British and Armenian agencies but were discontented in the desert environment so different from their native highlands. Although the British authorities allowed Gidur to engage in relief activities, they withheld granting him official recognition. He was also disadvantaged by the lack of financial support from the Armenian government, although a portion of the money gathered for Armenia in the United States was apparently sent to him via the Armenian Republic's delegation in Paris. In August 1920, Gidur warned of rising tension between the refugees and the Arab nationalists who had surrounded the camp. Through his good relations with the British, he was able to have 2,000 Armenians and Assyrians armed. The refugees defended themselves for eight days before the Baghdad government intervened to halt the fighting. Gidur then petitioned the British authorities to transfer the Armenian refugees to a safer site at Nahr Omar on the Shat-al-Arab near the port of Basra, where many moved in the following months.[10]

Meanwhile, in the United States, there was a moment of euphoric exuberance when former Prime Minister Hovhannes Kajaznuni, heading a delegation of the Armenian Republic, and a joint military mission that included General Antranig (Andranik) Ozanian, uplifted the Armenian American community that had suffered through the First World War without knowing the fate of loved ones left behind in their native towns and villages. Kajaznuni and his colleagues first testified in a measured and effective manner before the same subcommittee of the Senate Foreign Relations Committee that was to make recommendations regarding recognition of and assistance to the Armenian Republic.[11]

The joint civil and military mission then travelled from community to community in a show of unity and appeals for assistance for the Armenian army. Unfortunately, dissension among the Armenian political parties and their non-Armenian supporters eventually led to two separate campaigns, one supported by the SDHP and Dashnaktsutiun and the other, by Antranig, the Sahmanadir Ramkavar and Verakazmyal Hnchakian parties, and the AGBU. While each campaign raised about a half million dollars (with purchasing power many times more than the present value) and some people contributed to both drives, the split in the Armenian community reinforced the alienation caused by the previous withdrawal of the SDHP and Dashnaktsutiun from the Armenian National Union.[12] The frequent coalescence of the Hnchakian and Dashnaktskan positions on key issues may seem somewhat surprising in view of the intense ideological and tactical hostility of the two parties during the years of Soviet rule in Armenia.

The same alignment existed in 1920 when it came to the plan of former US Ambassador Henry Morgenthau and other Armenophiles to secure an American mandate for Armenia, even if this required a combined American protectorate over Armenia, Constantinople and possibly even Turkish Anatolia. By then, it was clear that the mandate proposal would fail to gain the approval of the Senate and that it might be better to seek direct US assistance to the Armenian Republic, including military, technical and financial aid. This was the strategy espoused by the American Committee for the Independence of Armenia (ACIA), supported by the SDHP and the Dashnaktsutiun, while the leaders of the other political parties, the Apostolic and Evangelical churches and the AGBU continued to call for a US mandate as the only way to guarantee the security of Armenia and the Armenian people. The Hnchakian and ARF press insisted that a mandate was not essential and criticized the incongruity of demanding national independence while at the same time seeking a foreign protectorate. With the ARF, the Hnchakians deplored the relief posters and films that exploited the image of starving Armenians in order to raise funds for relief. However well intended, they stated, by depicting helpless and hopeless people, these only played into the hands of those hostile elements that were irreconcilably opposed to US political and military involvement in Armenia.[13]

While the SDHP would later make its accommodation with communism and Soviet Armenian statehood, during the period of the First Armenian Republic, the Hnchakian leadership maintained a strong anti-Bolshevik stance. During the abortive Bolshevik uprising to seize power in Armenia in May 1920 (immediately following the Sovietization of Azerbaijan in late April), the SDHP joined all other legal political parties in condemning the perfidious opportunism and appealing to the population to squelch the treacherous subversion and support the Armenian government and army against all those who would subvert Armenian independence.[14] Yet, even at that time there was at least one Hnchakian leader in Tiflis who favoured the overthrow of the Armenian government and a few members in Yerevan who joined in the anti-governmental communist-led May Day demonstrations.[15]

On the broader scene, the Bolshevik challenge to the Armenian Republic served to intensify collaboration between the ARF and SDHP, as attested in their joint celebrations of the second anniversary of independence on 28 May 1920, in Yerevan itself and in rallies from coast to coast in the United States and in Armenian communities worldwide. By that time, most Western Armenians, including Boghos Nubar and the National Delegation, had also come to acknowledge the symbolic and factual importance of the existing Armenian Republic and participated, at least formally, in ceremonies marking the anniversary. These manifestations of Armenian unity were welcomed enthusiastically by the public.

Finally, during the Turkish invasion of the Armenian Republic in the fall of 1920, the Hnchakian party, with all others – Zhoghovrdakan, Socialist Revolutionary, Marxist Social Democrat Specifist, Ramkavar and non-partisan unions appealed to the populace to take to arms and defend the hard-won independence of the Armenian homeland.[16]

On 1 October 1920, the SDHP joined in the formation of an interparty council in Yerevan and issued individual and joint appeals for a national crusade against the unholy alliance of 'Turkish pashas and Bolshevik commissars'. Hnchakian leader Lazo (Hakob Ghazarian) travelled to Ashtarak, Echmiadzin and Oshakan as a part of a deputation to organize patriotic rallies.[17] With bitterness, the Armenian press echoed the views expressed by an opposition Socialist Revolutionary spokesman: the Armenian democracy, he exclaimed, had to depend on its own means to preserve its existence, especially as the European imperialists seemed to be 'loyal friends' only during banquet toasts and speeches. The national crisis required that political differences be laid aside. 'We must forget everything and concentrate only on one endeavor, the defense of the front.'[18]

Such exhortations were destined to be little consequence. Armenia was defeated and then partitioned through a series of treaties between December 1920 and October 1921. Only about half of Russian or Eastern Armenia was spared and continued to exist as the Armenian Soviet Socialist Republic. The SDHP quickly accommodated and attempted to collaborate with the new Armenian communist leadership, taking an active role in the Committee for Assistance to Armenia (*Hayastani Ōgnut'ean Komitē*), as well as the subsequent post-Second World War repatriation (*nergaght*) campaign. Perhaps this was the continuance of the overriding principle to support Armenian national statehood regardless of what group was at the helm. The Soviet period lasted for seven decades until 1991, with the Hnchakian party remaining faithful, despite occasional barbs and sarcastic criticism from the Soviet authorities.

Now several decades into the Third Republic (considering Soviet Armenia to be the Second Republic), many of the lessons that may be drawn from the trials and tribulations of the First Republic of Armenia still remain to be heeded. And the opportunities for loyal opposition parties to participate in state-building and to influence the course of events remain as complex and elusive as ever. Be that as it may, the stance of the SDHP during the short lifespan of the First Republic may, by and large, be considered to be exemplary in pointing the way to constructive political conduct.

Notes

1 See Richard G. Hovannisian, *Armenia on the Road to Independence* (Berkeley and Los Angeles: University of California Press, 1967), esp. chapters 4–9.
2 Richard G. Hovannisian, *The Republic of Armenia*, 4 vols. (Berkeley. Los Angeles. London: University of California Press, 1971–96), vol. 2, 253–4.
3 See especially Sabah-Gulian's articles and editorials in *Eritasard Hayastan* [Young Armenia] 2 August–8 October 1919, and in other Hnchakian organs published in Europe and the Near East in 1919-1920.
4 Hovannisian, *Republic of Armenia*, vol. 2, 254.
5 Hovannisian, *Republic of Armenia*, vol. 2, 353–4.
6 See *Maintenance of Peace in Armenia: Hearings before a Subcommittee on Foreign Relations, United States Senate, Sixty-sixth Congress, First Session, on S. J. R. 106. A Joint Resolution for the Maintenance of Peace in Armenia* (Washington, D.C.: Government Printing Office 1919), 3–62.
7 Hovannisian, *Republic of Armenia*, vol. 2, 378.
8 See Hayastani Hanrapetut'ean Patuirakut'ean Arkhiv, File 296/3, *Azgayin Patuirakut'iwn, 1919 t. Banakts'ut'iwnner Azgayin Patuirakut'ean ew Hayastani Hanrapetut'ean Mijew* (Boston, 1920).
9 See, for example, *Erkir* [Homeland], 16 December 1919; *Eritasard Hayastan*, 14 and 25 February 1920.
10 For materials on the Armenian mission in Mesopotamia and Arsen Gidur's activities, see especially Hayastani Hanrapetut'ean Patuirakut'ean Arkhiv, File 403, *H. H. Zhamanakawor Nerkayats'uts'ich' Iragum, 1920 t.* [Provisional Representation of the Republic of Armenia in Iraq, 1920], and File 236/135, *Copies des Lettres, 1920*. See also Hayastani Azgayin Arkhiv, Fund 200/1/499 and 200/1/575. See also Arsen Gidur,

Patmut'iwn S.D. Hnch'akean Kusakts'ut'ean, 1887-1962, 2 vols (Beirut: Shirag Press, 1962-3).
11 *Maintenance of Peace in Armenia*, 109-24. See also *Koch'nak Hayastani* [Clarion of Armenia], vol. 19, 18 October and 8 November 1919.
12 *Koch'nak Hayastani*, vol. 20, January 1920. For details regarding the fund-raising campaigns and the partisan journalistic feuds, see the newspaper issues of December 1919-April 1920 of the four major Armenian political parties active in the United States: *Eritasart Hayastan* (Hnchakian); *Hayrenik'* (Dashnaktsutiun); *Azg* (Ramkavar); *Pahak* (Verakazmyal Hnchakian).
13 Hovannisian, *Republic of Armenia*, vol. 2, 391-7.
14 There is extensive literature on the May rebellion in Armenia. For an overview, see Hovannisian, *Republic of Armenia*, vol. 3, 209-53, including numerous Soviet and non-Soviet sources in the notes.
15 Gidur, *Patmut'iwn S.D. Hnch'akean Kusakts'ut'ean*, vol. 1, 486-8.
16 *Haṛaj* [Forward], 7 October 1920; Hagop Der Hagopian, *Hayastani Vērjin Aghetĕ* (Constantinople: M. Der Sahagian Press, 1921), 53, 60-3.
17 *Haṛaj*, 9 October 1920.
18 Der Hagopian, *Hayastani Vērjin Aghetĕ*, 55-6.

Section II

Regional and Local Histories

The following section deals with the SDHP activities in the central and eastern provinces of the Ottoman Empire and South America. Within the historiography of the Armenian revolutionary parties there is a dearth of research on regional studies. Most of the literature tends to concentrate on the events in Constantinople such as the Bab-ı Ali Demonstration and the Ottoman Bank siege and disregards the history of these parties in the central and eastern provinces. Although the following section does not aim to cover the activities of the SDHP in all the provinces and the diasporic communities, it does provide examples from regions of Central and Eastern Anatolia, and from towns such as Musa Dagh, Aintab, Kesab and the mountainous region of Sasun. It is through examining the regional history of the party that one gets an intimate picture of the situation on the ground and the nature of SDHP's activities which were conditioned by local, regional and transnational exegesis. One sees how the party attempted to enlist non-Armenian elements in the eastern provinces during its anti-Hamidian activities. Whether using placards or direct contact with different Muslim elements of the eastern provinces, the SDHP tried to present the Armenian cause within the larger context of depredations and persecutions suffered by all ethno-religious groups of the empire.

The first article in this section by Toygun Altıntaş deals with Hnchak pamphleteering in Central Anatolia. He discusses how, through the medium of pamphlets, Hnchak revolutionaries on the ground spoke to multiple audiences transcending religious and ethnic boundaries. With the aim of encouraging resistance toward the local corrupt officers, they aimed to weaken the legitimacy of the Ottoman government. Altıntaş's article is important in that it demonstrates that violence was not the only path that the SDHP adopted in raising awareness about the depredations, persecutions and injustices suffered by the Armenians as well as other Muslim peasants; pamphleteering and the placing of placards were also used by the party as a tool for propaganda. In this process, the revolutionaries used Ottoman Turkish, Armenian and Armeno-Turkish on their pamphlets and placards to reach a wider audience. Their aim was also to establish cordial relations with Muslim peasants and denizens. Through pamphleteering, the revolutionaries also targeted the anti-revolutionary elements within the Armenian communities: the clergy and the bourgeoisie class.

The second article in this section by Varak Ketsemanian challenges the historiographic approaches to the Sasun massacres that mainly view the episode through a binary approach of 'freedom lovers vs. evil oppressor'. He argues that the violence in Sasun could only be understood against the backdrop of Armeno-Kurdish relations. Ketsemanian contends that social and economic factors as well as environmental fluctuations played a dominant role in the violence in the region. While the Ottoman authorities relied on the medium of violence to alter the rural social order by revamping Armeno-Kurdish relations, the SDHP reoriented violence by providing it with political clout. Thus, Ketsemanian argues that the SDHP adapted to the existing resistance rather than creating it from zero as it has been perceived in mainstream historiography. His article provides a rare glimpse into the revolutionaries' interactions with the political ecology of Eastern Anatolia.

The fourth article in this section by Ümit Kurt discusses the foundation of the SDHP branch in Aintab in the province of Aleppo. The Hnchaks mobilized both professors and students to their ranks by proselytizing in Armenian and foreign educational institutions. Aintab became the centre of the SDHP activities in the province of Aleppo, turning into the key to the establishment of branches in Urfa, Marash, Zeytun, Kilis, Birecik, Antioch, Kesab and Aleppo. Kurt argues that during the 1895 massacres in Aintab, the number of casualties was low due to the self-defence activities of the SDHP. Similarly, during the Adana Massacres of 1909, the Hnchaks put away their differences with the Dashnaks and organized self-defence units to protect from imminent attacks. During the First World War, the entire membership of the SDHP was arrested along with those of the ARF, while all the Armenian population was deported. After the return of the remaining refugees to Aintab in the post-war period, SDHP played an important role in resettling the refugees. Later, due to the Kemalist onslaught on Cilicia, Armenians once more found themselves as refugees. The Hnchaks focused all their efforts to help Armenians leave the city securely for Aleppo and Beirut.

Another important region where the SDHP was active was Musa Dagh, where the party attempted to win over the inhabitants through propaganda and indoctrination. In the beginning Musa Dagh was not the target. It happened to be on the way to Zeytun, where the SDHP was planning an uprising in order to attract the attention of the European powers to the plight of the Armenians. In this article, Shemmassian demonstrates how through the efforts of Hnchak leader Aghasi (Garabed Tursarkisian), most of the Armenians of Musa Dagh joined the SDHP. He discusses in detail the activities of the Hnchak revolutionaries and the measures that were taken by the government to thwart them. Shemmassian demonstrates that opposition to the Hnchaks and their activities did not come only from the authorities but also from the Armenian notables as well as clergy, who were fearful that the party was disrupting the status quo that existed in the region. Similar to other regions, the Hnchaks here too tried to mobilize Muslim elements in order to delegitimize the Hamidian regime. For example, they began negotiating with their Alawi neighbours for joint actions against the local authorities with the aim of establishing an independent Armenian-Alawi region. Even though this failed, it demonstrates how the party was cognizant of the plight of non-Armenian groups who were suffering under the Hamidian regime.

The last article in this section offers a glimpse into the activities of the SDHP in the diaspora through its insertion in South America. Vartan Matiossian's article deals with the history of the SDHP in Argentina, Uruguay and Brazil, where Armenian communities were established in the post-genocide period. Similar to other diasporic communities, the activities of the SDHP took place in an environment of cooperation/contention with other Armenian political parties such as the ARF and philanthropic organizations such as the AGBU. Matiossian demonstrates how the SDHP, through the medium of education and philanthropic activities, strove to preserve the identity of the Armenians and to aid the newly arriving refugees from Cilicia. Partisan politics also struck hard in the South American communities. The inter-party tensions that existed in the Ottoman Empire were now exported to these communities. All attempts to form a unified front by all the Armenian parties, organizations and churches failed. In this competition of winning over public opinion, the SDHP employed both print media and radio to influence its constituents. While today the activities of the SDHP in South America have dramatically declined, Matiossian's article demonstrates that in the earlier period, the SDHP in the region was a force to be reckoned with.

5

Armenians, Muslims, Citizens

Hnchak Pamphleteering in Central Anatolia

Toygun Altıntaş

The last decade of the nineteenth century marked an important turn in the development of Ottoman Armenian politics. Revolutionary parties entered the political realm, which had theretofore been dominated by the Apostolic Patriarchate, the Armenian National Assembly [hereafter ANA], and local institutions that were organically connected to them.[1] The National Assembly and the Patriarchate were widely thought to be incompetent and/or unwilling to address the worsening of the land grabs in the eastern provinces and the crushing tax burden on the peasantry throughout Ottoman Armenia.[2] Furthermore, both institutions were intricately linked with the Ottoman palace and bureaucracy, which had shown little interest in offering redress to the ailing Armenian peasantry.

The socialist and nationalist founders of the revolutionary parties, the majority of whom hailed from the Russian Empire, sought to appeal to such unaddressed grievances to the detriment of the Hamidian administration and the Armenian notability.[3] The Social Democrat Hnchakian Party [hereafter SDHP] established its presence in the political landscape of the Ottoman Empire with the organization of the Kumkapı Demonstration in 1890, three years after its formation. During the nineteenth century, the political landscape of the Ottoman Empire had been irreversibly integrated into a trans-imperial structure dominated by the established Great Powers of Europe through a combination of economic agreements, diplomatic treaties, and semi-colonial institutions such as the Public Debt Administration [hereafter PDA].[4] The Hnchak programme espoused a project of nationalist and socialist liberation by targeting imperial and international structures of oppression. The end goal was to bring about the establishment of an independent Armenia through the utilization of a wide array of tactics such as propaganda, terrorism and instigating foreign intervention.[5] Despite several episodes of intensive repression and internal division, the SDHP would become one of the two major revolutionary parties to influence Ottoman Armenian politics in the next two decades.

The secondary literature on the history of the SDHP in its formative years remains scarce when considering its importance in local and imperial society and politics.[6] It focuses on the founding cadres from Russian Armenia, which played an indispensable role in initiating the organizational spreading of the party throughout Ottoman Armenia, edited and published the organ *Hnch'ak,* and established contacts with liberal and socialist intellectuals and journalists in Western Europe.[7] As important as the founding cadres were the organizers and revolutionary propagandists of this period, the majority of whom hailed from Ottoman Armenia. They populated the ranks of the secret revolutionary committees sprawled throughout Central Anatolia and Ottoman Armenia, the armed bands that waylaid passers-by to cull financial resources for the party, and cells of assassins that targeted Armenian informants and anti-revolutionary notables. These Hnchak revolutionaries 'on the ground' were simultaneously engaged with multiple audiences in their efforts to build up a popular base among local Armenian communities, encourage disobedience and resistance towards local authorities and weaken the power and legitimacy of the Ottoman government. In addition to following directives from the central committee of the party, which was in Athens at the time, they operated with considerable autonomy and attention to local dynamics.

Using Ottoman and British archival sources, this chapter traces the pamphleteering and broadside campaign of Hnchak revolutionaries in Central Anatolia in the party's formative years. First, the chapter seeks to highlight the composite local, imperial and international dynamics of revolutionary organization while focusing on a particular region. In other words, the analysis of the revolutionaries' activities will be built up from their local engagements to the implications of their efforts on the larger imperial and international scales. In doing so, it will decenter the role and involvement of the central committee in the administration and popularization of the SDHP. Second, it attempts to dissect revolutionary venues of opposition and organization apart from violence. Much of the focus on the history of the Armenian revolutionary movement has revolved around the question of the utilization of attentats, self-defence and robberies.[8] Although violence was undoubtedly a central component of revolutionary politics, other modes of propaganda and engagement broadened the appeal of the SDHP. Furthermore, attention to such propaganda will shed light on the multiplicity of the goals and challenges of revolutionary opposition during this period. Third, the chapter seeks to expand the geography of the historiography of the Armenian revolutionary movement to include Central Anatolia. The historiography of the activities of both the Social Democrat Hnchakian Party and the Armenian Revolutionary Federation (ARF) has focused on the eastern provinces of the Ottoman Empire, where Armenian communities were more populous and the problem of land grabs by Kurdish tribes was particularly acute.[9] However, the Ottoman provinces of Ankara and Sivas were among the most significant zones of Hnchak organization and activity in the last decade of the nineteenth century. Revolutionary assassins regularly targeted Armenian informants and anti-revolutionary notables and armed bands roamed the countryside, robbing official mail couriers and passers-by, while organizers relentlessly worked to expand a fledgling network of revolutionary committees that assisted each other in the dissemination of political literature, expertise and arms and ammunition. Pamphleteering and broadside affixing were also common features of Hnchak activities.

Pamphlets and Propaganda

Pamphlets, posters and broadsides entered the arsenal of politicians and revolutionaries in the early modern period.[10] In civil war England and revolutionary France, mass-produced polemical literature became a fixture of political life. Pamphlets were considered essential to the making and shaping of public opinion, hailed by some historians as the harbinger of modern propaganda. Professional pamphleteers prospered during and after the English Civil War.[11] Although the legality of the ideas espoused in some radical pamphlets remained ambiguous, and their authors could be persecuted by the authorities, the pamphlet itself emerged as a legal medium through which intellectuals and polemicists would engage one another and the general public. By the late eighteenth century, it was expected that thousands of copies of a single pamphlet were to be sold, reaching ever higher numbers of readers and listeners.[12] Pamphleteering was certainly an integral part of the political process in the early modern period well into the nineteenth century. Its significance and impact were heightened during moments of acute political and social crisis. It was not until the emergence of a popular press with a high degree of freedom of expression that pamphlets became marginal to the political cultures of France and Britain in the late nineteenth century.

The defining qualities of political pamphlets were their openly polemical structure and content, their relative brevity in relation to lengthier tracts and essays on the nature of politics, and their engagement with the immediate social and political context. The evolution of the pamphlet as a particularly polemical form of propaganda can be attributed to the volatile and contested social and political contexts which gave rise to it as a prevalent form of political media. In other words, pamphlets were authored and viewed as components of a larger literature of disjuncture and contestation. As documents of contestation and polemics, pamphlets also tended to be relatively short with specific aims and goals. The brevity of pamphlets was not necessarily universal, however, particularly in the late eighteenth and early nineteenth centuries, at which point the genre was well-established and had come to include political treatises produced for mass readership.[13] In relation to the latter, some historians have referred to the pamphlet as 'the history of the moment'.[14] As a large body of literature of disjuncture and contestation produced during times of crises, pamphlets shaped and responded to particular events and developments at local and national scales. As such, their relevance and importance were somewhat ephemeral: when the crisis was subdued or a compromise was reached, a popular pamphlet could sink into obscurity.

As primary sources, however, their polemical nature and intrinsic connection to the immediate political and social context afford them a unique value. Pamphlets allow the historian to glimpse into the political culture of the pamphleteers and the diverse communities they sought to engage. As localized documents of propaganda, they provide insight into the making of discursive strategies of agitation and popularization. The themes they draw upon, their declared and undeclared audiences, their reception by the authorities and their tone and language shed light on the dynamics of oppositional politics that are not apparent in party programmes and official correspondence. In addition, pamphlets constitute indirect and distorted approximations of the sensitivities of largely illiterate populations. In the case of revolutionary France, for example, pamphleteers were aware of the significance of reaching out to illiterate rural populations. Many pamphlets were written and recited by cultural intermediaries that attempted to render propaganda legible and relatable to the peasantry. In turn, the peasants were not passive recipients of political propaganda; they proved time and again their ability and willingness to establish and manoeuvre between tactical alliances and cooperation with different interest groups from the larger cities.[15] The Ottoman Empire in the early modern and modern periods presents a comparable case in terms of the spread of literacy among its population.[16]

Another significant feature of popular literature in the Ottoman Empire was the limited use of the printing press. As a result, the available numbers of pamphlets and treatises were limited until the second half of the nineteenth century. Nevertheless, the eighteenth century marked the emergence of the medium of the *mecmua*, which was a collection of texts on a particular topic. The presence of such manuscripts attests to the growing significance of written materials, whether they were read, recited or both, in the public discussion of contentious issues. These compilations were written in vernacular Turkish to address particular and local issues of contention. Notable subjects included the widespread consumption of tobacco and coffee. Texts from such compilations were read aloud in coffeehouses. The manuscripts themselves became constituted media in the making, as the marginalia became cites of further debate and remarks. Although the eighteenth-century *mecmua*s were not explicitly political, it is noteworthy that they revolved around indirectly political subjects such as tobacco and coffee consumption, or local politics of notability. Anonymous leaflets and posters were employed to tarnish the reputation of local figures. The widespread popularity of tobacco and coffee brought about the regulation of their trade and consumption from the early modern period. The attitude of the authorities ranged from outright bans on tobacco and coffee to the clandestine monitoring of the spaces in which they were consumed.[17] In some ways, the *mecmua* became a literary coffeehouse, a medium in which controversial social issues and inconsequential trivia were discussed, simultaneously representing and shaping public opinion.[18]

With the onset of the nineteenth century and the spread of nationalist movements throughout the Ottoman Empire, pamphlets and broadsides entered the arsenal of the opponents of the Ottoman state. The word used for pamphlets and broadsides was *yafta*. It had been used to describe the public declarations affixed to the bodies of political prisoners that were executed in the eighteenth and early nineteenth centuries. As such, the *yafta* originated as a medium of state propaganda to legitimize its violence and showcase its power over its opponents. In time, however, its definition came to include any broadside or poster that made an appeal to the public and/or the state to take action on a given matter. As a result, broadsides that sought to attract the attention of government authorities to particular acts of abuse in the provinces when petitioning failed to achieve the desired results, or posters that were disseminated to tarnish the reputation of a local political rival also came to be referred to as *yafta*. The Ottoman government invested resources in the suppression of *yafta*-affixing after the Greek War of Independence, during which Greek nationalists called for public support in their struggle against the Ottoman Empire. Despite its increasing use during the nineteenth century, the anti-government *yafta* remained a sporadic phenomenon for most of the nineteenth century. In other words, except for certain instances of its use during the Greek War of Independence by nationalists, there was no concerted effort for its use as part of a revolutionary and/or seditious programme.[19]

Pamphlets and revolution

After the Kumkapı Demonstration in Istanbul, the SDHP committed its energies to the expansion of its operations in Central Anatolia.[20] Several revolutionary leaders arrived in the region in the early 1890s with instructions to expand the Hnchak network of revolutionary committees. In addition to this work of extensive organization, the revolutionaries conducted widespread pamphleteering in order to engage with the local population. There had been sporadic earlier attempts by local Armenian patriotic circles to encourage local Armenians to arm themselves. An example was a pamphlet distributed in Van that called on Armenians to consider their future and prepare for war.[21] However, the frequency of appearance and the number of revolutionary pamphlets that appeared in Central Anatolia from the early 1890s until the Hamidian massacres, suggest that the local revolutionaries were using this medium at an unprecedented scale. They employed a variety of discursive strategies in Ottoman Turkish, Armeno-Turkish and Western Armenian to different ends in order to weaken Ottoman legitimacy and authority, and reinforce the image of the party as a viable and powerful alternative to the state institutions. However, Hnchak pamphleteering was not simply aimed at agitation. It was a composite campaign with divergent appeals to different communities in a region where the rates of literacy among the targeted populations were low. The appearance of seditious pamphlets and posters in a tightly regulated political environment ensured that their content would be communicated to the public in some form.

Colonial Bengal, in the early twentieth century, presents a comparable case of extensive pamphleteering in a society, in which the levels of literacy were low. The spread of pamphleteering in Bengal was directly related to the expansion and popularization of the revolutionary nationalist movement in a campaign of violence that targeted British colonial officers there. Violence was conceptualized as a means to dispel the aura of invincibility that surrounded the ruling class and its representatives. Initially, the revolutionaries utilized the political press to advance their agenda and influence public opinion in favour of their attacks. As the colonial administration introduced a stricter regime of censorship in the regular periodical press to combat sedition, the revolutionaries were compelled to publish and disseminate their propaganda in the form of pamphlets. Hundreds of pamphlets were distributed in the cities and the countryside over the course of the decade after the partitioning of Bengal in 1905. The pamphleteers represented the struggle between the colonial administration and the nationalists as one between a virtuous national collective and its oppressive enemy in order to justify the attentats and attacks against British officials and targets. They also utilized religious and scriptural references by framing the revolution as 'a Hindu religious sacrifice (*Jagna*) for which the revolutionaries were asked to give blood in order to propitiate a wounded mother-goddess'.[22] Although the movement was suppressed by the British, it succeeded in instigating anti-British sentiment and placing the question of independence at the centre of politics in India.[23]

The Hnchak pamphleteering campaign did not have a similar unifying theme such as the legitimization of revolutionary violence. The pamphlets varied significantly in style and content. In addition, they were written for audiences that were not within the networks of the revolutionaries and their sympathizers. For that the revolutionary committees maintained a clandestine transfer of the party organ, the monthly editorials of which served simultaneously as the tactical and strategic vision of the party as espoused by the central committee, which was in Athens during the period in question. However, the central committee had little direct control over the production and distribution of revolutionary pamphlets and broadsides with the important exception of the placards that were posted in several towns and cities in the winter of 1892. In almost every other case, the authors of the pamphlets were anonymous local revolutionaries often signing the documents under aliases or the title 'Hnchak Revolutionary Society'. In other words, most of the pamphlets were produced for specific social and cultural contexts by local revolutionaries. In most cases, the intended audience was the Muslim community, although the revolutionaries occasionally employed pamphlets and posters to engage the local Armenian population.

The indirect audiences for the Hnchak pamphleteering campaign were the Ottoman administration and the diplomatic representatives of the Great Powers. Most of the revolutionary broadsides and pamphlets would eventually be seen by government officials and foreign diplomats. The revolutionaries were aware that their pamphlets and broadsides would eventually be confiscated by the authorities who had adopted harsh measures against the suppression of revolutionism and political dissent. Their brazen and persistent attempts at distributing pamphlets were a direct challenge to the authority of the state. The challenge was compounded by the particularly seditious language of the pamphlets, which often ridiculed local authorities and foretold the imminent collapse of the Ottoman Empire. Diplomatic representatives of the Great Powers were also among the undeclared (and possibly unintentional) audiences of the revolutionary pamphlets. The British vice-consul in Ankara received copies and translations of several pamphlets through local contacts. In cases where he had no access to the physical copies, he received intelligence on the manner of the dissemination of the pamphlets, their tone and content. The reactions and attitudes of these undeclared audiences were instrumental in elevating local disputes, agitation, sedition and propaganda to the imperial and international stages.

Appealing to Local Muslims

One of the most pressing concerns of the revolutionaries in Central Anatolia was the attitude of local Muslims towards Armenians and the government. The Hnchak programme briefly touched upon the significance of securing the sympathy of Muslim communities in order to realize the party's goals. The revolutionaries on the ground, however, found that Muslim–Armenian relations in general and the local Muslims' view of the revolutionary committees in particular would have a profound effect on their struggle and the efficiency of the Ottoman state's suppression of Armenian dissent in the provinces.[24] Therefore, many of the pamphlets, broadsides and placards prepared by the revolutionaries were directed towards the local Muslim population. This was in accordance with other Hnchak activities in the early 1890s.

Arsen Gidur argues that the famed Hnchak Jirair Boyajian had achieved some minor successes in promoting the image of the revolutionaries among the rural Muslim population in the countryside around Yozgat and Tokat. Many of the grievances of the Armenian and Muslim peasants were socio-economic. They both resented the burden of excessive taxation at the hands of government officials, and the extortionate terms of credit imposed on them by local notables and moneylenders. These commonalities had made possible the appearance of the revolutionaries in the countryside as a potential boon to the Muslim peasants. Gidur adds, however, that the period for Muslim approval or support for the revolutionaries was brief as Muslim notables and local authorities intervened to address the situation. They simultaneously intimidated and appeased the Muslim peasantry to prevent the cultivation of further pro-revolutionary sentiment.[25]

Considering the aforementioned significance of the attitude of local Muslims and the proportionally smaller communities of Armenians in Central Anatolia, it is not surprising that Muslims constituted the major audience for revolutionary pamphleteering there. In the early days of January 1893, numerous copies of two separate placards appeared in several Central Anatolian towns and cities. The first was signed by 'The Committee of the Patriots of Islam', although it was nominally addressed to Ottoman subjects at large. It stated that Sultan Abdülhamid II had stained the religion of Islam and the Ottoman state. It concluded that 'a great Power that rules over millions of Moslems is coming' to the Ottoman subjects' assistance. The text of the other poster was more cryptic. It praised the 'Indian remedy' for 'disease of the heart, paralysis, throat ailments, fear, and all other diseases which daily and hourly affect men, and which yearly brings death to thousands of patriots'. It foretold the imminent administration of this 'remedy' to the Ottoman Empire, as a result of which it claimed 'the whole of Turkey will then attain prosperity and live in tranquility'. The second poster was signed 'The Indians who seek the salvation of the people of Islam.'[26]

The 'placard affair' was followed by several months of government investigation and resulted in the first major trial of the revolutionaries in the Ottoman Empire. The Ottoman prosecutor focused his efforts on the exposure of the revolutionary committees and their armed bands that had been especially active in Merzifon and the countryside. However, the defendants also included the network of Hnchak sympathizers who had assisted the revolutionaries in the dissemination of the placards throughout Central Anatolia. Almost all of them claimed that they had been threatened with physical violence or assassination in case of refusal to help the revolutionaries. While it is likely that the revolutionaries intimidated the unwilling to assist them, it is also true that any admission of culpability in court would have guaranteed imprisonment.[27] The efficacy of Hnchak sympathizers throughout Central Anatolia was a testament to the success of the revolutionaries' proselytizing in the countryside. Several of the sympathizers received sentences of one to three years of imprisonment with hard labour.

The central committee was likely to have been involved in the authoring of the placards.[28] By publishing the placards, the central committee attempted to propagate the benefits of foreign intervention, specifically, a British one. Securing direct foreign intervention to enforce administrative reform in the Ottoman Empire was an important political goal for the Hnchaks. In addition to the obvious resistance of the Hamidian regime, though, the revolutionaries were aware that there was considerable hostility to foreign intervention by the local Muslim community. Therefore, the Hnchaks wanted to pose as a Muslim revolutionary group and portray Great Britain as a Great Power with a long history of benevolent government over millions of Muslims.

Another likely motive was to encourage Muslim hostility towards the government and arouse the suspicion of the local authorities towards the Muslim population. The texts had been published in *Hnch'ak* several months before their appearance in Central Anatolia.[29] The *Hnch'ak* editorial board had claimed to have received the posters from Muslim revolutionaries in the Ottoman Empire. The notion that a secret Muslim revolutionary committee was responsible for the placard affair was maintained until the trial. Letters to *Hnch'ak* from local revolutionaries stipulated that the government was blaming Armenian revolutionaries to persecute the Armenian community in general.[30] However, the trial and the central committee's erroneous publication of the placards in the party organ several months before they were distributed in Central Anatolia dispelled the spectre of a Muslim revolutionary group in public opinion and government circles. It is likely that the central committee had planned it as a means of promoting anti-government sentiment among the Muslim population while provoking the local authorities to take harsh measures against Muslims they deemed suspicious. Although the placards revealed the extent of the revolutionary network and the trial served as a platform for the revolutionaries to publicly declare their goals, the ultimate goal of cultivating tensions between the government and the Muslim community failed. The 'placard affair' was the only major episode in Hnchak pamphleteering that can be clearly traced to the central committee in Athens.

Establishing good relations with the local Muslim community continued to be a priority for the revolutionaries. Calls for cooperation with the Muslims were often coupled with declarations denouncing the sultan, the Ottoman bureaucracy and local government officials. Corruption and venality were common accusations levelled at local officials. At the end of 1893, several pamphlets were left at the doorsteps of local Muslim notables or broadsides affixed to the walls of some buildings signed by a 'Justice-Loving Committee'. The pamphleteers addressed their audience as 'our Muslim citizens'. The pamphlet stated that 'it is our sacred duty to spill the last drop of our blood to preserve liberty and peace in our homeland as a unified body of Muslims and non-Muslims'. The propensity of government officials towards bribes and their cruelty towards the common folk necessitated united action. According to the pamphleteers, the time of differences based on ethnicity and confession had passed; the Ottoman citizenry had to act in unison against a state apparatus that had been taken over by a corrupt elite whose interests directly clashed with those of the masses. The Ottoman government under Sultan Abdülhamid II was harming Muslims and Armenians alike.[31]

The call for Muslim–Armenian cooperation against the Hamidian regime had been toned down to a call for the cessation of inter-communal enmity by early 1895.

In a pamphlet that was widely distributed in Amasya, the revolutionaries called on their 'Muslim brothers' to set aside the question of religious differences. In civilized countries, they argued, individual rights and freedoms reigned supreme and set the basis for constant progress. In the Ottoman Empire, however, injustice and tyranny had taken over. Only revolution and struggle could overcome these obstacles to progress. It did not matter that the government defined the revolutionaries' conduct as evildoing. The revolutionaries paid no heed to the declarations of the government. What was particularly egregious was that the Turkish folk had been deceived by the government propaganda. The pamphleteers claimed that their Turkish compatriots had been cajoled by the government to participate in the perpetuation of its injustice and tyranny, while the Armenians suffered in prisons or the gallows. The pamphlet concluded with a call for Muslims to wake up and take heed of their position vis-a-vis the government and the revolutionaries. It stated:

> We Armenians will continue to struggle until our last breath to realize our Revolution. God willing, the time for its success is near. Do not waste time just standing by. Cease the enmity between nation and religion. Work for the fatherland and heed our cries. You will also benefit from it.[32]

The revolutionaries were aware that the deterioration of inter-communal violence and mass violence against the Armenians would have dire consequences for the future of the movement and the conditions of Ottoman Armenians at large. Therefore, they sought to secure the sympathy, if not the explicit support of the Muslim population. On the one hand, they emphasized the venality of local government authorities who, they claimed, were only serving themselves in their positions. On the other hand, they attempted to conjoin their nationalist revolutionary struggle with the general march for social, cultural and political progress. The local Muslims had the chance to hasten and participate in the process by opposing the Hamidian regime and making common cause with the revolutionaries.

During the same period, another pamphlet was disseminated in the city of Sivas and its surrounding villages. It started with a curse of unbelief for those that would turn it over to the authorities without reading it or admitting its truth. It justified the growing popularity of the revolutionary movement among Ottoman Armenians on the basis of the state of lawlessness and arbitrary use of government force. Because the Ottoman government had fallen into a state of injustice and tyranny and its officials were primarily motivated by bribes as opposed to a sense of duty, Armenians had placed their hopes in the event of a general revolution. The pamphleteers grieved the Muslims' indifference to the same abject conditions that affected them. They stated: 'You make yourselves the victims of a Government formed of vile officials who kill while they pet you, and you still are faithful to such a Government.'[33] The growing tensions between Muslims and Armenians were primarily the work of the Ottoman government in order to prevent the creation of a united front against them. The authorities were cultivating the idea that the revolutionaries were waging war against Islam and Muslims, that they sought independence under foreign tutelage, and that they would commence the final stage of their plan by staging a massacre of Muslims during the Eid al-Fitr.

The pamphleteers dismissed such allegations. They asked Muslims to look carefully to the activities of the revolutionaries and the targets of their attentats. The majority of their victims had been Armenians. 'If our aim was against Mahommedans or Mahommedanism' they asked, 'why should we kill the Armenians?'[34] It is striking that the revolutionaries included anti-revolutionary Armenian notables and merchants among their chief adversaries along with the local authorities. It was true that the overwhelming majority of the revolutionaries' targets in the early 1890s had been other Armenians. It was unprecedented, however, that they used that fact as a means to assuage Muslim anxieties about the revolutionaries' challenge to existing ethno-confessional hierarchies or the prospect of an independent Armenian state. The revolutionaries represented themselves as a political group that was primarily motivated by their opposition to Hamidian repression and sought to improve the conditions of all Ottoman subjects to their Muslim audience. By doing so, they aimed to counter the Hamidian strategy of cultivating Muslim anxieties of Armenian resurgence. Following this line of logic, the pamphlet concluded with a denial of the government's allegations that the revolutionaries aimed for political independence. 'Are we foolish enough to have the idea of national independence?' the pamphleteers asked. 'No, no. Crushed, oppressed, plundered, Mahommedan neighbors, before being Christians we are men. Being men both of us, we wish not to be robbed in daylight of our most holy rights.'[35] The revolutionaries underscored the socio-economic oppression of Armenians and the authorities' oppressive policies, while denying the existence of what was one of the foundational goals of the SDHP – complete independence for Armenians.

The revolutionaries distributed another pamphlet in the town of Amasya in the spring of 1895. It clearly reflected the frustration of the revolutionaries with the lack of support and sympathy for them among local Muslims. The preamble invoked the wrath of Prophet Muhammad on all those that would turn it over to the authorities without comprehending its description of the injustices suffered by the Muslim and non-Muslim subjects of the Empire and enlightening other Ottoman citizens. The utilization of Islamic references to convince Muslims to pay attention to the revolutionaries' propaganda mirrored the other pamphlet in Sivas. The pamphleteers then described the state of local government in some length. According to them, the company of local officials was telling of the character of the local authorities. Since they employed the services of local brigands, thieves and extortioning moneylenders, the integrity of government officials was compromised. In fact, the vice-governor of Amasya himself hailed from such a background, according to the revolutionaries. He was a brigand in the vicinity of Samsun, notorious for having ridden off into the wilderness on a horse he claimed he was interested in purchasing. 'Which one of us from the revolutionary committee has engaged in such conduct?' the revolutionaries asked.[36] Whoever attributed such activities to the revolutionaries committed slander. The pamphlet was aimed at establishing the moral superiority of the revolutionaries over local officials whose past, the pamphleteers claimed, was ridden with criminality and self-aggrandizement at the cost of the common folk. It was simultaneously an effort to tarnish the reputation of the imperial government and an appeal to the local Muslims' sense of justice and propriety.

A few months later, another pamphlet, signed by 'The Homeland Committee', was distributed on the streets of Sivas. It stated that the majority of the Ottoman population had been reduced to abject poverty in recent times. The government and its corrupt and bribe-seeking local officials were responsible for that state of affairs. Although every Ottoman subject was suffering from the malevolent administration, Armenians were vocal about their complaints and demands for change. It was for that reason that the government sought to 'sow the seeds of discord and enmity between two citizens'.[37] The lack of security on the roads and general disorder in the cities and towns could only be attributed to the policies of the government, according to the pamphleteers. The short pamphlet concluded with a call for joint action to remove the Ottoman 'yoke, and raise high the flag of liberty'. The revolutionaries were once again calling on Muslims to join them against the Ottoman state in open defiance and rebellion.

The call was even more pronounced in a broadside affixed in several towns in Central Anatolia in August 1895. It was addressed to Muslim 'citizens' of the Ottoman Empire and signed openly by the 'Armenian Revolutionary Society'. It followed other pamphlets in its reiteration of the common concerns of Muslims and Armenians under the oppressive and exploitative administration of Ottoman government officials. The argument was supplanted by a short explanation of the damage caused to the Ottoman economy at large by the free trade agreements signed with the Great Powers. Despite its natural resources for mining and rich agricultural land, the Ottoman economy lagged woefully behind its European counterparts. The only concern of local officials, however, was the preservation of their positions through the heavy taxation of the Muslim and Armenian peasantry alike. Neither the government nor its local administrators had any interest in the economic advancement of its people. The pamphleteers claimed:

> Citizens! We were not born to suffer under the caprices of these government officials. The government does not work for our progress. Muslim citizens, let us cast aside religious and national differences now. Let us work together, for perilous days are near. When all is taken into consideration, it will be understood that the Sublime State will collapse suddenly. Let us struggle to stop the oppressors and secure the progress of our country as the people![38]

Although Hnchak pamphlets and broadsides had assumed populist undertones since the beginning of the campaign, direct class-based agitation with references to the international capitalist system was a new development. The revolutionaries also declared openly that the Ottoman Empire would not survive for much longer, and called for Muslim cooperation under a new administrative arrangement in order to form a unified body politic.

The SDHP ran an aggressive pamphleteering campaign in Central Anatolia. Although the initial pamphlets were authored by the central committee in Athens and affixed and distributed as part of an effort to cultivate discord between local Muslims and government officials, the rest of the campaign was overseen by local revolutionaries. Common themes included the venality and corruption of government officials, the weak state of the Hamidian regime, and vigilance towards official efforts to sow enmity between Muslims and Armenians. In order to assuage Muslim anxiety about the increasing popularity of an Armenian political organization and the prospect of the collapse of the existing social order, the revolutionaries highlighted the socialist aspect of their platform. They called for Muslim cooperation in addressing common problems of over-taxation, bribery and administrative caprice. Furthermore, the revolutionaries prevaricated on the question of the creation of an independent state. Although the Hnchak programme clearly stipulated that complete political independence from the Ottoman Empire was one of the party's main goals, the revolutionaries downplayed its significance or flatly denied their interest in attaining it in order to calm Muslim anxieties. The pamphlets addressed to local Muslims display a significant degree of Hnchak awareness of the importance of Muslim public opinion and interest in shaping it in accordance with the party's political programme.

SDHP engagement with Armenian communities

The Ottoman Armenian community, unlike the Muslim majority, constituted both the agent and object of revolutionary change for the SDHP. As a result, the Hnchak engagement with local Armenian communities took multiple forms. Leading revolutionaries circulated political literature for members of the local branches. The cornerstone of political literature was undoubtedly the journal *Hnch'ak*, which was the party organ. Furthermore, party instructions and organizational documents were circulated in order to provide blueprints in the spread of the organization into smaller towns and villages. Raffi's works constituted another popular body of political literature for the education and motivation of new recruits.[39] Finally, there is evidence that the Hnchak central committee in Athens oversaw the translation and distribution of political treatises by famous European socialists.[40] A treatise by Ferdinand Lassalle was found among the confiscated documents of the Hnchak branch in Sivas in 1893.[41] The preface to the translation stipulated that the SDHP believed in the necessity of the political education of the Armenian people to realize its liberation. Only through such political education would the people be able to comprehend their own political interests. The treatise was a combination of the summary of Hegelian dialectics and the 'iron law of wages', and a polemic against Karl Marx and Friedrich Engels' proposition that the liberation of the working class could only be achieved by the public ownership of the means of production. Lassalle argued that such a proposition necessitated total revolution. Since this project of total revolution had failed, change through reform and expansion of democratic political rights had become the norm among European socialists, spearheaded by those in Germany.[42] While Raffi's works were thought to inspire the popularization of nationalist sentiment and demand for self-determination, Lassalle's treatise is likely to have served as an educational tool to introduce recruits and sympathizers to the recent debates within the socialist movement. It is not clear whether the central committee considered the gradualism of German social democrats a more palatable platform than the push for total revolution and wholesale social transformation.

In addition to party-sponsored political literature and Raffi's influential works, local revolutionaries took initiative in the production of propaganda material. Although Hnchak's efforts to recruit and appeal to the Armenian community usually adopted more direct forms than pamphlets, posters and public declarations, local revolutionaries occasionally authored and disseminated/affixed short texts to strengthen their image.

Armenian communities of Central Anatolia were addressed in a number of pamphlets and placards to broaden the appeal of the SDHP and to intimidate opponents of the revolutionaries. The pamphleteers also wrote about the weak state of the Hamidian regime and the corruption of its local representatives. Moreover, they attempted to justify their violent methods against anti-revolutionary Armenians. The pamphlets provided the revolutionaries with an alternative medium to reach the Armenian community that was different from the party organ in a few important ways. First, the pamphlets and placards were deliberately distributed in an open and public manner. This allowed the revolutionaries to address their audience and challenge government authority overtly. Second, the revolutionaries utilized the pamphlets to address specific concerns and localize the presence and power of the SDHP in the Armenian imaginary. In other words, the pamphlet served as a tool to materialize the revolutionaries' claim to represent the Armenian community on a local basis, while the party organ was written with the general strategic concerns of the central committee in mind. Finally, the pamphlets provided the revolutionaries with the medium and opportunity to engage in polemics to interject in the making of local public opinion and to attempt to shape it. The image and character of missionaries, government officials or Armenian notables were made and remade in the pamphlets. This section will analyse a few pamphlets and posters that were distributed by the revolutionaries in an attempt to dissect the dynamics of Hnchak propaganda among Central Anatolian Armenians.

Shortly after the trial of the revolutionaries in Ankara in the summer of 1893, a series of posters were affixed in public spaces in the mining town of Keskin (modern-day Kırıkkale). The posters were written in Armenian and addressed to the Armenian residents of the town. Signed by the 'Reform Committee', the posters focused on the gross injustices committed by Ottoman courts. So long as government courts failed in delivering justice, pamphlets and posters would continue to spread. The failure of the courts was a thinly veiled reference to the harsh sentences passed during the Ankara trial on revolutionaries and their sympathizers. The pamphleteers also criticized and insulted Sultan Abdülhamid II himself, calling him a cruel and oppressive villain. Salvation from such injustice and barbarity lay in the organization of Christians against the Hamidian regime. 'Christianity has awoken', a poster read, 'for injustice and prejudice has affected even the babes in the cradle'. The revolutionaries and their followers could not hold back any longer. The pamphleteers declared that such public declarations would continue to emanate from the committee so long as the struggle against the Hamidian regime continued. An important aspect of the series of posters in Keskin was their decided emphasis on the centrality of Christian self-determination and organization in defying oppression and effecting social and political change. Formal and informal ethno-confessional hierarchies that marginalized non-Muslims were utilized to mobilize local communities against government officials.[43]

The affixing of the posters in Keskin was a brazen act of sedition and a direct affront to government authority. The frequent insults to the royal persona, the confident assertion of further public declarations and statements on the growing membership of the revolutionary committees all served to agitate local and central government officials. The pamphleteers even alluded to the possibility of the establishment of an independent kingdom with a just Christian monarch. Such open acts of defiance also were designed to appeal to local Armenian communities and promote the image of the SDHP as an alternative political structure. The pamphleteers and revolutionaries aimed to show that political activism and revolutionism could be carried out despite the heavy-handed suppression of dissent by the government. This is why the pamphleteers declared that there would be future posters and pamphlets regardless of the countermeasures taken by government officials. They also hoped to secure the sympathy and allegiance of the majority of local Armenian communities by convincing them that the harsh court sentences, corrupt and cruel government officials or the sultan himself could not stop the single-minded struggle of the revolutionaries. The committees were more than a sum of the individuals that constituted them; therefore, the incarceration or even the execution of individual revolutionaries, no matter how influential or powerful they were, could not suppress the movement.

Approximately a year and a half later, a revolutionary pamphlet was circulated among the Armenian community of Merzifon. The pamphlet started with accusations of bribery and corruption levelled against local government officials. The pamphleteers specifically targeted the unofficial practice of rounding up prominent Armenians only to release them in exchange for bribes. The vice-governor of Merzifon bore the brunt of the revolutionaries' accusations, as he was the main beneficiary of this rapacious practice, as well as the arbitrary taxation of the peasants in the countryside. The pamphleteers alleged that the subgovernor had been a brigand himself a decade ago and had only risen within the ranks of the local Ottoman administration through coercion and deception. However, those same methods had sparked the flame of revolution, according to the pamphleteers and would only lead to the demise of the vice-governor and the regime he represented.[44]

Government officials were not the only target of the revolutionaries. The pamphleteers openly declared that they would assassinate Armenian notables and informants for their complicity in the Ottoman administration. Although they had initially sought to limit conflict within the Armenian community and direct their efforts solely against the Hamidian regime, Armenian notables and informants had made common cause with government officials in their zeal of imprisoning and executing revolutionaries. Therefore, they would respond in kind:

> Eye to eye, limb to limb . . . But we will not make the Aghas unquiet. No, no: we will make them very quiet, eternally quiet. This is our decision, from our heart of hearts, first and foremost to murder (or torment!) these Armenian Aghas; not for one day or one year, but at once, continually, and for ever.[45]

The pamphleteers' explicit threat served two important functions. First, it reminded the Armenian community of the intent and capacity of the revolutionary committees to enact severe punishments on those it deemed treasonous. Therefore, the committee could mirror the physical and mental violence utilized by the government to deter Ottoman Armenians from the party. Second, the revolutionaries were marking the boundaries of Armenian community and nationhood in accordance with their political goals. They sought to purge some members of the notability that had acquired official and unofficial positions to represent the community and assume it for themselves.

The pamphleteers also responded to some of the criticism levelled against them by Apostolic and Protestant priests and missionaries. Anti-revolutionary clergymen told their congregations that members of the revolutionary committees were infidels and sought to eradicate religion from society. Such accusations had the potential to profoundly tarnish the reputation of the SDHP among the Armenian community because the Apostolic Patriarchate and its prelacies occupied central positions in Armenian cultural and social life. The pamphleteers responded to the accusations by questioning the moral authority of their critics. A particularly virulent critic of the revolutionaries, the bishop of the district of Divriği (in modern-day Sivas), was accused of ignoring the plight of the Armenian community and succumbing to the comfort of material wealth, which reached him in the form of salaries and taxes. The missionaries also received their share of derision from the pamphleteers. They were described as 'stable-cleaners and street-sweepers of America' who arrived in Armenian communities in 'palatial style', with exorbitant salaries while trying to sell Christianity to Christians. The revolutionaries, on the other hand, were attempting to root out inequality in religion throughout the Ottoman Empire.[46] Therefore, it was not surprising that missionaries and corrupt clergymen considered the revolutionaries atheists and infidels, for they clearly had divergent views of religion and integrity.

Pamphlets and posters would continue to be utilized to publicly denounce anti-revolutionary clergymen and notables. In the summer of 1895, several posters were affixed to public places in Yozgat to denounce the former head of the town's lay council and one of his aides. Both men had participated in a petitioning campaign to draw the attention of the palace, the patriarchate and representatives of the Great Powers to excessive taxation and abuse of the peasantry in the countryside.[47] However, it is likely that by early 1895, they had turned against the revolutionaries in response to pressure from the government. The pamphlet stated that Avedis Arslanian and Yaver Efendi Damadian and their families would be assassinated and their houses burned down with kerosene because they had exposed the secrets of the revolutionary committee. Although the fates of Arslanian and Damadian and their families cannot be ascertained from archival evidence, it should be noted that such declarations were not empty threats. Several Armenian notables and informants were assassinated in this manner in Central Anatolia in the early 1890s.[48]

Hnchak pamphleteering was not the primary form of communication between the Armenian community and the revolutionaries. In rural areas, the revolutionaries could establish direct contact with peasants. In cities and towns, they could utilize the mediation of their sympathizers to reach representatives of the community and notables. Among some confiscated documents by the Ottoman authorities in Sivas, there was the transcript of a speech delivered by a revolutionary to a small circle of followers and sympathizers. The speaker predicted the imminent collapse of the Ottoman Empire and advised his audience to stay on course until the realization of their holy ideal.[49] The pamphlets were still significant, however, in the polemical articulation of the interests of the local committees. This included responses to anti-revolutionary clergymen's attempts to delegitimize the revolutionaries, accusations against the biased makeup of Ottoman courts or the corruption of government officials. Simultaneously, pamphlets were a means of projecting and legitimizing revolutionary violence. In other words, the revolutionaries were able to foreground and justify the assassination of Armenian notables when that became the focus of their activities.

Conclusion

Armenian revolutionaries engaged in a variety of activities to promote their political platform, expand the social base of their movement and weaken their chief adversary in the last decade of the nineteenth century. The recruitment of armed bands, the distribution of modern weapons among the Armenian peasantry, the organization of a loose network of secret revolutionary committees throughout Ottoman Armenia and the assassination of the party's opponents were among the arsenal of the revolutionaries during this period. Furthermore, they conducted an expansive campaign of pamphleteering in order to engage with the local population at various levels. Although the Central Committee of the SDHP exerted some influence over the content and tone of the first pamphlets, local revolutionaries took on the reins of the process afterwards. They imagined the local Muslim and Armenian communities as different political agents and audiences and utilized different tones, descriptions and calls for action to appeal to them.

Local Hnchaks were keen on securing the sympathy of the local Muslim population. They feared the local and imperial officials' efforts to integrate segments of Muslim communities into their policing and suppression efforts. Furthermore, they suspected the Muslims' tacit approval of government efforts to subdue all Armenian dissent. Muslim anxieties about Armenian resurgence, whether they had been cultivated by government officials or local notables, threatened the appeal of the Hnchak platform as a viable political project. The pamphleteers authored treatises and posters in which they attempted to tarnish the reputation of the Ottoman state. To that end, they focused on the venality and corruption of local government officials, the heavy tax burden faced by all Ottoman subjects, the oppressive political structure that silenced all dissent, and weakness of the Hamidian regime. They alternated between open calls for Muslim cooperation against the Ottoman state and resistance against the government's efforts to co-opt Muslims in its suppression of Armenian dissent. Meanwhile, government officials and several Muslim notables had been fostering general hostility against the Armenians, arguing that the end goal of the revolutionaries was the massacre of Muslims and the establishment of Christian domination. In order to combat such efforts and assuage Muslim anxieties, the pamphleteers even openly declared that the victims of their attentats had mostly been other Armenians. They also prevaricated on the question of the establishment of an independent state. Claiming that it was an unrealistic goal, the pamphleteers stated that the revolutionaries' chief aim was to realize the collapse of the corrupt Hamidian regime along with its local representatives.

The revolutionaries thought of the Armenian community as an entirely different kind of political audience and actor. It was the chief object and subject of revolutionary change. Therefore, the pamphleteers adopted a different tone when they addressed the Armenian community. The criticism of the Ottoman state and its officials took on a more aggressive and comprehensive manner. Furthermore, the pamphlets and posters reflected the revolutionaries' active efforts to reshape Armenian communities and redraw the boundaries of inclusion and notability in order to erase the influence of the Ottoman state in its administration. The heavy-handed criticism of anti-revolutionary clergymen and explicit threats against notables and merchants that were not 'supportive' enough of the revolutionary movement fulfilled this important function.

From its inception, the SDHP engaged in the ambitious political project of national independence and social revolution. Although the party maintained a centralized hierarchy, local recruits and revolutionaries had a profound influence on the party's conduct and the articulation of its goals. They utilized a wide array of tactics and methods to expand their social base and influence and weaken the imperial government. Pamphleteering was a salient component of their overall strategy. The numerous pamphlets the revolutionaries have left behind provide the historian with the opportunity to delve into the complexities of revolutionary politics in particular settings. Further research on this subject in other geographies such as the imperial capital or the Ottoman East has the potential to shed light on the parameters of the revolutionaries' engagement with various communities they sought to shape and influence.

Notes

1 For a general history of the Armenian Revolutionary Movement see Louise Nalbandian, *The History of the Armenian Revolutionary Movement: The Development of Armenian Political Parties through the Nineteenth Century* (Berkeley: University of California Press, 1963). For a general history of the SDHP and a chronological account of the institutional expansion of the ARF, see Arsen Gidur, *Patmutʻiwn S.D. Hnchʻakean Kusaktsʻutʻean, 1887-1962*, vols. I and II (Beirut: Shirag Press, 1962–3); Hrach Dasnabedian, *History of the Armenian Revolutionary Federation: Dashnaksutiun 1890/1924* (Milan: Oemme Edizioni, 1990). For a detailed discussion of the party programmes of the SDHP and the ARF, see Gerard Libaridian, 'What Was Revolutionary about Armenian Revolutionary Parties in the Ottoman Empire?' in *A Question of Genocide: Armenians and Turks at the End of the Ottoman Empire*, eds. Ronald G. Suny, Fatma M. Göçek and Norman M. Neimark, 82–112 (New York: Oxford University Press, 2011).
2 For a history of the Armenian Constitutional Movement and its socio-economic bases, see Hagop Barsoumian, *The Armenian Amira Class of Istanbul* (Yerevan: American University of Armenia, 2007).
3 For a discussion of the Russian nihilist and socialist influence on the Armenian revolutionary parties, see Ronald Grigor Suny, *Looking Toward Ararat: Armenia in Modern History* (Bloomington: Indiana University Press, 1993), 67–79.
4 For the economic angle, see Charles Issawi, *An Economic History of the Middle East and North Africa* (New York: Columbia University Press, 1982), and Roger Owen, *The Middle East in the World Economy, 1800-1914*, (London: I.B. Tauris, 1993). For the diplomatic angle, see M. S. Anderson, *The Eastern Question, 1774-1923: A Study in International Relations* (London: St. Martin's Press, 1966).

5   For a reprint of the original Hnchak programme, see Gidur, *Patmut'iwn S.D. Hnch'akean Kusakts'ut'ean*, vol. I, 32–7. For a translation of the programme into Ottoman Turkish, see Y.MTV. 74/84, undated.
6   This is also partly attributable to the party's lack of a central archive, unlike the Armenian Revolutionary Federation.
7   Suny, *Looking Toward Ararat*; Nalbandian, *The History of the Armenian Revolutionary Movement*.
8   For an edited volume on the ARF's attempt on Abdülhamid II, for example, see *To Kill a Sultan: A Transnational History of the Attempt on Abdülhamid II (1905)*, eds. Edhem Eldem, Henk de Smaele and Houssine Alloul (London: Palgrave Macmillan, 2018).
9   For a recent contribution to the history of Armenian revolutionaries, whose focus lies outside the Ottoman East, see Varak Ketsemanian, 'The Hunchakian Revolutionary Party and the Assassination Attempts against Patriarch Khoren Ashekian and Maksudzade Simon Bey in 1894', *International Journal of Middle Eastern Studies* 50, no. 4 (2018): 735–55.
10 For a general history of political propaganda in print in the nineteenth century, see Ian Haywood, *The Revolution in Popular Literature: Print, Politics, and the People, 1790-1860* (Cambridge: Cambridge University Press, 2014).
11 For a history of pamphleteering in Civil War England, see Jason Peacey, *Politicians and Pamphleteers: Propaganda during the English Civil War and Interregnum* (Aldershot: Ashgate, 2004).
12 Harvey Chisick, 'The Pamphlet Literature of the French Revolution: An Overview', *History of European Ideas* 17, no. 2/3 (1993): 149–66, and Kenneth Margerison, *Pamphlets and Public Opinion: The Campaign for a Union of Orders in the Early French Revolution* (Indiana: Purdue University Press, 1998).
13 Two famous examples from the early nineteenth-century Istanbul on the subject of administrative and military reform are the Kabakçı Mustafa pamphlet, which was transliterated with a commentary in Aysel Yıldız, *Asiler ve Gaziler: Kabakçı Mustafa Risalesi* (İstanbul: Kitap Yayınevi, 2007), and the Koca Sekbanbaşı Risalesi, which was published in Abdullah Uçman, *Koca Sekbanbaşı Risalesi* (İstanbul: Tercüman, 1974).
14 Shukla Sanyal, *Revolutionary Pamphlets, Propaganda and Political Culture in Colonial Bengal* (Cambridge: Cambridge University Press, 2014).
15 For the impact of literacy and the response of peasants to pamhpleteering, see Vivian R. Gruder, *The Notables and the Nation: The Political Schooling of the French, 1787-1788* (Cambridge, MA: Harvard University Press, 2008), 292–323.
16 For studies of literacy in the late Ottoman period, see Ami Ayalon, *Reading Palestine: Printing and Literacy, 1900-1948* (Austin: University of Texas Press, 2004), and Benjamin Fortna, *Learning to Read in the Late Ottoman Empire and the Early Turkish Republic* (Basingstoke: Palgrave Macmillan, 2011).
17 For techniques of social control in the Ottoman Empire in the early modern period and the nineteenth century, see Betül Başaran, *Selim III, Social Control and Policing in Istanbul at the End of the Eighteenth Century: Between Crisis and Order* (Leiden: Brill, 2014) and Cengiz Kırlı, *Sultan ve Kamuoyu: Osmanlı Modernleşme Sürecinde 'Havadis Jurnalleri,' 1840-1844* (İstanbul: İş Bankası Yayınları, 2009).
18 Fikret Turan, 'El Yazması Mecmualarda Gündelik Hayat, Güncel Sorunlar ve Günlük Dil: 18. Yüzyıl Osmanlı Edebiyatında Mahallileşmenin Kapsamı', *Fatih Sultan Mehmet İlmi Araştırmalar İnsan ve Toplum Bilimleri Dergisi* 2 (2013): 343–65.
19 Abdullah Bay, '19. Yüzyılda Osmanlı'da Propaganda ve Protesto Kültürü: "Teşviş-i Ezhân ve Fesadâmiz Müdhiş" Yaftalar', *Kebikeç* 41 (2016): 14.

20 The Kumkapı Demonstration was one of the first major demonstrations organized by the SDHP. Several Hnchak revolutionaries stormed the Apostolic Patriarchate during the Divine Liturgy on 27 July 1890. The revolutionaries read a list of demands from the Ottoman state to alleviate the conditions of Ottoman Armenians in the presence of the congregation. Then, they attempted to deliver the list of demands to the Sublime Porte in the company of the Armenian Apostolic Patriarch and an armed guard. The Ottoman authorities responded with force, leading to several deaths on both sides. There was a clampdown on Armenian political activities in the Ottoman capital afterwards, which resulted in the flight of many revolutionaries to the countryside or abroad. For a detailed account of the events from the perspective of the revolutionaries and the list of Hnchak demands at the demonstration, see Gidur, *Patmut'iwn S.D. Hnch'akean Kusakts'ut'ean*, 53–9.
21 Bay, '19.Yüzyılda Osmanlı'da Propaganda', 28.
22 Sanyal, *Revolutionary Pamphlets*, 9.
23 For a collection of essays that address various aspects of the Bengali revolutionary movement, see Peter Heehs, *Nationalism, Terrorism, Communalism* (New Delhi: Oxford University Press, 2000).
24 The local authorities in Central Anatolia employed local Muslims in order to pursue revolutionaries and search Armenians' homes for 'incendiary publications' in the same period. See Toygun Altıntaş, 'The Placard Affair and the Ankara Trial: The Hnchak Party and the Hamidian Regime in Central Anatolia, 1892-3', *Journal of the Ottoman and Turkish Studies Association* 4, no. 2 (2017): 326–7.
25 Gidur, *Patmut'iwn S.D. Hnch'akean Kusakts'ut'ean*, 99–100.
26 The National Archives. FO 424/175, no. 44, 13 April 1893, Sir Ford to Earl of Rosebery, incs no. 2 and 3.
27 Devlet Arşivleri Başkanlığı Osmanlı Arşivi (BOA), Y. PRK. UM. 27/35.
28 Varak Ketsemanian points to the possibility of the involvement of a Young Turk faction, which may have cultivated relations with the SDHP to use its networks. The erroneously early publication of the placards in the revolutionary organ and the lack of evidence pointing to such partnership – as opposed to later periods where ARF-Young Turk or ARF-CUP collaborations were attested to by participants on both sides – make this unlikely. Ketsemanian, 'The Hunchakian Revolutionary Party', fn. 20, 751.
29 *Hnch'ak*, 25 September 1892, Year 6, no. 9.
30 *Hnch'ak*, 28 February 1893, Year 6, no. 3.
31 Bay, '19. Yüzyılda Osmanlı'da Propaganda', 38.
32 Ibid., 31.
33 The National Archives, FO 424/182, no. 17, Sir Nicolson to the Earl of Rosebery, inc. 3, 12 January 1894.
34 Ibid.
35 Ibid.
36 Ibid.
37 Bay, 'Osmanlı'da 19. Yüzyılda Propaganda', 38.
38 BOA, Y. PRK. UM. 30/43, Revolutionary Poster, 22 August 1894.
39 A confiscated letter sent from the Arapkir Hnchak committee to the Sivas committee requested that Raffi's works be sent. The programme of the Sivas Hnchak committee also stipulated that the distribution of Raffi's works among the committees in Ottoman Armenia was of paramount importance. BOA. Y. PRK. UM. 29/36, 18 February 1894.
40 BOA, Y. PRK. UM. 30/14, Revolutionary Treatise, 22 May 1895.

41 For biographical information on Ferdinand Lassalle, see Subrata Mukherjee and Sushila Ramaswamy, *A History of Socialist Thought: From the Precursors to the Present* (Thousand Oaks: Sage Publications, 2000).
42 BOA, Y. PRK. UM. 30/14, Revolutionary Treatise, 22 May 1895.
43 BOA, Y. PRK. BŞK. 32/19, The Subgovernorate of Keskin to the Yıldız Palace, 19 July 1894.
44 BOA, Y. A. HUS. 300/14, The Sublime Porte to the Yıldız Palace, 14 June 1894.
45 The National Archives, FO 424/182, no. 17, Sir Nicolson to the Earl of Rosebery, inc. 4, 12 January 1894.
46 Ibid.
47 Their interrogation reports after the Yozgat pogrom are compiled in a file. BOA. Y. EE. 179/5.
48 Bay, 'Osmanlı'da 19. Yüzyılda Propaganda', 30.
49 BOA. Y. PRK. UM. 30/43, 20 August 1894.

6

Peasants, Pastoralists and Revolutionaries

Hnchakians and Armeno–Kurdish Relations in late Ottoman Eastern Anatolia

Varak Ketsemanian

From July 1894 until the spring of 1895, the district of Sasun in the Ottoman province of Bitlis in south-eastern Anatolia attracted the attention of the press in the United States, the United Kingdom and the rest of Europe. Events there led to unprecedented mobilization by intellectuals and philanthropists in support of thousands of Armenians who had fallen victim to brutal massacres by Kurdish tribal militias and Ottoman troops in the summer of 1894.[1] This article asks then how such a remote geographical corner became a theatre of violence and what does it tell us about early Hnchakian activities and Armeno-Kurdish relations in this part of the empire.

The late 1880s and the early 1890s are known in the scholarship on late Ottoman history as the era of the Armenian revolutionary movements. Armenian political parties, the institutional articulation of this moment, emerged at the end of the nineteenth century with the aim of providing a new direction to the Armenian community of the Ottoman Empire. The study of these organizations, however, has been among the most polarizing themes within the literature.[2] Historians have been unable to imagine a history that accounts for the complexities that the Ottoman state and the Armenian parties each faced.[3] Existing narratives often fail to capture the intricacies of the Ottoman socio-economic milieu and to provide a viable analytical framework for the dynamics of violence that intensified in 1890s in Constantinople and in the Eastern Provinces.

Nationalist Turkish historians portray these parties as 'separatist/secessionist' and/or 'nationalist', thereby legitimizing the Ottoman state's violence against the revolutionaries and rendering them as enemies who were alien to the empire, even as Armenian political parties were active agents in Ottoman social and political life. Armenian mainstream historiography, on the other hand, describes them as heroic attempts in thwarting the destruction of the Armenian community within the empire with ethnicity often serving as the sole axis of analysis.[4]

Such a binary is not only problematic but also methodologically unsound since both historiographies attribute unjustifiably large weight to the print culture and ideology of state and non-state elites. Correspondingly, they overlook the necessity to understand more critically the situation on the ground of struggle, where the concepts of the literate elites do not operate as dominant. The existing literature has often ignored the average militant on the ground who operated within the fissures of the Ottoman system. Therefore, through an interpretation of rural violence against the background of Armeno-Kurdish relations, this article aims to fill this historiographical lacuna by shedding light on the revolutionaries' interactions with the political ecology of Eastern Anatolia.

Contrary to the dominant 'ethnic paradigm' in the study of violence in late Ottoman societies, this article argues that escalating violence in Sasun from the 1880s until 1894 ought not to be understood in solely ethnic or ideological (nationalism, centralization, colonization) terms, but rather fundamental social and economic factors were at stake and played a critical role in determining the various actors, dynamics, time and scale of the conflict. Unlike Robert Melson's claim that Sultan Abdülhamid II relied on violence to maintain the existing social order in Sasun, this work shows that Ottoman authorities relied on violence and force *because they wanted to alter* the existing rural order by reconfiguring Armeno-Kurdish relations, rather than preserving them.[5] By analysing the socio-economic fabric of Sasun as a microcosm of intra- and inter-communal relations, we can begin to sketch new answers to questions such as 'what do clashes in Sasun tell us about Armeno-Kurdish relations at the *fin de siècle*?' and 'how did the Hnchakian militants contribute to the reconfiguration of inter and intra-ethnic tensions?'[6]

As Marxists, the Hnchakian founders saw in Sasun the pre-conditions for the historical unfolding of a nationalist and subsequently a socialist revolution.[7] Sasun remained a region where a 'feudal' relationship and an asymmetry of power existed among the Kurdish nomadic tribes and the sedentary peasant population of which the Armenians constituted a significant majority.[8] They argued that the 'feudal' relations between Armenian villagers and nomadic Kurds obstructed the productivity of Armenian peasants, as Kurdish tribal lords plundered the already precariously held means of production of the Armenian peasant class. This, in turn, impeded the latter from attaining a national consciousness and subsequently reaching the progress of the 'civilized world'.

Eastern Anatolia in the late nineteenth century

The Ottoman destruction of the Kurdish emirates of Eastern Anatolia in the 1840s created a political vacuum in the region which the smaller Kurdish nomadic-pastoralist tribes came to fill. A large group of actors including sheikhs, lower local-level notables and tribal leaders benefitted from this process.[9] Consequently, a niche overlap occurred after the Ottoman Army defeated the Kurdish Emirate of Bedr Khan/Bedir Han in Bo(h)tan (modern-day Cizre).[10] In other words, the security of the region deteriorated as nascent tribal families supplanted their former Kurdish *emirs*. This sociopolitical transformation accelerated the partial transition of hitherto pastoralist Kurdish tribes to sedentary life. However, despite Ottoman (re)settlement attempts –

often by force – of the tribes, many retained their nomadic lifestyle, a status known as transhumant. Subsequently, competition for the same resource environment increased among the newly settled Kurds and the local peasant population of which Armenians formed a significant plurality. The size of the pastoralists' herds determined not only their economic power but also their social and political status. As such, they became important sociopolitical actors within the Ottoman East.

Starting in the 1880s, Ottoman authorities integrated selected tribal leaders and their followers into the system of rule, backing these individuals with force and other resources when necessary.[11] Given the geopolitical significance of Bitlis as a frontier region with a considerable Armenian population, the Ottoman officials ensured that Kurdish and Islamic supremacy would reign in the region by sanctioning their activities at the expense of local Armenian peasants.

The arrival of Muslim refugees (*muhacirin*) from the Balkans and the Caucasus starting in the mid-century exacerbated the situation. Armenian complaints about violent infringements commenced in the 1860s when the resettlement of *muhacirin* as well as government programmes for the sedentarization of nomads aggravated conflicts over farmland and pastures. Thus, by the 1870s the emergence of Kurdish *beyliks* and the arrival of Muslim refugees rendered the economic aspect and dynamics of the Armeno-Kurdish relations a key element of conflict in Eastern Anatolia.[12] Subsequently, the Armenian peasantry faced massive land usurpations and diverse forms of oppression as many of these *muhacirin* were resettled in districts populated by Armenians.

In the years leading to the 1878 Russo-Turkish War, the horizontal diversity of actors in Eastern Anatolia gradually became replaced by a vertical one, a transformation that brought about differences in class to the forefront of the socio-economic dynamics.[13] Armed Muslims thus competed for scarce resources with an existing, mostly unarmed Christian population, whom they associated with the 'Christian enemies' (primarily Russia and the Balkan states) that had expelled them from their previous homelands.[14] Therefore, Tolga Cora's observation that the background of the Armeno-Kurdish conflict must necessarily include a discussion revolving around economic classes is an important contribution to the literature and a useful framework for this article.[15] The inclusion of 'class' helps us then understand the dynamics that existed among the two different ethno-religious groups and the changing power balance in their relationship. Furthermore, it helps us divide the Armenians themselves, into different socio-economic groups and assess their changing relations with the Kurds accordingly.

Impoverished by the breakdown of the former emirates, Kurdish *beys* now depended upon the sedentary villagers for material sustenance, maintaining thus a relationship that is often referred to as 'Kurdish feudalism' in Eastern Anatolia.[16] This situation in turn generated two simultaneous yet conflicting processes; on the one hand, the sociopolitical changes in the aftermath of the war (1877–8) accelerated the dynamics that were to shape the relations between the Armenian villagers in Sasun with the neighbouring Kurdish tribes throughout much of the 1880s and the early 1890s. They included a transformation in the local power structure and an accompanying increase in the importance of land ownership.[17] On the other hand however, social transformations on the local level provided the Ottoman government with a further impetus to devise a strategy that Stephen Duguid calls 'the politics of unity', whereby the centre sought to control and administer tribal groups in the 'unruly' east.[18] In other words, lacking the necessary resources to maintain a strong presence, the Ottoman centre cultivated a working relationship with several Kurdish tribal notables in the collective terrorization and disciplining of recalcitrant local Armenians.

Through a power devolution of this task to local agents, the authorities ensured that Armenian 'sedition' would not threaten state interests, exempting Kurdish tribes from any punishment for violence committed against Armenians writ large. As Stephan Astourian rightly points out, 'the Armenian Question was fully embedded in a number of other "questions"; the agrarian and Kurdish questions, the demographic Islamization of Anatolia during the period under scrutiny, and the attempts of the Ottoman state at modernizing and centralizing the empire'. He concludes that 'the Armenian Question was as much a Kurdish and Ottoman question as it is an Armenian one'.[19] It was against this background that Hunchakian militants made inroads into Sasun around 1891.

Sasun

Sasun, the mountainous extension of the Mush lowland, belonged to the southern peripheral zone of the outer margin of the Armenian Plateau.[20] In his 1912 study of Eastern Anatolia, Hovhannes Ter-Martirosyan described the area thus:

Sasun is a vortex of lofty mountains and deep valleys crisscrossing and interlaced, violently bisecting and cutting into each other. Like a single looming mass, the city rises above the Earth in the south of the Mush Valley, about halfway up the Taurus Mountains. All the way from Mush to Sasun, the road winds around mountains that crowd together and rise on top of each other. The road leads travellers up the flanks towards the blue sky, up towards the Dzirngadar Summit, then down into a large valley, then up and down again, past more hills and summits. Every time a traveller turns a corner, new gorges, new hills and mountains and new valleys appear before him in an endless procession.[21]

Home to a mixed population of Armenian and Muslim peasants and pastoralists, Sasun had close cultural and economic connections with Mush and other regional-urban centres including Diyarbekir and Aleppo through trade, education, pilgrimage and seasonal migration.[22] In return for a tribute (*hafir*) paid in kind to Kurdish tribal chieftains, many Armenian peasants who grew grains and herded sheep, cattle and goats, expected protection from outsiders.[23] During internecine or inter-tribal clashes, such bonds of clientage produced solidarity that cut across religious and ethnic lines. However, such 'traditional' tributary payments constituted a heavy burden on Armenian peasants, some of whom had also paid tithes and the sheep tax (*adet-i ağnam*) to official tax collectors or tax farmers.[24]

The regional demographics underwent seasonal changes as Kurdish pastoralists, from the southwest and the southeast (via the district of Siirt) arrived in increasing numbers during summers to graze their flocks in the highlands of Sasun.[25] According to one source, until the late 1870s and the early 1880s, many Armenian headmen of

Sasun rented off some of the pastures to the incoming Kurdish tribes who herded their flock with the former's special consent.[26] Sedentary and nomadic Kurdish *ağa*s ruled over the remaining areas that fell outside the control of the Armenian headmen.[27]

Local power brokers played a decisive role in shaping the various aspects of Armeno-Kurdish relations. Among such actors were the Armenian village headmen, known as *Res* or *Ishkhan*. According to contemporary sources, these men were the descendants of rich influential families and/or were affluent landowners.[28] Moreover, they served as adjudicators of local inter- and intra-communal disputes.[29] Not only did each *res* control a few villages in Sasun but procured a number of men armed with old-style *çakmaklı* (flintlock) rifles during clashes.[30] Gunpowder was usually bought from the village of Tsronk around Mush, whereas lead was purchased in Diyarbekir.[31] These weapons were especially effective against similarly armed Kurds in 1880s but were no match against the regular imperial army.[32]

Despite seasonal clashes in the summer throughout the 1880s, the obsolete weaponry of the local population accounted for why the Armeno-Kurdish conflict did not drag long.[33] This would change in the early 1890s as the subsequent sections will discuss. Disputes over livestock often led to small-scale skirmishes between Kurdish pastoralists and Armenian peasants. One such incident occurred in the fall of 1887 when the Kurdish inhabitants of Tapig were accused of having stolen over 200 sheep from the Armenians. Tensions escalated between the two sides, pushing the Ottoman authorities to intervene and deter Kurdish attacks, at least for the time being.[34] Such occasional fighting in the late 1880s was instrumental in the shaping of a culture of resistance among the Armenian peasants, a feature that the Hnchakian revolutionaries would capitalize on starting in the early 1890s. In other words, they attempted to reorient localized Armenian grievances against Kurds, Ottoman gendarmes and tax collectors to the Ottoman state writ large.

With the Great Powers displaying an interest in the Armenian Question by the early 1890s, the Hamidian regime took proactive measures to suppress Armenian revolutionary activism by co-opting the Kurdish rural notability. Practices of prevention that had occasionally placed government officials on the side of Armenian peasants, such as stopping Kurdish pastoralist access to the summer pastures of Sasun, were eroding by the early 1890s. Therefore, the proximity of Armenian and Kurdish populations and their often-symbiotic relations became increasingly alarming to the Ottoman authorities.

In his dispatch to Constantinople, Mehmet Safi Bey, the district governor of Siirt, argued that the sedentary Kurdish peasants of Sasun had remained Muslim only in name and that a thorough reform of the mountainous area was essential. He was shocked to see that many of the Kurds even spoke Armenian.[35] Safi Bey, who was leading an Ottoman force to secure the allegiance of the Reşkotanlı tribe, recommended the construction of a mosque, a school and other administrative buildings to restore Sunni orthopraxy.[36] He believed that Kurdish tribes could be convinced to stop their internecine conflicts and swear loyalty to the Ottoman state. He argued that the allegiance of the Kurds would create a powerful bulwark against any 'Armenian sedition' in the region.[37]

Socio-economic changes by the *fin de siècle*

In an area where the summer pastures (*yayla*) were high up on the mountains of Sasun and near the Armenian villages, pastoralist Kurds and Armenian villagers herded their flock on shared grasslands.[38] Until the early 1890s, the Bekranlı and Badikanlı tribes had been banned from entering the pastures around Armenian villages because they forced the peasants to pay them tributes in kind or stole their livestock. A report by the Ottoman chief of the general staff of the Seventh Infantry Division indicated that by the mid-1880s, the 'protection' of the Armenian peasants of Dalvorik/Talori had changed hands from the Bekranlı to the Khiyan tribe.[39] It stated that Armenians used to seek refuge in areas under the control of Sasun and Khiyan tribes when they were attacked by other pastoralists.[40]

The situation changed in the early 1890s however, as the Ottoman authorities lifted the ban enabling the inflow of many tribes who wintered in the province of Diyarbekir to the pastures in Sasun, [K]hulp and Genc.[41] Ottoman ministries even changed the official terminology used to hitherto describe Kurdish tribes. Thus, instead of portraying them as 'barbarian' or 'uncivilized', correspondence in the early 1890s stressed 'their loyalty to the Sultan, their martial capabilities, hospitality as well as their discipline'.[42]

In addition to limited agricultural production (tobacco, wheat), one of the dominating economic activities of the Armenians villagers remained livestock breeding.[43] The local sedentary population was divided between various local chieftains and headmen. Those, who 'belonged' to a Kurdish *ağa* were called *maraba*.[44] They had to pay the protection tax (*hafir*) to their Kurdish overlords.[45] These peasants were now subject to ill-treatment at the hands of not only Kurdish tribal notables but also Ottoman provincial administrators and security forces in the form of the gendarmerie and tax farmers (*mültezim*s). The combination of these practices resulted in the eventual emergence of a landless Armenian peasantry that lost its lands upon delaying the payment of taxes.

The Ottoman authorities did – or could – not make any serious attempts to curb the powers of the local Kurdish *ağa*s.[46] As Edip Gölbaşı argues in his work on the Hamidiye militias, created in 1891, because of the Ottoman state's scarce resources, Abdülhamid devised a strategy of power devolution in the east, whereby pastoralist Kurdish tribes were among the first to benefit.[47] The central government did not have sufficient power to enforce drastic changes against larger-scale resistance. To be implemented, therefore, changes including the Armenian reforms stipulated by the Treaty of Berlin of 1878 had to be negotiated with local power wielders particularly Kurdish tribal chiefs.

The heavy reliance of the Armenians and Kurds on livestock meant that they often competed for control over the limited grazing lands. Pastoralists such as the Bekranlıs used force to prevent Armenians from blocking roads that they had traditionally relied on to drive their herds to the summer pastures. Not having a claim over these lands was a real threat to pastoralist survival, since their sheep could not remain in the winter pastures of Diyarbekir that turned very hot in the summer, with temperatures as high as 45° C in July and August.[48] Thus, most confrontations among Armenians and pastoralist Kurds occurred starting in June when the pasturing season opened, and the two groups came in closer proximity. Kurdish tribesmen could have recourse to arms, whereas the Armenian peasants had no access to institutions that would guarantee their fair share of the pastures. With the active intervention of the central authorities, the preferential practices and the co-optation of Kurdish tribes became a matter of official policy that further limited the Armenians' recourse to any local or imperial institutions. *Hnch'ak* (Bell), the official organ of the Hnchakian Party, reported on how local Ottoman officials were co-opting some of the most notorious Kurdish sheikhs of the area.[49] According to one letter sent from Muş, the Ottoman administrators were recruiting Hacı Tayyib (Muş), Mehmet of Zilan (Khiyan) and Ömer of Duder (Hulp), who wielded a strong influence over the Bekran and the Badikanlı tribes respectively.[50]

Subsequently, one of the momentous results of this policy was the empowerment of the Kurdish tribes and their further entrenchment in local power structures helping thereby the Ottoman government to resolve local problems often at the expense of Armenian peasants.[51] As Safi Bey's memorandum had tacitly sanctioned, while Kurdish tribesmen and notables who partook in the dispossession of Armenian peasants were able to continue their conduct without fear of serious repercussions, Armenians who were involved in armed skirmishes against Kurdish pastoralists faced punishment.[52] This is evident in a report that Rauf Pasha, the governor of Bitlis, sent to the Yıldız Palace where he lauded the authorities' efforts at preserving Islamic influence in the region at the expense of the local Armenians, whom he described as 'seditious'.[53]

Mihran Damadian (1863–1945): A revolutionary in Sasun

Mihran Damadian, a Hnchakian militant, arrived in Sasun in early 1892.[54] A fugitive himself, Damadian was one of the participants of the Kumkapı demonstration that the Hnchakian Party organized in Constantinople in July 1890. After fleeing to Athens in the aftermath, Damadian succeeded in returning to the Ottoman territories. Subsequently, the party leadership sent him to Sasun, where he arrived disguised as a porter from Muş under the name Melkon [K]hurşid.[55] Damadian's previous tenure as a teacher in Muş in the mid-1880s and his recent experience in political activism in Constantinople provided him with the full skills and purpose as he worked towards the creation of a united Armenian militia in the region.[56]

A piece in *Hnch'ak* in January 1892 stated: '[t]he theoretical understanding of the historical moment is what should lead the men through a revolutionary process. The theories formulated are intended to help the people understand the socio-political state in which they are, and the reason as well as the methods required for the change desired'.[57] Thus, the leadership understood Damadian's presence in Sasun as the historical moment when Armenian peasants would grasp the true theories and the inevitability of the imminent class revolution. Unless a true revolutionary spirit was attained, the article continued, the progress of the 'nation' (*azg*) could not come about.

Damadian and the Armenian villages of Sasun

Once in the area, Damadian started touring Shenig, Semal and Geliguzan, the Armenian strongholds of Sasun.[58] Hostilities were frequent when Damadian first arrived since there was no solidarity between the *res* as each would stand idle when Kurdish tribes attacked neighbouring Armenian villages.[59] Such intra-Armenian tensions hampered any effective cooperation against Kurdish presence particularly in the summers even when they were getting tremendous supplies from the government.[60] Writing under the pseudonym *Mdrag*, Damadian's reports on Armenians in Mush and Sasun were published regularly in *Hnch'ak*.[61] On March 1892, *Hnch'ak* provided a detailed account of over-taxation in the villages of the Mush Valley. Some of the subsequent issues were dedicated to the region with several articles on Kurdish depredations against Armenians.[62] For Damadian, the mass imprisonment of Armenian teachers and notables was not simply the result of a government effort to destroy the revolutionary threat, but rather a more concerted attack on Armenians in general, since many in education and standing had been targeted regardless of their affiliation with the revolutionary circles.[63]

Against this background of exacerbating Armeno-Kurdish relations in the region, a devastating famine struck the provinces of Erzurum, Bitlis and Van in 1893 following the harsh winter of 1891–2.[64] In the aftermath of war and ecological catastrophes, it was the nomadic Kurds who suffered the most. It was they whom the Ottoman government failed most seriously when it failed to maintain order and the machinery of economic recovery in Eastern Anatolia. As Zozan Pehlivan's environmental analysis of the region shows, pastoralists in late Ottoman Kurdistan were more susceptible to extreme variations in heat, cold and precipitation and suffered greater harm from such crises than agriculturalists.[65] Therefore, in an ecosystem where the Kurdish tribes depended on the agricultural products of the peasant population, famine was not only catastrophic but also a catalyzer of existing tensions.

One indication of this was the degree of relative public order prevalent in the period 1885–92, during which they were no major outbreaks between Kurds and Armenians. However, the summers of 1892 and 1893 saw increasing levels of violence among Armenian peasants, Kurdish pastoralists and Ottoman gendarmes.[66] Thus, violence was becoming an integral part of this landscape since in an area where the reach of government control and institutions remained limited, violence became a norm and the medium through which people resolved their local problems.[67]

As a primary economic commodity, the appropriation of land became a feature of life that contributed significantly to the level and shaping of violence in the larger region.[68] Therefore, in the absence of viable legal institutions, violence pushed many to try to seize whatever estate – including pastures – they could. What the Hnchakian Party did then in Sasun was (re)orienting the violence to a particular direction – Kurdish tribes and Ottoman authorities writ large – rather than create it *ex nihilo* or 'bring with them' as Turkish mainstream historians claim. Therefore, looking at the situation in Sasun in the early 1890s in terms of a series of continuous social and economic transformations rather than an abrupt inter-ethnic havoc that erupted in the summer of 1894 provides a more solid basis for understanding the escalation of conflict as a convergence of these changes rather than *a priori* preparation for a rebellion or Armenian nationalist indoctrination.

From tension to conflict

From the previous analysis it is now safe to presume that any ecological and/or economic disruption of the status quo between Kurdish pastoralists and Armenian peasants intensified already existing tensions sparking occasional conflicts over already scarce resources. Subsequently, a vicious cycle emerged whereby Kurdish predations – consented if not outright encouraged by local Ottoman officials begat among Armenians a logic of reliance on arms, thus rendering violence, in this process, a legitimate practice.[69] Consequently, any increase of arms in the region alarmed the government and Kurdish chiefs of an imminent rebellion and hence, we see a return to violence, perpetrated in the name of 'quelling' insidious elements.[70] Yet, Ottoman and Kurdish forces often made no distinction between militants and civilians, rendering the peasant population a legitimate target, particularly during the massacres of 1894.[71]

In a report that *Hnch'ak* published in June 1892, an anonymous correspondent touched upon a major social issue that plagued the people of the Mush Valley, namely, the migration of the male population to urban centres as seasonal workers. With the local Ottoman authorities' inability to accommodate the needs of the population during environmental crises such as drought, crop failures and famine, many families decided to resettle elsewhere.[72] Moreover, because of the double-Kurdish and state-taxation system and their landless situation, many men were forced to leave their homes and assume the burden of seasonal work elsewhere.[73] With all forms of economic activity other than subsistence agriculture constricted by lack of markets, and continuous deflation, seasonal workers known in Armenian as *pandukht*s engendered an economy of remittances from urban to rural areas.[74] Without these precarious finances, peasant families who remained back home would be even less able to meet their fiscal obligations than they were already, while purchasing power for goods and services of whatever nature would be yet further reduced. Moreover, the contraction of the regional economy (from the 1860s until 1890s) was large enough on its own to exacerbate the 'parlous' economic situation which had come to prevail in the Ottoman East.[75]

The social and economic repercussions of this outward migration put the peasant population in a dire situation. The exodus of the male population drained the manpower of the Armenian villages significantly, leaving the remainder women and children defenceless against Kurdish predations. In response to the siphoning out of manpower from the region, a correspondent for *Hnch'ak* wrote in the summer of 1892 that if people were armed, they could defend their properties and hence, they would not be forced to leave their villages and families behind and go to urban centres.[76] During this period, the pages of *Hnch'ak* and *Drōshak,* the organ of the Armenian Revolutionary Federation (*Hay Heghap'okhakan Dashnakts'ut'iwn* /ARF) were replete with short reports about sporadic violence and killings of men in the vicinities of villages or forests.[77] It is quite probable that the victims were men journeying back to Eastern

Anatolia carrying little money from their seasonal work. This may explain many of the murderous assaults on humble people passing through the area.

Hampartsoum Boyajian (1860–1915): Resisting pastoralist Kurds

While the social and economic situation of the region worsened by the 1890s, the year 1893 proved consequential. Mihran Damandian's comrade in arms and a fellow Hnchakian militant, Hampartsoum Boyajian, known by his nom de guerre *Medzn Murad* (Murad the Great), joined the former in Sasun.[78] A student at the *Mekteb-i Tıbbiye-i Şahane* (the Imperial Medical School in Constantinople), Murad had been one of the organizers of the Kumkapı demonstration and had fled Constantinople in its aftermath.[79] He arrived in Sasun in early 1893 and met with Damadian in the village of Vartenis. The notorious Kurdish Musa Bey had killed the *Res* of Vartenis, Ohan, in the village of Godni in 1889, so there was already a widespread anti-Kurdish grudge in the village, which may explain why the residents welcomed the Hnchakian revolutionaries.[80]

The poor economic conditions of the Armenian peasants in and around Sasun, however, rendered them vulnerable to government cooptation and rewards in exchange for information about Armenian militants. Often accusations or charges of being a 'revolutionary' were placed on people in expectation of some monetary remuneration from local Ottoman authorities. A report in *Hnch'ak* in the summer of 1892 stated that: 'The informants of the government are everywhere. The state promises big rewards for those who can provide information on revolutionaries. Last week the price of betrayal was 20 *liras*, whereas this week it got up to 200. Although the informant is protected by the state, he knows that his time will come.'[81]

In response to the network of informants that the authorities employed, one of the first measures that Damadian and Murad undertook was the creation of an 'assassination squad' whose targets primarily included Armenian informers, Turkish and Kurdish *mültezim*s and Kurdish *hafir* collectors.[82] A letter sent in May 1892 from Mush reported that a Kurd named Kuli, who had participated in a raid on the Armenian church of the village of Haygerd, had recently been killed and his body displayed at the entrance of the church. Damadian, the author of the article, described it as a 'valiant act'.[83]

Conflict emerged, however, between the Hnchakian leadership in Europe and Damadian, when the latter found out that his confidential party correspondence appeared in *Hnch'ak* in May 1892. Through the publication of internal reports with often exaggerated facts and numbers, Avetis Nazarbekian, the chairperson of the Hnchakian Central Committee, made Damadian's position in Sasun much more tenuous and visible to the Ottoman authorities. The Ottoman police often stopped many of the cargos that contained the smuggled issues of *Hnch'ak* and confiscated materials about Armenian revolutionary activism.[84] Such interceptions made the Ottoman authorities much more aggressive as they assessed the threat to be much more dangerous than it really was.[85]

In the first months of 1893, Damadian and the Armenian headmen of Sasun agreed on sending Murad to the Caucasus to procure modern weapons for the peasants. Murad returned with no major success. He brought to Sasun only eight rifles he was able to get his hands on.[86] The ARF, recently created in Tbilisi in 1890, had reportedly refused to help Murad in his endeavours insisting that if any operation were to take place in Sasun, it was to be under the ARF's name rather than the Hnchakians'. Subsequently, in a letter he sent to the editors of *Drōshak*, Hrayr Tzhokhk (Armenag Ghazarian), an early Hnchakian militant native of Sasun, vehemently criticized the short-sightedness of the ARF leadership and its refusal to help Murad with the acquisition of arms.[87]

Although it is quite probable that Damadian and Murad had once shared the theoretically inspired views of the Hnchakian founders, their presence on the mountains rapidly taught them what the realities motivating local actors were and how they differed from their world view. In the investigation that ensued from the 1894 massacres, a certain Ohannes elaborated on the social and economic motives behind his decision to join the Hnchakian committee. According to his testimony, he hailed from a family of peasants. A Kurdish notable had 'purchased' his family and their labour and had confiscated their oxen. After experiencing some harassment, he petitioned the Ottoman authorities for some assistance, but nothing came of it. Eventually, he left his home in search of work in Constantinople where he met Damadian and journeyed back to Mush. After joining Damadian's band, Ohannes started living in Dalvorig. He avoided going back to his village for fear of the usurers and the Kurds.[88] While this case was pertinent to a single individual, it was representative of the larger pool of peasants who ended up joining the revolutionary networks. Ohannes's story was characteristic of the mundane concerns and motives that many of the villagers had upon their membership to the revolutionary parties.

In his memoirs, Damadian recalled how the peasant population of Eastern Anatolia had very little idea about the socialism to which the Hnchakian founders attributed so much importance.[89] Therefore, in a period when clashes with pastoralists Kurds intensified, the Armenian *res*' approval of Damadian's and Murad's residence in an area where they remained in partial control might well have had pragmatic and more prosaic motives including but not limited to access to larger networks of weapons and armaments.

Damadian's arrest

With the worsening economic situation and Armeno-Kurdish clashes in the summer of 1893 near Dalvorig, the Armenian villages of Shenig, Semal and Geliguzan stopped paying taxes to the government.[90] It is plausible that the refusal of payments was a deliberate response to Damadian's arrest in the spring of 1893. While on a tour of inspection of Armenian villages with his friend Sogho, a certain Kurdish Derviş Rızıl Ağace *Ağa* intercepted Damadian, arrested and handed him over to the Ottoman authorities in Mush. Damadian was eventually taken to the central prison in the provincial capital of Bitlis.[91] Shortly before his capture, Damadian had attended a meeting in Dalvorig, the Armenian stronghold of Sasun, where the headmen of the neighbouring villages were also present. They decided that if any Ottoman forces or Kurdish Hamidiye regiments marched on Dalvorig, all the armed men would muster there to protect this strategically important position.[92] Shortly after, Damadian was arrested on his way to Semal.[93]

Damadian's assassination squad was responsible for killing a certain Sofu [K]hurşid, who was roaming the vicinities of Sasun searching for a healer named Beydo, a resident of Geliguzan. Suspicious of his activities, the group killed him in September 1892.[94] Subsequently, the government summoned all the headmen of Sasun to hold the culprits accountable. Anticipating an imminent arrest at the government council in Mush, Damadian dissuaded these men from attending. While all agreed, *Res* Gorgeh of Semal, notwithstanding Damadian's pleas, went to Mush, where the local authorities immediately apprehended him. He eventually died in prison in late 1893.[95] Despite the local Ottoman authorities' investigation of the murder, local Armenian peasants refused to acknowledge any knowledge of the incident, perhaps fearing retaliation from the Hnchakians.[96] However, their reluctance to assist the authorities can also be interpreted as evidence of their sympathies for the revolutionaries.

Hostilities resurged between Semal and the other Armenian villages in the aftermath of Damadian's arrest. When Dervish *Ağa* and two other Kurdish tribesmen (from Khiyan) captured Damadian in Semal, Gorgeh's brother, Davo, arrived at the scene and invited the Kurds and the policemen over to the village for negotiations. Depoyan interprets this event as Davo's efforts to win some time in Semal and eventually liberate Damadian. However, given the context and the period (May 1893) in which these events occurred, it is more likely that Davo's move was a deliberate attempt of bargaining for Gorgeh's release against Damadian's capture.[97] It should be highlighted that the peasants' as well as the headmen's sympathies towards the revolutionaries were not unequivocal. Damadian's presence was not only a challenge to Gorgeh's position in the village but was also an opportunity to show loyalty to the Ottoman authorities. When Dervish *Ağa* refused to stay long in Semal, the villagers had no option but to let Damadian go with the gendarmes.[98] Consequently, hostilities erupted between the peasants of Semal and those of Shenig, Dalvorig and Geliguzan, who accused the former of treason for handing Damadian over to the Ottoman authorities and terminated all relations.[99]

After staying in Bitlis for a few months, the governor, Tahsin Pasha, began Damadian's interrogation, where he provided the authorities with detailed information of his own activities as a revolutionary.[100] However, he refused to provide the names of his hosts in Mush or Sasun.[101] The Ottoman police had intercepted letters that Damadian had written back in 1890 about the Sultan. The prosecutor presented them in court as evidence against him. Nevertheless, rivalries among Ottoman officials and particularly between Tahsin Pasha and the Minister of Police Nazım Pasha played out in Damadian's favour. The governor wanted to bring the police force of Bitlis under his direct control so that he would be the first to receive the information, yet Nazım Pasha had supposedly resisted. Upon learning that Damadian's correspondence contained information about a plot against Sultan Abdülhamid, Tahsin Pasha turned this into an opportunity for discrediting Nazım Pasha by demanding that Damadian testify in court in Constantinople that the conspiracy was planned in Athens by the Greeks.

Hence, Tahsin Pasha wanted to use Damadian's letters to show the police's ineptitude in gathering intelligence about possible subversion.[102] As Owen Miller notes, 'Tahsin Paşa used the Armenian issue for his own pecuniary ends.'[103]

Once Damadian accepted the terms, arrangements were made to send him to Constantinople to testify. The Sultan granted him amnesty in return for his knowledge of the Armenian revolutionary movement. Subsequently, the Ottoman authorities offered Damadian, the wanted fugitive, an administrative job in the bureaucracy, which he took.[104] Damadian provided information on the location of the Hnchakian Central Committee in Athens, the name of one of its founders, Rupen Khan-Azad, and an outline of its negotiations with other organizations. However, the only names of comrades and collaborators that he provided were either individuals who had been killed or captured by the government or ones that had fled Ottoman realms.[105] Damadian remained in Constantinople until 1895 and fled only a day before the *Bab-ı Ali* demonstration on 30 September 1895.[106]

The clashes of 1893

With Damadian gone, Murad and Hrayr Tzhokhk assumed the leadership of the local militia. Violent confrontations followed Damadian's capture in Sasun in the summer of 1893 as the Badikan, Sasun, Khiyan and Reşkotan tribes went up the mountains for their traditional pasturing cycle.[107] In the ensuing clashes between 300 Kurdish tribesmen and 600 Armenian peasants, a total of nine casualties were recorded (five Armenian and four Kurdish).[108] The Ottoman government intervened and dispatched a military company to stop the clashes.[109] Tahsin Pasha, the governor of Bitlis, also travelled to the region to report on the violence.[110] In his dispatch to the Interior Ministry, he claimed that the Armenian peasants had killed several pastoralists 'in brutal fashion' (*suret-ı feciada*).[111] Subsequently, the Armenians had retreated to the safety of the mountains.

The governor summoned the tribal chiefs and requested that they withdraw to their wintering grounds, whereas the peasants who had abandoned their villages were asked to return upon the assurances of the local Ottoman officials.[112] Many remained on the mountains, however, until the spring of 1894 fearing Kurdish reprisals.[113] Despite his acknowledgement of the Kurdish tribal presence as a trigger to the 'skirmishes' (*harekat-ı kıtaliye*), the governor underscored the fact that Armenian truculence could only be explained by the presence of foreigners and instigators among the peasants and that their actions were 'a provocation against the Muslim community' (*cemiyet-i islamiyeyi galeyana göturecek derecede*).[114]

The mediation of Kurdish notables, such as Hişman *Ağa*, was helpful for making Armenians return to their villages.[115] They had sought refuge among the sedentary Kurds of Sasun. The Ottoman authorities feared the potentiality of increased British pressure in the case of a general military manoeuvre against the Armenians because of the contemporaneous Ankara Trials. Therefore, a dispatch to the Sultan signed by the Ottoman foreign minister and the Grand Vizier highlighted that local Ottoman officials were forced to suppress the matter without arresting anyone as these were co-occurring with the Ankara Trials.[116] Therefore, despite the volatility of the situation, no formal investigation was launched in the summer of 1893 and after. As a matter of fact, Tahsin Pasha was rewarded for his 'complete restoration' (*Talori meselesi kamilen ref' ve izale*) of public order in Sasun.[117]

The primary economic capital that the Armenian peasants possessed was livestock. They used to go to Mush and Diyarbekir, sell the sheep and hence make a living for themselves in the winters.[118] However, with the arrival of the Kurdish tribes in the summer and the closure of the Diyarbekir trade route, Armenian peasants suffered a devastating economic blow.[119] Being aware of the vitality of this economic lifeline, the Kurds primarily targeted the flocks of the Armenian peasants, who in turn retaliated.[120]

The analysis so far suggests that as a newcomer, Murad's social and military clout was much more limited and depended on the cooperation of the *res* and other locals. This brings us to the modest role that the Hnchakian Party played in the region and discards claims about 'bringing the revolution' to Sasun.[121] As noted earlier, it is more helpful to think of the Hnchakians' influence in terms of creating unity among various scattered villages and reorienting the nascent culture of resistance towards local Kurdish authorities rather than a full-scale arming of the local population.

Therefore, it is worth reiterating that the intensification of seasonal clashes in Sasun in 1893–4 resulted primarily from a combination of three major factors. First, there were environmental and climatic oscillations that deteriorated the economic and social position of the peasant population. This led to an increasing presence of many Kurdish pastoralists once the ban was lifted and whom the Ottoman authorities openly supported. Their survival depended on their access to the summer pastures. Furthermore, the Ottoman state's perception of an 'Armenian threat' in the east and the excessive reliance on force bred new cycles of violence. Local struggles over grazing lands were now gaining imperial significance in the face of continued presence of Armenian revolutionaries and sustained Armenian resistance to pastoralist intrusions. Therefore, in the late nineteenth century, when Armenian national consciousness was in its rudimentary stage, the local clashes of 1893–4 remained a narrowly limited affair with exclusively local focuses and ends.

From clashes to massacres

The situation became extremely volatile by late 1893, yet the radical shift occurred throughout the summer of 1894 when Ottoman troops, some Hamidiye regiments and other Kurdish tribal forces participated in the massacre of the Armenians in Sasun.[122] While a detailed discussion of the actual killings falls outside the scope of this article, a few factors may account for this exponential increase of violence.[123]

First, Damadian's capture and the ensuing interrogation provided the Ottoman authorities with enough information to convince them that the Armenian threat was real and had to be eradicated. Second, the Hnchakian Party's attempts to assassinate the Armenian Patriarch in Constantinople in March 1894 and the chairman of the Armenian Civic Council in May of the same year exacerbated fears of a reshuffling of intra-Armenian politics as new provincial actors were emerging in the political arena.¹²⁴ Abdülhamid clearly understood that the emergence of revolutionary groups disrupted the political balance that he had been hitherto maintaining vis-à-vis the Armenian *millet* through its two main political institutions, the Armenian Patriarchate and the Armenian National Assembly.¹²⁵ Third, the pattern of violence in 1892–3 provided the Armenian peasants of Sasun with more experience in dealing with Kurdish predation. This consolidated intra-Armenian solidarity. Subsequently, local authorities lifted previous restrictions on pastoralists' incursions into Armenian areas of Sasun that they considered under the influence of the revolutionaries. Fourth, in 1894 the Ottoman government reissued the 'Tax Constitution (*nizamname*) of 1886' by which it stripped local notables (including *Res*, *muhtars*, priests, village councils) of their entitlements in collecting taxes on behalf of the government. Consequently, this task fell on the gendarmerie, presenting thus another challenge to an already fragile local power balance.¹²⁶

While future environmental histories of the region may confirm this, it is plausible that the famine in Erzurum, Van and Bitlis, three provinces with an economy based heavily on agriculture and trade, and the Armenian villagers' refusal to pay the state taxes in 1892–4 compelled the Ottoman officials in extracting more resources for additional revenues, often by sheer force.¹²⁷ This last point is corroborated by a report from *Hnch'ak* describing the famine in Bitlis and the increase in wheat prices. With agriculture primarily in peasant hands, tribal raids on windmills increased throughout the end of 1893, and early 1894. The report speculated that with the continuous inflation and the constant Kurdish incursions, the famine was most likely to continue well into 1894. The dire economic situation of the east compelled the authorities to control the wheat trade by stocking it in local storages. Subsequently, Kurdish nomadic tribes were left with no option but to attack the livestock of Armenian peasants, as an alternative to their survival.¹²⁸

It was against these social and economic changes that clashes in Sasun broke out in the early summer of 1894. In late spring, Murad received news that the government was sending masons to repair the Satan Bridge destroyed by Dalvorig Armenians a few years before.¹²⁹ Through this renovation, the Ottoman authorities were reopening the main way up to the Armenian stronghold in Sasun. The clashes around Dalvorig started when the Armenian peasants attacked the soldiers and workers on the bridge killing seven gendarmes in an ambush.¹³⁰ This provided the government with a pretext for the adoption of military measures, as peasant mobilization and resistance practices were inscribed in the official state narrative as a general Armenian rebellion.¹³¹

Skirmishes in the vicinities of Shenig, Semal and Gelîguzan continued between the Kurds and the Armenians until July.¹³² The tribesmen arrived in some numbers from the southeast and southwest, encircling the Armenian villages and creating a virtual state of siege. The pastoralists appear to have been motivated by a combination of the work of influential Kurdish sheikhs, rewards for their behaviour by the governor of Bitlis, and a general sense of rage against openly defiant Armenian peasants. Sheikh Mehmet of Zilan, who had been recruited by the Ottoman officials for his strong influence over the Bekran tribe, was one of the main culprits for the incursions in the summer of 1894. Almost a year before the actual atrocities, Sırrı Pasha, the governor of

Diyarbekir, had reported that the sheikh had claimed that he would avenge the killings of his kinsmen in 1893 by leading a large group of men.[133]

Peasant militias were quickly mobilized. The clashes were fierce with numerous casualties on both sides, though the Armenians held their ground against the pastoralists who failed to break their lines. Local Armenian notables, particularly *Res* Grko, led the defensive operations.[134] Some sedentary Kurdish lords such as Hişman and Hüseyin *ağa*s (of Khiyan) were reluctant to isolate and attack the Armenian peasants and even took them under their protection during the clashes.[135] Many of the villagers retreated to Mount Andok, a repetition of the pattern in 1893. The Ottoman officials interpreted this as a sign of rebellion. Once the pastoralists failed to break the Armenian defence, the Ottoman military assault on Sasun began on 24 August.[136] Over the course of two weeks, the soldiers and the tribesmen killed over a thousand Armenians and laid to waste over a dozen villages.[137]

Conclusion

To conclude, it is worth reiterating that agrarian and economic relations played a central role in the emergence of the Armenian Question and shaping the dimensions of the conflict in the early 1890s, particularly in Sasun. With the deteriorating situation in the eastern provinces and a shift in Ottoman domestic policy, relationships between the Kurdish tribesmen and the Armenians became much more strained. Nevertheless, this is not to suggest the inevitability of massacres. The Hamidian regime's very attempts to bring its order to the provinces for systematic tax collection and power brokerages only exacerbated existing social and political cleavages. Such a system *normativized* violence rendering it an essential element that shaped the relationships between Armenians and Kurds. Furthermore, during this period, the government's overriding security concerns defined most of its policy choices, which increasingly led the region towards instability. As this article demonstrated, crucial social and economic factors were at stake and were decisive in shaping the escalation of violence from the 1880s until 1894.

I have re-casted some of the terms in the historiography and history of the Armeno-Kurdish relations in Eastern Anatolia in light of the socio-economic transformations that marked the late nineteenth century. Such a model provides a viable and historically grounded alternative to the 'freedom lovers vs. evil oppressor' approach among mainstream historians. By integrating the socio-economic paradigm to the political and intellectual history of the Armenian revolutionary movement at the *fin de siècle*, I have attempted closing an important historiographical lacuna; instead of reducing violence to manifestations of nationalist agendas and *a priori* inter-ethnic hatred, this work analysed the local context in which violence was shaped, used and transformed. Factors from environmental fluctuations to economic changes, all contributed to the re-moulding of Armeno-Kurdish relations in an important imperial periphery. Therefore, combining an exploration of the ecological, social and economic dynamics, the article adopted a 'bottom-up' perspective that brought the agency and interests of the local actors to the forefront of historical research.

Upon arriving in Sasun in 1891–2, the Hnchakian militants found a milieu where villagers were periodically galvanized by the ethnic, social and economic peculiarities that characterized the configuration of the region. Thus, the Hnchakians attempted to adapt to the existing practices of resistance rather than create it *ex nihilo*. Yet, the Ottoman authorities perceived the peasants' presence and control over pastures, at the expense of pastoralist Kurdish tribes, as a matter of internal security. The ability of Sasun Armenians to navigate local ethnic relations and tensions and establish themselves as a social and economic force placed them beyond the pale of obedient imperial subjecthood.[138]

Therefore, the presence of an umbrella organization-albeit with limited resources-marked the institutionalization of provincial violence, in the absence of viable political and legal institutions. Under such circumstances, individuals in Sasun started reinterpreting their status in a new light, one that re-defined their relationship with their surroundings and the Ottoman state. The violence that accompanied modernization projects, power devolutions and centralization efforts provided a further impetus for the existence of revolutionary parties as alternative organizations capable of expressing 'provincial' grievances. With the limited outreach of the Armenian Patriarchate, the existence of revolutionary committees and their cooperation with local power brokers in remote corners of the empire meant that a new language of political articulation was evolving, one that would soon reach the imperial capital.

Notes

1 Boris Adjemian and Mikaël Nichanian, 'Rethinking the "Hamidian massacres", The Issue of the Precedent', *Études Arméniennes Contemporaines* 10 (2018): 19–29.
2 For a critical overview of this historiography and the inherent methodological problems, see Varak Ketsemanian, 'Ideologies, Paradoxes, and *Fedayis*, Historiographical Challenges, and Methodological Problems in the Study of the Armenian Revolutionary Movement (1890-1896)', in *Kurds and Armenians in the Late Ottoman Empire*, eds. Ara Sarafian and Ümit Kurt (The Press at California State University, Fresno, 2020), 119–60.
3 Gerard J. Libaridian, 'What Was Revolutionary about Armenian Revolutionary Parties in the Ottoman Empire?' in *A Question of Genocide, Armenians and Turks at the End of the Ottoman Empire*, eds. Ronald G. Suny, Fatma Müge Göçek and Norman Naimark (Oxford: Oxford University Press, 2011), 82.
4 Hrant Kankrouni, *Hay Heghap'okhut 'iwnĕ Ōsmanean Bṛnatirut'ean Dēm (1890-1910)* (Beirut: G. Doniguian, 1973); Hrach Dasnabedian, *Patmut 'iwn Hay Heghap'okhakan Sharzhman ew Hay Heghap'okhakan Dashnakts'ut'ean* (Beirut: Vahe Setian Press, 2009).
5 Robert Melson, *Revolution and Genocide, On the Origins of the Armenian Genocide and the Holocaust* (Chicago: University of Chicago Press, 1992), 51–3.
6 Even Garo Sasuni, a native of Sasun and an active revolutionary in the early 1900s, mentions the economic aspects only in passing. He over-stresses the Armeno-Kurdish relations as a pure case of ethnic strife; Garo Sasuni, *Patmut 'iwn Tarōni Ashkharhi* (Beirut: Publications of the Daron-Duruperan Compatriotic Union, 1956), 557–60.

7 For the ideological background of the Hnchakian founders, see Ashot G. Hovhannisyan, 'Hnch'akeanneri Kazmaworman Gaghap'arakan Armatnerĕ', *Patma-Banasirakan Handes* 2 (1968): 19–39.
8 Vardan Petoyan, *Sasunn Ants'ealum ew Sasuni Azatagrakan Sharzhumnerĕ* (Yerevan: Lusakn Press, 2005), 86.
9 Hans-Lukas Kieser, 'Réformes ottomanes et cohabitation entre chrétiens et kurdes (1839-1915)', *Études rurales*, juillet–décembre 2010, 48; Martin Van Bruinessen, *Shaikh, and State, The Social and Political Structures of Kurdistan Aghas* (London: Zed Books, 1992), 175–85.
10 Stephan Astourian, 'The Silence of the Land, Agrarian Relations, Ethnicity and Power', in *A Question of Genocide*, eds. Ronald G. Suny, Fatma Müge Göçek and Norman Naimark (Oxford: Oxford University Press, 2011), 56.
11 A British report dated 1884 made the case that 'the government would have to discard its present fatal policy of supporting *agha*s. These are the real disturbing elements of the country, and these once suppressed, the country would soon settle down, if not harassed by bad governors, as in that case a modus vivendi for the Kurds and Armenians would be very quickly found, since these people are not radically antipathetic'; Foreign Office Archives [hereafter FO] 424/141, Inclosure 3, no. 14 (4 January 1884).
12 Ueno Massayuki, 'For the Fatherland and the State, Armenians Negotiate the Tanzimat Reforms', *International Journal of Middle East Studies* 45 (March 2013): 93–109. For Armenian petitions regarding the insecurity caused by Kurdish pastoralists, see Bibliothèque Nubar [hereafter BNU]. APC/CP22/5, Document 195 (19 January 1856); BNU. APC/CGPR 81, document 10 (1 September 1863) BNU. APC/CP22/5, Document 247 (5 December 1880); Between 1860 and 1870, 529 petitions were sent from the Armenian Patriarchate in Constantinople to the Sublime Porte complaining of Kurdish and Circassian predations and abuses; Garo Sasuni, *K'iwrt Azgayin Sharzhumnerĕ ew Hay-K'rtakan Haraberut'iwnnerĕ* (Beirut: Hamazkayin Press, 1969), 135.
13 Brad Dennis, 'Patterns of Conflict and Violence in Eastern Anatolia', in *War and Diplomacy, The Russo-Turkish War of 1877-1878 and the Treaty of Berlin*, eds. Hakan M. Yavuz and Peter Sluglett (Salt Lake City: University of Utah Press, 2011), 278.
14 Astourian, 'Silence of the Land', 56.
15 Yaşar Tolga Cora, 'Doğu'da Kürt-Ermeni Çatışmasının Sosyoekonomik Arkaplanı', in *1915, Siyaset, Tehcir, Soykırım*, eds. Fikret Adanır and Oktay Özel (İstanbul: Tarih Vakfı Yurt Yayınları, 2015), 129.
16 FO 424/178, no 260, (15 October 1894); Gerard Chaliand, *A People Without a Country, The Kurds and Kurdistan*, trans. Michael Pallis (New York: Interlink Pub Group Inc, 1993), 15.
17 Janet Klein, 'Conflict and Collaboration, Rethinking Kurdish-Armenian Relations in the Hamidian Period (1876-1909)', *International Journal of Turkish Studies* 13 (2007): 155.
18 Stephen Duguid, 'The Politics of Unity, Hamidian Policy in Eastern Anatolia', *Middle Eastern Studies* 9–2 (May 1973): 131.
19 Astourian, 'The Silence of the Land', 56.
20 Henry Lynch, *Armenia, Travels and Studies, vol. 2, The Turkish Provinces* (London, New York: Green, & Co., 1901), 158.
21 A-Do (Hovhannes Ter-Martirosyan), *Vani, Bit'lisi ev Ērzrumi Vilayet'nerĕ* (Yerevan: Kultura, 1912), 119.

22 Estimates for the district region of Sasun list some 40,000 Armenian inhabitants to a roughly equal number of Kurds. The area that witnessed the most outbreaks of mass violence in 1894 were home to roughly 10,000 Armenians; Tigran Martirosyan, 'Armenian Demographics of Sassoun in the Late Ottoman Period', *Armenian Review* 57, no. 1–2 (Winter–Fall 2020): 59–92; Raymond Kevorkian, 'The Armenian Population of Sassoun and the Demographic Consequences of the 1894 Massacres', *Armenian Review* 47, no. 1–2 (Spring–Summer 2001): 41–53.
23 Edwin M. Bliss, *Turkey and the Armenian Atrocities, A Reign of Terror* (Philadelphia: Edgewood Publishing Company, 1896), 373; FO 424/178, no 260 (15 October 1894).
24 The Armenian peasants of Sasun paid the state taxes once a year in a lump sum until 1890; Sargis Bdeyan, Misak Bdeyan and Aghan Daronetsi, *Harazat Patmutʻiwn Tarōnoy* (Cairo: Sahag-Mesrob Press, 1962), 8–9.
25 Evropayi Hay Usanoghakan Miutʻiwn, *Apsdamb Sasunĕ* (Geneva, 1903), 11.
26 Ibid., 12.
27 Petoyan, *Sasunn Antsʻealum*, 86.
28 Sasuni, *Patmutʻiwn*, 105.
29 For an extensive list of *res* households, see Sasuni, *Kʻiwrt*, 390–1. A source from 1903 states that there were overall sixty-seven Armenian notables (*ereveli*) in the villages of Sasun; Miutʻiwn, *Apsdamb Sasunĕ*, 6.
30 FO. 424/162, Inclosure in No 80 (29 August 1889); Lynch, *Armenia*, 432; Vahan A. Bayburdyan, *Hay-Kʻrdakan Haraberutʻiwnnerĕ Ōsmanean Kaysrutʻiwnum* (Yerevan: Hayastan, 1989), 62; Sasuni, *Patmutʻiwn*, 531. According to an ethnographic study published in *Arakʻs*, the districts of Kavar and Shadakh could produce up to 1,000 armed men; *Arakʻs 1894-1895, Girkʻ I* (St. Petersburg: Y. I. Liberman Press, 1895), 70–3.
31 Haygaz Poghosyan, *Sasuni Patmutʻiwn 1750–1918* (Yerevan: Hayastan Press, 1985), 165.
32 Created in 1891, Hamidiye regiments and Kurdish pastoralist tribes received modern rifles which significantly affected the outcome of the conflict and the damage inflicted upon the peasant population; Janet Klein, *Margins of Empire, Kurdish Militias in Ottoman Tribal Zone* (Stanford: Stanford University Press, 2011).
33 Sasuni, *Patmutʻiwn*, 483–90.
34 Cumhurbaşkanlığı Osmanlı Arşivleri (hereafter COA) DH.MKT 1467/26 (30 November 1887).
35 This observation is corroborated by an ethnographic study published in 1894, where it is stated that the Pirik Kurdish tribe in the district of Kavar spoke the local Armenian dialect in addition to their native Arabic; *Arakʻs*, 84.
36 COA.Y.PRK.UM 19/64 (13 November 1890).
37 COA.Y.PRK.AZJ 17/116 (13 November 1890). To reinforce his point, Mehmet Safi Bey highlighted that 80 per cent of the region was made up of Muslims and only 20 per cent were Christians.
38 Bayburdyan, *Hay-Kʻrdakan*, 42; Azat Hambaryan, *Agrarayin Haraberutʻiwnnerĕ Arewmtean Hayastanum* (Yerevan: Armenian SSR Academy of Sciences, 1965), 59.
39 By the early 1890s, Kör Süleyman Ağa was the chief of the Khiyan tribe; Bdeyan et al., *Harazat*, 8.
40 COA.Y.EE. 159/94 (15 December 1894).
41 Toygun Altıntaş, 'Crisis and (Dis)Order, Armenian Revolutionaries and the Hamidian Regime in the Ottoman Empire, 1887-1896' (PhD diss., University of Chicago, 2018), 112.
42 COA.Y.PRK.MYD. 12/36 (28 January 1893).

43 Sasuni, *Patmut'iwn*, 328.
44 Nadir *Ağa* of the Bertran tribe owned eleven villages in Prnashen; Hambaryan, *Agrarayin Haraberut'iwnnerě*, 59.
45 *Arak's*, 78; Remitted yearly in produce or artisanal products, the *hafir*, often exceeded the amount of taxes levied by the government; Astourian, 'The Silence of the Land', 60; Armenians paid *hafir* to the Bekranlı, Badikanlı, Khoşekanlı, Garzanlı and Khiyanlı tribes; Owen Miller, 'Rethinking the Violence in the Sasun Mountains (1893-1894)', *Études arméniennes contemporaines* 10 (2018): 106.
46 In 1889, the British consul of Erzerum, Colonel Chermside, reported that 'the outrages by the Kurds on the Christians, inter-tribal feuds, highway robbery, cattle lifting, all exist'; FO 424/162, No 80 (14 September 1889).
47 Edip Gölbaşı, 'Hamidiye Alayları, Bir Değerlendirme', in *1915, Siyaset, Tehcir, Soykırım*, eds. Fikret Adanır and Oktay Özel (İstanbul: Tarih Vakfı Yurt Yayınları, 2015), 174.
48 Justin A. McCarthy, Ömer Turan and Cemalettin Taşkıran, *Sasun, The History of an 1890s Armenian Revolt*, (Salt Lake City: University of Utah Press, 2014), 14. For a discussion of the impact of climatic changes on pastoralist animals, see Zozan Pehlivan, 'El Niño and the Nomads, Global Climate, Local Environment, and the Crisis of Pastoralism in Late Ottoman Kurdistan', *Journal of the Economic and Social History of the Orient* 63, no. 3 (2020): 316–56.
49 Starting in 1887 *Hnch'ak* was published in Athens until November 1894. It then moved to London.
50 *Hnch'ak*, April 1892, no. 4, 29; Hulp remained the center of most of these Kurdish sheikhs; *Hnch'ak*, 2 February 1892, 14–16.
51 Elke Hartman, 'The Central State in the Borderlands, Ottoman Eastern Anatolia in the Late Nineteenth Century', in *Shatterzone of Empire, Coexistence and Violence in the German, Habsburg, Russian and Ottoman Borderlands*, eds. Ömer Bartov and Eric D. Weitz (Bloomington: Indiana University Press, 2013), 176.
52 Owen Miller, '"Back to the Homeland" (Tebi Yergir), Or, How Peasants Became Revolutionaries in Mush', *Journal of Ottoman and Turkish Studies Association* 4, no. 2 (November 2017): 287–308.
53 COA.Y.MTV. 44/55 (29 July 1890).
54 Arsen Gidur, *Patmut'iwn S.D. Hnch'akean Kusakts'ut'ean*, vol. I (Beirut: Shirag Press, 1962), 135–6, and Mihran Damadian, *Bir Ermeni Komitecinin İtirafları* (İstanbul: Timaş Yayınları, 2009), 24, claim 1891 and 1892 respectively.
55 For the Kumkapı Demonstration, see Gidur, *Patmut'iwn*, 53–63; Mihran Damadian, *Im Hushers* (Beirut: Democratic Liberal Party Club, 1986), 75–93; *Hnch'ak*, August 1890 (entire issue).
56 In the late 1880s, Damadian was the superintendent of the Nersesian School in Mush; Bedros Depoyan, *Mihran Tamatean* (Cairo: Arewi Terton, 1956), 31–8.
57 *Hnch'ak*, January 1892, no. 1.
58 Depoyan, *Mihran Tamatean*, 41.
59 Ibid., 43; Sasuni, *Patmut'iwn*, 554–5.
60 *Hnch'ak*, February 1892, no. 2. This report overlaps with the creation of the Hamidiye Regiments.
61 According to the memoirs of Sarkis Bdeyan, a close collaborator of Damadian in the region, the latter handed the letters to him, which he in turn sent them to his brother Misak in Constantinople. Misak then forwarded the reports to the Hnchakian center in Europe (Bdeyan et al., *Harazat*, 57).

62 *Hnch'ak*, December 1891, no. 12, 3 and 8; February 1892, no. 2, 14–16, 4; April 1892, no. 4, 28–32.
63 *Hnch'ak*, April 1892, no. 4.
64 *Hnch'ak,* January 1893, no. 1.
65 Pehlivan, 'El Niño and the Nomads', 319.
66 German reports have indicated the presence of Ottoman [official] tax collectors since the late 1870s. See Tessa Hofmann and Gerayer Koutcharian, 'The History of Armenian-Kurdish Relations in the Ottoman Empire', *Armenian Review* 39 (1986): 10.
67 The British ambassador, Sir Philip Currie, described Sasun, which was in the district of Genc, as 'the worst governed Mutessarifat of the Empire'; FO 424/178, no. 260 (15 October 1894).
68 Klein, 'Conflict and Collaboration', 159.
69 FO 424/178 Inclosure 2, no. 97 (15 April 1894), no. 271 (13 October 1894).
70 COA.Y.EE. 159/94 (15 December 1894).
71 Mehmet Polatel, 'The Complete Ruin of a District, The Sasun Massacre of 1894', in *The Ottoman East in the Nineteenth Century, Societies, Identities, and Politics,* eds. Yaşar Tolga Cora, Dzovinar Derderian and Ali Sipahi (London: I.B. Tauris, 2016), 180.
72 COA.DH.MKT 190/71 (25 December 1893); COA.BEO 388/29073 (21 April 1894); FO 424/141 Inclosure 3, no. 14.
73 *Hnch'ak*, July 1892, no. 7.
74 On *pandukht*s from Sasun, see Vahram Shemmassian, 'The Sasun Bantoukhds in Nineteenth-Century Aleppo', in *Armenian Baghesh/Bitlis and Taron/Mush*, ed. Richard G. Hovannisian (Costa Mesa: Mazda Publishers, 2001), 175–91.
75 Christopher Clay, 'Labor Migration and Economic Conditions in Nineteenth-Century Anatolia', *Middle Eastern Studies* 34, no. 4 (October 1998): 3–4.
76 *Hnch'ak*, July 1892, no. 7.
77 *Drōshak,* September 1891, no. 2; *Drōshak*, February 1892, no. 3.
78 For a biography of Hampartsoum Boyajian, see Sirvard, *Metsn Murat* (Providence: Graphic Composition, 1955); *Hnch'ak*, January 1895, no. 1.
79 Before 1890, Damadian and Boyajian were members of a secret organization in Constantinople; Yusuf Sarınay (ed.), *Osmanlı Belgelerinde Ermenilerin Sevk ve Iskanı (1870-1920)* (Ankara. T.C. Başbakanlık Devlet Arşivleri Genel Mudurluğu Osmanlı Arşivi Daire Bakanlığı, 2007), 23.
80 Sasuni, *Patmut'iwn*, 483–7, 554–5, 542–3. After the killing, eight Armenian village headmen from the Mush valley petitioned the Ottoman authorities requesting Musa Bey's exile as the only way to protect their lives, honour, and property. COA. DH.MKT 1617/42 (9 April 1889).
81 *Hnch'ak*, June 1892, no. 6.
82 Gegham Hovhannisyan, *Hnch'akean Kusakts'ut'ean Patmut'iwn (1887-1915)* (Yerevan: History Institute, 2012), 61; One of the victims was the Kurdish Ishak Çavuş *Ağa* of Avzan village of Mush. He was killed in late 1892; COA.BEO 138/10323 (15 December 1892). *Drōshak* mentions another assassination and the story of *Res* Grbo, who was killed on 6 September 1892 in Mush for being an informant to the local Ottoman council; Damadian, *Bir Ermeni Komitecenin*, 24; *Drōshak*, March 1893, no. 4; *Hnch'ak*, March 1893, no. 3.
83 *Hnch'ak*, May 1892, no. 5.
84 For examples of Ottoman police's interception of *Hnch'ak* see COA. A.MKT.MHM 751/12 (26 October 1895); COA. A.MKT.MHM 751/12/4 (22 March 1895).

85 Hovhannisyan, *Hnch'akean Kusakts'ut'ean Patmut'iwn*, 61.
86 Garo Sasuni, *Hrayri Derĕ Hay Azatagrakan Sharzhman Mēj* (Beirut: Atlas Press, 1964), 16.
87   *Drōshak*, July 1895, no. 9.
88 COA.Y.EE 168/9 (18 May 1895), cited in Altıntaş, 'Crisis and (Dis)Order', 281.
89 Damadian, *Im Hushers*, 83.
90 *Hnch'ak*, June 1893, no. 6; *Drōshak*, March 1893, no. 4; *Miut'iwn, Apsdamb Sasunĕ*, 14. Jelle Verheij claims that the Armenian *res* had stopped paying taxes to the state since 1870; Jelle Verheij, '"Les frères de terre et d'eau", sur le rôle des Kurdes dans les massacres arméniens de 1894-1896', *Islam des Kurdes*, -special issue of *Les Annales de l'Autre Islam*, eds. M. van Bruinessen and Joyce Blau (Paris: Institut national des langues et civilisations orientales, 1999), 239.
91 COA.Y.PRK.UM. 24/111 (13 June 1893).
92 Antranig Chalabian, *Revolutionary Figures* (USA: n.p., 1994), 31.
93 *Hnch'ak*, January 1894, no. 1-2.
94 *Drōshak*, March 1893, no. 4. The provincial yearbook (*salname*) of Bitlis mentions one Khurshid, who was a member of the district council of Genc; *Salname-i Vilayet-i Bitlis* (1893), 253.
95 Depoyan, *Mihran Tamatean*, 49; Sasuni, *Patmut'iwn*, 565-6.
96 For the investigation on Khurshid's murder, see Altıntaş, 'Crisis and (Dis)Order', 116-18.
97 According to *Drōshak*, Damadian's capture also involved the actions of some local Armenians; *Drōshak*, April 1893, no. 5.
98 Armed groups in other villages made hasty preparations to rescue Damadian while he was taken to Mush. The attack on Dervish *Ağa* and the rescue attempts were unsuccessful, however. As a result, Colonel Iskender *Ağa* of Mush retaliated and sent forces to Shenig to capture *Res* Grigor. A skirmish ensued (*Hnc'hak*, January 1894, no. 1-2). Dervish *Ağa* was promised a monetary remuneration of 10,000 Ottoman *kuruş* for his services. Yet he petitioned Constantinople and demanded his reward in November 1896. After an investigation, it became clear that the money that was sent from Constantinople to Bitlis was divided among the governor Tahsin Pasha (6,000) and the district governor (4,000) of Mush. The Ottoman authorities ordered an immediate follow-up to the issue claiming that otherwise the reputation of the Sultan would be tarnished. COA.DH. TMIK.M 22/ 37 (2 November 1896); COA.DH. TMIK. M 23/2 (19 November 1896); COA.DH. TMIK.M 23/ 2 (23 November 1896).
99 Depoyan, *Mihran Tamatean*, 58; Damadian, *Bir Ermeni Komitecinin İtirafları*, 50.
100 In his dispatch to Constantinople, Tahsin Pasha described Damadian as an agitator who attempted to incite rebellion among the Armenians; COA.Y.EE. 155/19 (19 June 1893).
101 COA.Y.EE. 172/10 (13 June 1893).
102 Chalabian, *Revolutionary Figures*, 40.
103 Miller, 'Rethinking the Violence', 17.
104 He was first sentenced to a capital punishment, but the verdict was changed; Hüseyin Nazım Paşa, *Ermeni Olayları Tarihi, Cilt I* (Ankara: Başbakanlık Devlet Arşivleri Genel Müdürlügü Osmanlı Arşivi Daire Başkanlığı, 1998), 34; COA.Y.EE.163/22 (3 December 1894).
105 Altıntaş, 'Crisis and (Dis)Order', 228-9. For the complete report see Sarınay, *Osmanlı Belgelerinde Ermenilerin Sevk*, 18-48.

106 Unaware of Damadian's new administrative job, the Hnchakian leader Avetis Nazarbekian summoned him to Europe in the summer of 1895; Grakanut'ean ev Arvesti T'angaran [hereafter GAT], Avetis Nazarbekian Fond, File 905.
107 *Hnch'ak*, February 1894, appendix.
108 COA.Y.PRK. A. 10/4 (27 March 1895).
109 COA. Y.EE. 159/94 (15 December 1894).
110 COA. Y.A.HUS. 277 /44 (5 July 1893).
111 COA.Y. EE. 155/22 (9 July 1893).
112 COA.Y.A.HUS. 277/141 (13 July 1893).
113 *Hnch'ak*, January 1894, no. 6; FO 424/178, no. 260 (15 October 1894).
114 COA.Y. EE. 155/22 (9 July 1893); According to the report of the *Mutasarrıf* of Genc, who was sent to Dalvorig to investigate the matter, these foreign 'instructors' could be distinguished from the local Armenian peasants from their cloths and form; COA.Y.A.HUS. 277/112 (9 July 1893). In February 1894, Tahsin Pasha reiterated that some Armenians had crossed into Ottoman territories from the Russian Empire and were provoking local Armenian peasants. Thus, he requested that the central authorities increase their support for spies and informers; COA. BEO. 361/27063 (18 February 1894).
115 Throughout the summer of 1894, local officials expressed concern over the leaders of these tribes – namely Hişman *Ağa* of Sasun and Hüseyin *Ağa* of Khiyan – who refused to isolate the Armenians. Allegedly, the *ağa*s retorted with disdain to official instructions that they refrain from associating with the Armenians. They stated that the Armenians were their subjects/clients under protection, and hence would not pay taxes to the state. In the aftermath of the massacres, Ottoman policy would make such a position untenable for Kurdish notables in the region; Toygun Altıntaş, 'The Abode of Sedition', Resistance, Repression, And Revolution in Sasun (1891-1904)', in *Age of Rogues, Rebels, Revolutionaries and Racketeers at the Frontiers of Empires*, edited by Alp Yenen and Ramazan Hakkı Öztan, 178–207 (Edinburgh: Edinburgh University Press, 2021).
116 COA.Y.PRK. A. 10/4 (1 April 1895). Despite the insistence in Ottoman documents that no arrests were made, British reports mention that in the aftermath of the clashes some Armenians were detained and a few died in prison; FO 424/178, Inclosure 1 in no. 112 (9 April 1893). In December 1892, flyers in Turkish were posted on the walls of Merzifon, Kayseri and Yozgat. Hundreds of Armenians were subsequently arrested and tried. These trials came to be known as the Ankara Tribunals; Toygun Altıntaş, 'The Placard Affair and the Ankara Trial, The Hnchak Party and the Hamidian Regime in Central Anatolia, 1892–1893', *Journal of Ottoman and Turkish Studies Association* 4 (2017): 309–37.
117 Y.Y.MTV 80/28 (18 July 1893). After the massacres of 1894, it was ordered to cover up the past atrocities. An Ottoman military report claimed that investigating the events of September 1893 would require the investigation of even earlier events. The Porte was probably anxious that such an investigation would reveal that the clashes between Armenians and the Bekranlı and Badikanlı tribes and the retreat of Armenians to the mountains were, in fact, an annual occurrence, and that only in 1894 had the Ottoman government chosen to treat the matter as a full-fledged Armenian rebellion; COA.Y.EE. 159/94 (15 December 1894).
118 FO 424/182, Inclosure 2 in no. 197 (26 April 1985).
119 *Apstamb Sasunĕ*, 18.
120 Throughout the early summer 1894, the Bekranlı and Badikanlı tribes who were involved in the attacks against the Armenian peasants had promised to return the

121 McCarthy et al., *Sasun*, 21.
122 Already by the summer of 1893, a report from Mush claimed that the situation in Sasun resembled a 'state of war' (*paterazmakan vijak*); *Hnch'ak*, January–February 1894, no. 2–3, *Hnch'ak*, March 1894, no. 3.
123 For an excellent account of the massacres, see Altıntaş, 'Crisis and (Dis)Order', 222–89.
124 On these attempts, see Varak Ketsemanian, 'The Hnchakian Revolutionary Party and the Assassination Attempts against Patriarch Khoren Ashekian and Maksudzade Simon Bey in 1894', *International Journal of Middle East Studies* 50 (November 2018): 735–55.
125 In 1863, the Armenian Constitution stipulated the creation of the Armenian National Assembly as the highest legislative authority of the Armenian *millet*.
126 Nadir Özbek, 'Abdülhamid Rejimi, Vergi Tahsildarlığı ve Siyaset, 1876-1908', *Doğu Batı* 52 (2010): 179.
127 According to British reports, gendarmes appeared in Dalvorig in the spring of 1894 to collect taxes in arrears. The people protested that, as consequence of the treatment they had received at the hands of the Kurds, they were unable to contribute, and while declaring their loyalty to the government, they stated that it was impossible for them to pay taxes if they were not protected by the authorities against the Kurds; FO 424/178, no 260 (15 October 1894).
128 *Hnch'ak*, January–February 1894, no. 1–2; *Hnch'ak*, July 1894, no. 10.
129 Chalabian, *Revolutionary Figures*, 79; Verheij, 'Les frères de terre et d'eau', 241.
130 *Hnch'ak*, November 1894, no. 12.
131 Altıntaş, 'Crisis and (Dis)Order', 240. It appears from the British consular reports that throughout August and September 1894, the British ambassador Philip Currie subscribed to the 'Armenian rebellion' narrative. However, he sent a strong protest to the Grand Vizier cautioning him on the usage of irregular [Kurdish] troops in the suppression of the uprising; FO 424/178, no 193 (31 August 1894), no 196 (3 September 1894). By 20 September, Currie reported to his superiors that 'the belief is that the importance of the disturbance has been greatly exaggerated by the local authorities of Bitlis, to which place Zeki Paşa has gone'; FO 424/178, no. 214 (20 September 1894).
132 A report in *Hnch'ak* described the increasing number of Armenian prisoners in Mush; *Hnch'ak*, July 1894, no. 10.
133 BOA.Y.EE. 155/21(29 June 1893); In a ciphered telegram sent to the Grand Vizier in September 1894, Sirri Pasha acknowledged that the Bekranlı and Badiklanlı tribes had been deliberately sent to Dalvorig by the *Mutasarrıf* of Genc to punish the 'bandits'; COA. A.MKT.MHM. 750/15 (16 September 1894).
134 McCarthy et al., *Sasun*, 23; Other Armenian *ishkhan*s who participated in the 1893-4 clashes included Bedo (Geliguzan), Katib Manoug (Semal), Kasbar (Dalvorig), Magar (Sbghank); Sasuni, *Patmut'iwn*, 345. Grko was killed during the clashes in the summer of 1894; Sasuni, *Patmut'iwn*, 518.
135 Altıntaş, 'Crisis and (Dis)Order', 241.
136 According to *Hnch'ak*, 12,000 Ottoman soldiers were involved in these clashes, *Hnch'ak*, January 1895, no. 1.
137 Raymond Kevorkian calculated that the military operations of the Ottoman troops and the Kurdish irregulars concentrated primarily on thirty-two localities in the

northwestern part of Sasun (Kevorkian, 'The Armenian Population', 49). In the aftermath of the massacres, pastoralists from the Bekranlı and Badiklanlı tribes looted and shared among themselves the properties, livestock and farms of the killed Armenians. Some were even taken to nearby urban centres for auction sales; COA.A. MKT.MHM. 750/15 (16 September 1894). After the brutal intervention of the Ottoman army in the summer of 1894, 22,455 Ottoman *liras* were collected by Hnchakian adherents in Constantinople as a relief to the devastated people (GAT, Arpiar Arpiarian Fond, File 668, page 1).
138 Altıntaş, 'Crisis and (Dis)Order', 256.

7

The Hnchakian Revolutionary Party in Aintab

Founders, Ideology and Structure

Ümit Kurt

The Social Democrat Hnchakian Party (SDHP or Hnchakian Party) was one of the first organized Armenian political parties. Established in Geneva in 1887, its founders, Avetis Nazarbekian, Maro Vardanian, Gabriel Kafian, Rupen Khan-Azad, Kristapor Ohanian and Gevorg Gharajian, were the first to adhere to the 'scientific socialism' of the time and try to implement this world view among the Armenians of the Ottoman Empire.[1] Despite being the first Armenian movement to develop a considerable grassroots organization and create a large network of underground cells inside the Ottoman Empire, the history of the SDHP has been inadequately covered by the scholarship on the social, political and economic life of the late Ottoman Armenians.[2] The official program of the party called for a 'broad democracy, political freedom and national independence' for Turkish Armenia – the six Armenian provinces in eastern Anatolia known as western Armenia: Sivas, Erzurum, Mamuret-ul-Aziz, Diyarbekir, Bitlis and Van – through revolutionary action, and 'denounced the exploitation of man by man and set socialism as the future objective of the Armenian people'.[3]

The field of activity of the SDHP was not only limited to eastern Anatolia but also extended to the region of Cilicia. Philipos Sarkisian and Avedis Shishmanian (both graduated from the Murad Rafaelian School in Venice) from Zeytun were the first Hnchak members who actively operated in Aintab.[4] Aintab in the province of Aleppo – situated on the boundaries of Cilicia and Syria, near the Gulf of Alexandretta – was an important city where the SDHP took roots. The Hnchakian chapter in Aintab was established at the Central Turkey College, the most important American-Protestant institution in the city, founded in 1876. It had numerous Armenian professors and students.[5] The chapter had an organizational structure that was controlled by military discipline and order. In a short period of time and as a result of meticulous efforts, a massive organization was established that was powerful in terms of both quality and quantity. The Aintab branch of the Hnchakian party came into prominence in 1890–2

A shorter version of this article appeared in the Armenian Review. See Ümit Kurt, 'History of Hunchakian Revolutionary Party in Cilicia: Aintab as a Case Study', *Armenian Review* 57, no. 1–2 (2020): 93–115.

and attracted many young Armenians who became directly involved in the party or sympathized with it.⁶

The party included representatives of all categories and classes. Operating in numerous fields ranging from education, religion, commerce and craftsmanship among others, the party maintained a strong presence with well-informed, discreet and disciplined members.⁷ The branch was led by Ghazaros Effendi Diradurian, who was the dean of Armenian language teachers at Aintab College, and his student Movses Hovsepian.⁸ The size of this branch was considerable. It had young members from Aintab, Aleppo, Marash, Kesab, Kilis, Talas, Urfa and other cities. It included female founders, among whom was Roza Levonian, the wife of Prof. Sarkis Levonian from the Central Turkey College. Another one was Ester Keshishian, a teacher at the American Girls' College of Aintab.

The Hnchakian branch in Aintab was an organization with appeal and credibility aiming to serve the Armenians of the city. They worked for the interest of both individuals and the public in fields such as church and education. They were closely concerned with people's problems. Through external advice and instructions from sister chapters in Europe and Egypt as well as various indicators, the Hnchakian branch in Aintab was managed quietly.

In addition to the Central Turkey College, the Vartanian High School for Boys, founded in 1882, was another centre of the SDHP activities in Aintab, which recruited multiple members from there.⁹ The repressive policies of Sultan Abdülhamid II (1876–1908) led the Armenian students in the Vartanian School to enrol in the revolutionary movement. Armenian students of the school met secretly and discussed revolutionary literature. At some point, the school became a meeting point for the youth and the hearth of revolutionary activities. The principal of the school and its teachers became Hnchak sympathizers. They included Sarkis Samuelian from Marash (killed in the 1895 massacres), Sarkis Turabian, Armenag Nazaretian and Nazaret Fistikchian. For example, an able intellectual, Sarkis Turabian, who acted as the principal of Vartanian in 1900, became the leader of the SDHP in Aintab.¹⁰ Another important Hnchakian figure was Vahan Kurkjian. Under his leadership, prominent members of the Aintab Armenian community such as Hrant Sulahian, Harutiun Jebejian, Hagop Hamalian and Sahag Sahagian joined the ranks.¹¹

The Aintab SDHP and the Zeytun resistance

The Aintab branch of the SDHP played a critical role in helping the Armenian self-defence movement in Zeytun. At the beginning of the summer of 1895, Aghasi (Garabed Tursarkisian), a prominent figure of the Hnchak movement, arrived in Aintab and started working towards self-defence measures.¹² According to Soghomon B. Bastajian, a leading figure of the party in Aintab, Aghasi's visit was aimed at strengthening the links between the central Hnchakian administration and the local branch and to receive financial support from Hnchaks for the region of Cilicia. Thus, the relation between local forces and the party was formalized; and largely upon the organization's request, both sides agreed on the need for material and moral support from abroad.

A five-person administrative board was formed, composed of Nazaret Kechejian, Harutiun Yemenijian, Sarkis Turabian, Hagop Kechejian and Soghomon Bastajian.[13] Other figures such as Khachig Bilejimian, Hagop Ohanian, Artush Tabakian, Nerses Kazanjian and Hagopdjan accompanied Aghasi in order to participate in the resistance movement in Zeytun. In the spring of 1895, Ghazaros Diradurian, along with his five students left Aintab to participate in the resistance movement in Zeytun.[14]

During Aghasi's visit to Aintab, prominent Armenian Apostolic and Protestant notables of the district gathered at Prof. Zenop Bezjian's house.[15] A secret meeting was held with sixty people led by Garabed Nazaretian, a prominent Armenian merchant, and teachers representing the Central Turkey College. A total of 400 Ottoman gold liras were raised with their support. This amount was handed to Aghasi, who took it with him to Zeytun.[16] Another important figure who donated a large amount was Harutiun Agha Nazaretian, a respected and beloved figure not only among Armenians but also the Turkish community.[17] Soghomon B. Bastajian reported that, as members of the Nazaretian family, the brothers Harutiun, Garabed and Nigoghos provided all kinds of material and moral support for the establishment of a Hnchakian branch in Aintab. Bastajian was also of the opinion that the Zeytun resistance was neither a show of brigandage nor adventure. On the contrary, he described it as a heroic struggle for self-defence and self-preservation against the imposition of political oppression.[18] The 1895 Zeytun resistance was treated as a collective and national movement. According to Bastadjian, it was a victory gained against the Ottoman administration that left a considerable mark on the European powers.

The massacres of November 1895 in Aintab were remembered as *Balta Senesi* (The Year of the Ax), as most Armenians were killed by blunt instruments – though firearms were also used.[19] The exact number of victims is unknown. According to various records, between 300 and 400 people were killed from 16 November to 19 November in Aintab[20] out of an Armenian population of 15,390 recorded in the 1895 Yearbook of Aleppo.[21] Due to the self-defence activities and the efforts of the Hnchakian leadership, the casualties were relatively lower in Aintab in comparison to other cities and towns in the region of Cilicia. As described earlier, Aintab already had an administrative organization in place; new and young forces were incorporated into this structure.[22]

Activities of the SDHP in Aintab after the 1908 Young Turk Revolution

After Abdülhamid II's abolishment of the Constitution and the Parliament in 1878, a group of reform-oriented political activists called the Young Turks, led by a network of exiles and reformers, established the Committee of Union and Progress (CUP) in 1889. During the summer of 1908, the CUP convinced the commanders of the Ottoman Third Army in Macedonia to revolt against the sultan. They threatened to march on Constantinople unless the group's demands were met. As a result, the sultan announced the restoration of the Constitution and established a parliamentary government, led by members of the CUP. More importantly, on 24 July 1908, civil and religious liberties were guaranteed to all citizens.[23] Shortly after the revolution, new political currents and empire-wide political changes resonated strongly in Aintab. With the declaration of the Second Constitutional era, the SDHP officially proclaimed itself as a political party in Aintab. It also had ardent members in various schools, including the Atenagan College and Cilicia Djemaran.[24]

In general, Armenians benefitted from the Constitution more than any other ethnic group.[25] Armenian language newspapers were freely published on all subjects, including articles on political, national, local, ideological and historical issues. Prior forms of censorship ceased and Armenian history and literature came into prominence. Poetry, odes and dramas on the national past were published and performed. Above all, critiques of the regime and its officials became possible.[26] Hnchakians also expanded their publishing and cultural activities in Aintab. Their activities engaged young Armenians. Prominent Hnchakians also visited Aintab. For instance, Paramaz (Matteos Sarkissian), a prominent leader of the party, enlightened Aintab party members and sympathizers about the new principles of the constitutional regime (equality, freedom and brotherhood) and the need to protect those principles.[27] He advised Hnchakian members to organize under any circumstances since he believed that the CUP would not abide by those principles. Therefore, for Paramaz, Armenians should always be alert and armed.

At the end of the school year, Central Turkey College discovered that Armenian students had formed a secret revolutionary society. Students who had allied with the local Armenian population in Aintab threatened to strike and promote their cause against the local Young Turk authorities. Approximately 200 individuals, almost all Apostolic and Protestant Armenians, belonged to the society. The president of the College, John Merrill, was forced to address the issue in a way that would placate growing CUP discontent with the American institution without ostracizing the local Armenian community. Following a recommendation from the faculty, Merrill closed the college for six weeks. When the college reopened, he refused to admit any students who possessed a connection to the society.[28]

'We had met our college difficulty firmly and settled it wisely', Merrill wrote to the Board of Trustees after the incident.[29] Because of this, he believed, the college had been spared further chastising from Constantinople. He continued: 'Had the college been full of young Armenian revolutionaries and the Turks of the city full of suspicions towards us and the Armenians . . . I do not believe the local government could have kept order.'[30] In Merrill's mind, the college had done all it could to promote order and maintain neutrality between the Armenian Christian population and the Young Turks. The reaction, while 'firm', did not dispel Turkish suspicions towards the institution. Missionaries in Aintab did not understand, asserts Joseph Grabill, that 'the existence of the society at Central Turkey, regardless of the school's disciplining it, convinced many Turks of missionary complicity in the Armenian insurrection'.[31]

Prior to the massacres that occurred in Adana and its outskirts in April 1909 and caused the death of over 20,000 Armenians,[32] the general political climate in Aintab was tense and volatile. On 14 April 1909, one of the officials of Aleppo's post office informed representatives of the SDHP and the ARF (Armenian Revolutionary Federation) about the Adana massacres. Representatives in Aleppo reported the unfortunate incidents that took place in Adana to both party administrators in Aintab and warned them to immediately leave everything aside and to take precautions in order to prevent the occurrence of similar massacres in the city. When the Armenians of Aintab heard the terrible news of the massacres, they immediately joined their forces and prepared for self-defence. Excitement over the declaration of the Constitution and freedom had completely faded and political fault lines had come to the surface. Along with the ARF, Hnchaks used all their efforts to supply weapons in order to put a strong self-defence against any potential attacks by the mob.[33]

The ideal positions and sites for self-defence from the residential areas on the west side of the city were established. The Armenian section of the district was divided into different zones, and at each post a band of fighters were stationed to stand guard day and night. Strategic locations were selected as self-defence positions.[34] Led by Hnchaks, Armenians organized in their assigned positions for a week during which no violent incidents occurred. Nerses Hagopian, a well-known Dashnak, states that eventually they received news that Turkish notables of the city were holding meetings with various groups and discussing preparations for massacres. According to rumours, some among the Turkish community opposed a potential massacre.[35] Since Armenians were no longer as defenceless and disorganized as they had been in November of 1895, 'the time for such cheap plundering, looting and easy slaughtering had now passed'.[36] Thus, no massacre took place in Aintab. The Armenians did not meet the fate of those in Adana and its surroundings and the city itself stayed relatively calm.[37] Despite the existence of a fragile ethno-religious coexistence, the Armenians of Aintab continued strengthening themselves against a potential onslaught.

On 11 April 1909, the annual meeting of the Evangelical Union (Protestants) was supposed to be held in the city of Adana with the participation of a dozen professors, teachers and respectable figures from Aintab's Protestant community. The group included such people as Professors Sarkis Levonian[38] and Setrak Ekmekjian from the Central Turkey College, as well as Pastors Zhamgochian, Bedrossian, Kuyuumdjian and Hagop Effendi Simjian.[39] On their way to Adana, they were burnt alive in Osmaniye's Protestant Church on 14 April 1909.[40] Among those killed were twenty-six leaders of thirty-three different Protestant congregations, pastors, ministers, delegates and professors, including Levonian.[41]

Hagopian cites a Turkish leader of Aintab who stated following this incident: 'You Armenians, you covered a long distance in modernism. We weren't able to follow your lead; we weren't able to rise up to your level . . . So we need to slaughter you every 20-30 years, to make you run with pace!'[42] This speech reflects the 'resentment' and 'envy' Muslim Turks had towards the overwhelming success of Armenians in the political, social and economic realms. To that end, it affirms the existence of such a mindset.

In mid-April, the Turkish muleteer who had gone with the Aintab delegates to Adana reported that all Armenians were killed in Osmaniye.[43] Having heard this terrible news, American missionary Fred Shepard wanted to leave for Hassan Beyli in order to help the poor over there, but he was convinced otherwise by his native and foreign friends who insisted him to stay, since a massacre might occur at any moment in Aintab too. The situation in the town was critical.[44]

The Severed Head Incident (Kelleci Olayı/Kesik Baş Vakası)

In the post-Adana massacres, there was another specific event in Aintab that further agitated the Muslim community, thereby escalating interethnic tensions in a way that could have led to a massacre similar to that of Adana. This attempt, however, failed. The event was called 'Kelleci Olayı/Kesik Baş Vakası' (The Severed Head Incident) among the people of the city.[45] Given the period and historical context that increased the level of violence against Armenians and led to massacres in Adana and its surrounding areas, it is important to dwell upon this event. It embodies the cautious relations between Armenians and Muslims and shows the tense state of relations between two different ethno-religious elements in Aintab.

In April, rumours of trouble broke out in Aintab. On 3 May 1909, a basket holding a severed head was thrown into the lot adjoining the Armenian Church in the Armenian Quarter, leaving the impression that an Armenian had murdered a Turk. The severed head was unrecognizable. A Turkish woman claimed that she saw a dead body missing its head in a place called 'Boklu Bostan', close to the church's neighbourhood.[46] This same woman cried out, 'Infidels killed this Muslim, cut his head off, and threw it to the garden', and ran to the Turkish neighbourhood wailing to break the news.[47] Her cries spread around the whole city. A number of police officers paid a visit to the church and took the severed head to the governor's palace, where the deputy governorate and the police headquarters were located. Upon hearing the news, the agitated Turks were filled with anger towards local Armenians. In response, Armenians closed their shops and withdrew to their homes. As previously decided, all Hnchak and Dashnak youth took their positions and prepared for an attack.[48] The *kaymakam* (local prefect), Ali Kemal Bey, demanded from the Armenian community to hand over the murderers.

Nerses Hagopian, a witness of this incident, noted how the Turks disrupted peace in the city. Armenians raised several questions to the kaymakam about the presence of the Turkish woman, who saw the dead body, at the location on a Monday morning. Furthermore, they wondered how she knew that the severed head belonged to 'a Turk'. However, Ali Kemal Bey insisted that they had looked into those questions and the killer had already confessed to his crime.[49] The Turkish-Muslim mob was adamant on taking revenge on Armenians. Meanwhile, an old Muslim woman approached the government palace asking to see the severed head. Upon examining the head closely, she discovered that one of the teeth was missing. Immediately, she recalled that her son had had a tooth removed the previous week and got up from her seat asserting, 'This is my son.'[50] Her son had been missing for two days. This further complicated the situation, for this woman clearly stated that the severed head belonged to her son. She blamed her son-in-law, who was also her son's business associate, for this crime. The police chief and other policemen showed up at his shop and arrested him. It was evident that the severed head came from the son-in-law's house, on the basis of the bloodstains found in his shop.⁵¹ Moreover, it was not hard to find the body, which was covered with a thin layer of dirt inside the stable of the brother-in-law's house. The arms and legs of the dead man were recovered in the Turkish cemetery nearby. Ultimately, the murderer was caught and brought to prison in shackles. Armenians were pleased with this result, for they were aware that they had narrowly escaped their fate.⁵² Yet, in any event, the self-defence activities of the Hnchaks were well-organized in the city against any potential attack.

The perpetrator of the 'severed head' case was tried in Aleppo. Many Aintab Armenians and Turks were present at the court. Known to be fond of Armenians, a prominent member of the local elite, Ahmed Agha (Deli Ahmed), also attended the hearings. At that time, killing someone – the act of murder – was punished by execution. Ahmed Agha and *kaymakam* Kemal Bey worked tirelessly to discover the truth and calm the agitated Muslims, who had been told that an Armenian had murdered a Muslim.⁵³ In addition, Muslim inhabitants, and administrators of the district, as well as the firm stance of the local CUP rulers played an important role in preventing the likelihood of anti-Armenian violence. Their efforts were appreciated by Armenians.⁵⁴ Kemal Bey used all his power to prevent the outbreak of violence in Aintab.⁵⁵ He was later rewarded with a letter of appreciation by the governor of the Province of Aleppo for his great efforts to maintain peace and public safety.⁵⁶ Additionally, Ahmed Agha succeeded in having the murderer of the 'severed head' case hanged at Arasa Market Square of Aintab in public view.⁵⁷

After the trial and execution, the tension between both communities was relatively eased; economic life resumed, and affairs became somewhat normal. Construction and related businesses started growing with new neighbourhoods. The district expanded towards the west, making valuable the lands that were once unavailable for residence. Compared to the previous year, there was a remarkable improvement in terms of living standards. Therefore, the relations between the two groups evolved into a 'relative state of normalcy'.

* * *

The next six years following the declaration of the Constitution was a constructive period of economic, cultural and educational improvement for Aintab – especially for Aintab Armenians. Equality, freedom and fraternity in the post-revolutionary period also entailed equality in the service of the ethno-religious groups in the army. The Armenians had wholeheartedly accepted the principle of enlisting in the Ottoman army. Additionally, the CUP government's decision to make military service mandatory for non-Muslims in 1909 had its consequences for the Armenians of Aintab. Among various positive developments to integrate Armenians into Ottoman society was the opportunity to have Armenians join the army and rise in its ranks and enrol in military schools. For them, military conscription meant a reaffirmation of equal rights among the groups. In the aftermath of the Adana Massacre, the ARF's relations with the CUP became more problematic, even though they signed an agreement of cooperation on 3 August 1909. According to Hovhannes Araradian, one of the prominent representatives of the ARF in Aintab, after the massacres in Adana an atmosphere of perpetual distrust reigned in the relations between the two parties.[58] The massacre undermined ARF's commitment to the constitutional process, as well as a possible alliance between both of them.[59] The official relations established by the initial freedom of the Second Constitutional Period eventually gave way to insincerity.

By 1915, the SDHP of Aintab was composed of 28–30 well-organized groups.[60] Each group consisted of seven to eleven members including the youth from the Atenagan College, Cilicia Djemaran and the Central Turkey College.[61] In addition, the Aintab Hnchakian branch had its own student and sports unions, women's clubs and auditoriums for conferences and lectures. It was the centre for Hnchakian committees in Urfa, Marash, Zeytun, Kilis, Birecik, Antioch, Kessab and Aleppo.[62] The SDHP of Aintab did not have peaceful relations with the Armenian Patriarchate at Constantinople and was always considered a rival to the Diocese.

On 29 April 1915, the CUP government sent orders to the local authorities, including those of Aintab that, especially considering the events in Zeytun, Bitlis, Sivas and Van, Armenian leaders were to be arrested and kept under supervision throughout the country.[63] According to such orders, all Dashnak and Hnchak committees and organizations were to be dissolved, their newspapers closed and their leaders arrested and brought before military tribunals. All Hnchak representatives in Aintab were arrested and imprisoned.[64] Those members who were not imprisoned were sent to work in the labour battalions. Almost everyone who remained in the city was deported to Deir el-Zor along with their families. Only one-third of the deportees managed to survive and return to the city.

In lieu of a conclusion: The post-genocide period (1918–22)

In the Sykes-Picot agreement, concluded on 19 May 1916, France and Britain carved up the Arab territories of the former Ottoman Empire into spheres of influence. Under this agreement, the Syrian coast and modern-day Lebanon went to France, while Britain would take direct control over central and southern Mesopotamia. Based on the Sykes-Picot agreement and the seventh article of the Mudros Armistice (30 October 1918), British forces occupied Aintab in December of the same year. The primary and most urgent tasks of the occupation forces were to facilitate the comeback of Armenians to their homes, to restitute their properties and assets and to find and return the Armenian women and children who had been held in Muslim households to their families or relatives. Armenian survivors started to return to their hometowns in December 1918. Some Armenians, including those of Aintab, chose to return to Cilicia. The Kilis refugees were the first to return.[65] In January 1919, other convoys of Armenians from Dörtyol, Mersin, Tarsus, Alexandretta, Kırık Han, Hajin (Hacin) and Toprakkalı began returning by train with the help and organization of the Armenian National Union (hereafter ANU) in Aleppo.[66] Moreover, the Ministry of Interior requested the Ministry of War to send 2,000 liras as Mobilization Allowance (*Seferberlik Tahsisatı*) for Aintab Armenians in order to compensate for their return expenses.[67]

In January 1919, the Allied High Command decided to repatriate all Armenian deportees from camps in Syria and Palestine to their hometowns in Anatolia. The majority of those survivors were natives of Cilicia. Among the deportees concentrated in Aleppo, some 6,000 came from Aintab and 3,000 from Kilis.[68] In early February, the process of repatriation intensified in Aintab. According to statistics provided by the Greek Ecumenical and Armenian Patriarchates early in 1919, there were 430 Armenians who had returned to Aintab.[69] On 12 May 1919, the director of the Central Service of Armenian Repatriation issued another order for the repatriation of Marash and Aintab refugees.[70] By 31 May 1919, 4,221 Armenians had returned to Aintab.[71] Between 1 January and 20 July 1919, a total of 5,607 Armenian refugees were repatriated to Aintab.[72]

The exact number of Aintab Armenians who returned to their homeland is unknown. There are various contradictory figures regarding the number of returnees from both Armenian and Turkish sources. According to Turkish sources, there were approximately 18,000 Muslims and 37,000 Armenians in Aintab in 1918-19, and the number of Armenians who returned with the support of the British was around 25,000.[73] Based on Armenian sources, overall, 18,000 Armenian survivors managed to return to Aintab by the end of 1919.[74] Additionally, 1,500 Armenians from Sivas, Gürün and Kayseri, as well as 600-700 Armenian orphans from various places, came to Aintab.[75] In 1920, these estimates were very important for the ANU Committee of Aintab, as it used the numbers to calculate the distribution of food rations as equally and economically as possible.[76] The Aintab branch of the Hnchakian Party played a pivotal role in helping Armenians return to Aintab.

On 15 October 1919, the British decided to cede the city to the French by signing the Syrian Agreement with the French government.[77] According to this agreement, the French forces would replace the British in October 1919, a situation that disrupted the restoration process. Local authorities became reluctant to return the Armenian properties to the survivors, even if ordered to do so by the Ministry of Interior. Occasionally, houses were returned to their rightful owners, but in most cases local authorities refused to evict the present occupants. Additionally, the rise of the Kemalist nationalist movement in the city in 1919-20 put a halt to the restitution process. In the face of French occupation, local nationalist-Kemalist forces instigated an armed struggle.

Over the course of the Kemalist onslaught on Aintab, Armenians systematically organized and fought. An administrative body named the National Union was formed with representatives of the three denominations (Orthodox, Protestant and Catholic) and three political parties (ARF, SDHP and ADL) for the purpose of managing the community and its religious affairs. Fr. Nerses Tavukjian became the president of the National Union.[78] As the supreme authority, the National Union formed a municipal council, police force, central provisions committee, judiciary body, sanitary commission, firefighters' group, financial committee and a group to distribute flyers. The Military Committee, which had come into being two months earlier, was under the command of two well-known Hnchaks, Adour Levonian and Avedis Kalemkarian.[79] Another noted Hnchak, Hagop Murekian, undertook an important mission and had a significant position in the National Union.[80] Other members of the National Union included Dashnaks and Ramkavars. In addition, there were four Hnchaks who constituted the Military Central Board: Avedis Kalemkerian, Adour Levonian, Kevork Baboyan and Rupen Yaghsizian.[81]

Throughout the Kemalist-French struggle in Aintab, which began on 1 April 1920, and ended with the Kemalist defeat and the city's surrender to the French military forces on 9 February 1921, the Armenians of Aintab allied with the French. However, on 4 November 1921, the French commanders made an official declaration to leave Aintab to the Turkish authorities, which created an atmosphere of great panic among the Armenians who relied on the French to help them against the much-feared Kemalist forces.[82] On 25 December 1921, when the French forces started leaving Aintab, the departure of Armenians from the city gained momentum. In early December 1921, 8,000 Armenians managed to leave Aintab by their own means.[83] The final French contingents left on 4 January 1922.[84] Yet, despite their victory, the French ultimately decided to retreat from the city in February 1921, abandoning it to the Kemalist forces in accordance with the Treaty of Ankara from 20 October 1921.

The activities of the Hnchakian Party in Aintab, along with the Dashnaks and Ramkavars, came to an end with the complete departure of the Armenians from the city in 1921–2, The Hnchaks spent all their efforts into helping Armenians leave the city securely for Aleppo and Beirut.

The Aintab branch of the SDHP was always an effective and influential political entity with its well-established structure and cadre in the political, social and cultural walks of Armenian life throughout the late nineteenth and early twentieth century. Even though the party suffered from internal strife in the aftermath of the Hamidian massacres in the 1890s, leading to the rise of the Dashnaks in the city, the SDHP continued to be a key political actor. For the genocide survivors, it used all its organizational capacity and manpower to facilitate their return to Aintab in 1918–19 and at such a critical period, never shied away from collaborating with the ARF for that purpose.

Notes

1 Louise Nalbandian, *The Armenian Revolutionary Movement: The Development of Armenian Political Parties through the Nineteenth Century* (Berkeley: University of California Press), 104–8; Ronald G. Suny, *Looking Toward Ararat: Armenia in Modern History* (Bloomington: Indiana University Press, 1993), 72–5.

2 For some of the works that discuss the establishment of the Hnchakian Party; see Abel Manoukian, *Hayrenik'i Azatagrut'ean Banakin Hamozuatz Zinuornerě* (Beirut: Araz Printing Press, 2014); Gegham Hovhannisyan, *Hnch'akean Kusakts'ut'ean Patmut'iwn (1887-1915)* (Yerevan: History Institute of the National Academy of Sciences, 2012); Arsen Gidur, *Patmut'iwn S.T. Hnch'akean Kusakts'ut'ean, 1887-1962*, vol. I (Beirut: Shirag Press, 1962); Rupen Khan-Azad, *Hushardz'an Nuiruatz Sots'eal Demokrat Hnch'akean Kusakts'ut'ean K'arasnameakin* (Paris: Imprimerie Turabian, 1930). I would like to thank Varak Ketsemanian for drawing my attention to these invaluable sources. See also Toygun Altıntaş, 'The Placard Affair and the Ankara Trial: The Hnchak Party and the Hamidian Regime in Central Anatolia, 1892-93', *Journal of the Ottoman and Turkish Studies Association* 4, no. 2 (2017): 309–37.

3 Anahide Ter Minassian, 'Nationalism and Socialism in the Armenian Revolutionary Movement (1887-1912)', in *Transcaucasia, Nationalism and Social Change*, ed. Ronald Grigor Suny (Ann Arbor: The University of Michigan Press, 1996), 150;

Varak Ketsemanian, 'Ideologies, Paradoxes, and Fedayis in the Late Ottoman Empire: Historical Challenges, and Methodological Problems in the Study of the Armenian Revolutionary Movement (1890-1896)', in *Armenians and Kurds in the Late Ottoman Empire*, eds. Ümit Kurt and Ara Sarafian (Fresno: The Press, at California State University, 2020), 122.

4 Kevork A. Sarafian (ed.), *Patmutʻiwn Ayntʻepi Hayotsʻ*, vol. II (Los Angeles: Union of the Armenians of Aintab, 1953), 943-4.

5 *Papers of the American Board of Commissioners for Foreign Missions* (hereafter ABCFM), reel 668-371, no. 468/1732; Sarafian, *Patmutʻiwn Ayntʻapi Hayotsʻ*, vol. I, 554–5; Sarafian, *A Briefer History of Aintab* (Los Angeles: Union of the Armenians of Aintab, 1957), 52; Turan Baytop, *Antep'in Öncü Hekimleri: Merkezi Türkiye Koleji Tıp Bölümü ve Antep Amerikan Hastanesi* (İstanbul: SEV Yayınları, 2003), 14. For the list of alumni of the College from Aintab see ABCFM, reel 668-400, no. 497/98; 497/99; 497/500; 497/501; 497/502.

6 Kevork H. Barsumian, *Patmutʻiwn Ayntʻapi H. H. Dashnaktsʻutʻean 1898-1922* (Aleppo: Tigris, 1957), 20.

7 Sarafian, *Patmutʻiwn Ayntʻepi Hayotsʻ*, vol. II, 936; Levon Chormisian, *Hamapatker Arewmtahayotsʻ Mēk Daru Patmutʻean,* Vol. 1, 1878–1908 (Beirut: Shirag Press, 1974), 232.

8 Sarafian, *Patmutʻiwn Ayntʻepi Hayotsʻ*, vol. II, 937.

9 Sarafian, *Patmutʻiwn Ayntʻepi Hayotsʻ*, vol. I, 665–70, 740–53; Chormisian, *Hamapatker Arevmtahayotsʻ Mēk Daru Patmutʻean*, 232.

10 Sarafian, *Patmutʻiwn Ayntʻepi Hayotsʻ*, vol. II, 944–5; Chormisian, *Hamapatker Arevmtahayotsʻ Mēk Daru Patmutʻean*, 232.

11 Chormisian, *Hamapatker Arevmtahayotsʻ Mēk Taru Patmutʻean*, 234.

12 Soghomon B. Bastajian, 'Zeytuni Apstambutʻiwnĕ ew Hnchʻakean Kusaktsʻutiwně', in Sarafian, *Patmutʻiwn Ayntʻepi Hayotsʻ*, vol. II, 936; Chormisian, *Hamapatker Arevmtahayotsʻ Mēk Taru Patmutʻean*, 231. At the time of Aghasi's visit to Aintab, Hnchakian local 'cells' were led by Armenag Nigoghos Nazaretian, Hrant Sulahian, Berj Momjian and Soghomon Bastajian. See Elie H. Nazarian, *Patmagirkʻ Nazarean Gerdastani (1475-1988)* (Beirut: Atlas, 1988), 162. Armenag Nigoghos Nazaretian would remain a Hnchak member until 1909. Later, he abjured of his revolutionary ideas and joined the Ramkavar Party.

13 Sarafian, *Patmutʻiwn Ayntʻepi Hayotsʻ*, vol. II, 936 and Barsumian, *Patmutʻiwn Ayntʻapi H. H. Dashnaktsʻutʻean,* 315. It should be noted that certain section of the Armenian community, particularly conservative notables, professors in the Central Turkey College, and Protestant clergymen (especially Manase Papazian among others) opposed to aid the Armenian resistance in Zeytun. They contended that since Ottoman military forces outnumbered Armenians, it would be impossible to resist them. They firmly believed that this movement would put the lives of many defenceless Armenians in jeopardy and cause their destruction. See Sarafian, *Patmutʻiwn Ayntʻepi Hayotsʻ*, vol. II, 949.

14 Ibid., 949.

15 He was a professor and faculty member of the Central Turkey College. In 1915, he became a civil representative of the Protestant community for the Ottoman Empire with a residence at Constantinople, where his family also joined him. ABCFM, reel 667-252, 287/1732.

16 Nazarian, *Patmagirkʻ Nazarean Gerdastani (1475-1988)*, 145; Chormisian, *Hamapatker Arevmtahayotsʻ Mēk Daru Patmutʻean*, 231-2. Artin Harutiun Nazaretian

was the second son of Kara Nazar Agha, who was one of the most well-known, affluent and respected figures of Aintab and its Armenian community. Primarily dealing in jewellery, Nazaretian family's assets in Aintab were remarkable. The house of the Nazaretian family was one of the largest and most magnificent residences of the city at the time.

17 Nazarian, *Patmagirk' Nazarean Gerdastani (1475-1988)*, 140; Barsumian, *Patmut'iwn Aynt'api H. H. Dashnakts'ut'ean*, 33; Chormisian, *Hamapatker Arevmtahayots' Mēk Daru Patmut'ean*, 234.
18 Sarafian, *Patmut'iwn Aynt'api Hayots'*, vol. II, 934.
19 Emre Barlas, *Doktor Mecid Barlas'ın Anıları* (İstanbul: Cinius Yayınları, 2010), 12; Şakir Sabri Yener, *Gaziantep Yakın Tarihinden Notlar Gaziantep Vilayet Merkezinin 76 Sene Evveline Kadar Olan Mahalli Maarif Hareketlerinin Kısa bir Tarihçesi* (Gaziantep: Gaziyurt Matbaası, 1968), 368; J. Rendel Harris and Helen B. Harris, *Letters from the Scenes of the Recent Massacres in Armenia* (London: James Nisbet & Co., Limited, 1897), 32. For a complete account of Hamidian massacres in Aintab in November 1895, see Ümit Kurt, 'Reform and Violence in the Hamidian Era: The Political Context of the 1895 Armenian Massacres in Aintab', *Holocaust and Genocide Studies* 32, no. 3 (2018): 404–23.
20 Sarafian, *Patmut'iwn Aynt'epi Hayots'*, vol. I, 923; Rev. Edwin Munsell Bliss, *Turkey and the Armenian Atrocities* (New York: Edgewood Publishing Company, 1896), 455–6; 553; F. D. Shepard to Alice Shepard, 18 November 1895, Houghton *ABCFM* 16.9.5 and Fuller to Smith, 25 December 1895, Houghton *ABCFM* 16.9.5; Harris and Harris, *Letters from the Scenes of the Recent Massacres in Armenia*, 32; Saunders to Terrell, 27 November 1895, United States Department of State, *Papers Relating to the Foreign Relations of the United States* (Hereafter FRUS), 1895, Vol. II, 1390; Rev. H. George Filian, *Armenian and Her People* (Hartford: Conn. American Publishing Company, 1896), 295; M. S. Gabrielian, *Armenia: A Martyr Nation. A Historical Sketch of the Armenian People from Tradition Times to the Present Tragic Days* (New York: Fleming H. Revell, 1918), 257–8; Turkey, no. 2, 1896, 318–37; Shadid Bey, *Islam, Turkey and Armenia and How They Happened* (St. Louis: C.B. Woodward Company, 1898), 201; E. Antoine, *Les Massacres d'Arménie* (Bruxelles: O. Schepens, 1897), 72–9; J. Arman Kirakossian, *British Diplomacy and the Armenian Question from the 1830s to 1914* (Princeton and London: Gomidas Institute Books, 2003), 261.
21 The total population of Aintab was recorded as 84,135 out of which 11,703 were Gregorian Armenians, 3,528 Protestant Armenians and 307 Catholic Armenians. *Salname-i Vilayet-i Halep, Ayıntap Kazası*, 1313/1895, eds. Cengiz Eroğlu et al. (Ankara: Global Strateji Enstitüsü, 2007), 187.
22 Sarafian, *Patmut'iwn Aynt'api Hayots'*, vol. II, 936.
23 For studies regarding the causes, initial phases of preparation and execution of the Young Turk Revolution of 1908, see Şerif Mardin, *Jön Türklerin Siyasi Fikirleri, 1895-1908* (Ankara: Türkiye İş Bankası, 1964); Şükrü Hanioğlu, *Bir Siyasal Örgüt Olarak Osmanlı İttihad ve Terakki Cemiyeti ve Jön Türklük* (İstanbul: İletişim Yayınları, 1986); Aykut Kansu, *1908 Devrimi* (İstanbul: İletişim, 2006); idem, *The Young Turks in Opposition* (New York: Oxford University Press, 1995); Feroz Ahmad, *The Young Turks: The Committee of Union and Progress in Turkish Politics, 1908-1914* (Oxford: Clarendon Press, 1969); Eric Jan Zürcher, *Unionist Factor: The Role of the Committee of Union and Progress in the Turkish National Movement, 1905-1926* (Leiden: E.J. Brill, 1984); Nader Sohrabi, *Revolution and Constitutionalism in the Ottoman Empire and Iran* (Cambridge: Cambridge University Press, 2011).

24 Barsumian, *Patmut'iwn Aynt'api H. H. Dashnakts'u'tean*, 23.
25 Sarafian, *Patmut'iwn Aynt'epi Hayots'*, vol. I, 972, 974.
26 Ibid., 974–5.
27 Ibid., 950.
28 Joseph L. Grabill, *Protestant Diplomacy and the Near East: Missionary Influence on American Policy, 1810-1927* (Minneapolis: University of Minnesota Press, 1971), 48.
29 Letter from John Merrill to the Trustees of Central Turkey College, 18 May 1909, *Research Publication from Wesleyan University Library*, ABCFM 16.9.6.1, 1817-1919, Unit 5, Reel 673, vol. 1, no. 1380.
30 Ibid.
31 Grabill, *Protestant Diplomacy in the Near East*, 48.
32 On the Adana Massacres, see Bedross Der Matossian, *The Horrors of Adana: Revolution and Violence in the Early Twentieth Century* (Stanford: Stanford University Press, 2022); Raymond Kévorkian with the collaboration of Paul B. Paboudjian, 'Les massacres de Cilicie d'avril 1909', in Kévorkian, *La Cilicie (1909-1921) des massacres d'Adana au mandat français* (Revue d'Histoire Armenienne Contemporaine, Tome III, 1999), 7–248; Hrachik Simonian, *The Destruction of Armenians in Cilicia, April 1909* (London: Gomidas Institute, 2012), and Hagop H. Terzian, *Cilicia 1909: The Massacres of Armenians* (London: Gomidas Institute, 2009).
33 Sarafian, *Patmut'iwn Aynt'api Hayots'*, vol. II, 978; Hovhannes Araradian, 'H. H. Dashnakts'ut'iwnĕ Aynt'api Mēj 1908-1915', in Sarafian, *Patmut'iwn Aynt'epi Hayots'*, vol. II, 988; Barsumian, *Patmut'iwn Aynt'api H. H. Dashnakts'ut'ean*, 37.
34 Sarafian, *Patmut'iwn Aynt'epi Hayots'*, vol. II, 978.
35 Ibid., 979.
36 Ibid.
37 Ibid., 538; Frank Andrews Stone, 'The Educational "Awakening" Among the American Evangelicals of Aintab, Turkey: 1845-1915', *Armenian Review* 35, no. 1–137 (1982): 43.
38 Sarkis Levonian, a venerable man and an illustrious person, was commonly known as 'Sarkis Hoja'. After studying at the Central Turkey College, he went to the United States in 1880 and studied three years at Yale University. He became a very capable and distinguished professor at the Central Turkey College, where he was chairman of the mathematics department. He was a highly respected leader of the Armenian Evangelicals, speaking often in their churches. See Vartan S. Bilezikian, *Abraham Hoja of Aintab* (Winona Lake: Light and Life Press, 1952), 44.
39 ABCFM, reel 668-463; January 1911.
40 Sarafian, *Patmut'iwn Aynt'epi Hayots'*, vol. II, 538; Bilezikian, *Abraham Hoja of Aintab*, 42–4; Stone, 'The Educational "Awakening" Among the American Evangelicals of Aintab, Turkey: 1845-1915', 42.
41 Letter from John Merrill to the Trustees of Central Turkey College, 18 May 1909. ABCFM 16.9.1, 1817-1919, Unit 5, Reel 673, vol. 1, no. 1324.
42 Sarafian, *Patmut'iwn Aynt'epi Hayots'*, vol. II, 979. It is very interesting that the same kind of conversation took place early in August 1908 between Ömer Naci Bey, a member of the Ittihad's Central Committee responsible for inspecting the local CUP branches, and Dashnak representatives in Van. In this conversation, Naci declared in a humorous tone: 'We Turks are lagging far behind European civilization, whereas you [Armenians] have made considerable progress. If it is true that it is indispensable to move forward together and live together as brothers, you will have to pause for a while and wait for us to catch up. If you don't, we shall have to latch on to your skirts

to prevent you from advancing.' See Vahan Papazian, *Im Husherě*, vol. II (Beirut: Hamazkayin Press, 1952), 225, in Raymond Kévorkian, *A Complete History of Genocide* (London: I.B. Tauris, 2011), 60.
43 F. D. Shepard, 'Personal Experience in Turkish Massacres and Relief Work', *The Journal of Race Development* 1, no. 3 (1911): 329.
44 Ibid., 329; Alice Shepard Riggs, *Shepard of Aintab* (Princeton: Gomidas Institute Books / Taderon Press, 2001),118.
45 Sarafian, *Patmut'iwn Aynt'epi Hayots'*, vol. II, 979; Barsumian, *Patmut'iwn Aynt'api H. H. Dashnakts'u'tean*, 36.
46 Sarafian, *Patmut'iwn Aynt'epi Hayots'*, vol. II, 1005; *Hay Ant'ēp*, vol. X, issue 6, no. 38 (1969): 12.
47 Sarafian, *Patmut'iwn Aynt'api Hayots'*, vol. II, 979, 1005; *Hay Ant'ēp*, vol. X, issue 6, no. 38 (1969): 12.
48 Sarafian, *Patmut'iwn Aynt'epi Hayots'*, vol. II, 951–2, 979–80; Barsumian, *Patmut'iwn Aynt'api H. H. Dashnakts'u'tean*, 37.
49 Sarafian, *Patmut'iwn Aynt'api Hayots'*, vol. II, 980.
50 Ibid., 980, 1005; *Hay Ant'ēp*, vol. X, issue 6, no. 38 (1969): 12.
51 Ibid.
52 Kevork Barsumian claims that this incident, known as the matter of 'Kelleci' in Aintab, was a Turkish fraud. Aintab's brave Cretan district governor explained that Armenians were able to evade a potential massacre without any loss, thanks to the testimony and insistence of the victim's mother and to the great sacrifices of Hamal Sarkis Jinbashian from the ARF. Another significant point Barsumian makes is the fact that those who attempted to provoke the Muslim community against the Armenians and those who put this plan into action by using this murder as an excuse were 'fanatical Unionist murderers'. See Barsumian, *Patmut'iwn Aynt'api H. H. Dashnakts'u'tean*, 36.
53 Fred F. Goodsell, 'What Might Have Happened', *Missionary Herald*, 1909, 139.
54 See the telegram sent by Dr. Avedis Nakashian, an Aintab Armenian, to the newspaper *Tanin*. *Tanin*, 27 May 1909, no. 263, cited by Ramazan Erhan Güllü, *Antep Ermenileri: Sosyal-Siyasi ve Kültürel Hayatı* (Ankara: IQ Yayınları, 2010), 256.
55 BNu [Bibliotek Nubar]/Fonds A. Andonian, P.J.1/3, liasse 9, *Aintab*, ff? Ali Kemal Bey was a former kaymakam of Duma (Palestine) and appointed to Aintab as a replacement to Necmeddin Bey on 7 December 1908; see BOA.DH.MKT 2677/47, 1326 Za 13 [7 December 1908]; Barsumian, *Patmut'iwn Aynt'api H. H. Dashnakts'u'tean*, 37.
56 BOA.DH.MKT 2861/50, 1327 Cemaziyülahır 11 [30 June 1909]. Interestingly enough, the same Ali Kemal Bey was dismissed from his post because of the complaint about him when he was a kaymakam in Duma. Allegedly, he got involved in acts of corruption when he was the sub-prefect of the Duma district. Since an investigation was open for these accusations, he was discharged from his post as Aintab kaymakam. See DH.MKT 2906/10, 1327 Şaban 3 [20 August 1909] and DH.MKT 2910/20, 1327 Şaban 8 [25 August 1909].
57 Sarafian, *Patmut'iwn Aynt'epi Hayots'*, vol. II, 980.
58 Ibid., 987. Although the ARF supported the Young Turk Revolution, this involvement did not bring mutual trust between the two political forces. The ARF was the only Armenian party co-operating with the CUP, but as Şükrü Hanioğlu noted, 'The CUP papers and available Ottoman documents reveal that the joint CUP- Tashnagtsutiun revolutionary activities were very insignificant and that the CUP never trusted the

Tashnagtsutiun . . .'. Hanioğlu, *Preparation for a Revolution: The Young Turks 1902-1908* (Oxford: Oxford University Press, 2001), 207.
59 Raymond Kévorkian, *The Armenian Genocide* (London: I.B.Tauris, 2011), 74.
60 Sarafian, *Patmut'iwn Aynt'epi Hayots'*, vol. II, 985.
61 Ibid., 987. The Student Association of the Central Turkey College was always an important element in supporting the Hnchak activities of Aintab ARF. See, Barsumian, *Patmut'iwn Aynt'api H. H. Dashnakts'u'tean*, 46.
62 Ibid., 986.
63 BOA.DH.ŞFR 52/96-97-98, coded telegram from interior minister Talat to the Provinces of Edirne, Erzurum, Adana, Ankara, Aydın, Bitlis, Aleppo, Hüdavendigar [Bursa], Diyarbekir, Sivas, Trebizond, Konya, Mamuretülaziz, and Van, and to the provincial districts of Urfa, İzmit, Karahisar-ı Sahib [Afyon], Bolu, Canik, Karesi [Balıkesir], Kayseri, Marash, Niğde and Eskişehir, dated 24 April 1915.
64 Among them were Tatul Kupelian, Avedis Khandzedian (died in prison), Khoren Varjabedian (died in prison in 1920), Armenag Maksudian, Garabed Zarigian, Dikran Poladian (died in Der Zor in 1916), Doctor Nerses Baghdoyan, Hovhannes Piranian, Hagopian Nazarian, Rupen Yaghsizian, Kevork Baboian and Hagop Murekian.
65 *Taragir*, Aleppo, 25 December 1918. Detailed lists of potential repatriates originating from various localities are found in France, Archives du Ministère des Affaires Etrangères, Nantes, Beyrouth: Cilicie 1919-1921, Cilicie-Alep, cartons 319–31; APA, Files 42. Kilis was a district of Aintab in 1918.
66 Formed in Egypt in early 1917 and promoted by the Allies, the Armenian National Union (ANU) brought together an array of Armenian organizations and political parties. The French in Cilicia and the British in Syria recognized the need of interlocutors 'who could fairly claim to represent the diverse components of Armenian society'. As soon as the Mudros Armistice was signed, both General Edmund Allenby, commander of the Allied forces in the Near East, and Georges Picot, the French commissioner, 'encouraged the formation of the branches of the ANU in all of the Allied-occupied areas' in which 'there was an Armenian population'. In Cilicia, the ANU and the representative of the Paris-based Armenian National Delegation, Mihran Damadian, were – in the view of the French administration – quasi-official spokesmen for Armenian interests. Vahé Tachjian, 'The Cilician Armenians and French Policy, 1919-1921', in *Armenian Cilicia*, eds., Richard G. Hovannisian and Simon Payaslian (Costa Mesa: Mazda Publishers, 2008), 542, fn 4.
67 BCA/TİGMA 272.00.00.74.68.37.5, 9 January 1919.
68 Archives of the Armenian National Delegation (cited hereafter as AND), in the BNu/Fonds, Microfilm/1, 'Statistiques des Arméniens d'Alep'.
69 APC/APJ, PCI Bureau, 367, list of the regions where the Armenians and the Greeks were repatriated, cited in Kévorkian, *The Armenian Genocide*, 748.
70 Barsamian and Gedzvanian on behalf of Ehnesh refugees to Aleppo ANU chairman and members, 16 January 1919; Barsamian on behalf of twenty-five Ehnesh refugees to Aleppo ANU chairman and members, 13 February 1919, in Vahram L. Shemmassian, 'Repatriation of Armenian Refugees from the Arab Middle East, 1918-1920', in *Armenian Cilicia*, eds. Hovannisian and Payaslian, 424, fn 19. Clouscard (director of the Central Service of Armenian Repatriation), announcement in Armenian regarding repatriation of Armenians to Aintab and Maraş, 12 May 1919. See also Clouscard to President of Inter-Provincial Committee of Aleppo, 8 June 1919 (Ibid., 424, fn 19).
71 NARA, RG 84, vol. 83, *Correspondence, American Consulate, Aleppo, 1919*, Jackson, Political and Economic Conditions, 31 May 1919; NARA, RG 59, 867.00/897.

72 NARA, RG 59, 867.48/1316, Jackson to Secretary of State, 23 August 1919; Harutiun Simonian (ed.), *Haweluats: Aynt'api Hayots' Patmut'iwn* (Waltham: Mayreni Press, 1997), 105.
73 Uğurol Barlas, *Gaziantep Tıp Fakültesi Tarihi ve Azınlık Okulları* (Gaziantep: Gaziantep Kültür Derneği, 1971), 14; M. Oğuz Göğüş, *İlk İnsanlardan Bugüne Çeşitli Yönleriyle Gaziantep* (Ankara: Cihan Ofset, 1997), 69, 306; Sahir Üzel, *Gaziantep Savaşının İç Yüzü* (Ankara: Doğuş Matbaası, 1952), 7. Another local source claims that 50,000 Armenians gathered in Aintab after the British occupation of Aintab. *Gaziantep Kültür Dergisi* III, Issue 28 (10 April 1960): 89.
74 Barsumian, *Patmut'iwn Aynt'api H. H. Dashnakts'ut'ean*, 331. Archpriest Nerses Babayan who reached Aintab on November 21, 1919, from his exile estimated the Armenian population in Aintab at 17,000–18,000; see Yervant Babayan (ed.), *Pages from my Diary/Archpriest Der Nerses Babayan* (Los Angeles: April Publishers, 2000), 31.
75 Babayan, *Pages from my Diary/Archpriest Der Nerses Babayan*, 51.
76 Sarkis Karayan, 'On the Number of Armenians in Aintab in 1914', in *Patmut'iwn Aynt'api Hayots'*, vol. III, ed. Babayan (Los Angeles: Abril Publishers, 1994), 17. An administrative body named the Armenian National Union Committee of Aintab was formed in early 1919. The Armenian National Union was founded for the purpose of managing community and religious affairs in Aintab; see Sarafian, *Patmut'iwn Aynt'api Hayots'*, vol. I, 1080.
77 Yaşar Akbıyık, *Milli Mücadele'de Güney Cephesi (Maraş)* (Ankara: Kültür Bakanlığı, 1990), 48–52; Gotthard Jaeschke, *Kurtuluş Savaşı ile İlgili İngiliz Belgeleri* (Ankara: TTK, 1991), 46.
78 Babayan, *Pages from my diary/Archpriest Der Nerses Babayan*, 32.
79 Ibid., 34.
80 Barsumian, *Patmut'iwn Aynt'api H. H. Dashnakts'ut'ean*, 53.
81 Ibid., 65, 240.
82 BNu/Fonds, Notes Sur La Cilicie, 1; Hayastani Azkayin Arkhiv [Armenian National Archive], A letter from Catholicosate Deputy Der Nerses Tavukjian to Arshag Chobanian, 14 November 1921, Catalogue no. 430/1/842, 6. In his significant letter to Chobanian, who was in Paris at the time, Tavukjian underlined how they were abandoned by the French, who did not fulfil their promises to protect Armenian life and properties. See Ibid., 7–9. For a similar letter written by Nerses Tavukjian and sent to the president of the French Republic Council on 16 November 1921, see Hayastani Azgayin Arkhiv, A letter from the Catholicosate Deputy Nerses Tavukjian to the president of French Republic Council, Catalogue No: 430/1/844, 16 November 1921.
83 BNu/Fonds, Notes Sur La Cilicie, 1. As of 14 November 1921, according to the number given by Der Nerses Tavukjian, there were 8,500 Armenians in Aintab; see Hayastani Azgayin Arkhiv, A letter from Catholicosate Deputy Der Nerses Tavukjian to Arshak Chobanian, 14 November 1921, Catalogue No: 430/1/842, 9.
84 Vahé Tachjian, 'The Expulsion of Non-Turkish Ethnic and Religious Groups from Turkey to Syria during the 1920s and Early 1930s', in *Online Encyclopedia of Mass Violence,* ed. Jacques Semelin, 6. http://www.massviolence.org/IMG/article_PDF/The-expulsion-of-non-Turkish-ethnic-and-religious-groups.pdf. According to the report of British Consulate in Aleppo, as of November 1922 there were still 3,000 Armenians living in Aintab; see FO 371, 'Diplomatic Records: Report on the forces exile of the remaining Armenians from Aintab and Marash', 15 November 1922; Hayastani Azgayin Arkhiv, Catalogue No: 430/1/838, 1922.

8

Absolute Monarchy

The Social Democrat Hnchakian Revolutionary Episode in Armenian Musa Dagh during the 1890s

Vahram L. Shemmassian

Political awareness and the resultant revolutionary societies among Armenians in the Ottoman Empire during the late-nineteenth and early-twentieth century did not evolve in a vacuum. Fertile soil existed, especially in the interior provinces, where Armenians had been discriminated against and oppressed by the government and ordinary Muslims (mainly Turks and Kurds) alike. Countless complaints lodged with the government via the Armenian Patriarchate of Constantinople remained unanswered or inconsequential. Unable to obtain redress through legitimate means, some Armenian groups resorted to arms to defend their people, property and rights in general. The government's inaction and continued maltreatment also led those groups to seek European intervention in a bid to force the government to implement reforms. This move coincided with the European Powers' own, competing interests and agendas vis-à-vis the Ottoman Empire. Be that as it may, the Ottoman government reacted with wide-scale massacres of innocent Armenian civilians as punishment and paid only lip service for reforms when pressured further. Greatly concerned with this abysmal situation, Armenian revolutionary organizations played a crucial role in preaching and raising awareness about nationalism, pressuring the government to effect reforms, and/or carrying out an armed struggle to free the nation from the Ottoman yoke.

In the case of the Musa Dagh and Kesab (Kessab/Kasab) population, they seem to have identified themselves as Christian rather than Armenian, because they referred to their dialects, which were similar, as *Kistinek*, that is, the language of Christians.[1] This self-perception of belonging to a religious entity rather than a nation may be explained by a long period of isolation, surrounded by Muslims, from other Armenian concentrations within the Ottoman Empire.[2] But that self-characterization gradually transformed from a faith-based understanding to an ethno-national concept first through revolutionary societies.

The first Armenian revolutionary society that concerned itself with Musa Dagh was the Social Democrat Hnchakian Party (SDHP). Founded in August 1887 in Geneva, Switzerland, by Russian-Armenian students enrolled at various European universities, the party aimed at 'the political and national independence of Turkish Armenia', which could only be achieved through revolution. It entailed 'Propaganda, Agitation, Terror, Organization, and Peasant and Worker Activities'.[3] The SDHP was strongly nationalistic yet also Marxist in orientation,[4] a paradox that resulted in the split of the party after 1896.[5]

In 1890, the SDHP decided to study the situation in the region of Cilicia (located in the Adana and Aleppo provinces) with the specific aim of starting an uprising at Zeytun to attract European interest in the worsening situation of Armenians in the Ottoman Empire. Accordingly, the party designated Garabed Tursarkisian, alias Aghasi, as regional agent to prepare the groundwork for armed struggle.[6] Born in 1871 in Hajin, Aghasi, after finishing the local elementary school, attended the Central School in Constantinople. There he became acquainted with many prominent Armenian figures and was influenced by the prevalent revolutionary fervour. Targeted by the Turkish secret police for engaging in extra-legal activities, he left the empire for Marseille, France, and enrolled in evening classes to learn French. It was from this port city that he embarked on his mission to Cilicia.[7]

Landing at Beirut, Aghasi organized an SDHP chapter with five members. From there he crisscrossed northern Syria and Cilicia for the next two years, founding new cells or reinforcing existing ones. He visited Beylan, Soghuk Oluk, Geozelli, Nargizlik, Fartisli, Aleppo, Kilis, as well as Aintab, Dörtyol, Iskenderun/Alexandretta, Marash, Hasanbeyli and other localities.[8] During one of his stays in Iskenderun, he became aware of the existence of the Armenian villages of Musa Dagh and around Kesab. Travelling to Antioch forthwith, he met with Boghos Seferian, a member of the municipal Administrative Council and an SDHP sympathizer. Through Seferian, Aghasi established contact with two individuals from Musa Dagh, Mardir Isgenderian and Yesayi Garigian, both of whom joined the SDHP.[9]

Whatever the exact details, Aghasi returned to Iskenderun, recruited a group of fourteen men, and went back to Musa Dagh in July 1893.[10] During a rare encounter he met with Catholicos Mgrdich Kefsizian of Cilicia, who was holidaying at Haji Habibli and Chevlik by the sea near Kabusiye. Expressing his 'deepest sympathy' for the emancipatory cause, Kefsizian pledged 400 Ottoman liras which he could not deliver due to his untimely death.[11] Aghasi and company hid in caves to maintain secrecy, but ultimately came out into the open and established their headquarters at Kheder Beg. They also kept in touch with affiliates in Kilis, Aintab, Aleppo, Iskenderun, Dört Yol, Antioch and Kesab through an extensive network of communications, sometimes sending and or receiving as many as forty letters a week.[12]

The Ottoman government was aware of the presence of Armenian revolutionaries in Musa Dagh and Zeytun as early as February 1893.[13] In light of these developments, Mustafa Nedim Effendi, Judge of the Court of First Instance of Aleppo province, prepared 'to open a case against the revolutionaries'.[14]

The reported return of previously exiled revolutionaries to Musa Dagh in early June 1894 prompted the Intelligence Unit officer in the area to alert the 5th Army Command.[15] Four months later, in October, he provided new details about the twelve revolutionaries who were back and 'in cahoots with local villagers', adding: 'A certain Garigian is facilitating hideouts for arms and ammunition for them'. The officer had 'no doubt that these bandits are being influenced by foreign powers. At least this is what the government of Aleppo province thinks'.[16]

A year later, in July 1895, the Antioch government informed the Aleppo provincial headquarters that the 3rd Infantry Division under Colonel Muhammad Ali Effendi was in the Svedia area investigating Aghasi's clandestine activity. It was believed that Aghasi had about 150 foreigners plus some fugitives from justice under his command. 'Armed to the teeth' with weapons and ammunition smuggled by Armenian merchants conducting business between Antioch and Aleppo, they freely roamed Musa Dagh. Meeting several times, their leadership 'had taken decisions as to how, where, and when to operate, regardless of our [Ottoman] military presence in the area'. Antioch complained that 'we have been reporting on these activities for a long time now, but have yet to see a serious effort by you [Aleppo] regarding sending a definitive military force to take care of this issue'.[17] In August, Governor Raif put the number of 'protesting' men in Musa Dagh at 745, adding: 'It seems that they were affected by what happened in the Zeytun sector of Marash county [in Aleppo province] where their coreligionists had been brought to justice when anti-government actions took place there'.[18]

The SDHP endeavoured to win over the highlanders of Musa Dagh through propagation, indoctrination, playing on fears and sometimes coercion. According to Frederic Poche, the United States consul in Aleppo, the revolutionaries were 'inciting the little nucleus of Armenians to make common cause with their compatriots to free the survivors of this [Ottoman exterminatory] campaign [of the 1890s], and their descendants, from the barbarian yoke of their oppressors'.[19] Furthermore, Aghasi, whose 'every word was received as an inspired utterance', and his comrades told large gatherings that 'thousands of Armenians were drilling in America, that abundant supplies of Martini Rifles were coming, that the English and American Governments were about to interfere on their behalf by force of arms, and many similar statements of misleading and dangerous character'.[20]

When news of the 1894 Sasun massacres in Bitlis province reached Musa Dagh, the SDHP sermons became louder. Arguing effectively, they stressed that unless the villagers armed themselves 'their wives and children would be butchered'.[21] Actual incidents of Turkish soldiers beating Armenian women in Kabusiye, whose husbands were on the run due to tax matters, created 'something like a panic ... on the subject of a possible Moslem uprising, but ... this idea has been carefully cultivated [by the SDHP?]'.[22] Henry D. Barnham, the British consul in Aleppo, summed up the situation as follows: 'These villagers have been worked up to believe that they are in real danger, and, actually, have taken steps which many of them were unwilling to take'.[23]

Foreign diplomats and missionaries stationed in the area wished to see a bloody confrontation between Musa Dagh and the Ottoman government averted. American Protestant missionary C.S. Sanders, who had free access to Musa Dagh and seems to have served as an informant to the British consulate at Aleppo during the SDHP episode, thought that, 'if it were possible, without letting the Government know the facts, to induce them to issue an order that Tax Collectors, Zapties or Soldiers were on no account to touch the [Musa Dagh] women, it would ... ease the situation considerably'.[24]

Despite such wishes on the part of foreign consuls and missionaries, the Ottoman government was concerned more about collecting taxes and the safety of collectors than addressing the heavy-handedness and abuses applied in the process. It was reported by a government official in October 1895 that the revolutionary committee 'instructed the village elders [of Musa Dagh] to do something against government tax collectors when the latter visited the area'.[25] Although the majority of elders reportedly refused to comply with those instructions and decided to remain loyal to the government, a minority dissented and sided with the revolutionaries.[26] It was believed that Bitias, which owed 37,000 kurush/piasters in taxes, could be the centre of such friction. The government accordingly informed and asked the foreign consulates in the area to persuade the Armenians to refrain from 'such foolish acts', while, at the same time, ordering General Muhammad Ali to be there with his forces 'so that he may take defensive measures' and 'prevent such attacks [on tax collectors] from happening'.[27] Muhammad Ali, himself, was reportedly targeted for assassination.[28]

While the consuls and Sanders sought ways to ease the tension, Aghasi and company embarked upon a successful membership drive. The bulk of the population initially received the revolutionaries 'with coldness and distrust, but they gradually made their way, and with such care that boys were frequently drawn into the movement without the slightest suspicion on the part of their parents'.[29] Within six months after Aghasi's arrival, 75 per cent of Musa Daghtsis had joined the SDHP,[30] and by March 1895 'nearly all the Armenians were enrolled'.[31] Interestingly, women, who at one point were admitted in droves of 250 at a time, constituted the most devoted and enthusiastic members.[32] Each and every member was required to take an oath of secrecy and kill anyone, including family members, if they betrayed the cause. This pledge was made before a 25 by 30 centimetres silken cloth bearing Armenian inscriptions, stamped on all four sides with the party seal, and covered with a pistol and a dagger superimposed like a cross.[33] Members also had to have a two-barrel shotgun, a revolver with 100 bullets, a sword, and several bags of gunpowder and lead. By the end of 1894, all Musa Dagh Hnchakians possessed at least a one-barrel shotgun and a sword.[34] Dubbed 'Maro',[35] most probably after Mariam (Maro) Vartanian, one of the party's founding members, the local militia were divided into groups for training.

The Armenians of Musa Dagh were not the only recruits. When the Catholic curate of Kesab, Nigoghos Beojekian, heard of Aghasi, he travelled to Kheder Beg to join the revolutionaries in their march to Zeytun. But Aghasi urged him to return to Kesab, where he could be more useful. According to Sanders, who was there between 15 March and 20 May, 'the villagers of Kessab sent word to Aghasee ... that they refused absolutely to have anything to do with revolution or even to contribute money'. So that Kesab 'was, to a man, opposed to the movement'.[36] This claim was not entirely true. For instance, Nusuhi pasha, the governor of Beirut province, based on information obtained from intelligence sources, reported the arrival in Kesab of Armenian revolutionaries carrying United States passports. Not only were the Hnchakians 'driven by foreign powers', but also 'American missionaries are helping these persons'.[37] The latter two claims were similarly untrue. Also, two envoys from Kesab invited the revolutionaries in Musa Dagh to visit them. When a deputation of three revolutionaries arrived, a large crowd welcomed them.[38] The SDHP soon formed a seven-member committee to coordinate local efforts. It also created a tribunal, assisted by a police force of four, to settle disputes besetting local society.[39]

The SDHP revolutionaries in Musa Dagh also considered the neighbouring Alawis (Nusayris) as potential allies. In fact, the latter approached the revolutionaries first. According to Aghasi, Alawi interest in the emancipatory cause began when they observed an improvement in Musa Dagh society brought about by the SDHP. As a result, some eight Alawis, former students of the Presbyterian mission school at Svedia, joined the revolutionary ranks and even assumed Armenian names, their leader now being called Ohannes.[40] Aghasi and Sheikh Ibrahim, the religious-political leader of Svedia Alawis, discussed the possibility of broader cooperation in a secret meeting. The Sheikh agreed to assume responsibility for the transportation of 5,000 Chassepot rifles that Aghasi believed he could procure from abroad. The Sheikh also guaranteed that he could raise an army of 10,000 Alawi fighters if Aghasi would recruit 2,000 well-armed Armenians for his part. With a combined force of 12,000 men, the Sheikh believed, Armenians and Alawis could occupy Antioch, confiscate a cache of 10,000 Martini rifles stored there, and capture Aleppo. The territory under control could later be expanded to include Hajin and Zeytun to form an independent Armenian–Alawi region.[41]

Diplomatic correspondence corroborates some Armenian–Alawi relationship. Barnham reported that the Alawis 'have become interested in the [revolutionary] movement, but, I believe, they have as yet taken no active steps in the matter'.[42] He later remarked: 'I should say that the extent of the movement will depend upon the action of the Ansariye Fellaheen, who form the majority among the population in the district. They are a Mussulman Sect intensely hostile to the Turks, and especially ill-disposed to some of the leading Turkish notables of Antioch. They particularly resent the conscription for the army'.[43] Joseph Dowek (Douek), the British vice-consul in Antioch, on 17 August 1895, wrote to his superior in Aleppo: 'I learn that they [the revolutionaries] are conscripting soldiers from other sects and paying them three pounds sterling per month; [and] that of the sect of the Nusairiyeh they have conscripted one hundred fifty or two hundred'.[44] Dowek's statement was grossly exaggerated, if not untrue. In any event, Armenian–Alawi negotiations hit a snag as Aghasi could not procure the promised Chassepot rifles.[45]

In any case, during their three-year stay in Musa Dagh, from 1893 to 1896, the SDHP revolutionaries established martial law terming it 'absolute monarchy [i.e., hegemony]'.[46] It forbade alcohol consumption except for medicinal use, wedding celebrations and holidays. Weddings were put on hold during crises or were allowed by permission only. No one could travel without prior consent. Religious disputes were outlawed, as was the customary felling of mulberry trees carried out to economically hurt personal foes. A police force and a civil court imposed these restrictions and resolved other local disputes. All family, inheritance, blood and business feuds were subjected to this tribunal, as were thieves and rascals. Criminals and their influential patrons were brought to justice.[47] Sometimes even neighbouring Greeks, Alawis and Turks submitted their cases to SDHP justice believing in its efficacy.[48] Punishment varied according to the nature and/or seriousness of the crime. Some offenders were simply warned, scared off, threatened or jailed. In one instance, a man from Yoghun

Oluk, who disregarded repeated warnings to come to his senses, was exiled together with his mother to Alexandria, Egypt. Others were beaten up and/or sentenced to death.[49] According to one account, sixteen people lost their lives during the SDHP episode.[50] As a result of these measures relative peace prevailed in Musa Dagh. Even the *kaymakam* (district governor) of Antioch, who visited Musa Dagh during inspection tours, turned a blind eye to the SDHP administration so long as it did not cause any major trouble or personal headache. Moreover, gendarmes refrained from visiting the Armenian villages for about two years.[51]

Taking advantage of the condition thus created, some emboldened Musa Daghtsis occasionally forayed into Turkish villages – sometimes without SDHP blessing despite their strictness – thereby reciprocating a traditional behaviour on the part of their Muslim neighbours. In one instance, a band of eighteen Armenians and Alawis attacked the village of Arsuz to the north, bringing along horses and food.[52] The government expressed serious concerns for the safety of the Muslim villages surrounding Musa Dagh. Beirut Governor Nusuhi reported that the adherents of the three religious denominations in Musa Dagh (Apostolic, Protestant and Catholic) threatened the said villages, inhabited mostly by Turkmens and some Alawis, as well as gendarmes, and proposed that special measures be taken to protect them. He also informed the French consulates in Beirut and Latakia of the situation. The United States consulate of Beirut received a similar notification especially given the fact that twelve of the Armenian revolutionaries carried American passports and were 'involved in subversive actions'. These notifications did not yield any 'tangible results'.[53]

The SDHP leadership faced opposition from some conservative notables, clergymen and ordinary citizens. Although most traditional notables had embraced the revolutionary cause, some were not sincere. Notables from Bitias and Haji Habibli, in particular, seized every opportunity to incite the lesser peasantry against the 'aliens'.[54] The extent of internal discontent can be gauged from an affidavit submitted in support of the Protestant pastor Sdepan Yarpuzlian of Yoghun Oluk. Written in 1898, the document was signed by forty-six clergymen and laymen, including 'the most prominent Gregorians [Apostolic Armenians], in a word a more representative set of signatures could not be found, and the whole is gathered up and confirmed by the seal of the Gregorian bishop of Antioch at the end'.[55] The Capuchin missionary Fedele Da Trieste of Kheder Beg, in turn, initially expressed sympathy for the plight of Armenians, who ought to be liberated 'once and for all from the Turkish tyranny', because 'it is here among them [Armenians] that it is possible to understand what it means to be under [the rule of] the Turks'. If need be, 'I too shall die with my dear children [i.e., flock]' in anticipation of Turkish massacres of Armenians and other Christians in the district, similar to the ones that had taken place in Sasun, Mush, Bitlis, Marash, Aintab and elsewhere.[56] But Da Trieste hoped that a French or British naval force in northwestern Syria would be able to provide security and strike fear among the Turks.[57]

Letting the Capuchin leadership, the Sacred Congregation for the Propagation of the Faith and Pope Leo XIII know and do something about Armenian aspirations would undoubtedly yield religious gains as well. Once emancipated, Da Trieste believed, the Musa Daghtsis, irrespective of their confessional affiliation, would convert to Catholicism en masse having seen Rome's genuine interest in their plight. Because

American Protestant missionary activity had not produced favourable results to date, Protestantism could hardly claim any admirers heretofore. Following the sad example of numerous Armenians in the general vicinity, the Musa Daghtsis could ultimately lose their Christian faith and identity under persistent duress. Accordingly, the British or the French ought to send serious commissions of inquiry 'to correct the bad Turkish regime' so fraught with functionaries of all ranks, from provincial governors down, usurping the people and religious institutions.[58]

Convinced as he was of the legitimacy of Armenian claims, Da Trieste cited other motives for walking along the revolutionary road. To begin with, although he had come to realize that 'the spirit of the revolution' had crept into the villages akin to 'a poisonous snake', and although he followed his superior's instructions to exhort 'public calm and tranquility', he failed to extinguish 'these new political passions'. In this situation, therefore, it would be unwise to navigate against the tide given the fact that his entire congregation had joined the revolutionary movement. Second, he claimed to be deceived by the Armenian Catholic priest of Kesab (Nigoghos Beojekian) into joining the revolutionaries. Third, contradicting the latter reason, he himself was curious to know, as an insider, what transpired within the movement. Fourth, he feared for his own life and accordingly assigned an armed night guard to his bedroom. For these reasons Da Trieste joined the inhabitants of Kheder Beg in watching the village passes against the anticipated army assault. But his visibility and betrayal by informants eventually drew the government's suspicion, after which he could no longer live as a free man.[59] Accordingly, he relinquished his post to a colleague by the name of Marcellino da Vallarsa and departed for Beirut, where he arrived on 16 July 1895.[60] Given his perceived strange behaviour at the time, his superior (and other colleagues), after concluding that 'his mind seems to be a little disturbed' which could force him 'to take a wrong step' or 'become a wild madman', decided to send him to his native Trieste.[61]

Marcellino da Vallarsa pursued a different course. Assisted by the French vice-consul in Antioch, Albert Potton, he persuaded his constituents to obey the voice of God and surrender to the authorities like true Christians. He explained that rebellion was a sin conducive to tragedy and destruction. Therefore, a due punishment was justifiable; that is why the European Powers could not protect them.[62]

Such advice notwithstanding, in the spring of 1895 new arrivals from the United States reinforced the SDHP ranks. When the scope of the 1894 Sasun massacres became known, *Hnch'ak* (*Bell*), the party's official mouthpiece, published an urgent appeal for Armenian émigrés in the United States to protect the orphaned children in the homeland. As a result, young volunteers from Boston, Lynn, Lowell, Worcester, Fitchburg, Providence and New York sailed to London on 1 January 1895. After a two-month stay in the British capital, they arrived on the island of Cyprus and split into two groups.[63] According to an Armenian source, the first group departed for Musa Dagh in April. Although their boat capsized due to a severe storm, they succeeded in swimming ashore. This scene of men struggling against waves left an awesome impression on some Muslim witnesses, who thought that an army of strangers had landed.[64] The second group, led by Shavarsh Shishmanian, alias Baron Avedis, arrived on 9 May. As the accompanying cargo consisted of large quantities of pistols, guns, powder, bombs and uniforms earmarked for Zeytun, it took about 400 natives and revolutionaries 18 hours to carry them to the mountain tops and store them in the caves overlooking Bitias.[65] Internal Ottoman correspondence indicates different dates regarding the revolutionaries' landing.[66]

When notified of these landings, the British ambassador to Constantinople, Sir Philip Currie, inquired about the revolutionaries and their provenance.[67] They were, he was told, 'Armenians some of whom at least were from America, and it does not appear that any were from IranoCaucasia'.[68] Cyprus was also notified. The British authorities there seemed to be quite aware of Armenian activities on the island. Armenian visitors had been coming in by *Messageries Maritimes* steamers from Marseille, the Austrian *Lloyd* steamer from Beirut, the *Bells* steamers from Alexandria, and the *Knott's Princes Line*.[69] Furthermore, Hakob Hovsepian, an important Hnchakian contact in the coastal town of Larnaca,

> who used rarely to be seen away from his [watch making] shop, has, during the past year [preceding September 1895], and still does, pay frequent visits to the Pier, Customs, Post Office, and the Bank, generally in company with other Armenians. ... He has presented Bank of England notes of 100£ each, and that he receives drafts from Constantinople, &, all of which are exchanged for gold.[70]

Citing this and another example, W.J. Ansell, the Acting Collector of Customs in Larnaca, believed that 'Cyprus has simply been used [by Armenians] as the means of obtaining information and distributing relief'.[71]

While those investigations were underway, all sorts of stories circulated in the Antioch district. Wires reaching the governor of Aleppo province, for example, spoke of a clandestine disembarkation of 400, 3,000 and even 5,000 English soldiers.[72] Sanders seemed to know much more. Charting a map of Chevlik and its vicinity, the landing area, he reported that in early May 1895 'a party of seventeen revolutionists had landed on the coast from Cyprus... having with them seven or eight rifles, a number of revolvers, known here as Kara Dagh (imitation of a very large Smith Wesson), and some ninety bombs!' He described the latter as 'round iron balls, of a diameter of about six inches, armed with nine nipples any of which they say would explode the bomb when it came in contact with the ground'.[73] It was also thought that on 26 May 'four boats (with) firearms from Cyprus attempted to land on the coast.... One boat containing 400 rifles was seized, the others escaped'.[74]

Such rumours or news caused euphoria in the district. The *müdür* (sub-district governor) of Svedia rushed to inform his superior at Antioch, who kept the *konak* (government house) in Aleppo abreast of the situation, 'thus causing the greatest excitement there'. Governor Hasan Pasha, in turn, remained 'in constant telegraphic communication with the Porte and the Palace on the subject'.[75] On 27 May 1895, the governor dispatched troops to Svedia for investigation.[76] Similarly, in the afternoon of 30 May the surveillance battleship *Arcadia* arrived in Latakia, took aboard 150 troops and a police agent, and sailed north after midnight. It first went to Arsuz, searched the area, and made a southwardly detour to Svedia, where the soldiers set up camp.[77] The corvette *Beyrouth* later joined the *Arcadia* at Alexandretta, and a transportation boat arrived to supply their charcoal needs. The search led to the discovery of some Henry Martini bullets and three bombs. However, the investigation continued without any arrests or collision taking place.[78]

All the rumours about the seizure of armed boats proved premature and were hence contradicted by the district governor himself.[79] Although the Armenians displayed 'a revolutionary inclination', they had 'shown no unsubordination [sic] to the Authorities'. Therefore, the kaymakam was scolded for being 'too hasty' in deploying troops, whose 'appearance … in the Armenian districts now is dangerous'.[80] The governor was also admonished for his poor judgement. His mishandling of the situation gave vent to the existing effervescence, which would certainly produce abroad 'an unfavorable impression on the state of the country'. Meanwhile, many Armenians in northwestern Syria lived in a state of heightened fear because the government collected their guns but not those belonging to Muslims. Furthermore, Christians in the area were molested and threatened with death as *giavur*s (infidels).[81] A representative of the Austro-Hungarian Empire assessed the situation as a powder keg: 'If ever a sinister thing happens in the interior, we will risk to see the birth of an aggression on the part of the mountaineers of Giavour Dagh, ignorant and fanatical men nourishing a great hatred for Christianity'. He therefore wanted a European warship sent to the region to prevent imminent hostilities.[82] Similarly, American missionaries, fearing for their lives and those of other Christians, asked their ambassador, A.W. Terrell, to mediate.[83]

The crisis had not dissipated entirely when a new incident rekindled the tension. At the end of July 1895 Turkish and Alawi peasants stopped two loads belonging to Armenian muleteers at a secondary road near Antioch.[84] An inspection at the municipality revealed that the loads, consisting of four travel trunks, contained about 800 Ottoman gold liras, a batch of letters, 'two bags of Winchester and Martini cartridges, various tools [such as breeches, screws and locks] for the manufacture of arms, two double barrelled shot guns, and three revolvers'.[85] One of the muleteers, who evaded capture, made his way to Musa Dagh and informed Aghasi of the mishap. In dire need of money, the revolutionaries decided to send a comrade named Melcon/Melkon Guedjian (Harputlu Melkon) disguised as a foreign merchant to claim the confiscated goods.[86] Upon entering Antioch on 3 August, Guedjian was arrested and, showing his American passport and pretending that he did not understand Turkish, escorted to the municipality. There he lodged a complaint before the kaymakam and his *majlis* (council) to the effect that, while transporting his belongings from Iskenderun to the interior, he was attacked and robbed by highwaymen and that he had the keys to the trunks which he had come to recover. He explained that the money was sent by an Armenian American society via London to be distributed among the poor Armenian peasantry of northwestern Syria to avoid a revolution because of their misery. As for the guns and bullets, they were to be used for self-defence only and by no means against the government.[87] Upon interrogation Guedjian confessed that, in addition to his assigned task of distributing arms and money as well as hiding some 200 Armenian revolutionaries from Svedia in Hajin, Sis, Aintab, Beylan and Iskenderun,[88] he would commission 'a rifle expert to tour the region and help in establishing an arms factory in the country'.[89]

In the end, the Antioch authorities sent Guedjian and the other muleteers to Aleppo, where they were tried and sentenced to long prison terms, Guedjian receiving 101 years.[90] Because, however, according to bilateral agreement the American consulate in Aleppo was not notified of Guedjian's case as that of an American citizen, the U.S. embassy in Constantinople claimed mistrial and demanded the immediate release of its protégé and the removal of the Aleppo governor. All requests were granted.[91] Guedjian departed Constantinople – where he had been transferred – for Marseille on 17 December 1895.[92]

At the time of the discovery of the above loads an outraged Muslim mob in Antioch, estimated at more than 2,000 armed men, 'precipitated on the Armenian quarter, knocked on the doors, uttering all sorts of menaces, and wanted to enter the Armenian church by force'.[93] In the absence of security forces, some city notables intervened to calm the crowd. Government agents then searched the Armenian church but found no hidden caches as it was feared.[94] Anti-Christian demonstrations continued on 1 August as Da Vallarsa ventured to enter Antioch. An ever-swelling Muslim crowd stopped him at the city gate and amidst degrading cries tried to pull him down from his horse, beat him up and take him to the police station. City notables finally escorted the Capuchin missionary to the French vice-consulate, where guards repelled the pressing ruffians.[95] Gravely concerned with their own well-being, the local Armenian community leadership sent a telegram to the Grand Vizier, the Aleppo governor and the Armenian Patriarch of Constantinople, and distributed copies of the same to the resident foreign diplomatic corps.[96]

This incident exposed the lack of security in Antioch as the government had 'no force at all at its disposal for the protection of the peace of the town' and especially Christians and foreign subjects.[97] At the same time, the French consul in Aleppo met with the governor to discuss public safety at Antioch and its vicinity and especially the well-being of the French vice-consul, people administered by him and foremost 'our missionaries'.[98] The governor responded by saying that a commission of inquiry had been dispatched to find and punish the troublemakers according to law and that, thanks to the sultan, 'public tranquility is perfect and ... there is nothing that can cause inquietude'. But, he added, the events had been started by aliens who had brought 'unacceptable things' into the country.[99]

The commission alluded to consisted of Mustapha Nadim Effendi and Alay Bey, the Colonel of the Gendarmerie of Aleppo, who 'are making private investigations as to the state of affairs, and the government is informed of all the proceedings and preparations of the Armenians, but is keeping appearances as if it did *not* know the facts'.[100] The district governor at the same time summoned all the religious heads of Antioch to read to them the Grand Vizier's response to the 1 August Armenian petition. The Vizier, it was learned, had ordered the district governor to calm the populace and to announce that 'the Government was presently occupied to prepare a plan for reforms'. The meeting adjourned following a brief sermon by the district governor exhorting tranquility and harmony.[101]

Potton praised the district governor for his moderation, prudence and canniness.[102] Be that as it may, the Turks continued to persecute the Armenians. During the second half of August 1895, the Turkish notables of Antioch held a meeting and sent a lengthy secret telegram to Constantinople and Aleppo. The cable accused the Armenians of 'thefts, assassinations, and giving asylum in their mountains to all sorts of criminals infesting the region'.[103] Potton vehemently denied the charges.[104] As a result, many Antioch Armenians, who had no faith in the promised security, gradually left town and took refuge in Musa Dagh.[105]

Meanwhile, revolutionary preparations in Musa Dagh continued with renewed intensity. The Armenians, it was reported, 'intend to provoke an uprising and have some of them killed in order to attract the attention of the European powers'.[106] An armed clash took place between government troops and some revolutionaries on 8 September 1895.[107] This general tense situation prompted the Hnchakians to send emissaries to Iskenderun, Payas and Aleppo in October to instruct Musa Dagh migrant workers 'to return home in readiness for action', a call which many heeded.[108]

Despite all the talk about imminent clashes, nothing significant transpired between the autumn of 1895 and February 1896. However, the arrest of an Armenian thief at the Turkish village of Mishraqiye on Svedia plain on the night of 29 February breached that calm. In retaliation, a group of revolutionaries and other youths from Yoghun Oluk and elsewhere began to fire on Mishraqiye. Fearing for their lives, its inhabitants surrendered one of their own as a hostage and asked the Svedia police to set the imprisoned Armenian free, but to no avail. Da Vallarsa on 4 March went to Yoghun Oluk to persuade the captors to release the Turkish hostage in order to avoid inevitable bloodshed which both sides, the government and the Armenians, were prepared to engage in. The revolutionaries remained adamant. Da Vallarsa then went to Antioch to consult with Vice-Consul Potton. They agreed to send two reports to the French consulate in Aleppo, one by Da Vallarsa on the tension in Musa Dagh and another by Potton on the menacing situation in Antioch, where thousands of axes were prepared and stored in mosques. In the meantime, the Musa Daghtsis beseeched Baron Avedis to release the Turkish hostage. He agreed provided the supplicants would pay 100 Ottoman piasters (420 francs) for the revolutionary cause.[109]

In March and early April fresh Turkish reinforcements arrived in Antioch district. While two Ottoman battleships monitored the coast, contingents 100 to 800 strong arrived from Aleppo, Zeytun, Latakia, Ordu and elsewhere, and took up positions in Antioch, Svedia, Kabakli and around the Armenian villages of Musa Dagh.[110] These forces consisted mainly of *redif*s (reserves), including Kurds and others who had participated in the recent Armenian massacres in Cilicia. Some soldiers stationed at Kabakli clashed with the Armenians for 'a trifling motive', and although several of the latter were arrested on 'no specific charges', the incident ended without further trouble.[111]

The 'only object' of the incoming soldiers, the Aleppo governor explained, was 'to search for and seize certain Armenian Revolutionaries'.[112] Having failed to do so, the government now pressed

> the Armenian villages in question for arrears of taxation, a demand with which, in their present destitute condition, it is impossible for them to comply, and they ... express the fear that such action may be intended to force the Armenians to

assume a so-called rebellious attitude, and thereby furnish the Authorities with a pretext for precipitating matters in a violent manner.

Therefore, 'the result of such a course would be not to procure the surrender of the 15 or 20 revolutionaries, but probably to bring about the destruction or massacre of a large number of guiltless and offenceless villagers'.[113] And should some of the Turkish troops native to Antioch be killed during the anticipated bloodshed, the whole region could be hit by tragedy.[114]

The attitude of the Muslim population vis-à-vis their Christian neighbours grew ominously more aggressive. A special inspector from Aleppo, while looking into the Armenian affair, circulated a telegram written by Diyarbekir Turks vowing to sacrifice their blood in case an impending reform plan by the government granted the Christians of the Ottoman Empire new rights. Very much excited by this telegram, and believing that between 500 and 600 Armenian fighters had arrived from Zeytun, the Muslims of Antioch continued to arm themselves with revolvers, clubs and knives,[115] 'openly and continually threatening the Christians that they will soon follow the example of their coreligionists at Aintab, Orfa, Biredjik and elsewhere, by massacring them all'.[116]

As before, foreign diplomats scrambled for security guarantees. Dowek implored his superior at Aleppo 'to ask the Governor General to provide special protection for us and other British subjects here [in Antioch] and at Swedeah for the defence and safety for our persons and property, as I fear we shall have a serious outbreak in Antioch soon'.[117] Although representations were made to the governor forthwith, Dowek took no chances and requested a British battleship at Svedia Bay.[118] As a result, the battleship *H.M.S. Barfleur* arrived, followed by the *H.M.S. Sybille* and *H.M.S. Hood*.[119] In the final analysis, the sight of a foreign naval force 'was of the greatest importance for the security of the whole district, Antioch included. It seems that, because of the presence of these British ships of war, the Turkish military leaders felt obliged to change their policy and plans, and so did not proceed to attack the [Musa Dagh] villages'.[120]

While military and diplomatic activities were in full swing, the mood in the Armenian villages remained tense.[121] The youth, considered 'inexperienced and shortsighted' by their elders, opted to fight, while the rest, cognizant of the risks involved, deemed it wise to give up.[122] In the absence of unequivocal support, the revolutionaries met to discuss their options. A confrontation with the government forces could be calamitous. Even if the Hnchakians surrendered, the Turks would slaughter the Armenian villagers, as they had done elsewhere. Furthermore, given the circumstances, outside rescue attempts were unfeasible. The sea constituted the only conduit to freedom; regardless, the Musa Daghtsis would meet certain death after the revolutionaries' departure.[123] As the latter vacillated, an assembly of seventy-five representatives from the six villages congregated in a church to find a solution to the seeming impasse. After deliberating for three days, the gathering ruled that the insurgents must give up and leave. A five-member deputation conveyed the ultimatum. But the revolutionaries refused to surrender unless the government guaranteed the highlanders' safety. The assembly concurred.[124]

The abovementioned meeting (or flurry of activity), which Da Vallarsa described differently, took place from 8 to 11 March 1896. As revolutionary agents spread news of an impending assault by a large Muslim mob, and accordingly issued a call to arms in Kheder Beg and Yoghun Oluk, Da Vallarsa refuted that claim and tried to ease the people's fears. Feeling 'deceived' by the 'false' rumour, the latter pondered ways with Da Vallarsa to get rid of the revolutionaries in their midst. Given the many opinions expressed, a consensus could not be reached immediately. Besides, fearing for their lives, no one wanted to be the first to confront the revolutionaries. In an effort to reconcile the opposing views, Da Vallarsa formed an eight-member committee, four each from the pro- and anti-revolutionary camps. Its task was to prepare a list of the heads of households with either inclination. Those who were against the revolutionaries were promised protection, whereas those who had pledged allegiance to them did not have to honour their oath because, after all, it was illegal, invalid, and against legitimate authority and 'God's rules'. For the people of Kheder Beg and Vakef this 'plebiscite' took place at a location designated by Da Vallarsa, whereas those of Yoghun Oluk met at the Apostolic church minus the Catholics, who joined their Kheder Beg coreligionists. The results were as follows: only 7 out of 187 heads of households from the Kheder Beg–Vakef group and 20 out of 200 heads of households from the Yoghun Oluk group were pro-revolutionaries. Accordingly, on 11 March Da Vallarsa summoned the most influential people to his residence to discuss ways of getting rid of four revolutionaries sheltered in the home of the Apostolic priest, Boghos Kiusbekian, at Kheder Beg. The four men voluntarily left the village for Haji Habibli after midnight.[125]

The government's position regarding surrender terms was ambivalent. In a letter dated 2 March 1896 to Augusto Toselli, an Italian civil engineer and director of the tobacco company *Régie* at Svedia who would play an instrumental role in the Armenian–Turkish negotiations, chief Turkish representatives Mustapha Nadim Effendi and Ali Riza explained their stance. The government intended to improve conditions in the Armenian villages provided they expelled the foreign agitators found among them. Those who surrendered peacefully would be dealt with respect. The native detainees would be tried before tribunals at Antioch and receive due punishments. As for the foreigners, they would be handed over to their respective diplomatic agents upon show of a passport, lodged wherever they wished, and expelled from the country after receiving authorization from the government. Should, however, the insurgents reject the offer, 'it is our duty to cleanse these villages with all the means possible'.[126]

Aleppo Governor Raif Pasha held a different opinion. Although the revolutionaries 'would consent to leave the country on the same conditions obtained by the Ambassadors at Constantinople in favor of the few Hnchakists of Zeitun; that is to say: to be allowed to proceed to Europe under the guarantee of a foreign power', he, the governor, 'has not recommended, and has no intention of recommending to his government such an agreement, being of the opinion that it is necessary to secure the unconditional surrender of these individuals, to be dealt with as the Ottoman Government may think fit'. Acting British consul A. Catoni agreed 'to a certain extent', but, he wondered,

> what will the consequence be if ... the Armenian villagers refuse to deliver up the agitators in question! Doubtless a conflict between the troops and the Armenians will then take place there, and judging from the present attitude of the Turks in

general, it is to be feared that a general outbreak will occur in the whole district of Antioch and Suedia.[127]

Hoping to defuse the tension, British ambassador Sir Philip Currie offered Ottoman Foreign Minister Tewfik Pasha his mediation through an interlocutor, but his offer was declined.[128]

Meanwhile, Potton, Da Vallarsa and Toselli were in constant communication with each other – and the latter two with the government emissaries – to prevent an army attack and ultimately find a peaceful resolution to the conflict. At this time, in late March and early April, 1896, three army battalions began to occupy strategic positions in and around Musa Dagh. Two of the battalions, which were returning from Zeytun, having sustained losses and been away from their families for months, had become 'wilder than wild beasts' seeking Armenians to cut them 'into pieces'.[129] On 8 April 1,600 soldiers surrounded Kabusiye.[130] Mustafa Nedim Effendi and Ali Riza ordered the village elders to show the insurgents' hideout, which they did. Eight revolutionaries and six other suspects surrendered without resistance[131] and were taken to Antioch two days later.[132] The remaining revolutionaries withdrew from the other villages to their fortification at Haji Habibli. This was, as the Turkish commanders soon realized, 'a kind of natural fortress, difficult of access and easy of defence'. Hence, to be able to subjugate Haji Habibli, the authorities needed a much larger force than the one at hand. They accordingly opted for negotiations.[133]

On 9 April, after accomplishing their mission at Kabusiye, the Ottoman forces entered Kheder Beg without warning. Commander Hilmi (Elmi) Pasha and other officers rested at the Capuchin residence for an hour and offered to keep some soldiers behind for Da Vallarsa's protection, which he declined. The troops then took up positions on a hilltop overlooking Yoghun Oluk. In the afternoon, Mustafa Nedim Effendi and Ali Riza arrived in Kheder Beg, stayed till evening, met with some family representatives, and asked Da Vallarsa and Toselli to go to Yoghun Oluk the following day, which they obliged. The government representatives, cognizant of the danger involved but trusting Da Vallarsa's and Toselli's diplomatic skills, now wanted them to proceed to Haji Habibli on a fact-finding and negotiating mission. Although reluctant to embark on such a risky journey, the two men acceded to the request.[134]

Unbeknownst to the beleaguered Armenians that such arrangements were already being made, they too sought Toselli's mediation for an honourable outcome. Two envoys, Garigian and a certain Soghomon, took off after dark, crossed the enemy lines undetected and delivered a four-point peace plan to the Italian in his residence at Svedia. According to the plan, 1) the revolutionaries would surrender if the government asked; 2) European observers must supervise the handover; 3) the fighters must be accorded military honours and safe passage to overseas; and 4) the authorities must guarantee the villagers' well-being. Toselli responded that he had already seen the Turkish commander the previous day and that the French vice-consul at Antioch had likewise expressed willingness to intervene. At the end, Toselli promised to meet with the Turkish commander the next day and write to Potton. Garigian and Soghomon returned to their headquarters before dawn.[135]

On Friday, 10 April 1896, Da Vallarsa and Toselli went to Haji Habibli for talks with the revolutionaries. Inside the meeting house were eight young men, all well-built, bearded, long haired, proudly disposed, and armed with weapons, bullet vests and swords.[136] Toselli eased their fears by stating that the European battleships stationed off the coast aimed to prevent any attempt at savagery, that the arrears would not be collected and that the Ottoman army would not occupy the villages.[137] At the end of the talks, which lasted four-and-a-half hours, the revolutionaries agreed to surrender provided they would be able to keep their weapons, treated as guests instead of prisoners and shipped to Europe escorted by a European till the port of departure. Da Vallarsa and Toselli returned to Kheder Beg the same day after presenting those conditions to the government representatives, who accepted them.[138]

On the following day, Saturday, 11 April, Toselli received a letter from the revolutionaries demanding new concessions. He refused to deal with them any further, but Da Vallarsa remained hopeful and resolute. He sent an ultimatum to Haji Habibli: unless the revolutionaries showed up at a designated location near Yoghun Oluk by 2:00 p.m., the whole deal would be off. The two men then went to Yoghun Oluk to inform the government representatives of the snag. The latter now decided to attack Haji Habibli on Tuesday, 14 April with 2,000 soldiers. Da Vallarsa and Toselli advised against such a plan, because the Armenians could even fight 5,000 troops with only 500 men from their strong positions. 'Indescribable massacres' could follow triggering a European naval intervention and further bloodshed across the entire region. Surrounding Haji Habibli and cutting off its water supply would be a better alternative to pressure the revolutionaries to surrender within a few days without bloodshed. While these options were being discussed, word came that the revolutionaries were now ready to give up. Da Vallarsa rushed to Haji Habibli, where many native armed men and women of all ages threatened him as a 'traitor' for surrendering the revolutionaries to the Turks. Others, however, who were unhappy with the revolutionaries, regarded Da Vallarsa as a new Moses sent by God to deliver them. Led by Da Vallarsa with a white flag in hand, the revolutionaries arrived in Yoghun Oluk on horseback and armed. They were greeted by the district governor of Antioch, Mustafa Nedim Effendi, Ali Riza, Toselli and other officials. Mustafa Nedim Effendi and the military commanders shook Baron Avedis's and Da Vallarsa's hands, offered everyone coffee and cigarettes and treated the revolutionaries in general as guests and not prisoners, as agreed.[139] On Monday, 13 April, Da Vallarsa, an Armenian priest and fifty soldiers escorted the foreign revolutionaries to Antioch 'on horseback and without handcuffs'.[140] For their central role in the peaceful resolution of the crisis, Potton, Toselli and Da Vallarsa received rewards from the sultan.[141]

The prisoners were detained in Antioch through the first week of May. Although not ill-treated, they were not shipped to Europe as agreed.[142] Instead, they were transferred to the penitentiary at Aleppo on 8 May.[143] From their cells, the Hnchakians secretly communicated with various foreign consuls, requesting their mediation.[144] At long last, the Armenian political prisoners, among them forty-nine Musa Dagh natives, gained their freedom on 26 December 1896, thanks to a general amnesty. Before being released, the foreign subjects were photographed, and all prisoners took an oath of allegiance to the sultan. Diplomatic circles received the news with satisfaction.[145] Be that as it may, nine of the Armenian detainees with U.S. citizenship were sent to Mersin and from there to America via Marseille.[146]

Back in the troubled region the government constructed a network of fortifications along the coast. *Nokta*s (military posts) were set up at Latakia, Kaladuran near Kesab, Svedia, Iskenderun and Payas under the supervision of a special committee from Constantinople.[147] Troop congestion was not diffused as desired. By September 1897, 300 reserves from the 72nd Jaffa regiment had encircled Yoghun Oluk and Musa Dagh, while more than 200 reserves from the 73rd Hassan-el-Akrad regiment had been deployed in the district of Ordu (including Kesab) and in Antioch.[148] This strict vigilance continued in subsequent years. Besides military surveillance, the government contemplated other administrative measures to maintain tighter control. For example, in addition to the *sanjaks* (counties) of Aleppo, Urfa and Marash in Aleppo province, it decided to create a fourth *sanjak* with headquarters at Antioch that would include the *kaza*s of Antioch, Jisr al-Shughur, Iskenderun and Svedia, thereby elevating the latter from the lesser status of a *nahiye* (sub-district).[149]

Despite the military measures (and later the purported administrative changes), rumours of a new SDHP landing at Musa Dagh in late March 1897 put the government back on emergency alert.[150] Several months later similar unconfirmed reports rekindled the tension. While in Cyprus en route to the United States, the former Protestant pastor of Yoghun Oluk, Rev. Sdepan Yarpuzlian, met some SDHP agents who reportedly informed him of an impending armed campaign to Musa Dagh. Hoping to avoid a new crisis, the pastor wrote forthwith to one of his friends there, urging him to notify the government.[151] Generally speaking, the district remained calm, and only a few revolutionaries continued to filter into Musa Dagh.[152]

Revolutionary activity in subsequent years does not seem to have receded. In the summer of 1904, an Antioch notable, Rifaat Agha, provided the local government with a list of thirty-six former Hnchakians and other Armenians from Musa Dagh, accusing them of sedition for allegedly storing large quantities of ammunition sent from Algeria to overthrow the Ottoman hegemony and establish French rule in Syria and Lebanon. Only five of the accused were arrested and jailed in Aleppo, while the rest became fugitives. When the Ottoman Constitution was reinstated in the summer of 1908, both groups returned home thanks to a general amnesty granted to *personae non gratae*,[153] but they did not remain inactive as the local SDHP chapter was resurrected sometime during 1910–11.[154]

The SDHP revolutionary episode during the 1890s left a lasting impact on Musa Dagh society. From the revolutionaries' perspective, the 'once-cowardly' and subservient mountaineers – with the exception of the inhabitants of Yoghun Oluk and Kheder Beg – were transformed into fearless fighters cognizant of their human rights. Much enthused with this overnight change, Aghasi shared his thoughts: 'It is wrong to think that (…) races are always born slave. Bravery (…) is a profession that requires a teacher, and the cowardly person, like a student, undergoes change from one day to the next.'[155] According to Baron Avedis, Aghasi's deputy and successor at Musa Dagh, the Musa Daghtsis, entertaining 'deep respect and noble compassion' vis-à-vis the revolutionaries, became aware of their rights within the course of one year, began to breathe freely, and stood up shunning 'soldiers, army, and cannon alike', as well as the spilling of their own blood.[156]

If the revolutionaries viewed the above phenomena through a positive prism, other observers decried all the negatives brought about or reinforced by the Hnchakians. Sanders, who abhorred things revolutionary and especially the Hnchakians, remained their most outspoken critic.[157] An Armenian reporter, covering Musa Dagh in 1911, likewise attributed some of the causes of pervasive social malaise to the Hnchakian era.[158]

The SDHP revolutionaries arrived in Musa Dagh on their way to organize an uprising in Zeytun. Their stopover, however, lasted a long time, during which they endeavoured to raise the national awareness of the natives, to arm and train them, and to have an armed confrontation with the government hoping to attract the attention of the European Powers to the plight of the Armenians in the Ottoman Empire. However, a strong European intervention in the Zeytun crisis and the safe conduit of Armenian revolutionaries to Europe set an example for all parties involved in the Musa Dagh imbroglio to follow. Musa Dagh was thus spared. As for domestic problems, the Hnchakian revolutionaries could not be blamed for the destructive feuds commonplace in Musa Dagh before their arrival. But despite their tight control of public life, the Hnchakians failed to create a lasting civic infrastructure for Musa Dagh society to function more responsibly after their departure. This vacuum allowed villagers to resume their personal vendettas with renewed intensity.

Notes

1 Shavarsh Shishmanian, 'Kilikean Suētia ew Hay Heghap'okhut'iwn', *Shirak*, no. 2 (July 1906): 91; Smpad Rsdigian, 'Musa Taghĕ (1894-1897)', *Hayrenik' Amsagir*, no. 6 (June 1952): 71.
2 *Asparēz*, no. 3 (11 December 1908).
3 Louise Nalbandian, *The Armenian Revolutionary Movement: The Development of Armenian Political Parties through the Nineteenth Century* (Berkeley: University of California Press, 1963), 104–14.
4 Ibid., 104.
5 Ibid., 128–31.
6 Arsen Gidur, *Patmut'iwn S.D. Hnch'akean Kusakts'ut'ean*, vol. I (Beirut: Shirag Press, 1962), 162.
7 Mardiros Kushakjian and Boghos Madurian, eds., *Hushamatean Musa Leṛan* (Beirut: Sevan Press, 1970), 261–3.
8 Gidur, *Patmut'iwn S.D. Hnch'akean Kusakts'ut'ean*, vol. I, 163–8.
9 Ibid., 169; Aghasi [Garabed Tursarkisian], 'Husher', in *Druagner Suētioy Antsʿealēn (1893-95 Heghap'okhakan Shrjanēn)*, ed. Mihran M. Seferian (Beirut: Ararad, 1957), 36–7.
10 Gidur, *Patmut'iwn S.D. Hnch'akean Kusakts'ut'ean*, vol. I, 170; Aghasi, 'Husher', 41.
11 Aghasi, 'Husher', 41–4, 52–3, 70–2.
12 Ibid., 49; Rsdigian, 'Musa Taghĕ', *Hayrenik' Amsagir*, no. 5 (May 1952): 21; Great Britain, Foreign Office (FO) Archives, Kew, United Kingdom, FO 195, File 1883, and FO 424, File 182, Barnham to Currie, June 1, 1895.
13 See for example the ciphered telegram sent by the governor of Aleppo Raif Bey to the Prime Minister's Office in Constantinople, 23 February 1893, Turkey, Başbakanlık Osmanlı Arşivi (BOA), İstanbul, Turkey, A.MKT.MHM.650.20.21, Serial no. 8650.

14 Ibid., A.MKT.MHM.650.20.8 and 9, telegram, Serial no. 8850-28, Ministry of Justice to Aleppo province, Constantinople, 12 March 1893. See also A.MKT. MHM.650.20.29.
15 Ibid., A.MKT.MHM.648.3.1, previously indexed as 1313.C.29, Intelligence Unit Officer telegram, Serial no. 1136, Aleppo Governorate, 5 June 1894.
16 Ibid., A.MKT.MHM.650.20.10, Intelligence Officer (signature), Serial no. 9062-360/235, to Ministry of Internal Affairs, 3 October 1894. See also A.MKT. MHM.650.20; A.MKT.MHM.650.20.30; A.MKT.MHM.650.20.13; A.MKT. MHM.650.20.14; A.MKT.MHM.650.20.31 through 34.
17 Ibid., DH.ŞFR.177.32.1-8, cyphered telegram, Serial no. 8048, from Antioch to Aleppo Province, 6 July 1895.
18 Ibid., DH.ŞFR.196.39, cyphered telegram, Serial no. 10479, Aleppo Governor Raif to Ministry of Interior Affairs, 12 August 1895. See also A.MKT.MHM.646.5, Serial no. 6482, Special no. 108, telegram Ministry of Interior to Aleppo Province, 1 September 1895; A.MKT.MHM.646.8.11, [Intelligence] Officer of Antioch District to the Ministry of Interior, 13 September 1895.
19 United States National Archives (USNA), Archives of the Department of State, Washington, D.C. (now in College Park, MD), Record Group (RG) 59, Despatches, vol. 59 (reel 58), #563, Frederic Poche to A.W. Terrell, 31 June 1895.
20 Great Britain, FO 195, File 1883, and FO 424, File 182, Barnham to Currie, 1 June 1895.
21 Ibid., 11 March 1895.
22 Ibid.
23 Ibid.
24 Great Britain, FO 195, File 1883, and FO 424, File 182, Barnham to Currie, 11 March 1895.
25 Turkey, BOA, DH.ŞFR.181.56.1-5, cyphered telegram, Serial no. 12677, 8 October 1895.
26 Ibid., A.MKT.MHM.646.3.1, Serasker Riza cyphered telegram, Serial no. 6439-40, to Aleppo Province, 8 September 1895.
27 Ibid., DH.ŞFR.181.56.1-5, cyphered telegram, Serial no. 12677, from Aleppo Governorate to Svedya Local Government Office, 8 October 1895.
28 Ibid., A.MKT.MHM.646.3.1, Serasker Riza to Aleppo Province, 8 September 1895.
29 Great Britain, FO 195, File 1883, and FO 424, File 182, Barnham to Currie, 1 June 1895.
30 Aghasi, 'Husher', 82.
31 Great Britain, FO 195, File 1883, and FO 424, File 182, Barnham to Currie, 1 June 1895.
32 Aghasi, 'Husher', 83.
33 Curia Generale dei Frati Minori Cappuccini, Archivio Generale de Cappuccini (hereafter AGC), Instituto Storico dei Cappuccini, Rome, H 93, Cartella V, Da Vallarsa to Rev. Father General, 19 April 1896.
34 Aghasi, 'Husher', 97–8.
35 *Hnch'ak*, 20 December 1895, 189.
36 Great Britain, FO 195, File 1883, and FO 424, File 182, Barnham to Currie, 1 June 1895.
37 Turkey, BOA, A.MKT.MHM.646.3.1, Seraskar Riza, cyphered telegram Serial no. 6439-6440, to Aleppo Province, 8 September 1895; A.MKT.MHM.646.3.2 and 3, information by Nusuhi Pasha; A.MKT.MHM.646.3.4, information by Nusuhi Pasha.

The quotations are from the latter document. See also idem, A.MKT.MHM.647.21.1, Officer Adel, cyphered telegram Serial no. 337, to Aleppo Province, 20 October 1895.
38 Shishmanian, 'Kilikean Suetia', *Shirak*, no. 3 (August 1906): 149–52.
39 Ibid.; Avedis Injejikian, 'Kesap ew ir Barbaṛě', in *Kesap*, comp. and ed. Hagop Cholakian, vol. III (Aleppo: Kesab Educational Association of California/Arevelk Press, 2004), 95–6.
40 Aghasi, 'Husher', 93–7; Gidur, *Patmut'iwn S.D. Hnch'akean Kusakts'ut'ean*, vol. I, 173.
41 Aghasi, 'Husher', 49, 94–5; Gidur, *Patmut'iwn S.D. Hnch'akean Kusakts'ut'ean*, vol. I, 162, 172. According to Aghasi, the number of Alawi fighters would be 60,000.
42 Great Britain, FO 195, File 1883, and FO 424, File 182, Barnham to Currie, 11 March 1895.
43 Ibid., 7 August 1895.
44 Great Britain, FO 861, File 28, Joseph Dowek to Henry D. Barnham, 17 August 1895.
45 Aghasi, 'Husher', 108–9.
46 Ibid., 82.
47 Ibid., 80–6; Shishmanian, 'Kilikean Suētia', *Shirak*, no, 4 (September 1906): 219; Shishmanian, 'Druagner Suētioy Ants'yalēn. Aṛants' Ginii Patarakě', in *Kilikean Taret'suyts'* (Constantinople: Keshishian, 1922), 283–9.
48 Shishmanian, 'Kilikean Suētia', *Shirak*, no. 4 (September, 1906): 219.
49 Ibid.; Aghasi, 'Husher', 81–6; Rsdigian, 'Musa Taghě', *Hayrenik' Amsagir*, no. 6 (June 1952): 73; Dikran J. Khrlopian, *Voskematean. Patmut'iwn Merdz[awor] Arewelk'i Hay Avet[aranakan] Miut'ean*, vol. I (Beirut: Armenian Evangelical Union of the Near East, 1950), 340.
50 Khrlopian, *Voskematean*, vol. I, 340.
51 Aghasi, 'Husher', 87–93.
52 Ibid., 87–91, 125–7.
53 Turkey, BOA, A.MKT.MHM.647.21.2, cyphered telegram from the Governor of Beirut Province, Nusuhi to Aleppo Province Governorate, 27 June 1895. See also idem, A.MKT.MHM.650.20.15 and 16, telegram Serial no. 2796, 2881, from Serasker Riza to General Army Command, 4th Subdivision, 8 March 1896.
54 Aghasi, 'Husher', 83–4, 104–6; Rsdigian, 'Musa Taghě', *Hayrenik' Amsagir*, no. 6 (June 1952): 72.
55 American Board of Commissioners for Foreign Missions (ABCFM) Archives, Houghton Library, Harvard University, Cambridge, MA, ABC: 16.9.5, vol. 14, C.S. Sanders to James Barton, 27 April 1898.
56 AGC, H 93, Cartella V, Da Trieste to V. Rev. Father Antonino, 22 February 1895.
57 Ibid., 1 March 1895.
58 Ibid., 10 March 1895.
59 Ibid., 21 April 1895, 20 July 1895; idem, Da Trieste, report written from Beirut to V. Rev. Father General Bernardo d'Andermatt, September 1895.
60 Ibid., Da Trieste to V. Rev. Father General, 16 July 1895.
61 Ibid., Giovanni Andrea da Caramagna to Rev. Father General, 20 August 1895.
62 Sacra Congregazione per le Chiese Orientali, Archivio Storico, Rome., Rubrica 105 (1), File 2, doc. 4543, Antonio da Reschio, 'Appunti', 30 October 1895; doc. 4825, Da Reschio to Cardinal Ledochowsky (Ledokowsky), 31 December 1895.
63 Rsdigian, 'Musa Taghě', *Hayrenik' Amsagir*, no. 5 (May 1952): 16–20.
64 Ibid., 14–15; Rsdigian, 'Heghap'okhakan Husher', *Asparēz*, 27 November 1908, 3; Aghasi, 'Husher', 101–2, 112; Shishmanian, 'Kilikean Suētia', *Shirak*, no. 2 (July 1906): 90.

65 Aghasi, 'Husher', 102–3, 111–20; Rsdigian, 'Heghap'okhakan Husher', 3. See also Salahi Ramsdan Sonyel, *The Ottoman Armenians: Victims of Great Power Diplomacy* (London: K. Rustem & Brother, 1987), 173.
66 Turkey, BOA, A.MKT.MHM.536.28.4.10, communique from Aleppo Province Governorate to the Adana Province and the Ministry of the Marine, 9 March 1895, and BOA, A.MKT.MHM.536.28.4.11, Serasker Riza communique, 21 March 1895.
67 Great Britain, FO 861, File 27, Currie to Barnham, 1 May 1895. See also FO 195, File 1883, Barnham to Currie, 6 June 1895.
68 Ibid., FO 195, File 1883, and FO 424, File 182, Barnham to Currie, 11 March 1895.
69 Ibid., FO 424, File 184, Inclosure 1 in no. 148, Arthur Young to Chamberlain, 2 October 1895.
70 Ibid., Inclosure 2 in no. 148, Extracts from a Report of the Acting Collector of Customs to the Chief Collector, Nicosia, 25 September 1895.
71 Ibid. See also Sonyel, *The Ottoman Armenians*, 123–4.
72 Austria, Osterreichisches Staatsarchiv, Die Akten des k.u.k. Ministeriums des Aussern, 1848-1918, Vienna, Carton 296, File *Beyrut, 1895*, Bertrand to Chevalier De Remy, 5 June 1895; G. Levanti to de Remy, 8 June 1895; Italy, Ministero degli Affari Esteri, Servizio Storico e Documentazione, Archivio Storico, Rome, Siria—Rapporti Politici, 1891-1899, File *Siria, 1895*, R. Bollati to Signor Ministro, 17 June 1895; E. Vitto to Ambassador in Constantinople, 10 June 1895, annex to the preceding document.
73 Great Britain, FO 195, File 1883, Barnham to Currie, 1 June 1895.
74 Great Britain, FO 195, File 1883, Barnham telegram, 30 May 1895.
75 Ibid.
76 Ibid., 1 June 1895; Austria-Hungary, Carton 296, File *Beyrut, 1895*, Bertrand to Chevalier De Remy, 5 June 1895; G. Levanti to de Remy, 8 June 1895; de Remy to Goluchowsky, 13 June 1895.
77 Austria-Hungary, Carton 296, File *Beyrut, 1895*, Alp. Geoffrey to De Remy, 4 June 1895; Levanti to de Remy, 8 June 1895.
78 Great Britain, FO 195, File 1883, and FO 424, File 182, Barnham to Currie, 6 June 1895, 21 June 1895.
79 Ibid., FO 861, File 27, Dowek to Barnham, 31 May 1895; FO 424, File 182, Currie to the Earl of Kimberley, 5 June 1895.
80 Ibid., FO 861, File 27, Dowek to Barnham, 31 May 1895.
81 Austria-Hungary, Carton 296, File *Beyrut, 1895*, Bertrand to De Remy, 5 June 1895; Levanti to De Remy, 8 June 1895.
82 Ibid., Levanti to De Remy, 8 June 1895.
83 USNA, RG 59, Despatches, vol. 60 (microfilm reel 59), # 627, Terrell to Richard Olney, 18 September 1895.
84 Great Britain, FO 861, File 28, Dowek to Barnham, 30 July 1895, 1 August 1895. In the first letter, Dowek reports that the incident occurred 'today', that is, on 30 July, but in his second letter, he indicates 'yesterday', that is, on 31 July. Moreover, whereas he mentions Harbiye (near ancient Daphne), some 3 miles south of Antioch, as the location of the arrests, during the detainees' trial in Aleppo later on it was revealed that they were stopped at two separate spots, one 'near the village of Haji Jilis in the commune of Suedie', and one 'at the place called Haj Getchen near Antioch'. See USNA, RG 59, Despatches, vol. 60 (microfilm reel 59), #630, Enclosure: 1/630, Translation of Indictment Marked 'e'.

85 USNA, RG 59, Despatches, vol. 60 (microfilm reel 59), #630, Enclosure: 1/630, Translation of Indictment Marked 'e'. See also Great Britain, FO 861, File 28, Dowek to Barnham, 30 July 1895, 1 August 1895, 8 August 1895.
86 Aghasi, 'Husher', 129–31; Rsdigian, 'Musa Taghě', *Hayrenik' Amsagir*, no. 5 (May 1952): 21–2; Shishmanian, 'Kilikean Suetia', *Shirak*, no. 4 (September 1906): 215. Aghasi and Rsdigian refer to Melcon Guedjian as Melkon Kejeian and Melkon Keojeian, respectively. On the other hand, Shishmanian and Anergiugh, 'Teghekagir Kilikiayi', *Hnch'ak*, no. 22 (1 December 1895): 181 mention Guedjian only as Kurken.
87 Great Britain, FO 861, File 28, Dowek to Barnham, 3 August 1895; FO 195, File 1883, and FO 424, File 183, Barnham to Currie, 7 August 1895; USNA, RG 59, vol. 60 (microfilm reel 59), # 630, Terrell to Olney, 24 September 1895; France, Archives du Ministère des Affaires Étrangères (AMAE), Turquie: Alep, vol. 10, *1893-1895*, Albert Potton to Le Ree, 7 April [must be 7 August] 1895. At one point Le Ree maintained that Guedjian had Austrian citizenship. See idem, Le Ree to Gabriel Hanotaux, 12 August 1895.
88 Turkey, BOA, DH.ŞFR.00177.009.001.001, 002.001, Aleppo Governor Hasan to Ministry of Interior, no date given.
89 Ibid., BOA, DH.ŞFR.00177.00, Aleppo Province cyphered telegram no. 7792 to Ministry of Interior, 4 August 1895. See also Bilâl N. Şimşir (ed.), *Documents diplomatiques ottomans: Affaires arméniennes*, vol. III (1895–1896) (Ankara: Imprimerie de la Société Turque d'Histoire, 1999), 238–9.
90 France, AMAE, Turquie: Alep, vol. 10, *1893-1895*, Le Ree to Hanotaux, 12 August 1895; USNA, RG 59, vol. 60 (microfilm reel 59), # 629, Terrell to Olney, 25 September 1895; Enclosure: 1/630, Translation of Indictment Marked 'e'; Terrell to Olney, 24 September 1895. Indicted with Guedjian were Kevork of Haji Jilis, son of Tujjar Mamas; Garabed of Beylan, son of Apraham; gunsmith Garabed, son of Babik of Aintab; Sarkis, son of Avedis of Aintab; Apraham, son of Boghos of Antioch; and Manoug, son of Hovhannes.
91 USNA, RG 59, vol. 60 (microfilm reel 59), # 627, Terrell to Olney, 18 September 1895; # 630, Terrell to Said Pasha, 23 September 1895; # 640, Terrel to Said Pasha, 23 September 1895; Terrell to Olney, 28 September 1895; # 643, Terrell to Olney 26 September 1895, 14 October 1895; Poche to Terrell, 3 October 1895; Terrell to Said Pasha, 23 October 1895; # 654, Terrell to Olney, 28 October 1895, 30 October 1895; # 657, Enclosure: 3/660, Said Pasha to Terrell, 30 October 1895; vol. 61 (microfilm reel 60), # 699, Terrell to Olney, 3 December 1895; Enclosure: 1/699, Seal of Ministry of Police of Stamboul to see Terrell (copy of translation), n. d.; Enclosure 2/699, Terrell to Olney, 3 December 1895; Enclosure: 2/712, Minister of Foreign Affairs to Terrell, 8 December 1895 (translation note verbale); *New York Times*, 28 September 1895, 1.
92 USNA, RG 59, Despatches, vol. 61 (microfilm reel 60), # 727, Terrell to Olney, 17 December 1895. Aghasi, 'Husher', 131, never found out how Guedjian was released or what happened to the 760 liras. That sum, in fact, was not returned to Guedjian, who was sent to Europe and from there to the United States with U.S. ambassador Terrell's own money.
93 France, AMAE, Turquie: Alep, vol. 10, *1893-1895*, Le Ree to Hanotaux, 5 August 1895.
94 Ibid.; Great Britain, FO 861, File 28, Dowek to Barnham, 1 August 1895; Italy, Archivio Storico, Armenia—Rapporti Politici, 1895, File *Armenia, Settembre 1895*, L'incident d'Antioche, resumé d'un rapport en date du 22 juillet (v. s.) 1895, arrive d'Antioche. See also *The New York Times*, 25 February 1896, 5.

95 Great Britain, FO 861, File 28, Dowek to Barnham, 1 August 1895; AGC, H 93, Cartella V, Marcellino da Vallarsa to Excellency, 1 August 1895.
96 Great Britain, FO 861, File 28, Dowek to Barnham, 1 August 1895; France, AMAE, Turquie: Alep, vol. 10, *1893-1895*, French consular agent at Antioch [Potton] to French consul general at Aleppo [Le Ree], 2 August 1895; Italy, Archivio Storico, Armenia—Rapporti Politici, 1895, File *Armenia, Settembre 1895*, L'incident d'Antioche, resumé d'un rapport en date du 22 juillet (v.s.) 1895, arrive d'Antioche. According to the Italian source, the attack on the Armenian quarter was premeditated.
97 Great Britain, FO 861, File 28, Dowek to Barnham, 1 August 1895.
98 France, AMAE, Turquie: Alep, vol. 10, *1893-1895*, French consular agent at Antioch to French consul general at Aleppo, 2 August 1895, and Le Ree to Governor General of Aleppo, 3 August 1895.
99 Ibid., Hassan to Le Ree, 4 August 1895.
100 Great Britain, FO 861, File 28, Dowek to Barnham, 17 August 1895.
101 France, AMAE, Turquie: Alep, vol. 10, *1893-1895*, Potton to Le Ree, April 7 [must be 7 August] 1895.
102 Ibid.
103 Ibid., 24 August 1895.
104 Ibid.
105 Ibid.
106 Great Britain, FO 861, File 28, Dowek to Barnham, 8 August 1895.
107 Turkey, BOA, A.MKT.MHM.646.8.3, telegram from Aleppo Province to Ministry of Interior, 9 September 1895.
108 Great Britain, FO 195, File 1883, Barnham to Currie, 16 October 1895; FO 424, File 184, Currie to Marquess of Salisbury, 17 October 1895.
109 AGC, H 93, Cartella V, Da Vallarsa to Rev. Father General, 19 April 1896. The two reports were sent on Saturday, 7 March 1896.
110 Great Britain, FO 861, File 29, Dowek to Catoni, 18 March 1896, 26 March 1896, 3 April 1896; Catoni to Currie, 9 April 1896; FO 195, File 1932, Catoni telegrams no. 41, 30 March 1896, no. 43, 6 April 1896, no. 44, 9 April 1896; Catoni to Currie, 19 March 1896; FO 424, File 186, Currie to Marquess of Salisbury, 31 March 1896; AGC, H 93, Cartella V, Da Vallarsa to Rev. Father General, 19 April 1896.
111 Great Britain, FO 195, File 1932, Catoni telegram no. 34, 12 March 1896; Catoni to Currie, 19 March 1896. The incident occurred probably as a result of an isolated Armenian-Alawi (Nusayri) friction. See FO 861, File 29, Dowek to Catoni, 18 March 1896; Rstigian, 'Musa Taghë', *Hayrenik' Amsagir*, no. 6 (June 1952): 74–5.
112 Great Britain, FO 195, File 1932, Catoni telegram no. 41, 30 March 1896; FO 424, File 186, Currie to Marquess of Salisbury, 31 March 1896.
113 Ibid., FO195, File 1932, Catoni to Currie, 9 April 1896; Catoni telegram no. 44, 9 April 1896.
114 Ibid., FO 861, file 29, Dowek to Catoni, 26 March 1896.
115 Ibid., FO 195, File 1932, Catoni telegram no. 35, 16 March 1896; FO 861, File 29, Dowek to Catoni, 18 March 1896.
116 Ibid., FO 861, File 29, Catoni to Currie, 19 March 1896.
117 Ibid., FO 861, File 29, Dowek to Catoni, 18 March 1896.
118 Ibid., FO 195, File 1932, Catoni telegram no. 41, 30 March 1896; Catoni to Currie, 9 April 1896; FO 424, File 186, Currie to Marquess of Salisbury, 31 March 1896; FO 861, File 29, Catoni to Dowek, 4 April 1896.

119 Ibid., FO 861, File 29, Dowek to Catoni, 3 April 1896; FO 424, File 187, R. Drummond Hay to Currie, 7 April 1896.
120 Ibid., FO 195, File 1932, Catoni to Currie, 21 April 1896.
121 Ibid., FO 861, File 29, Dowek to Catoni, 18 March 1896.
122 Garigian, *Druagner Suētioy Heghap'okhut'ean Patmut'enēn* (Paris: Abaka Press, 1921), 4–5.
123 Ibid., 6–8.
124 Ibid., 11–12.
125 AGC, H 93, Cartella V, Da Vallarsa to Rev. Father General, 19 April 1896.
126 USNA, RG 59, Despatches, vol. 64 (microfilm reel 62), #1129, Ali Riza and Mustafa Nedim Effendi to [Augusto] Toselli, 2 March 1312 [1896].
127 Great Britain, FO 195, File 1932, Catoni to Currie, 9 April 1896. See also Catoni telegram no. 44, 9 April 1896.
128 Ibid., Catoni telegram, no. 43, 6 April 1896; FO 424, File 187, Currie to Marquess of Salisbury, 14 April 1896.
129 AGC, H 93, Cartella V, Da Vallarsa to Rev. Father General, 19 April 1896.
130 Ibid.
131 Ibid.
132 Great Britain, FO 195, File 1932, Catoni to Currie, 21 April 1896; Garigian, *Druagner*, 23–7. The FO source mentions thirteen revolutionaries, two of whom foreigners.
133 Ibid., FO 195, File 1932, Catoni to Currie, 21 April 1896.
134 AGC, H 93, Cartella V, Da Vallarsa to Rev. Father General, 19 April 1896.
135 Garigian, *Druagner*, 31–7.
136 AGC, H 93, Cartella V, Da Vallarsa to Rev. Father General, 19 April 1896. A Foreign Office document mentions Saturday, 11 April 1896, as the meeting date. See Great Britain, FO 195, File 1932, Catoni to Currie, 21 April 1896. Given the fact that Da Vallarsa actually participated in the negotiations, 10 April must be the correct date.
137 Rsdigian, 'Musa Taghě', *Hayrenik' Amsagir*, no. 6 (June 1952): 76. The Hnchakian leadership at the time consisted of Shavarsh Shishmanian (chairman), Smpad Rsdigian, and Yesayi Garigian, for Aghasi and a small team of comrades had left Musa Dagh for Zeytun in the summer of 1895. For Aghasi's departure, see France, AMAE, Turquie: Alep, vol. 10, *1893-1895*, Potton to Le Ree, 20 September 1895; Aghasi, 'Husher', 135–41; Shishmanian, 'Kilikean Suētia', *Shirak*, no. 3 (August 1906): 154; Rsdigian, 'Musa Taghě', *Hayrenik' Amsagir*, no. 5 (May 1952): 22.
138 AGC, H 93, Cartella V, Da Vallarsa to Rev. Father General, 19 April 1896.
139 Ibid.
140 Ibid.; Great Britain, FO 195, File 1932, Catoni telegram no. 45, 13 April 1896; Catoni to Currie, 21 April 1896; Shishmanian, 'Kilikean Suētia', *Shirak*, no. 5 (October 1906): 272. On 14 October, Da Vallarsa visited British Vice-Consul Dowek to deliver him the Hnchakian objects that Baron Avedis had left with him. Dowek, however, refused to receive the parcel without permission from his superior at Aleppo. See FO 861, File 29, Dowek to Catoni, 15 April 1896. Also, Da Vallarsa does not mention that an Armenian priest accompanied him while escorting the revolutionaries to Antioch.
141 AGC, H 93, Cartella V, Da Vallarsa to Fr. General, 26 January 1897.
142 Great Britain, FO 861, File 29, Dowek to Catoni, 6 May 1896.
143 Ibid., FO 195, File 1932, Barnham telegram, 9 May 1896.
144 Ibid., Barnham to Currie, 18 May 1896.
145 France, AMAE, Syrie-Liban, vol. 104, *Dossier général, 1896-1897 juin*, H. Pognou to G. Hanotaux, 27 December 1896.

146 USNA, RG 59, Despatches, vol. 64 (microfilm reel 62), # 1151, Horace Lee Washington to Terrell, 23 January 1897; Terrell to Olney, 6 January 1897. As seen in the text, different sources have provided different numbers (12 and 9) regarding the revolutionaries carrying U.S. passports.
147 Great Britain, FO 195, File 1932, Barnham to Currie, 25 May 1896.
148 Ibid., FO 861, File 31, Establishment of reserves in Vilayet of Aleppo; Return Shewing the Number and Stations of All Troops Quartered in the Vilayet of Aleppo.
149 Great Britain, FO 195, File 2054, Barnham to N.R. O'Conor, 21 May 1899.
150 Ibid., FO 195, File 1976, Barnham telegrams no. 18, 31 March 1897, no. 19, 1 April 1897; Barnham to Currie, 14 May 1897; Austria-Hungary, Carton 306, File *Aleppo, 1897*, [illegible] to Agenor von Goluchowsky, 1 April 1897.
151 Great Britain, FO 195, File 1976, Barnham to Currie, 1 October 1897; FO 861, File 31, Sanders to Barnham, 6 September 1897; ABCFM, ABC: 16.9.5, vol. 11, a newspaper clip; vol. 14, Sanders to Judson Smith, 20 September 1898; Sanders to James Barton, 27 April 1898; affidavit from forty-six clergymen and notables from Musa Dagh to 'the Christians of America'. For a somewhat different version of the incident, consult France, AMAE, Syrie-Liban, vol. 105, *Dossier général juillet-décembre 1897*, Le Gerant du Consulat d'Alep [name illegible] to Hanotaux, 18 October 1897. The Hnchakians persecuted Yarpuzlian in the United States, accusing him of embezzlement of relief funds earmarked for Musa Dagh, of conversion to Islam, and of treachery. See, especially, the ABCFM documents *supra*.
152 Turkey, BOA, DH.TMIK.M.75.49.3-5, cyphered telegram Serial no. 1016 from Serasker Riza to General Military Command, 7 August 1899.
153 Zora Isgenderian, *Husher Patmut'ean Hamar* (Beirut: Sevan Printing House, 1974), 11–20. In April 1904, it was reported that 'eight Armenian revolutionaries who had escaped to Europe have returned to the Svetya littoral at Arsuz through Egypt. One of them, Hagop son of Koko, is from Yoghun Oluk village'. See Turkey, BOA, DH.ŞFR.667.77, Adana Province to Interior Ministry, telegram Serial no. 1298, 9 April 1904.
154 *Eritasard Hayastan*, 11 March 1921; *Hnch'ak*, no. 17 (May 1936) and no. 3 (March 1935).
155 Aghasi, 'Husher', 89.
156 Shishmanian, 'Kilikean Suētia', *Shiruk*, no. 3 (August 1906): 148–9 and idem, no. 5 (October, 1906): 271.
157 Great Britain, FO 861, File 31, Sanders to Barnham, 3 May 1897. See also ABCFM, ABC: 16.9.5, vol. 14, Sanders to Smith, 20 September 1898.
158 *Biwzandion*, 27 April 1911.

9

The Hnchakians in South America

Early History

Vartan Matiossian

The 125th anniversary of the foundation of the Social Democrat Hnchakian Party (hereby SDHP) in 2012 coincided with the 100th anniversary of the foundation of its oldest South American chapter in Buenos Aires. This article constitutes the first attempt at outlining the early history of the party in South America (Argentina, Uruguay and Brazil). It is noteworthy that local archival materials are not accessible and press collections are either non-existent or outside public availability. On the other hand, secondary sources, either in Armenian or local languages (Spanish and Portuguese), are plagued with contradictory information.

The Buenos Aires chapter of the Armenian General Benevolent Union (AGBU) was founded in April 1911 and the Armenian Apostolic Church was established after the first Divine Liturgy held in April 1912, the same month as the local chapter of the Armenian Revolutionary Federation (ARF) was established. The latter was reorganized in December 1912.[1] Meanwhile, Hovannes (Onnig) Gulbenkian, correspondent of *Kohak* – a SDHP newspaper edited by Hmayag Aramiants in Constantinople – wrote in his first report from Buenos Aires in August 1912: 'No efforts are spared to found a S.D. Hnchakian chapter and we will probably succeed in the near future; the arrangement of the well-known pending issues will contribute much to our success (...).'[2] In his next report (May 1913), Gulbenkian announced that thirty-one members from Everek, a village near Caesarea (today's Kayseri), had formed the chapter, but did not mention the date.[3] The prevalent view, according to the testimony of Sdepan (Panos) Shkherdemian, an elder member who settled in Argentina before the First World War, is that a group of Armenians from Everek, led by Jivan Tokatlian, founded the Hnchakian chapter in late 1912.[4]

According to Sahag Bakchejian (Bakchellian, 1888–1963), who arrived in 1913 and became a leading party figure for the next half century, the community counted 2,000 people by 1914.[5] The party underwent a process of organization parallel to the influx of Armenian immigrants prior to the First World War and entered the fray of internal politics. Between March and August 1915, the main organizations of the community – the Parish Council of the Apostolic Church and the ARF on one side and the AGBU and the SDHP on the other – worked separately to raise funds for the Armenian volunteers and the victims of the genocide.[6] In the next six months, there was a concerted effort to achieve a degree of cooperation in the field. A reporter for *Koch'nak*, in New York, wrote that the organizations had developed 'a conciliatory spirit of unity towards each other, and a new effort to work cooperatively in order to satisfy the demanding needs of our wounded homeland'.[7] It was short-lived, however; in March 1916, the AGBU and the SDHP reportedly boycotted a fundraiser of the Parish Council and the ARF Committee.[8]

The community was weakened by the emigration of half of its members to the United States due to the economic crisis in Argentina. Internal strife and disorganization continued until the last months of the war.

After the Armenian National Union (ANU) was founded in the United States (April 1917), the SDHP and the ARF undertook informal contact to organize the Buenos Aires community on its model with the AGBU.[9] An official meeting initiated by the SDHP was held in March 1918 with the participation of the ARF, the Reformed Hnchakian Party – date of foundation unknown – and the AGBU.[10] However, the Unión Nacional Armeniana, chaired by Hnchakian member Hampartsoum Kechejian, only included the SDHP, the 'new' board of the Parish Council aligned with the non-ARF side, the Evangelical Church – date of foundation unknown – the AGBU, and the Hajin Society, founded in 1915 and also chaired by Kechejian.[11] It appears that the Union had initially included the ARF and the ARF-controlled 'old' board of the Parish Council, but the Hnchakian drive to power had apparently forced them to quit.[12]

Internal disputes triggered a crisis in July 1918; the Union was reorganized in September through the efforts of Israyel Arslan (1879–1953) and renamed Unión Nacional Armenia (UNA). It regarded itself as the Argentinean chapter of the ANU of America and followed its bylaws. Accordingly, it included six religious, political and charitable organizations: the Apostolic Church, the Evangelical Church, the SDHP, the ARF, the Reformed Hnchakian Party and the AGBU. The SDHP was represented by Nazaret Khesulmunian (Khulmunian),[13] who later moved to Montevideo, where he was a speaker at the celebration of the second anniversary of the independence (1920).[14]

The internal situation of the UNA in Buenos Aires reflected the looming problems within the North American organization, where an anti-partisan stance led to disputes with the SDHP and, subsequently, the ARF, resulting in the withdrawal of the former in early 1919. The crushing ARF victory in the elections for representatives to the Armenian National Congress in Paris (1919) was marred by purported attempts of electoral fraud by the non-ARF faction. After the rejection of its proposal to elect the board by popular vote, the ARF also left the ANU.[15] The Reformed Hnchakian Party remained as its only political support.

The thirty-first Representative Assembly of the American Regional of the SDHP (1918) had decided to divide America into five sections, with California and South America temporarily linked to the Executive Body of the American Regional.[16] The party chapters in Buenos Aires 'followed the same course suggested by the Armenian American organ of their party'.[17] Both the SDHP (May 1919)[18] and the ARF (March 1920) left the UNA, arguing that none of them was any longer represented at the ANU, on which the Argentinean organization depended.[19] They were the main organized political forces in Buenos Aires and constituted an Inter-Party Body in February 1920 led by three members, two from the ARF and one from the SDHP (S. Shkherdemian). It worked to assist the fledgling Republic of Armenia in open competition with the National Union.[20]

According to the 25 April session of the ARF committee, the SDHP submitted a proposal to jointly celebrate the second anniversary of the independence.[21] A few days later, Etienne Brazil, diplomatic representative of the Republic of Armenia for South America, who was headquartered in Rio de Janeiro (Brazil), wrote to the Inter-Party Body: 'Your [April] 23 letter made me very happy after seeing that two powerful parties which represent the true strength of our nation have joined forces. . . . Your idea of the May 28 celebration is much praised.' He added some comments that were quite characteristic of the rousing enthusiasm of those times:

> Never be interested in those Armenians who remain indifferent towards any pro-Armenian events. Our republic has already been recognized. The Armenian who carries in his veins the blood of a true Armenian sooner or later will embrace our tricolor flag, which today waves on the heights of the Ararat, colored by so many traces of blood.[22]

The Inter-Party Body issued several circulars that appear to have inflamed the spirits in the community. According to the AGBU minutes, '[their] content is completely contrary to the spirit of true Armenians and they have labeled the other party and organizations as traitor and retrograde, as if the republic were their property and only Hnchakians and Dashnaktsakans were entitled to celebrate'.[23] Two different celebrations of the independence were separately organized by the two parties[24] and by the National Union and the AGBU on 28 May 1920.[25] The former collected almost 30,000 francs,[26] while the National Union-AGBU event raised around 29,000.[27] The money was mostly sent to the Armenian government, while a small share went to the Armenian population in Cilicia, which was fighting in self-defence against Kemalist forces after the French-Turkish pact of 1920.[28]

An inter-party fundraiser to help Cilician Armenians began on 29 June 1920.[29] The two parties also created the Committee of Aid to the Armenian Army on 16 July chaired by Shkherdemian.[30] More than 23,000 francs were collected during a rally and sent to Avetis Aharonian, president of the delegation of the Republic of Armenia.[31]

An effort to mend the community rift led to a general meeting on 4 July when the National Union decided to rename itself Unión Nacional Armenia de Argentina (Armenian National Union of Argentina) and adopt new bylaws, thus ending its dependence on the United States. At a new general meeting held on 14 July the executive board of the National Union was again formed by the Apostolic and Evangelical Churches, the three political parties (ARF, Hnchakian and Ramkavar), and the AGBU. The meeting approved the new bylaws and resolved to include two non-partisan board members.[32]

The disputes were still ongoing. E. Brazil wrote to the Inter-Party Body on August 5:

Since you belong to different currents, I don't consider appropriate to intervene in your internal struggles, because a nation is dead without conscientious internal struggle; however, I would only suggest that, when it comes to an external issue, you must work cooperatively to defend national interests before foreigners. Consequently, I request that you form a committee with two members from each current to manage Armenian internal and external affairs until new indications are given. I have also written a similar letter to the National Union.[33]

He repeated his request three days later, with the addition that the committee should also include a fifth non-partisan member.[34] The ARF committee adopted a variant of this proposal on its 12 September meeting:

[T]o propose that the five members of the board are elected by popular vote and the three political parties, Hnchakian, Ramkavar, and Dashnaktsakan, have one representative each. The newly formed board will provisionally manage the external and internal affairs of the community until the arrival of the representative of the Republic of Armenia. After his arrival, the parties will retire their representatives and the remaining five members of the board will manage the internal affairs of the community.[35]

Suggestions and negotiations would be ineffective. At a community assembly on 17 October 1920, the reading of a report on the activities of the Union was followed by the announcement that the ARF and the SDHP were leaving it.[36] The reasons are unclear. Dissatisfied with non-partisan hegemony, the political parties, despite their small membership, may have preferred to continue working alone.

The failed negotiations triggered the collapse of the National Union. Despite some efforts to revive it in 1923, the institution continued a nominal existence until 1933. Its president and secretary exclusively signed official paperwork and identity documents, since it was the only Armenian institution officially recognized by the government with authority to issue such papers.[37]

Meanwhile, after a year of uncertainty that echoed the general chaos lived by Armenians everywhere, several meetings in November and December 1921 resolved the formation of an 'Armenian House' (*Hay Tun*), later called 'Armenian Community Center' (*Hay Gaghut'ayin Kedron*) as a new umbrella organization without religious and political distinctions. A five-member committee was charged with the writing of the bylaws; the only party member was H. Kechejian.[38] A foundational meeting was held on 25 January 1922, and a general meeting elected the board on 7 May.

The Center mentioned as its first purpose 'to keep national and religious feelings awake', and to work 'to care for the national education of Armenian children and youth'.[39] In May 1922, S. Bakchejian suggested the opening of schools in four key neighbourhoods of Buenos Aires: Palermo (AGBU offices), San Juan (SDHP club), Liniers (Khacher Mardoyan's home) and Barracas.[40] In July it was considered 'enough for now' to ask for facilities in the first three areas.[41] The resolution to open classes was set into motion, although, according to the annual report of the Center (May 1923), '. . . the result of our partial inquiries has shown us that our children do not make significant number in any neighborhood'.[42] Bakchejian became chairman of the Armenian Community Center in 1925-6.

The establishment of the Soviet regime in Armenia in December 1920 created a shift of forces abroad, particularly within the ARF and the SDHP. The membership loss in the ARF was essentially the result of disillusionment about the future viability of the party and its policies towards Armenia, while the process in the SDHP was part of the internal debates on the party's rapprochement to the new regime.[43] In 1924 Garabed Keshishian, secretary of the Armenian Community Center, wrote in a report to *Koch'nak* that 'both parties have their clubs and activities, which have some usefulness, but however, it is painful to see that partisanship, the mistake of putting the party above the interests of the nation has also taken a very obvious turn here', and expressed the wish that 'our parties (. . .) awaken and change the form and the course of their activities'.[44]

Despite the paucity of material, we can give an outline about the Argentinean chapter of the SDHP, which published the first Armenian-language newspaper in South America, the collotype monthly *Khorhrdayin Hayastan*. Its name, meaning 'Soviet Armenia', was an obvious indication of pro-Soviet sympathies by a current within the party. Mihran Seferian first dated it 1922[45] and then 1923, with Apraham Krajian as editor,[46] whereas Ardashes Der Khachadurian gave the date 1922-3 and wrote that it published at least five issues.[47] The date 1922-3 appears more accurate for various reasons.[48]

In July 1923, a communiqué released by the SDHP and the Armenian Workers Party – the Armenian section of the Workers Party of America, the predecessor to the Communist Party USA – announced their unification under the name of the Armenian Federation of the Workers Party of America.[49] In South America, the ongoing internal conflict, as well as the need to fit into the Argentinean political environment led to a different outcome. *Khorhrdayin Hayastan* was replaced by a printed weekly. The new publication adopted the name of *Arzhēnt'inean Mamul* (Argentinean Press) and has been commonly claimed to have been the first Armenian-language newspaper in Argentina and South America.[50] Stepan Shkherdemian, its editor, wrote decades later:

> It was necessary to have a printed newspaper, even if small and modest. But how? Everything was lacking: Armenian fonts, layout, typesetters, and even . . . a more or less capable editor. We bought a few kilos of unused typefaces owned by the local AGBU chapter. We mixed them with Latin characters 'seemingly' Armenian and we had enough typefaces to publish the newspaper[51]

This paper was actually the first *printed* Armenian-language newspaper, published between 7 October 1923 and 6 April 1924.[52] It was typed in the Hnchakian club and printed at *La Internacional*, the organ of the Communist Party of Argentina, reflecting the growing Hnchakian and Communist contact at the time. The pro-Soviet wing of the SDHP executed a takeover in late 1923, as announced by a letter quoted in the Soviet Armenian press months later. The anonymous writer was probably Zarmair Kiwtnerian, cited by Shkherdemian as having been a member of the editorial board:[53]

On the eve of the third anniversary of Soviet Armenia, we three Communist comrades were able to put *Arzhent'inean Mamul* at our disposal. The first issue under my editorship was published on December 2 [1923]. I had no responsibility for the issues previously published. Comrade Moshe [M. Oshin] will soon arrive as editor of *A[rzhent'inean] Mamul*.⁵⁴

On 30 December 1923, *Arzhent'inean Mamul* became the 'organ of the Social Democratic Hnchakian Party of the Armenian Federation of the American Workers Party'.⁵⁵ However, this did not last long. Following the break-up of the short-lived Hnchakian-Communist agreement in the United States,⁵⁶ the 30 March 1924 issue was published as 'organ of the Buenos Aires chapter of the S.D. Hnchakian Party' and declared that Kiwtnerian was no longer related to the paper. Shkherdemian was editor again, this time on a temporary capacity.⁵⁷ The last issue of 6 April announced the arrival of M. Oshin (Mihran Uzunian) as editor.⁵⁸ According to Shkherdemian, *Arzhent'inean Mamul* folded because of 'economic difficulties'. However, it resurfaced on 17 April, under Oshin's editorship and with the new name *Nor Erkir*.⁵⁹ It is likely that the change was the result of a comeback by the leftist wing; Kiwtnerian seems to have returned either as Oshin's deputy editor⁶⁰ or successor.⁶¹

The ideological rift came to a formal break-up in Buenos Aires when a group of 'Hnchakian comrades that had reached class awareness' left the party and founded the Armenian section of the Argentinean Communist Party on 1 May 1924.⁶² A correspondent to the weekly *Zart'ōnk'* of Alexandretta attested that the Hnchakian Party had suffered a division after joining the Workers Party in North America, and the Hnchakians had followed that pattern in Argentina: one part had remained within the party and the other had formed a communist cell, with *Nor Yerkir* as the latter's organ.⁶³

Another Hnchakian group left the party in September 1924 and formed the 'Shahumian' chapter of the Armenian Section, with Oshin himself as secretary.⁶⁴ A month later, a correspondent to the daily *Aṛawōt* of Constantinople mentioned 'the Communist printed weekly *Nor Erkir*' as part of the Armenian press of Buenos Aires, which, along with '*Karmir Astgh*, collotype, fight the Communist struggle, but their orientation is moderate'.⁶⁵ In December, the AGBU chapter decided to ask back the typefaces rented to the party, 'because they are not in use'.⁶⁶ They were returned in March 1925.⁶⁷ It is likely that *Nor Erkir* had already ceased publication by the time.

According to Kiwtnerian, who had just moved to France, in February 1925, most of the fifty members of the Armenian Section were former Hnchakians, along with four or five former ARF members.⁶⁸ A letter sent to the Hnchakian weekly *Ardzagang P'arizi* in Paris reported that the Hnchakian chapter of Buenos Aires had been reconstituted with twenty-five members.⁶⁹

The growing influence of the pro-Soviet current in the community, reinforced by the foundation of the Buenos Aires chapter of the Committee of Aid to Armenia (*Hayastani Ōgnut'ean Komitē*, HOK) in 1924, challenged the SDHP hegemony in the non-ARF political arena during the 1920–30s. Mgrdich Hagopian described the party schism in a speech of 1936:

> A group of restless people, who used to make pointless noise from the very beginning, with pretentions of having made a big discovery and other 'perspectives,'

one day stood up, led by well-known *Panchoonie* Zarmayr Kiwtnerian, to deliver the 'beautiful' message that the Hnchakian Party has nothing to do [any more].[70] Of course, this had some impact on party members, and also became the reason for some others to isolate themselves. However, conscientious comrades were solidly grappled to their party, as they had faith and hope in what it could do and the role it could play.

The group that set the division, which had no political value, after long wanderings and an equal number of name changes, found shelter under the redeeming umbrella of the HOK. The outcome of those games was very costly for us. The enemy,[71] which did not have a remarkable value until then, took advantage and started a fast progress. Twelve years have passed since that meaningless 'struggle' and this period has sufficed for Armenian workers to study the things and the events, to see evil and good, and we are very happy to declare that the same workers trusted their vote to the Armenian Marxist political party, the Hnchakians, as the authentic defender of their cause.[72]

In 1930, the chapter of Buenos Aires undertook a new reorganization with seventy-two members. According to the news report, 'the chapter had almost stopped activities due to the known issues', but the editorials of *Eritasard Hayastan*, the central organ in the United States, had allayed doubts and contributed to the reorganization.[73] The chapter also had the theatre group 'Sabah-Gulian' and the Student Union,[74] as well as a club and a library.[75] In 1937, the party expanded to five chapters. Four of them were in different neighbourhoods (Sabah-Gulian, in Palermo; Paramaz, in downtown; Murad, in Villa Soldati; and Sarkis Dkhruni, in Boca and Barracas) and the fifth, Jirayr, was located in the nearby suburb of Valentin Alsina.[76]

The Ninth World Assembly of the party decided to create the Regional Committee of South America in 1934.[77] This decision acknowledged the growing importance of the regional chapters. The Executive Body of the Hnchakian Party decided to move the monthly *Kaytz* from São Paulo to Buenos Aires in 1935, and the First Representative Assembly of the South America region, held in Buenos Aires in July 1936, seconded this move.[78] However, the decision was postponed for a year, and *Kaytz* was finally closed in May 1937 after twenty-two issues by the decision of the second Representative Assembly of South America, held in Buenos Aires. It was going to be reissued in Buenos Aires as an organ of the South American chapters.[79]

Sharzhum, founded by Sahag Bakchejian,[80] was the successor to *Kaytz* and published its first issue on 19 June 1937.[81] It appeared in Armenian – except for a government-mandated Spanish column from 1943–55 – and became bilingual (Armenian and Spanish) in the 1970s, sporadically featuring articles in Portuguese too. It appeared as a four-page broadsheet between 1937 and 1980, when it became a tabloid (eight to twelve pages). It had a run of 1,000 copies in 1954[82] and 1,500 in 1974.[83] The first editor was Dajad Kntuni,[84] followed by Yervant Mkhitarian (Garmrag) from São Paulo, who remained as a field worker and editor for six months after the South American Representative Assembly of 1937,[85] and Mgrdich Hagopian.[86] Apraham Eolmez became editor in 1939 until his sudden death in May 1958.[87] Vahan Zeituntsian succeeded him as editor from January 1959 until his death ten months later.[88] He was followed by Nazaret Guzhnuni (Jerejian), who resigned in June 1962;[89] Giwregh Achabahian, mentioned as editor in November 1962,[90] and Albert Keoseyan, who was fired in September 1965.[91] Afterwards, the weekly was edited again by Guzhnuni (1966–9), followed by Varuzhan Ajemian (1969–76),[92] and Samuel (Samo) Sarkissian (1976–91).

Sharzhum ceased publication in June 1991 after fifty-four years of uninterrupted publication. It was the third newspaper in the Armenian press of South America for its longevity after *Armenia* and *Nor Hajin*.

The SDHP had a chapter in Cordoba, 600 kilometres north of Buenos Aires. A letter of 1 October 1929, informed that the newly constituted chapter had received the approval from the Central Executive Body of the party, and there had been board elections. The chapter had thirty members.[93] The party club was opened in February 1930 and the theatre group 'Jirayr' was also formed,[94] followed by a new theatre group, 'Paramaz', in 1934.[95] In late January 1936, party antagonism peaked after the victory of the Popular Front, also integrated by the SDHP, in the elections of the Armenian Community Center, which provoked the division of the community. The ARF was excluded and founded a second church and a school. Hnchakian militant Apraham Eolmez continued as director of the community school until his move to Buenos Aires in 1939.[96] In this year, the party had a youth branch, the Kaytz Youth Union.[97] The division continued until it was solved in 1943 due to the intervention of Sahag Bakchejian, then chairman of the Administrative Institution of the Armenian Church in Buenos Aires.

The other South American communities saw the birth and growth of their local chapters in this period. The Hnchakian chapter of Montevideo was founded in the neighbourhood of Cerro, which was the first concentration of the community, in 1926. It moved out in the 1950s and finally settled in its current location in November 1962.[98] The number of its members is said to have reached up to 150.[99] The newly created Central Administrative Council of the Armenian Diocese of Uruguay was under Hnchakian control from 1937 to 1939.[100]

In 1932, the SDHP founded the Haigazian School,[101] which was under the sponsorship of the Central Administrative Council in 1942 and had sixty-five students.[102] An Armenian Student Union was founded in 1938 and had thirty members in 1943, and a youth section was created with female (1939) and male branches (1942), counting seventy-five members in 1943.[103] Printed media were always short-lived in the community, which depended on the Armenian newspapers of Buenos Aires for printed information and always relied on radio programmes that historically belonged to different sectors: 'If the schools are there to educate and enhance Armenianism [*sic*] in the youth, the radio stations play an essential role in maintaining the sense of community in a land where assimilation has taken its toll.'[104] At the same time, the radio programmes were bound to become a central player in the political struggle. The first radio hour of the community, Radio Armenia, founded on 15 June 1935, was a joint venture by Hnchakian Party member Harutyun Rupenian and sympathizer Hovannes Ateshian.[105] Rupenian later became the sole owner of the radio programme, which in 1947 was broadcasted four times a week for a total of eight hours.[106] After various moves, Rupenian bought the Independencia radio station in 1957 and turned

Radio Armenia into a daily programme, with Armenian and Spanish sections, which he directed until his death in 1993. His widow Araksi continued it until the demise of the radio hour in July 2007.[107]

The SDHP-sponsored radio hour Voice of the Armenian Community started in November 1938 and was still on the airwaves in 1943,[108] but had disappeared by 1947.[109]

In Brazil, the beginning of organized Hnchakian presence was marked by the foundation of the chapter of São Paulo (1928), the main centre of the community, with forty members. The majority of the nine founders were from Cilicia (Hajin and Marash).[110] It was followed by the foundation, in 1930, of the Sabah-Gulian club[111] and the Vanig Student Union, which gathered the young membership of the party,[112] although it did not have a single student in its ranks.[113] After the disruption of their activities by some members moving to the interior or abroad, with others leaving the party to found the local chapter of the Committee of Aid to Armenia,[114] the chapter and the Student Union were revived after the election of new boards in April 1931. The São Paulo Police Department approved the statutes of the Union in May 1932.[115] The Sabah Gulian club was reopened in 1933.[116]

In November 1932, the Student Union bought the collotype machine that had belonged to *Erand* (1928–31), the first Brazilian Armenian monthly journal published by the defunct Armenian Co-Ed Youth Union. *Kaytz*, the monthly of the Student Union, started publication in January 1933 with twenty pages and a circulation of 300 copies. Hagop Azadian, M. Mardirosian and Yervant Mkhitarian were the members of the editorial board.[117] It published twenty-five issues until April 1935. The First Representative Assembly of the party in Brazil decided to turn *Kaytz* into a printed publication in March 1934, but the delay in the arrival of the typefaces from the United States postponed the decision until August 1935.[118] The director was Bedros Nazarian, and the editor, Y. Mkhitarian. It ran 1,000 copies.[119] It was published until May 1937, as we saw, and the last issues seem to have been published on a weekly basis, judging from a picture of its cover.[120]

A party member, Antranig Budakian, published the first Armenian newspaper in Portuguese, *O Dominante,* in 1934–5. It was devoted to the promotion of Armenian and Brazilian cultures and may have also had an Armenian section.[121]

In March 1934, the First Representative Assembly of the party had also resolved to open a school.[122] The Kilikia School of São Paulo opened its doors in October 1935 with Y. Mkhitarian as acting principal, then replaced by H. Kalayjian. It was officially sponsored by the Educational Society formed under the aegis of the Student Union, with seventy students and Armenian and Brazilian sections. According to Vartanian, the school lasted just three years and was closed due to financial issues and government pressure.[123] The same writer also mentioned other party-affiliated organizations, such as the Ararat Sport Union, with a two-year life; the Vanig theater group, which lasted until the end of 1937; the Arshaluys Youth Union (co-ed) and the Committee of Reconstruction of Soviet Armenia (1935–6).[124] Most Armenians were concentrated in the state of São Paulo. The second Hnchakian chapter was founded in Lins, a town in the state more than 400 kilometres from the city of São Paulo, in July 1929. After a fast growth, it started disintegrating at the end of 1934 due to the move of its members.[125] The chapter had a theatre group called Banvor.[126] In

1931 another chapter was founded in Araçatuba (more than 500 kilometres from São Paulo) and Hnchakian groups were created in Garça (a newly founded town in the state) and Santos (capital of the state). Outside the state, there was a newly founded chapter in Campo Grande (capital of the state of Mato Grosso) and a group in Rio de Janeiro.[127]

The resolution to move *Kaytz* to Buenos Aires was probably connected to the political situation of the country, which would deliver a fatal blow to the activities of the Hnchakian Party. Getulio Vargas had already shown dictatorial tendencies after coming into power following the revolution of 1930 and winning the presidential elections of 1934. He asked Congress for continuous renewal of the state of emergency resulting from a botched communist coup attempt in 1935. This led to the suspension of civic rights, imprisonment of the opposition and the concession of extraordinary faculties to the government. Vargas followed up with a self-coup in November 1937 and established the authoritarian corporatist regime of the *Estado Novo* ('New State', 1937–45), which followed the model of Italian fascism. In December 1937, Vargas signed a decree dissolving all political parties. The activities of all foreign clubs, newspapers and schools were prohibited.[128] Native or naturalized Brazilians who were children of immigrants were forbidden to become members of foreign institutions in 1938.[129]

During the Second World War, Brazil gradually sided with the Allies and declared war on Germany and Italy in August 1942.[130] The paradox was not missed; liberal sentiments kept growing and Vargas responded by moving away from repressive policies. He promised substantial liberalization after the end of the war, which would bring about the downfall of the *Estado Novo* and his resignation in 1945. The subsequent democratic elections returned political freedom to the country. Hnchakian members had a leading role in the Repatriation Aid Committee (1946–7) that worked towards organizing the settlement of community members from Brazil in Soviet Armenia.[131]

Armenian political parties did not make a visible comeback but made themselves heard through newspapers. The typefaces of *Kaytz* were used for the publication of *Hayastani Dzayn* on 11 January 1947. The six-page broadsheet monthly – four pages in Armenian and two in Portuguese – published twenty-two issues until 1950, with Hagop Kayserlian as owner, B. Nazarian as director and Y. Mkhitarian as editor.[132] It was the last Hnchakian newspaper in Brazil.

Conclusion

The catastrophic years 1915–23 generated a second wave of refugees towards South America, the only corner of the world that favoured almost unrestricted immigration. By 1932, the number of Armenians was estimated to be about 15,000 in Argentina,[133] 4,000 in Uruguay[134] and 3,000 in Brazil.[135] The new wave expanded and reinforced the organizational structure of the Argentinean community and turned the minuscule Armenian groups of Brazil and Uruguay into structured communities.

Besides institutional work, which included the development of satellite organizations (youth, cultural, educational, etc.), and the ideological struggle around

Soviet Armenia and national symbols, the SDHP engaged in power struggle for community control, directed towards institutions (e.g. compatriotic societies), day schools and churches.

Claims of hegemony or preeminence by this or that party have been a staple in the history of the political currents in the Diaspora. The case of the SDHP in Buenos Aires was of particular interest, as it maintained a tactical alliance with the Progressives to keep the political equilibrium vis-à-vis the ARF. Both sides established a regime of cohabitation in the Administrative Institution of the Armenian Church (the Diocesan Council) from 1938 to 1947, including chairmanship by party members, Sahag Bakchejian (SDHP, 1942–5) and Mgrdich Belorian (ARF, 1945–7). In the run up to the elections of May 1947, the ARF refused the demand of the non-ARF sector for the allocation of equal number of seats to each political force. The cohabitation ended and the SDHP-Progressive alliance headed by Bakchejian (52.5 per cent of votes) won the election and governed the institution alone until 1951 when a new regime of cohabitation was put in place for the next seventeen years.

The inner dynamics of that alliance is one of the many issues of the Hnchakian history in South America that expect further inquiries.

Notes

1 See Narciso Binayan (Carmona), *La colectividad armenia en la Argentina* (Buenos Aires: Alzamor Editores, 1974), 121; Narciso Binayan Carmona, *Entre el pasado y el futuro: los armenios en la Argentina* (Buenos Aires: n.p., 1996), 237; Vartan Matiossian, *Harawayin Koghmn Ashkharhi. Hayerě Latin Amerikayi Měj Skizbēn Minch'ew 1950* (Antelias: Press of the Catholicosate of the Great House of Cilicia, 2005), 68–9.
2 *Kohak*, 29 August /11 September 1912, 371. The 'well-known pending issues' are unclear.
3 *Kohak*, 16/29 June 1913, 290.
4 *Sharzhum*, 16 December 1961, 4; Binayan, *La colectividad*, 121 (cf. Binayan, *Entre el pasado*, 237). I have not found any source yet to confirm the date November 1912, which appeared in a recent news report about the celebration of the party's 130th anniversary. See *Armenia*, 13 December 2017. www.diarioarmenia.org.ar/el-partido-Hnchakian-celebro-el-130-aniversario-de-su-fundacion (Accessed on 20 November 2022). Another elder member, Mgrdich Hagopian, gave the date 1913 and added the erroneous information that no other Armenian political current existed in Buenos Aires. See *Eritasard Hayastan*, 24 June 1936, 4.
5 Y. Poghosian, *Hachěni Ěndhanur Patmut'iwn ew Shrjaka Gozan-Taghi Hay Giwgherě* (Los Angeles: Central Commission of the Compatriotic Union for Reconstruction of Hajin, 1942), 795.
6 *Koch'nak*, 28 August 1915, 742; *Armenia*, 21 April 1934, 2.
7 *Koch'nak*, 11 March 1916, 272.
8 *Hayrenik'*, 22 April 1916, 2.
9 *Ardzanagrut'ean Tomar Haykakan Baregortsakan Ěndhanur Miut'ean*, Buenos Aires, minutes of 7 November 1917.

10 Ibid., minutes of 24 February 1918. See also *Armenia,* 28 January 1970, 1. The latter was the first of a nine-part series of unsigned editorials, entitled 'Puēnos Ayrēsi Hay Gaghut'ě ew H. Y. Dashnakts'ut'iwně', and published by editor Ashot Artsruni between 28 January and 6 February 1970.
11 *Ardzanagrut'ean Tomar,* minutes of 8 March 1918; *Armenia,* 1 June 1934, 2.
12 *Ardzanagrut'ean Tomar,* minutes of 30 June and 3 July 1918.
13 Letter from the Armenian National Union to Boghos Nubar, 4 November 1919 (National Archives of Armenia, file 430, catalogue 1, folder 646).
14 *Koch'nak Hayastani,* 24 July 1920, 958.
15 Manoug Hampartsoumian, 'Amerikahay Gaghut'ě (Verjin Tasnameakě)', *Hayrenik' Amsagir,* June 1923, 71–4.
16 *Eritasard Hayastan,* 24 April 1918, 379.
17 *Koch'nak Hayastani,* 12 August 1919, 995.
18 *Pahak,* 6 June 1919, 2.
19 I. A. [Israyel Arslan], 'T'ē Inch'pēs Tsnund Aṛaw H. A. E. Hogabardzut'iwně?', *Hay Kedron,* April 1942, 56.
20 *Armenia,* 26 June 1934, 2.
21 *Armenia,* 30 January 1970, 1.
22 *Armenia,* 17 January 1955, 2.
23 *Ardzanagrut'ean Tomar,* minutes of 2 May 1920.
24 *La Razón,* 28 May 1920, 6; *La Prensa,* 28 May 1920, 13.
25 *La Razón,* 27 May 1920, 5.
26 Binayan, *La colectividad,* 33; Binayan, *Entre el pasado,* 97.
27 Arslan, 'T'ē Inch'pēs', 56; Ashot Artsruni, *Tarets'oyts' Har. Amerikahayots'* (Buenos Aires: Ararat, 1943), 21.
28 Genocide survivors had returned to Cilicia after the armistice of Mudros, counting on the promise of the Allies protection. They stayed in Cilicia during the brief period of the French mandate (1919-1920), until the attacks of the Turkish nationalist forces headed by Mustafa Kemal led to French retreat and the massacre and evacuation of the Armenian population in 1920-1921.
29 *Armenia,* 30 January 1970, 1.
30 Binayan, *Entre el pasado,* 97.
31 *Armenia,* 24 June 1934, 2.
32 Arslan, 'T'ē Inch'pēs', 56–7. The Buenos Aires chapter of the Armenian Democratic Constitutional Party (*Hay Sahmanadir Ṛamkavar Kusakts'ut'iwn*) was formed in February 1919 (*Armenia,* 30 January 1970, 1) and mentioned with the name of Armenian National Democratic Party (*Hay Azgayin Ṛamkavar Kusakts'ut'iwn*) in March 1920 (*Ardzanagrut'ean Tomar,* minutes of 11 March 1920). The 14 July 1920, meeting decided to include the Democrats (*Ṛamkavar*) in the board 'when they are able to send a representative' (Arslan, 'T'ē Inch'pēs', 57), which indicates that the organization was not functional at that time.
33 *Armenia,* 17 January 1955, 2.
34 *Armenia,* 19 January 1955, 2.
35 *Armenia,* 6 February 1970, 1.
36 Arslan, 'T'ē Inch'pēs', May 1942, 74.
37 Matiossian, *Harawayin Koghmn Ashkharhi,* 91–2.
38 Arslan, 'T'ē Inch'pēs', June 1942, 91.
39 *Ardzanagrut'ean Tomar Hay Gaghut'ayin Kedroni,* 'Hay Gaghutayin Kedroni Tsragir'. See Arslan, 'T'ē Inch'pēs', June 1942, 92.

40 See *Ardzanagrut'ean Tomar Hay Gaghutayin Kedroni*, minutes of 30 May 1922, and the AGBU response in *Ardzanagrut'ean Tomar Haykakan Baregortsakan Ĕnthanur Miut'ean*, minutes of 4 June 1922.

41 *Ardzanagrut'ean Tomar Hay Gaghutayin Kedroni*, minutes of 4 July 1922. Arslan only mentioned the first three places and the date 1924 (Arslan, 'T'ē Inch'pēs', November 1942, 105, followed by Binayan, *La colectividad*, 40; Vartan Matiossian, 'La iglesia armenia en Buenos Aires (1912-1938): bosquejo histórico-organizacional', in *Los armenios en América del Sur. Primeras Jornadas de Estudio*, ed. Vartan Matiossian (Buenos Aires: Instituto de Investigación Armenológica, 1991), 87; Binayan, *Entre el pasado*, 111). I have corrected it in Matiossian, *Harawayin Koghmn Ashkharhi*, 171. A misreading of Arslan's mention turned Mardoyan into a Hnchakian member and created an inexistent joint secretariat of the AGBU and SDHP (Nélida Boulgourdjian-Toufeksian, 'The Armenian Church and the School Network in Buenos Aires: Channels for the Preservation of Identity', *Journal of the Society for Armenian Studies* 10 (1998-9 [2000]): 117).

42 *Ardzanagrut'ean Tomar Hay Gaghut'ayin Kedroni*, Report of the Armenian Community Center, May 1922–May 1923.

43 Apraham Krajian (1905–73), a SDHP member arrived in Buenos Aires in 1922, became one of the founders of the Armenian section of the Argentinean Communist Party in 1924 and was the editor of the weekly *Shirak* of the Committee of Aid to Armenia (1933-1936). Krikor Geōnjian, one of the founders of the SDHP chapter in São Paulo in 1928, left the party and moved to Buenos Aires, where he became one of the leaders of the Armenian Section and the director or editor of the pro-Soviet weeklies *Verelk'* (1937–9), *Hay Mamul* (1945–50, 1955–9), *Nor Geank'* (1960–1), and *Sewan* (1961–90) until his death in 1966.

44 *Hayastani Koch'nak*, 3 June 1924, 719.

45 Prptogh [Mihran M. Sēfērian], 'Ts'uts'ak Hnch'[akean] Mamulin 1887-1938', *Usanoghats' Taregirk'*, third year, Beirut, 1938, 138; Mihran Sēfērian, 'S. D. Hnch'akean Kusakts'ut'ean K'arozch'akan Gortsōnēut'iwnĕ (1887-1952)', in *Yisnameak Eritasard Hayastani 1903-1953* (Boston: Eritasard Hayastan, 1953), 163.

46 Mihran M. Seferian, 'S. D. Hnch'akean Kusakts'ut'ean Propakant-K'arozch'akan Kortsunēut'iwnĕ (1887-1952)', *Hnch'akean Matean*, fourth fascicle, January 1954, 95. Hovhannes Petrosian followed Seferian, but created a move of *Khorhrdayin Hayastan* to New York, where the Society for Material Assistance to Soviet Armenia published an unrelated printed monthly, also called *Khorhrdayin Hayastan* (Hovhannes Petrosian, *Hay Parberakan Mamuli Bibliografia (1900-1956)*, vol. 2 (Yerevan: ASSR State Chamber Book, 1957), 381; cf. Amalia Kirakosian, *Hay Parberakan Mamuli Matenagitut'iwn (1794-1967)* (Yerevan: ASSR Al. Miasnikyan Library, 1970), 303). The New York-based *Khorhrdayin Hayastan* started publication in August 1923 as 'Year 1, No. 1' (*Hayastani Koch'nak*, 11 August 1923, 1078), which precludes the possibility of any move from Buenos Aires.

47 Ardashes Der Khachadurian, *Hay Mamuli Ts'uts'ak* (Los Angeles: Hamazkayin, 1987), 46. For the idea of a move to New York, see Ardashes Der Khachadurian, *Sots'eal Demokrat Hnch'akean Kusakts'ut'ean Mamulĕ (1887-1992)* (Beirut: SDHP Dkhruni Student Youth Union, 1992), 26.

48 The first issue of *Arzhent'inean Mamul* announced in its masthead 'Continuation of *Khorhrdayin Hayastan*' and 'Year 2, No. 1'. See *Arzhent'inean Mamul*, 7 October 1923, 1. It implied that the monthly had been published since 1922. Moreover, the SDHP weekly *Erkunk'*, published in Athens, mentioned *Khorhrdayin Hayastan* in

January 1923 among several other party publications. See *Erkunkʻ*, 21 January 1923, 2.
49 *Banvor,* 28 July 1923, 1-2.
50 See, for instance, Binayan, *La colectividad,* 101; Albert Kharatian et al., 'Hay Parberakan Mamulĕ', *Haykakan Sovetakan Hanragitaran,* 'Sovetakan Hayastan' volume (Yerevan: Haykakan Sovetakan Hanragitaran, 1987), 459; Der Khachadurian, *Hay mamuli,* 19; Carlos Hassassian, 'Panorama de la prensa gráfica armenia en Argentina y Uruguay', in *Los armenios en América del Sur. Primeras Jornadas de Estudio,* ed. Vartan Matiossian (Buenos Aires: Instituto de Investigación Armenológica, 1991), 104; Binayan Carmona, *Entre el pasado,* 272; Nélida Boulgourdjian-Toufeksian, *Los armenios en Buenos Aires. La construcción de la identidad (1900-1950)* (Buenos Aires: Centro Armenio, 1997), 154; Carlos Hassassian, 'La prensa', in *Armenia, Una cultura milenaria en la Argentina,* ed. Manrique Zago (Buenos Aires: Manrique Zago, 1999), 100.
51 *Sharzhum,* 16 November 1961, 4, where the first issue of the newspaper was dated 23 October 1923. The 27 kilograms of typefaces, acquired by the AGBU in the United States, were actually leased and not sold. See *Ardzanagrutʻean Tomar Haykakan Barekortsakan Ĕndhanur Miutʻean,* minutes of 18 March and 14 August 1923.
52 Matiossian, *Harawayin Koghmn Ashkharhi,* 192, where I have listed a variety of inaccurate dates in secondary sources. The correct date appeared for the first time in Binayan, *Entre el pasado,* 272, from a verbal communication after I reviewed the only collection of the newspaper, kept at the Mekhitarist monastery of Vienna, in 1995.
53 *Nor Ōr,* 18 March 1969, 3.
54 *Khorhrdayin Hayastan,* 16 March 1924, 2.
55 *Arzhentʻinean Mamul,* 30 December 1923, 1.
56 *Banvor,* 9 February 1924, 2-3; *Banvor,* 22 March 1924, 4.
57 *Arzhentʻinean Mamul,* 30 March 1924, 2.
58 *Arzhentʻinean Mamul,* 6 April 1924, 1.
59 *Nor Ōr,* 18 March 1969, 3. Unfortunately, the only collection of *Nor Erkir,* housed at the Mekhitarist monastery of Vienna, was not available at the time of my visit in 1995. I calculated the date counting down from the fourth issue of 8 May 1924, mentioned in Hassassian, 'Panorama', 104. For the suggested dates '1922(?); from 1924 (new cycle),' see Garegin Levonian, *Hay Parberakan Mamulĕ (1794-1934)* (Yerevan: Pethrat, 1934), 21. Those dates were later turned into a fact, as if the newspaper had been actually published from 1922-5, along with *Arzhentʻinean Mamul.* See Petrosian, *Hay Parberakan,* 379 (in the Russian abstract, '1922-1924'); H. Kankruni, 'S. D. Hnchʻ[akean] Kusaktsʻutʻean Mamulĕ' 134 Tʻertʻ 41 Erkirneru Mēj', *Ararat Grakan,* 8-9-10, 1960, 398; Kirakosian, *Hay Parberakan,* 144; Manvel Babloyan, *Hay Mamuli Hamahawakʻ Tsʻutsʻak* (Yerevan: ASSR Academy of Sciences Press, 1986), 148; Kharatian et al., 'Hay Parberakan', 459; Hrant Kankruni, *Yanun Hayrenikʻi 1887-1987* (Beirut: n.p. 1990), 190.
60 Levonian, *Hay Parberakan Mamulĕ,* 121; Hassassian, 'Panorama', 104; Dēr Khachadurian, *Sotsʻial Demokrat,* 32.
61 Seferian, 'S. D. Hnchʻakean', 163; Petrosian, *Hay Parberakan,* 379; Kirakosian, *Hay Parberakan,* 144; Babloyan, *Hay Mamuli Hamahawakʻ,* 145.
62 *Ardzanagrutʻean Tomar Haykakan Baregortsakan Ĕndhanur Miutʻean,* minutes of 11 May 1924; *Banvor-Pʻariz,* 1 November 1924, 3. The Armenian members of local communist parties did not form a party in community politics of the Diaspora, but

became the leading force of the pro-Soviet faction, which used the self-denomination 'Progressive' (*Yarajdimakan*).
63 *Zart'ōnk'*, 10 September 1924, 8. Thanks are due to Mihran Minasian (Yerevan) for bringing this article to my attention.
64 *Proletar*, 18 October 1924, 4.
65 *Aṛawōt*, 24 November 1924, 2.
66 *Ardzanagrut'ean Tomar Haykakan Baregortsakan Ěndhanur Miut'ean*, minutes of 21 December 1924. The newspaper has been dated both 1924 (Hassassian, 'Panorama', 104; Binayan, *Entre el pasado*, 274; Hassassian, 'La prensa', 100) and 1924-5 (Sēfērian, 'S. D. Hnch'akean', 63; Dēr Khachadurian, *Sots'ial Demokrat*, 32).
67 *Ardzanagrut'ean Tomar Haykakan Baregortsakan Ěndhanur Miut'ean*, minutes of 8 March 1925.
68 *Banvor- P'ariz*, 1 Febuary 1925, 2-3.
69 *Ardzagang P'arizi*, 8 March 1925, 8.
70 Comrade Panchoonie was the hero of a trilogy of epistolary novels by famous satirical writer Ervant Odian (1869-1926), who has become the prototype of revolutionary activists who just damage their party and the people who they proclaim to serve. The phrase 'has nothing to do any more' was a reference to former ARF activist and prime minister of the first independent Republic of Armenia, Hovhannes Kajaznuni (1868-1938), who had written a damning criticism of the party, entitled *The Armenian Revolutionary Federation Has Nothing to Do Any More* (1923).
71 The word 'enemy' (*t'shnami*) refers, in all probability, to the A.R.F.
72 *Eritasard Hayastan*, 24 June 1936, 4.
73 *Eritasard Hayastan*, 20 September 1930, 3.
74 *Eritasard Hayastan*, 13 June 1931, 4.
75 *Eritasard Hayastan*, 25 July 1931, 3.
76 *Sharzhum*, 6 June 1983, 4.
77 *Sharzhum*, 6 July 1983, 4.
78 *Eritasard Hayastan*, 19 August 1936, 4; *Eritasard Hayastan*, 22 August 1936, 2-3. An editorial of *Sharzhum* claimed in 1983 that the regional meeting resolved to keep *Kaytz* in São Paulo and publish local organs in Buenos Aires and Montevideo (*Sharzhum*, 6 July 1983, 4), but I have not been able to confirm this through another source.
79 Eznig Vartanian, *Prazilioy Hay Gaghutě* (Buenos Aires: Sipan, 1948), 250; Arsen Gidur, *Patmut'iwn S.D. Hnch'akean Kusakts'ut'ean*, vol. II (Beirut: Shirag Press, 1963), 234. The closure of the newspaper has been also dated June 1937 (Yessai O. Kerouzian, 'Armenians in Brazil', *Ararat*, Autumn 1984, 59).
80 Artsruni, *Tarets'oyts'*, 49. See also *Nerka*, January–February 1963, 45. Hassassian has also given the name of Garabed Ekshian as founder (Hassassian, 'Panorama', 107).
81 It has been inaccurately asserted that the first issue was published on June 20, 1937 (Binayan, *La colectividad*, 103; Kevork Karamanoukian, 'The Armenian Press in Argentina', *Ararat*, Autumn 1984, 32; Hassassian, 'Panorama', 107; Binayan, *Entre el pasado*, 276).
82 *Boletín Oficial de la República Argentina*, 29 April 1955, second section, 4.
83 Binayan, *La colectividad*, 103; Karamanoukian, 'The Armenian Press', 33.
84 Seferian, 'S. D. Hnch'akean', 95.
85 Gidur, *Patmut'iwn S.D. Hnch'akean Kusakts'ut'ean*, vol. II, 234.
86 His name was mentioned in an editorial of 1961 (*Sharzhum*, 18 November 1961).

87 *Yushamatean Abraham Ēōlmēsēkean (1901-1958)* (Buenos Aires: Ararat, 1959), 20.
88 *Nerka*, November–December 1961, 15.
89 *Surhandak*, 16 June 1962, 2. I have divided Guzhnuni's tenure in two periods of three years, since his biography mentioned him as having edited *Sharzhum* for six years (*Nor Hachĕn Patmagirk' 1921-1973* (Buenos Aires: Ararat, 1974), 197).
90 *Eritasard Hayastan*, 29 March 1963, 3. Achabahian was director of *Sharzhum* in June 1963. See *Nerka*, June 1963, 26. It is not unlikely that he was acting editor after Keoseyan's firing.
91 *Sharzhum*, 4 September 1965, quoted in *Nerka*, August–September–October 1965, 62.
92 Varuzhan Ajemian, personal communication (April 1999). His stint has been also noted as 1973–6 (Hassassian, 'Panorama', 107).
93 *Eritasard Hayastan*, 30 November 1929, 3.
94 *Eritasard Hayastan*, 5 April 1930, 3.
95 *Eritasard Hayastan*, 7 July 1934, 3; *Eritasard Hayastan*, 29 December 1934, 4.
96 *Eritasard Hayastan*, 15 April 1936, 3.
97 *Sharzhum*, 4 February 1939, 2.
98 *Eritasard Hayastan*, 29 March 1963, 3. A correspondent wrote in 1936 about the creation of 'three male and two new female chapters, each of them with 30-40 comrades, and you can consider the addition of a dozen of existing chapters irrefutable proof of the achievements of the Hnchakian ideology'. See *Eritasard Hayastan*, 19 September 1936, 1. It appears that the original chapter had broken down into various chapters due to the expansion of party activities.
99 Kankruni, *Yanun Hayrenik'i*, 158.
100 *Armenia*, 3 September 1965, 2.
101 Ibid., 159. The Haigazian School has been inaccurately claimed to have been the first school of the community. See Gidur, *Patmut'iwn S.D. Hnch'akean Kusakts'ut'ean*, vol. II, 247. However, the Mamigonian School had been founded in 1931 with 135 students, and in 1932 there were also the Mesrobian (77 students) and Apkarian (44 students) schools (*Armenia*, 18 June 1932, 1).
102 Artsruni, *Tarets'oyts'*, 270.
103 Ibid., 290.
104 *AGBU News*, January 1992, 10.
105 *Eritasard Hayastan*, 19 September 1936, 1; *Sharzhum*, 15 January 1938, 2. The foundation of Radio Armenia has been ascribed to the Armenian Student Union (Binayan, *Entre el pasado*, 280), which was actually founded in 1938.
106 *Lraber*, 29 May 1947, 1.
107 The broadcasting of Turkish music by Radio Armenia in its first three decades was regarded as natural by a Turkish-speaking cross section of the community and as totally unacceptable to Armenian speakers. It became a matter of bitter controversy and partisan struggle until the radio hour stopped such broadcasting in 1965 (*Nerka*, August–September–October 1965, 47) through the personal intervention of Vazken I, Catholicos of All Armenians (Zohrab Matiossian, personal communication, 1985). In the words of an observer, 'in those years there were unrestricted broadcasts with Armenian, Turkish, Arabic and Greek music. The Armenians of the time freely experienced the hybrid past of their people in Cilicia. However, religious authorities requested that only Armenian music should be broadcast even though not many of the station's audience could understand the language very well. Listeners were not necessarily pleased, but this became the rule given the community's hierarchical

structure' (E. Alvarez, *Los recién llegados*, unpublished manuscript, Montevideo, 1988, 15, quoted in Felipe Arocena and Adriana Topalian, 'Young Armenian-Uruguayans: Identity and Participation in the Community', *Journal of the Society for Armenian Studies* 19, no. 1 (2010): 109). Radio Armenia apparently also broadcasted religious sermons in Turkish in the early years. See Carlos Hassassian, 'The Armenian Community in Uruguay', *Ararat*, Autumn 1984, 73. This was not odd, given that the language was mostly rooted in Cilicia, especially Marash, with a majority of Turkish speakers who read the Bible in Armeno-Turkish.

108 Artsruni, *Tarets'oyts'*, 276. It is noteworthy that the party radio hour coexisted with a private radio hour directed by a party member. Gidur gave the inaccurate date 1935 for the foundation of Voice of the Armenian Community and claimed that 'its direction was in the hands of Der Krikorian, Khulmunian and Rupenian' (Gidur, *Patmut'iwn S.D. Hnch'akean Kusakts'ut'ean*, vol. II, 246). His book has no mention of Radio Armenia, perhaps reflecting Rupenian's personal disagreements with the party leadership.

109 *Lraber*, 29 May 1947, 1.
110 *Eritasard Hayastan*, 21 September 1929, 1.
111 *Eritasard Hayastan*, 12 July 1930, 3.
112 Gidur, *Patmut'iwn S.D. Hnch'akean Kusakts'ut'ean*, vol. II, 222–3.
113 Vartanian, *Prazilioy*, 247.
114 Gidur, *Patmut'iwn S.D. Hnch'akean Kusakts'ut'ean*, vol. II, 223.
115 *Eritasard Hayastan*, 9 July 1932, 3.
116 Gidur, *Patmut'iwn S.D. Hnch'akean Kusakts'ut'ean*, vol. II, 226.
117 *Eritasard Hayastan*, 15 April 1933. See also Vartanian, *Prazilioy*, 247–9. Ardashes Der Khachadurian first accepted (Der Khachadurian, *Hay Mamuli*, 19) and then rejected the date January 1933 (Der Khachadurian, *Sots'ial Demokrat*, 27). For the inaccurate claim that the monthly was founded in November 1931 and the first issue appeared in December, see Gidur, *Patmut'iwn S.D. Hnch'akean Kusakts'ut'ean*, vol. II, 226.
118 Gidur, *Patmut'iwn S.D. Hnch'akean Kusakts'ut'ean*, vol. II, 226.
119 Vartanian, *Prazilioy*, 250.
120 Ibid. The periodical was advertised as 'weekly of the S. D. Hnchakian South America region' in 1937. See *Eritasard Hayastan*, 13 January 1937, 4.
121 Mihran Minasian, 'Hay Parberakan Mamuli 33 Norayayt Anunner', *Haigazian Armenological Review* 21 (2001): 359.
122 Gidur, *Patmut'iwn S.D. Hnch'akean Kusakts'ut'ean*, vol. II, 226.
123 Vartanian, *Prazilioy*, 246. Despite Gidur's assurance that the school was closed in July 1936, after one year (Gidur, *Patmut'iwn S.D. Hnch'akean Kusakts'ut'ean*, vol. II, 227–8, 230), it was mentioned among the organizers of the anniversary of the twenty Hnchakian Martyrs of 1915 in July 1937, and the event was held on its premises. See *Eritasard Hayastan*, 31 July 1937, 3.
124 Vartanian, *Prazilioy*, 246–7. See also Gidur, *Patmut'iwn S.D. Hnch'akean Kusakts'ut'ean*, vol. II, 228.
125 Gidur, *Patmut'iwn S.D. Hnch'akean Kusakts'ut'ean*, vol. II, 223. See also *Eritasard Hayastan*, 2 November 1929, 1.
126 *Eritasard Hayastan*, 29 November 1930, 3.
127 Gidur, *Patmut'iwn S.D. Hnch'akean Kusakts'ut'ean*, vol. II, 226.
128 *Hayastani Koch'nak*, 16 January 1943, 64. See also Robert M. Levine, *The Vargas Regime: The Critical Years, 1934-1938* (New York and London: Columbia University Press, 1970), 167–8.

129 Taura Regina de Luca, 'Inmigración, mutualismo e identidad: São Paulo (1890-1935)', *Estudios Migratorios Latinoamericanos* 29 (1995): 201.
130 This was somehow reflected by Y. Mkhitarian's startling declaration in an article published in the United States two months later: 'Our republic, with the *competent leadership of its energetic and visionary great president*, H.E. Dr. Getulio Vargas, continues the course of progress and tightens its relations with the neighbor sister republics day after day.' See *Eritasard Hayastan*, 14 October 1942, 1. The italics are mine. In 1942-3, a group of Hnchakian militants broadcasted the Ararat radio hour, directed by Mkhitarian, with purely cultural contents. Gidur, *Patmutʻiwn S.D. Hnchʻakean Kusaktsʻutʻean,* vol. II, 235.
131 Vartanean, *Prazilioy*, 549-50.
132 Seferian, 'S. D. Hnchʻakean', 167; Kirakosian, *Hay Parberakan*, 341; Kharatian et al., 'Hay Parberakan', 459; Der Khachadurian, *Hay Mamuli*, 46; Kankruni, *Yanun Hayrenikʻi*, 189 (1946-50 on page 127); Der Khachadurian, *Sotsʻial Demokrat*, 40.
133 Hovhannes Amirents, 'Haraw[ayin] Amerikayi Hay Gaghutʻē', in *Endardzak Taretsʻoytsʻ Azgayin Hiwandanotsʻi* (Istanbul: Aprahamian, 1932), 232.
134 N. A. [Nubar Aharonian], 'Montʻevitēoyi Hay Gaghutʻi Vichakagrutʻiwnē', *Armenia*, 7 May 1932, 2.
135 Amirents, 'Haraw[ayin] Amerikayi', 230.

Section III

Ideology

A multi-layered analysis of the ideology of the SDHP cannot be done without understanding the ideologies of the ARF and to a lesser extent that of the Ramkavars (Armenian Democratic Liberal Party). The founders of the SDHP, similar to those of the ARF, were influenced by Russian political ideologies that were alien to the Armenians living in the Ottoman Empire. The eastern provinces of the Empire became the laboratory in which they attempted to test their contradictory ideologies. The articles in this section analyse the paradoxes faced by the SDHP since its foundation. These paradoxes were not endemic to the SDHP; the ARF too faced similar paradoxes in its attempt to dictate the course of history and bring a positive change into the lives of the Armenians of the eastern provinces.

In the first article in this section, Gerard Libaridian discusses the paradoxes within the SDHP as it relates to Western/Eastern Armenian realities, to the Church, and to Marxist ideology. He demonstrates how the founders of the party were alien to the situation of the eastern provinces. As a matter of fact, none of the founders had ever set a foot in those regions. They attempted to bring change to a territory that they were totally unfamiliar with. While the SDHP seemed to be devoted to the Marxist ideology of creating a classless society as a path to achieve socialism, it advocated a contradictory policy of national independence. This conundrum between nationalism and socialism would cause a rift within the party. Finally, in their relation to the church, they tried to create an alternative source of legitimacy. The SDHP chose Zeytun as the first area in which they could implement their vision. However, as discussed in the different chapters of this volume, the project failed due to multiple causes. It seems that there was a deep gap between the theoretical vision of these parties and their practical application on the ground.

Gaïdz Minassian's article goes more into depth in analysing the ideology of the SDHP in tandem with that of the ARF. Through a social scientific approach, he provides a fresh look at the Armenian revolutionary movement, which in many respects contains certain permanence from one century to the next. He argues that it is impossible to understand the SDHP without understanding the ARF. Through using the approach of *aide-mémoire*, Minassian demonstrates the links that connect the two parties together. In this article, he introduces the term *haïtadism*, which he considers synonymous with the 'Armenian Question'. He analyses the ideologies, successes, and failures of both parties in relation to *haïtadism*. He argues that both parties attempted to use universalistic ideologies based on contemporary thinking (Owen, Marx, Engels, Lavrov, Comte, Durkheim, Plekhanov among others) to situate *haïtadism* on the global level. He traces the sources of agreements and disagreements between both parties that went beyond ideological discrepancies to include a battle of egos that hampered any type of cooperation. According to him, while Kristapor Mikaelian and Stepan Sabah-Gulian embodied rationalism, after the former's death and the latter's marginalization, both the ARF and the SDHP embodied *haïtadist* and communist messianism.

Discussion and dissemination of the SDHP ideologies in tandem with contemporary political thought were not endemic to party intellectuals – student organizations also played an important role in promoting contemporary ideologies in general and that of the Hnchaks in particular. The third article in this volume concentrates on *Kaytz* (1911–14), which was the periodical of the Istanbul Students' Union of the Social Democrat Hnchakian Party. Through analysing the content of this periodical, Yaşar Tolga Cora demonstrates how the newspaper devoted large sections to discuss the philosophical roots of historical materialism and scientific trends in Europe. The aim was to help students develop Marxist thought. Cora argues that the newspaper did not publish only theoretical articles, but also dealt with such topics as domestic and foreign policies pertaining to the Ottoman Empire and the condition of the working class in Turkey. Cora contends that *Kaytz* used neologisms in developing new terminology to explain the socialist ideology to its constituents.

The final article in this section deals with the total eradication of the history of the SDHP from the lexicon of the Turkish left. In this article, Kadir Akın dissects the history of the Turkish left, whose past was based on denial. By denial, we do not mean here the denial of the Armenian Genocide, but that of the existence of other socialist movements like that of the SDHP that contributed to the development of socialism in the Ottoman Empire and modern Turkey. Akın demonstrates how for the Turkish left history began with Hüseyin Hilmi, supposedly the founder of the socialist movement in Turkey. He demonstrates how members of the CUP who were culprits of the Armenian Genocide became leaders of the Turkish Communist Party (Türkiye Komünist Partisi, TKP). Akın contends that the reason why the TKP had denied the existence of other socialist parties such as the SDHP in the Ottoman Empire is because it would compel them to take a position against their suffering and oppression. In this article, he calls upon the Turkish left to revisit its own history and the history of socialism in the Ottoman Empire and integrate the other socialist parties like that of the SDHP with the larger narrative of the true history of socialism in the Ottoman Empire and modern-day Turkey.

10

Ideology and Reality

Hnchakian Paradoxes at Birth[1]

Gerard J. Libaridian

Modern Armenian history is rich with personalities and groups that have adopted or expounded on to ideologies that compensate for their inherent strategic vulnerabilities. In their coherence and seeming universality, ideologies provide intellectual and spiritual strength to those upholding them when they are, in fact, weak and lack the necessary resources to bring about change on their own. In their attempts to act according to ideologies, such individuals and groups run counter to realities on the ground and some way or another come to terms with them, more often than not creating paradoxes that they learn to live with.

This article will discuss three of the major paradoxes dealing with the early years of the founding of the Social Democrat Hnchakian Party (SDHP, Hnchakians) the first Armenian political party, beginning in 1887.[2] These paradoxes appear to dominate the gap between the world view of the founders of the party and the relevance of that world view to Western Armenian/Eastern Ottoman realities, to the Church and to Marxist ideology. These paradoxes explain much about the difficulties the SDHP faced as well as those that challenged the Armenian people following the Congress of Berlin in general.[3]

These paradoxes are relevant for our understanding of (a) how the Hnchakians perceived issues at the time, (b) how they proposed to resolve them, and why they thought they could resolve them, and (c) how the Armenian polity resolves problems today.[4] The following are the paradoxes this article will focus on:

1. The founders of the Hnchakian Party that proposed to save Western/Ottoman-occupied Armenia were Eastern/Russian Armenians; as far as this author has been able to determine, none of these founders had ever been in Western Armenia. Their sense of the circumstances under which Ottoman Armenians were living – circumstances that required 'salvation' – derived from newspaper articles, reports by others who had visited the region, or through personal correspondence.
2. The SDHP adopted Marxist ideology – rather, what they understood to be Marxist ideology – that placed class struggle above all else as the mover of history

and the means to achieve socialism; yet the party advocated the independence of Armenia, an otherwise classic nationalist goal.
3. True to the Marxist interpretation, the SDHP programme shunned religion and the Church as a real agency in the future development of history; in fact, there is no mention of religion or church in the party programme. Yet their first actions were closely linked to the Armenian Church, seeking to benefit from its privileges within and trying to engage it as an ally against the Ottoman state.

Russian and Ottoman Armenians

It has been noted before that it was Russian Armenians who founded the first Armenian political party, one that proposed to save Ottoman Armenians.[5] There have been a number of explanations for this phenomenon, such as the idealism of youth (the founders were all university students) and the increased interest among Russian Armenians in Ottoman Armenian life following the 1877–8 Russo-Turkish War and the treaties of San Stefano (February 1878) and Berlin (July 1878).

Yet there is one dimension in this story that has not been really appreciated. That is Russian Armenian youth with close understanding of the Russian populist movements that were primarily peasant-oriented and readily saw the problem in essence as a problem of rural Armenians, the basis of Armenian society in the historic Western Armenian territories.[6] Some historians have noted the connection of Russian Armenian university students, founders of the Hnchakian and the Armenian Revolutionary Federation (ARF or Dashnaktsutiun, Dashnak) parties, to the People's Will (*Narodnaya Volya*) secret organization in Russia without recognizing agrarian crisis in the rural areas as the basis of the origins of the Armenian Question. This dimension was not one the Great Powers cared about, nor did the relatively stable Armenians in Istanbul or other major Ottoman cities. This is not to say there was no recognition by urban liberal intellectuals, some segments of the middle class and a few clergymen from the provinces of the threat to the communal base of the rural Armenian economy. But for the founders of the Hnchakian Party that dimension constituted the basis of Armenian grievances.

It is important to note that this agrarian dimension of the problem in Ottoman Armenia has been lost to the parties in question as well as to most historians. Under the traumatic effect of the Genocide, what has survived for most urban Armenians, including historians and inheritors of the parties, is the nationalist and existential aspect. Soviet Armenian historians who, similar to the founders of the Hnchakian Party, imagined and wrote within the sphere of a socialist ideology, recognized the agrarian dimension more readily.[7]

The question arises: why did a national party not arise among Western Armenians with the same concerns? The answer may be logistical. The Ottoman state had a dominant presence in Ottoman Armenian life; any organization that was based in the Ottoman territory would be easily discovered and destroyed. There were also too many Armenians who thought it was not possible, wise or beneficial to oppose the state. It was not difficult for the state to make use of all of these Armenians, and of the internal spy system, to make the rise of an Armenian national political party based in the empire impossible.

It is also possible that Ottoman Armenian political thought had not reached the point where it could imagine radical action such as an armed opposition, rebellion or revolution. In most areas where Armenians lived, non-Armenians and Muslims were either dominant or overwhelming. Power relations here and any sense of 'justice' depended on the submissive relationship the most conservative Armenian elements and institutions held with Ottoman and local authorities. The reform movements – Ottoman and Armenian millet-based – did attract the most daring but the absence of a political imagination beyond what the Ottoman Armenian leadership could offer could not easily attract the youth that was radicalized by the time the Hnchakians were ready to call for a radical approach. The reformist movements took Ottoman rule for granted in a society where the Church had the dominant role, a role that was also circumscribed by the state.[8]

Meanwhile, as we shall see later, underlying an established tradition of Russian Armenian interest in Ottoman Armenians and their plight was a territorialization as well as a historicization of Armenian identity, bringing that identity closer to modern nationalism. Within that perspective, borders were irrelevant.[9]

Thus, being Russian or Ottoman Armenian was altogether irrelevant, as far as the founders of the SDHP were concerned, to their quest to resolve the problem of their brethren across the border. As noble as it sounded, such an attitude tended to disregard the real differences between the two segments of the Armenian people, differences that compelled the party founders and organizers to make adjustments later in their strategy. When no adjustments were forthcoming, the party split, as in 1896, after the 1894–6 massacres in Ottoman Armenia. One wing, made up predominantly of Ottoman Armenians, split from the 'mother' party to constitute the 'Verakazmyal' (Reformed) Hnchakian Party; the latter accused the party leadership of having emphasized socialism too much at the expense of the existential struggle needed in the Ottoman lands. Such emphasis, they noted, gave the Armenian struggle an unduly anti-Western character that in turn, made the movement suspicious in the eyes of the Great Powers, all anti-socialist.

Marxism and Armenian independence

What distinguished political parties of that time from organizations devoted to specific causes or sets of goals is the adoption of a world view or an ideology as the basis of the organization's strategy and, to some extent, tactics. The world view or ideology a party adopted was fundamental because it is through its prism that the party will (1) define the struggle they will be engaged in, including their enemies and potential partners, (2) interpret the forces and factors that affect the environment within which they will be functioning, (3) determine the solution they will be seeking to the problem and (4) thus design the strategy they will be following to achieve their goals.

The founders of the Hnchakian Party were followers of the Marxian world view, or what they understood to be the Marxist view. That is an ideology that considered class struggle as the prime mover of history that looked upon the exploitation of the majority of the people by a minority class as the main problem and a classless society, through class struggle, as the solution to that problem. On many levels, Marxian socialism was the antithesis of the nationalist world view that regarded the nation as the ultimate and absolute value.

The Hnchakian founders' experience in Russia, mentioned earlier, was a major factor in their adoption of socialism, at the time the most progressive and liberationist ideology, particularly appealing to the weak. The universalist perspective and appeal of Hnchakian socialism is also the reason why the party's name did not include the term 'Armenian'. Thus, as a matter of belief, albeit couched in scientific garb, according to SDHP, history had always moved because of class struggles and to succeed in one's struggle one had to have the support of the logic of history with you – thus neutralizing your relative weakness in power relations – and not only side with the class that is destined to win in history but also the morally right one. The moral underpinnings of class struggle had an eschatological progress. Humanity had moved from the very bad toward the better; and it was bound to reach the best, and the best strategy to be part of history was to participate in it the right way; classless society, inevitable because socialists had understood the positive laws of social development, would constitute the ultimate in human progress. The Hnchakian ideologues took for granted that Armenians were part of humanity and subject to the same laws as the rest.

Logically, therefore, the Hnchakian programme should have called upon Armenians in the Ottoman Empire to wage class warfare as members of the exploited classes against all exploiters regardless of their ethnicity or religion. Instead, they called upon the establishment of an independent Armenia.

The manner in which these two goals – socialism and independence – were reconciled was quite ingenious, and it constitutes a precursor for national liberation movements later in more than one continent: the relationship between empire and oppression and exploitation of subject nations as a class. The Hnchakians separated the two seemingly conflicting goals by spreading them over time. Independence was an immediate goal, while socialism was the ultimate goal. The Hnchakians were erudite enough to understand that the struggle on the basis of scientific socialism could be waged in capitalist societies that also had a proletariat, although a peasantry – the experience they were exposed to in the Russian Empire speaks to this – could be a substitute for an industrial proletariat. But they asserted that the Ottoman Empire was too backward to be the scene for a class struggle; thus, the goal of waging socialist struggle itself required that an Armenia be created, one where capitalism and other prerequisite conditions could exist for the long-term goal of waging class struggle and creating a socialist society. In that way, Armenians would be participating in the making of future humanity on the right side of history.

This paradox becomes even more intriguing when the arrangement between nationalism and socialism is projected into the field of action. In seeking resources for the creation of the first goal, independence, the Hnchakians appealed to all layers of Ottoman Armenian society. One of these was the 'princes' of Zeytun, the impoverished local leaders of a mountainous district in Cilicia that had retained a degree of autonomy within the Ottoman dominion. Zeytun was one of the very rare areas where one could see remnants of the Armenian nobility as well as a fighting spirit reminiscent of the past. Armenians imagined the 1862 Zeytun Rebellion against the Ottomans as the first sign of the political and military renaissance of the ancient and independent Armenian people. In fact, that rebellion was primarily one of the last acts of a dying Armenian 'feudal nobility' – represented by the mainly impoverished *ishkhans* (princes), who wished to preserve their privileges and were able to summon the defensive instincts of the population under their administration against the centralizing policies of the Ottoman Empire in the throes of reform. The Hnchakians made great efforts to win the very old and very conservative Zeytun leadership to their side, the side of a battle for the independence of Armenia because it was a ready-made resource that could be used for the short-term goal.

It is not all that clear that the Hnchakian leaders were conscious of the paradox at this level. They certainly were aware of the major conflict between nationalism and Marxian socialism; they would also become more sensitive to that after the 1894–6 massacres, when many Western Armenians who had rallied to the SDHP believing in its immediate goal challenged the relevance of socialism for the Ottoman Armenian condition. The founding fathers and one mother of the Hnchakian Party do not seem to have been aware of the dangers of ideology 'going native' when it made concessions to national history and local mentalities and sacrificed – from an ideological point of view – the ultimate goal to promote tactical gains. One important advantage ideologies have over simple political programmes is that they are internally coherent. Real conditions and experiences are filtered and turned into elements that sustain a system of interpretations and projections or constructs for the future. Ideologies do impose new realities; they also bend because of realities on the ground.

A key dimension in the SDHP's ideological conundrum was that while the individuals were enamoured by socialism, as an organization the object of their concern was 'the Armenian people'. It was not the working class of the Ottoman Empire or of the other empires where Armenians lived; it was not the Armenian working classes and peasants in any of those places. The historical category they were trying to 'save' was the Armenian people. Furthermore, their programme called for the independence and reunification of all three segments of historical Armenia: territories under Ottoman rule, the major part of historic Armenia; those under Russian rule; and those under Persian rule. That they started out with Ottoman Armenia was a tactical decision dictated by the existential threat to the Armenian people posed by the situation in that part of historic Armenia.[10]

Hnchakians and the Church

The SDHP programme as eventually published in the *Hnch'ak* monthly does not mention religion or the Armenian Apostolic Church that had emerged as the dominant Armenian institution in Armenian life for a long time, since the collapse of the Armenian kingdoms. Perhaps this was a way for Hnchakians to manifest their ideological purity or devotion to the most universal of values, socialism. In fact, establishing a political party was a form of rebellion against that dominant Church; in essence, the SDHP was a challenge to the religious institution's claim, taken for granted until then, to speak for Armenians. By creating a new institution, the Hnchakians were also creating a new principle of legitimacy. The absence of the Church and religion from the programme indicated that the party, both as a new institution and as the bearer of a new world view, had no use for religion or for the Church.

Yet at the first encounter with Ottoman authorities of field workers sent to the Ottoman Empire to spread the new gospel, in 1889 the field workers sought sanctuary in the Armenian Church of Trebizond. Their first political action, the demonstration against the Ottoman government at Kumkapı in July 1890, began with a bizarre act: The leaders of the demonstration invaded the church of the Armenian Patriarchal seat in Istanbul, interrupted mass and asked the Patriarch to lead a demonstration against the Ottoman government at Kumkapı. Patriarch Khoren Ashekian refused. He was roughed up, physically; unwillingly he did proceed at the head of the angry demonstrators, mostly migrant workers from the provinces, the lumpenproletariat of Istanbul, although they did not know that term. Following this brazen action, the Patriarch offered his resignation, which was rejected by the Ottoman government. As one can guess, the leaders of the demonstration were imprisoned.

It is significant that a political party that starts out by ignoring religion and Church decides to make itself known by trying to make use of the Church, to garner the Church's legitimacy, rather than organizing an activity that would more closely reflect its ideology. One could argue that once the idea of an independent Armenian state was adopted, albeit as an ostensibly short-term goal, then the party leadership would permit itself to use any tactical means available, including the Church and remnants of the feudal lords. The question is, at what point does the tactical becomes the dominant definer of a party? The issue would haunt the Hnchakian Party for a long time to come.

One explanation for these paradoxes is the connection of the birth of the SDHP – as well as soon after of the ARF – to the internationalization of the Armenian issue through the Treaty of San Stefano in February and the Treaty of Berlin in July 1878; that is, the birth of the so-called 'Armenian Question'. Once Armenians, that is, at that time the Church, gave up their hopes for internally inspired reforms in the Armenian provinces that could be implemented through the Ottoman government, eyes were turned toward the Great Powers that assumed responsibility for pressing the Sultan to implement reforms required by the 1878 Treaty of Berlin. Yet a decade passed and the Armenian Question was practically forgotten. The SDHP was the expression of both the frustration of Armenians with the non-implementation of a reform programme and the perception that the internationalization of the Armenian issue could and should be used as a strategy to achieve the tactical goal of independence. The Church, specifically the Patriarchate of Istanbul, had been the mechanism for the internationalization of the Armenian Question; and in the Balkans, former Ottoman territories had escaped the Sultan's rule through rebellions and bloodshed. Hence the assignment of important roles to the Church and the princes, two institutions that were not only ignored in the party programme but were also implied to be historically regressive forces within the framework of the advent of socialist society.[11]

What ideologies are and do

On a deeper level, though, ideology constituted a source of power, real and/or imagined, for the weak. For the Hnchakians, as later in more practical terms for the ARF and to a lesser extent Ramkavars, ideology was a way of participating in (a) Western, European ('civilized') discourse, (b) in positivist thinking: history is moving forward toward a better future, progress was inevitable, (c) it was time for Armenians to join the march. There was, therefore, hope for Armenians; they only needed to be on the right side of history.

Ideologies and systems of thought have the advantage of providing wholesome explanations of the world around you, of forces that control your life, that help you understand where you can be part of the making of your own future, where you can become an agency of that future. But that which is their advantage, their wholesomeness and coherence, is the vulnerable point of ideologies. Socialism and Marxism explained capitalism and to some extent the kind of imperialism that evolved out of capitalism. So the SDHP could understand the large forces and interests at play, ideally. But no ideology or system explains everything at every level; not accurately and fully for all instances. That which explains everything, it is said, explains nothing. Ideologies, especially those that have predictive power, provide the impression that one understands the complex processes around you, that one's decisions – derived from a correct understanding of the laws of history – are bound to produce the end that the ideology predicted. Thus, one relies on the illusion that somehow one is in control of one's destiny even though one is being massacred.

Ideologies also endow adherents with a sense of empowerment that energizes and leads to acts of heroism. Yet in case one's resources are not sufficient to produce the desired change, those acts are celebrated as acts of martyrdom and produce a sense of martyrdom and victimhood that can be mistaken for success.

The Ottoman Empire was characterized as the 'Sick Man of Europe', implying that it was weak. The Ottoman Empire was weak, indeed, but only relative to any of the Great Powers. But it was not weak relative to some of its subject peoples, such as Armenians. And it provided a number of opportunities to Armenians to have a false sense of being right; they had, after all, followed the dictates of an ideology, as if the purpose of the struggle was to be faithful to the ideology.

The aftermath

It is not the purpose of this article to trace the SDHP's ideological equivocations following their birth in 1887. But it is useful to mark a few significant moments. As indicated earlier, the Hnchakian Party split in 1896, following which it lost its position in the revolutionary movement to the ARF that had manifested a more flexible attitude regarding ideology. Both wings of the Hnchakian Party continued to be present in the Armenian political spectrum. The 'mother' party, as the SDHP is called, did find some way to manifest its socialist identity by being more alert to the nationalist dimensions of the Young Turk, especially the Committee of Union and Progress (CUP, Ittihad ve

Terakkı) ideology and organizing Armenian workers in Russian cities and Baku later on. But they, just as the ARF, continued to be dogged by the duality of their cause: born to save Western Armenia and Western Armenians, they felt at home in the Russian Empire.

In 1909 the SDHP dropped its goal of establishing an independent Armenia in the Ottoman Empire: The Young Turk Revolution of 1908, it argued, indicated that you could have a bourgeois revolution in the Ottoman Empire and an independent Armenia was no longer necessary for the party's ultimate goal to be pursued. That optimism gave way to severe pessimism by 1911 as the CUP failed to deliver on the promise of the Young Turk Revolution. In 1915, twenty Hnchakian leaders were hanged in Constantinople for having plotted the assassination of Ottoman government leaders.[12] By that time, the SDHP had already made its peace with the Church as well, although the Patriarchate was more under the influence of the ARF. By 1915 Marxism had become negotiable, even for the mother party, and the Church proved to be incontrovertible.

The Genocide beginning in 1915 became the great equalizer. Paradoxes, policies and ideologies became irrelevant. Armenian political parties left their original liberal ideas and progressive ideologies under the ashes of Western Armenia. The weight of the past – including that of specific policies and overarching conceptualizations in a diasporan setting that was constantly shifting demographically and geographically – has made ideologies irrelevant and past ideologies better forgotten.

Much of the movement toward liberalized thinking – socialism should be counted as the most progressive in this direction[13] – would give way to more traditional attitudes, as Armenian institutions, including the political parties, adopted preservation of culture and identity as the new agenda. The party whose founders included a woman, Maro Vardanian, said to have contributed significantly to the ideological grounding of the party, never produced another woman as a leader, although it is possible that there remained more women rank-and-file members in the SDHP than in any of the others.

Nonetheless, the SDHP did continue, as ideologically motivated parties tend to do, to find solutions to its paradoxes. At the end of its political prevarications and to conclude the first phase of its history as a party in historic Armenia, in August 1920 the SDHP decreed the 'Act of Self-Government of Cilicia', an act that lasted a few days only;[14] there had also been a Ramkavar declaration of independence by Mihran Damadian. Furthermore, the SDHP returned, in a way, to its ideological origins and in 1921 recognized Soviet Armenia as the realization of its ultimate goal.[15] Soviet Armenia was both socialist and an Armenia, even if somewhat independent. Now made up largely of Western Armenians, there was no longer a paradox; more importantly, there was no longer a Western Armenian population to save: they had been massacred or turned into refugees elsewhere. Strangely, it was Western Armenian Hnchakians supporting an Eastern Armenian state. Henceforth, the SDHP considered it its patriotic duty to support Soviet Armenia. Western Armenia, as territory, was not a matter of strategic considerations or struggles: in foreign and security policy issues, that meant following the USSR line. That issue was raised briefly in 1945, but more resolutely after the 1960s, when the Soviet Union needed legitimation of the Soviet government in Armenia through nationalist rhetoric; communist ideology and the building of socialism were no longer adequate to maintain any semblance of legitimacy. Support for Soviet Armenia also meant strong support for the All-Armenian Catholicosate in Etchmiadzin in the Diaspora in the battles with the American and ARF-supported encroachments by the Catholicossate of Cilicia, in Lebanon since 1921, against the Mother Church's jurisdictions in the diaspora.

Conclusion

Today it is difficult to visualize, even for a historian, the important role ideologies played in the rise of the Armenian revolutionary movement. One reason – the diasporization of Armenian life – was mentioned earlier. A second reason may be that nineteenth-century style positivist ideologies have been discredited. Thus, we really lack systematic studies of the role of ideologies in the minds of Eastern Armenians who, unlike their equally idealistic Western Armenian brothers, reached out to guns through a different intellectual process than the early fedayees.

As indicated earlier, socialism, as the ideology of the SDHP and later the ARF, was also used as a critical tool to understand the wider forces around them, both economic and imperial. Diasporan agendas are not open to interpretations beyond those 'sensed' by Armenians; an 'ideology' is too big a word and too large a world to be relevant. Ideologies have been replaced by 'national visions'. One universalist ideology that survived the longest is the communist one, entrenched in Soviet Armenia for some seven decades. But that too lost its lustre by the 1960s and power by the late 1980s. By the 1960s the Communist Party of Soviet Armenia, as those elsewhere in the USSR, had to call upon national history, identity and issues too in order to preserve a sense of legitimacy.

These and related issues require a much more detailed investigation than is intended in this article. But there is no doubt that these ideologies, however conflictual and full of paradoxes, were significant in the minds of not only those who adopted them but also others, watching them. The Sahmanadir Ramkavar Party would be created in 1908, as a counterbalance to the SDHP and the ARF, to represent the interests of the Armenian bourgeoisie. The founders of the former clearly indicated that they were creating the new party to oppose socialism, as well as the revolutionary methods, of the two existing parties.

The shifting fortunes of ideologies became evident in the first major conflict in the post-genocide diaspora: To support or to struggle against the Communist Party rule in Soviet Armenia. The Hnchakians, as mentioned earlier, and the Ramkavars joined hands to support the new, Soviet Armenia, the former as a matter of ideology, the latter as a matter of practicality. The ARF opposed it. For decades, along with the churches they controlled, these three parties scrounged for ideological grounds for their positions. That battle led them to fall into a new trap, the Cold War, the ultimate 'ideological' struggle. While domestically all parties and institutions subscribed to the new religion of preservation of culture and language, they turned over the reins of their intellectual bearings to the dictates of the East–West confrontation. Their initial connection, to what one may label as universally valid ideologies, was now mediated by forces even less accessible to them than what they had in the Ottoman Empire.

Universal ideologies became altogether irrelevant to Armenian political thought after the collapse of the USSR. One might say the rise of the Genocide recognition campaign after the 1970s overcame any remnants of differences between the parties; it also dominated the way Armenian political parties, including the SDHP, connected to the world. And since the birth of the Third Armenian Republic in 1991, ideologies have been replaced by 'orientations', Eastern/Russian versus Western/European. The position of the first group is consolidated by the essentialist interpretation of the Genocide, that is, that Turks killed Armenians because they were Turks and that Armenians were victims because Armenians are always victims; and, therefore, Armenians are under constant threat of annihilation by Turkey, as Turks are still Turks and Armenians are still Armenian. Therefore, fate has determined Armenia's future to be with and, if necessary, under Russia. That is the Russian orientation, supported by and large, in so many words, by all three political parties of the Diaspora and, of course, the remnants of the communists and those plagued with nostalgia for Russians or Soviets. The Karabakh Committee that led Soviet Armenian to independence, transformed into the Armenian National Movement, represented the only revival of an alternative, self-determining agenda that looked to a future of Armenia as a liberal, European-style democracy in peace with all its neighbours. That is the closest we have come to a new ideology, however, limited to the Republic of Armenia. The future of that vision is very doubtful, even in Armenia.

The greatest paradox is that ideologies, intended to bring Armenians closer to progressive humanity or the 'civilized world', may have helped Armenians become victims or accept the victim status, when transformed into a shell because of the Genocide and loss of the connection to the universal except for alignment with international forces that could only make use of Armenians, as they did in the Ottoman Empire, but only more so.

The spectre of the Treaty of Berlin still dominates.

Notes

1 This article was originally presented at a conference held in 2012 on the occasion of the 125th anniversary of the founding of the Hnchakian Party.
2 As important as the Armenakans (established in Van in 1885) were, they can best be characterized as a political organization rather than as a party; they also never became a national organization. They espoused some important values but did not develop a national programme of action.
3 This article does not intend to present a history of the Hnchakian Party. Prior to the publication of this volume and other sources mentioned here, there have been four works that are significant for that history: Hagop Turabian's sketchy three-article series in 1916; Louise Nalbandian's unpublished MA thesis at Stanford University, 1949 (limited to the issue of the introduction of socialism in Armenia, to 1947); Hnchakian leader Arsen Gidur's two volume history in Armenian (Beirut, 1963), a somewhat tentative and uneven work; and Soviet Armenian historian Ashot Hovannisyan's important article on the origins of the party. Please see the bibliography for full details on these works.

4 The basic tenets of the Hnchakian Party can be found in the leading article of the first issue of the official organ, *Hnch'ak* ('Hratarakut'ean Masin', November 1887), the leading article of the second issue ('Brnapetut'iwn. Heraka ew Motaka Npatakner ew Mijots'ner', *Hnch'ak*, January 1888, no. 2 and 'Tzragir', *Hnch'ak*, October–November 1888, no. 11–12.
5 Russian Armenians would also establish the second party, the Armenian Revolutionary Federation (ARF) in 1890.
6 For the Great Powers, the Armenian Question was a subheading of the Eastern Question, that is, how to divide up the Ottoman Empire and who would get Constantinople.
7 See, for example, H. G. Vardanyan, *Arevmtahayeri Azatagrut'ean Harts'ě* (Yerevan: Haykakan SSH GA Hratarakch'ut'yun, 1967) and A. A. Hambaryan, *Eritt'urk'eri Azgayin u Hoghayin K'aghak'akanut'iwně ev Azatagrakan Sharzhumnern Arevmtean Hayastanum (1908-1914)* (Yerevan: Haykakan SSH GA Hratarakch'ut'yun, 1979).
8 See Gerard J. Libaridian, 'The Changing Armenian Self-Image in the Ottoman Empire: *Rayah*s and Revolutionaries', in *The Armenian Image in History and Literature*, ed. Richard G. Hovannisian (Malibu: Undena Publications, 1981), reproduced in Gerard J. Libaridian, *Modern Armenia* (New Brunswick: Transaction Publishers, 2004); and Gerard J. Libaridian, 'The Ideology of Armenian Liberation. The development of Armenian Political Thought before the revolutionary movement (1639-1885)' (unpublished PhD diss., UCLA, 1987).
9 Kristapor Mikaelian, one of the founders of the ARF, would later characterize the borders between the Russian and Ottoman Empire as being drawn by bandits.
10 This was an approach that 'real' Marxists, Bolsheviks would reject. Their point of departure would be the class struggle and would, at best, relegate ethnic/national identity to a tertiary role. There were also Marxists who would be recognized as 'Specifists', who considered that under some circumstances, such as when an ethnic group was targeted for exploitation and/or oppression, special consideration should be given to the ethnic/national unit as such within the framework of class struggle. See Libaridian, *Modern Armenia*, 89–112.
11 Ibid. The ARF would deal differently with this issue. Less ideologically constrained, it assigned all members of Armenian society, from the rich to the poor, the priest and the merchant, the teacher and the women a role in the struggle that was shaping up. Of the historical Armenian political parties, only the Democratic Liberal or Party assigns the Armenian Church such an important role in Armenian life. Bolsheviks later would find another solution: the national question was an imperialist plot; in the specific case of Armenians, the question was framed wrong; besides, it could not be resolved, not even by Russia, but especially by Russia, because Russia too was an imperialist power whose interests colluded but also coincided with those of Western imperialists states. Thus, only by changing Russia, and after Russian, the world revolution, could the Armenian question be resolved.
12 See Gerard J. Libaridian, 'What Was Revolutionary About Armenian Revolutionary Parties in the Ottoman Empire?', in *A Question of Genocide: Armenians and Turks at the End of the Ottoman Empire*, eds. R. G. Suny, F. M. Göçek and Norman M. Naimark, 82–112 (New York: Oxford University Press, 2011).
13 See Nigol Shahgaldian, 'The Political Integration of an Immigrant Community into a Composite Society: The Armenians in Lebanon, 1920-1974' (unpublished PhD diss., Columbia University, 1979).

14 Antranig Genjian, *S. D. Hnchʻakean Kusaktsʻutʻiwně ew Kilikean Inkʻnawarutʻean Akʻtě. 1919-1921* (Beirut: Ararat Press, 1958). The term 'inkʻnawarutʻiwn' may also be translated as 'autonomy'.
15 The SDHP would return to Armenia after the 1991 independence.

11

SDHP-ARF

Fraternal Twins or Semi-identical Twins?

Gaïdz Minassian

What was going on in the minds of Hrair Tzhokhk (1864–1904), Simon Vratsian (1882–1969) and Hrair Maroukhian (1928–98), three leaders of the Armenian Revolutionary Federation (ARF) at different times, when they talked about the relationship between their political formation and the Social Democratic Hnchakian Party (SDHP)? The first one, a military leader of Sasun, a former member of the SDHP, and a young recruit of the ARF in the *Yerkir*, wrote a long letter published simultaneously in July 1895 in *Hnch'ak*, organ of the SDHP, and in *Drōshak*, organ of the ARF: 'What do you have?', he addressed the two parties from the depths of Sasun. 'What do you have? What is this idea that distinguishes you from each other? What is the point of divergence in your two conceptions for which you exhaust yourselves instead of unifying your pitiful forces and for which you destroy the house of the miserable people entrusted to your protection? It is shameful, it is an offense, a crime.'[1]

A few years later, in his hometown of Nor-Nakhichevan in the Caucasus, under Russian administration, the young Simon Vratsian, who in 1920 was to become the last prime minister of the First Republic of Armenia (1918–20), recounted in his memoirs, published in 1955 in Beirut, how he joined the ARF in 1898. Within twenty-four hours of each other, Simon Vratsian participated in two clandestine meetings of two different revolutionary organizations but with offices side by side in the same building. The first meeting he attended was that of the SDHP. Thus, when he went upstairs to attend his second meeting, not remembering the exact office where he had made contact, he hesitantly walked across the landing and knocked on a door, without knowing that he was at the wrong office and therefore the wrong organization. But he entered, took a seat and participated in the discussions. Moreover, it was only after this second meeting and only when his interlocutor handed him the ARF programme at the end of the exchanges that Vratsian realized that he was at an ARF meeting. Beginning from that moment on, he never left the party until his death in 1969.[2]

Many decades later, back from Soviet Armenia, Hrair Marukhian, the general secretary of the ARF, a banned organization in the Soviets, stated at a public meeting in Vienna, Austria, on 18 October 1988, that the Ramkavar party is a liberal party and from an ideological point of view there can be no compatibility between the Ramkavars and the ARF since the ARF is a socialist party, i.e., it doesn't believe in any other way but socialism. Like the SDHP, from an ideological point of view . . . in fact, I mean that at some point the Hnchakians and Dashnaktsakans, will have to change their names, because they have the same ideology. When you talk to a Hnchakian, you can sometimes get confused and wonder: are you talking to a Dashnaktsakan or to a Hnchakian?[3]

Thus, these three examples demonstrate that the comparative approach between the SDHP and the ARF is not an artificial one; it has been legitimately discussed since the origins of the revolutionary movement and it even stretches throughout the twentieth century. Whether it is the letter of Hrair Tzhokhk, the memoirs of Simon Vratsian or the speech of Hrair Maroukhian, the question of the convergence between these two formations does not cease to nourish the reflection on the circumstances of their foundation, nature and evolution throughout the ordeals crossed in the Ottoman, Russian and Persian empires, as well as in exile during the Soviet period of Armenian history. Everything leads us to believe that the SDHP and the ARF constitute two distinct but parallel itineraries, as in a relationship within the same sibling between the younger and the older brother, where similarities and dissimilarities interpenetrate, forming a sort of grey zone between fraternal or semi-identical twins, a sort of in-between, a median space that is all the more dense because one does not know in this singular sibling who is the eldest and who is the youngest. If we look at the birth certificates of the two formations and their strategies, the SDHP is the elder, born in 1887 in Geneva, Switzerland, while the ARF is the younger, since it was founded in 1890 in Tbilisi, in the Russian Empire. But if one looks at other criteria such as power, strength and authority, the roles are reversed: the ARF enjoys the right of birth and the SDHP is the 'little brother', certainly rebellious but condemned to play a secondary role in the development of the political and social history of Armenians between the end of the nineteenth century and the fall of the USSR in 1991.[4]

So, what exactly this dynamic of convergence and the real empowerment of these two brothers, the Hnchakian Party and the Dashnaktsakan, are? At first, the uniqueness of the revolutionary movement in history gives weight to the idea of a community of destiny between these two forces of *haitadism* (taken from the words *Hai Tad* or Armenian cause), close enough to go through the same ordeals but distinct enough never to be diluted in each other. Conversely, the empirical approach to the two trajectories in place reveals different strategic and practical choices that distance them from each other without ever breaking the fraternal link that unites them. Hence the idea of a revolutionary paradox that characterizes the history of these two political formations, which in 2022 reached the canonical ages of 135 and 132 years respectively, making them two of the oldest political organizations in the world.

How many anecdotes, memories, but also settling of scores, incidents, confrontations and verbal jousts run through the history of these two political formations? The examples are many, but the aim of this contribution is not to list them, nor less to tell *histoire croisée* (in the meaning that Michael Werner and Bénédicte Zimmermann have outlined)[5] of the SDHP and the ARF, but to demonstrate the particular link that connects these two organizations, which are more than a hundred years old, by using history as an *aide-mémoire* (aid to memory) to support an approach that is more a matter of political science than that of pure historical research.

Towards a coherent history, politics, revolution and Haitadism

The Armenian revolutionary movement (1878–1914) – composed essentially of the Armenakan party, the SDHP and the ARF – was the heir of two dynamics, sometimes complementary, sometimes contradictory.[6] On the one hand, the universalism of the Enlightenment, the era of revolutions (French, American, Industrial), the birth of the Eastern Question, the liberal reforms in the Russian and Ottoman Empires, the wars and defeats of the Ottoman Empire, the rise of new ideas based on *Reason* as the driving force of *History*, and the emergence of a generation of students, intellectuals and publicists who were more open – as they attended universities abroad – than their elders. On the other hand, the despotism of the Russian and Ottoman Empires in their respective remote provinces, the unequal policies of the central powers, the conservatism of the Armenian Church, the absence of an industrial fabric in Turkish Armenia, the rigidity of the traditional Armenian family model, and the isolated mentalities of the plateau populations cut off from the realities of the world. How did the three Armenian organizations combine the thread of universalism with the needle of particularism, the two tools necessary to sew a new national narrative and propose a new iconography that would bring Armenians together? Simply by the irruption of politics, like a revolutionary thrust into the field of possibilities in the service of a new actor: Armenia. From then on, history, politics, revolution and Armenia were one alchemy, one new paradigm. Together, these revolutionary organizations offered the Armenians to take a great leap in history by facing the harshness of the power relationship, of reality. Why use this image of the great leap? Because until the turning point of the Russo-Ottoman war in 1877–8, Armenians, on a collective scale, projected themselves into the future, not from a political perspective, in order to confront reality, but from the cultural one. It was through the cultural that national thought was expressed, particularly under the direction of the ecclesiastics who were in the majority among the elites and were the only authorities recognized by the imperial powers. So much so that the projection into the future through the cultural allowed to bypass or avoid the rigidity of reality whereas the projection through the political constituted, for the pioneers of the Armenian Revolution (Abovian, Nalbandian, Khrimian Hairig, Raffi, etc.), a confrontation with reality, the end of the false pretences, a strong and frank act without knowing the consequences or measuring its responsibilities. Hence the idea of the great leap.[7]

This leap was defined above all, if not as a break, at least as a distancing from Armenian monism, that system of thought composed of a single substance, the spiritual or religious, which suffocated all other spheres (the political, the social, the cultural, the economic). This Armenian monism or the 'church-nation'[8] unified the different fields of activity and broke the distances in order to prevent their autonomization: the political was religious, the cultural was religious, everything was religious. However, throughout the nineteenth century, the will of the first secret societies, confirmed by the three Armenian revolutionary organizations, consisted precisely in valorizing the political to the detriment of the religious and in marking a break with the old order. This liberation movement presented itself as the bearer of a new history, one written by reason and the hand of man to the detriment of religion and the hand of God. But this autonomization of politics was not identical, especially between the three main formations. The Armenakan party, the SDHP and the ARF progressed in scattered order. If for the SDHP (Marxist and internationalist) the break with the Old World was radical in the name of the revolution of the 'I' and the advent of social sciences, for the Armenakan party (traditionalist and regionalist), it was out of question to break with the religious order and classicism. If the SDHP marked a break between the religious and the political to the benefit of the latter, the Armenakan party rather made the religious and the political cohabit to the benefit of the former, as if it presented itself as the political arm of the Armenian Apostolic Church. If the SDHP wanted to defend the workers against the bourgeoisie and the royalty, the Armenakan party defended the peasantry without antagonizing the bourgeoisie and even less the idea of monarchy. If the SDHP wanted to be the vanguard of a social revolution in which the use of violence constituted the vector of a social transformation, the Armenakan party was for the reification of a national revolution in the name of the (self-) defence of a tradition. If the SDHP favoured the empowerment of actors (individuals and people), the Armenakan party defended their dependence on tradition and the nation. In short, for the SDHP, history was rupture; for the Armenakan party, history was cyclical. For the ARF, however, history was neither rupture nor cyclical, but tragic. This reference to Hegel is not accidental, since the revolutionary movement was at the same time the result of a Comtian approach – theological with the evolution of the Armenian Church, metaphysical with the irruption of political culture and the beginnings of the liberation movement in the nineteenth century, and positive with the materialization of the revolutionary movement – but also of a Hegelian approach: the Armenakan thesis, the Hnchakian antithesis and the Dashnaktsakan synthesis. So much so that halfway between the Armenakan party and the SDHP, the ARF did not decide between politics and religion, between nationalism and internationalism, between tradition and modernity, between rurality and urbanity, between nation and people, between self-defence and revolution. To tell the truth, if Simon Zavarian leaned towards the Armenakans by rural, national, conservative, clerical and fundamental inspiration and, on the contrary, if Rostom recognized himself more on the side of the internationalist, radical, anticlerical, progressive, urban verb of the Hnchakians, Kristapor, the main founder of the ARF, recognized himself neither through a fundamental nor a radical approach to the revolution but through an instrumental approach.

In addition to this great common leap in the name of the primacy of social sciences, the forces of the revolutionary movement also recognized themselves in a common national sociopolitical field, which could be considered as the political system proper to the Armenians: *haitadism*, a neologism cousin to the expression – more diplomatic and less popular and less sacralizing – of 'Armenian question', itself a younger daughter of the Eastern Question, that vast plan of dismemberment of the Ottoman Empire concocted by the European powers. This neologism marked a turning point in the development of politics, as it dusted off the concept of system among Armenians and introduced the Westphalian principles of territoriality and sovereignty, as well as the process of secularization of identities. As a new concept, *haitadism* is in turn set up as a proto-system and is presented in part as the heir of pre-medieval and medieval dynasticism, due to the fusional relationship between rulers and lands but also the central place of the family in this new collective emancipation. Compared to Westphalian principles, *haitadism* was a break with the imperial principle of deterritorialization of Armenians, since it proposed instead to territorialize Armenian identity. Henceforth, one speaks of 'territory' and no longer of 'land'. Finally, concerning the process of secularization of identities, *haitadism* introduced the revolution of the 'I' and the fundamental freedoms where the individual and the people became in theory new actors of history. However, did they really achieve this in reality? In other words, who led the reins of politics? The nation, therefore, the Church and the 'elites', or the people without the ecclesiastics and the bourgeoisie? As long as Armenians did not answer this question, *haitadism* remained in limbo between modernity and tradition. Its modernity was set in motion but was not irreversible, because while it favoured the passage from the spiritual to the temporal (secularization), it did not sever nation from people and therefore did not break with the religious. In other words, *haitadism* synthesized tradition and modernity, and the whole of the actors that it contained respected this balance, perhaps with the exception of the Marxist elements of the SDHP and the ARF – starting with Rostom, called 'the Marxist' by his comrades – turned towards anticlericalism. Still, this distancing was theoretical for them; it was translated into facts with difficulty, or when it took shape, it simply ended in their split.

The term '*haitadist* system' refers to the relationships between elements identified by specific characteristics; this ensemble is subject to the influences and constraints of its environment. The reason for using this term *haitadist* is that like other specific analytical frameworks, it is political in the sense that its elements (roles, institutions, apparatuses) and the relations between these elements (balance, communication, negotiation) contribute to the realization of a new political order. The best configuration for grasping *haitadism* in its genesis and construction, its delimitations and scope, its actors and their strategy is to stick to a structural-functionalist approach, notably that of the American sociologist Talcott Parsons.[9] According to the AGIL (Adaptation, Global Attainment, Integration, Latency) system conceived by him, any model, whether *haitadism* or not, must fulfil four functions in order to move from a society to a political system:

a) It must draw its necessary resources from external systems in order to develop or transform them according to its needs; in exchange, it must provide its products. This is what Parsons' model calls *Adaptation* (adapting to international and economic fluctuations, to globalization).
b) To define its goals and mobilize its resources to achieve them. This is what Parsons calls *Goal attainment* (gathering the Armenians into the Armenia of the Treaty of Sevres or Wilsonian Armenia, an avatar of the Empire of Tigranes the Great).

c) To maintain the coordination between the parts and the coherence of the *haitadism*, protecting it from brutal changes and disruptions (world wars, revolutions, Cold War, third world crisis, etc.). Parsons gives the name *Integration* to this stabilizing dimension of the system.
d) Finally, ensuring that actors remain faithful to the norms and values of *haitadism*; Parsons refers to this motivation and maintenance of the model as *Latency*.

Thus, as a specific Armenian model, *haitadism* takes the form of a national political system. This national *haitadism* contains several actors and approaches, sometimes converging, sometimes diverging. Indeed, as a whole, *haitadism* rests on two pillars: the territory and the population or the homeland and the people or territorial haitadism and social haitadism. At first glance, the difference did not appear because haitadism was intended as a tool for re-acculturation of the achievements of the Armenian heritage (language, culture), which the three formations shared around a new press and a promotion of vernacular Armenian. They also presented themselves as an instrument of territorialization of the Armenian identity, marking a break with the imperial order (Ottoman and Russian), which was based on the extra-territoriality of minorities and the autonomy of management of religious communities. Integrating the population into the territory brought together the different revolutionary tendencies, but what was the priority: liberating and unifying the territories or liberating the people? Territorial rights or people rights? Territorial *haitadism* or social *haitadism*? The SDHP and the ARF did not take a decision and made the two perspectives coexist, even if the former insisted on freedom for the people (demand for independence), while the latter placed them at an equal distance until 1907 and found itself rather in the camp of freedom for the people from the Young Turkish Revolution in 1908 until the fall of the empires in 1917–18. In 1919, at its ninth congress, the ARF still avoided a decision, but adopted the final objective of the creation of a free, independent (people's rights) and reunified Armenia (territorial rights).

The choice between those two poles of attraction was all the more difficult for them as the Armenian revolutionary movement was structured in a space of liberation deprived of a political centre. At that time, the official Armenian discourse could not be linked to an urban centre recognized by the whole social body: Constantinople? It was the capital of the Ottoman Empire, even though it was home to a large number of Armenians. Tbilisi, where the ARF was founded? This city, one of the largest ones in the Russian Empire, was not in Armenian territory. Yerevan? It was more a South Caucasian town than a centre of power redistribution. St. Petersburg? It was the capital of tsarist Russia, too far from Armenia. Not to mention Geneva, where the SDHP was founded, also far from the *Yerkir*. That leaves Van, where the Armenakan party was founded, but which was isolated from the rest of the world, or Erzerum, which was the mythical capital of Armenians, the centre of gravity of Armenia's strategic rebirth, but difficult to reach for the revolutionaries. Deprived of any industrial fabric in Armenia, of the unwavering support of the Armenian bourgeoisie, as a social group spread over several empires, and practically devoid of mutual knowledge between the Armenian societies of Turkey and Russia, but also of a single centre of power, the new paradigm (politics, revolution, Armenia) suffered from a major deficit in the mobilization and identification of Armenians with a delimited space.

This deficit aggravated the traumatic relationship that Armenians had with the balance of power, which the SDHP and the ARF tried to overcome by resorting to violence (guerrilla warfare, terrorism) and diplomacy (action with governments and the Second International). However, before addressing their common strategy, a detour through the weight of the empire is worthwhile to understand the specificity of the Armenian case. Like the Bulgarians, Greeks, Macedonians and other peoples under Ottoman domination, the Armenian revolutionary movement had the particularity of being implanted on the straddle of three empires, essentially two, often rivals and sometimes partners: the Russian Empire and the Ottoman Empire and incidentally the Persian Empire. This interaction between the empires themselves on the one hand and between the empires and the national emancipation movement on the other amplified the phenomena of Armenian instrumentalization by one empire against another, as well as the repression against Armenians by the coalescing empires. The more the empires competed, the more the Armenian revolutionary forces were instrumentalized by one power to the detriment of the other, as in the case of the Russian utilization of the ARF and the SDHP between 1912 and 1917 during the reactivation of the Armenian question on the European diplomatic agenda and the formation of the Armenian volunteer battalions (five to be exact, four Dashnaktsakan and one Hnchakian). The more the empires cooperated with each other, the more the revolutionary movement was subjected to relentless repression orchestrated by the central powers, as it was the case with the massacre of the *fedayees* (freedom fighters) from the three organizations in Van in 1896 (Avedisian-Armenakan, Bedo-ARF, Mardig-SDHP). The Armenian revolutionary movement never managed to overcome this imperial paradox, despite attempts to polarize it on Turkish Armenia in order to spare Russia from Armenian agitation in the Caucasus. This impotence, or at least this imperial constraint in which the game of princes thwarts the strategies of revolutionaries, can be read as a necessity and a possibility.

The necessity was the one that forced both formations to register in the international law, namely the reforms in the six Eastern Ottoman provinces (Turkish Armenia) that the European concert imposed on the Ottoman Empire in 1878, 1895 and 1914, respectively after the Russo-Turkish War (treaties of San Stefano and Berlin), in the midst of the Hamidian massacres when 250,000 Armenians were massacred, or after the Balkan Wars and the Russo-German initiative against the Sublime Porte on the eve of the First World War. Although there were voices within both formations claiming against this positive law associated with capitalist and imperial powers, the SDHP and the ARF demanded the implementation of reforms to advance *haitadism* and give it full legitimacy.

Incidentally, this watered down their revolutionary identity and insurrectionary message, even though – this was the other side of their strategy, that of possibility – the SDHP and the ARF advocated the use of guerrilla warfare and excelled in terrorism. The Hnchakian and Dashnaktsakan commandos claimed countless attacks during the Ottoman and Tsarist periods, including those against their own members for supposed treason or settling of scores: the most famous was the murder of Arpiar Arpiarian, a

Hnchakian writer of the late nineteenth century, on 12 February 1908, by a Hnchakian commando. The adduced reason was to have betrayed the party by splitting it at the time of the creation of the Hnchakian Reformed Party (*Verakazmyal*), in London, in 1896. On several occasions, Arpiarian escaped assassination attempts by Dashnaktsakan cells who accused him of being an intelligence agent in the service of the Ottoman Empire. In addition to terrorism, the SDHP and the ARF also used guerrilla warfare and general insurrection to develop the Armenian Revolution. The SDHP organized the first insurrection in 1894, which unleashed the Hamidian massacres;[10] the ARF organized the second in 1904, which was crushed by the Ottoman army supported by Hamidiye Regiments. One character was central to both insurrections: Hrair Tzhokhk, who was Hnchakian during the first uprising and switched to the Dashnaktsakan side just after its failure. More than a hundred years after his death, Tzhokhk is still sung by both organizations, even though he had distanced himself from the SDHP, whose recourse to street demonstrations seemed ineffective to him, whereas he advocated large-scale armed action.

Not only Tzhokhk can be considered an interface between the two organizations, but from the very beginning, he accurately established that the strategy of the actors, that of the two main founders, Avetis Nazarbekian (1866–1939) for the SDHP and Kristapor Mikaelian (1859–1905) for the ARF, was practically the same. In the aforementioned letter sent to both leaderships in 1895,[11] Tzhokhk raised the question of the ego of leaders, denounced their pride and mainly targeted those two leaders. Both were brilliant students well versed in the social sciences, who had travelled through Europe and various universities like most of their contemporaries. Coming from humble backgrounds, they both frequented for a while in the Russian populist circles; they were thirsty for ambition and sought to enter history through the big door of Revolution. Therefore, when the ARF met in 1890 during its founding congress, Mikaelian obtained the agreement of the SDHP, represented by Rupen Khan-Azad (1862–3–1929) to join the new organization, the Federation of Armenian Revolutionaries (FAR). However, as soon as he returned to Geneva, the SDHP delegate was strongly criticized by its leader, Nazarbekian, after having reported to him on the meeting in Tbilisi.[12] According to the compromise between Mikaelian and Khan-Azad, the newspaper *Hnch'ak*, which was already established, would be a theoretical organ edited in Geneva and the new publication *Drōshak* would be a general information newspaper edited in Tbilisi. Nazarbekian rejected this idea and dismissed any form of alliance with the ARF considering that it had nothing to do with socialism, let alone Marxism. Although Khan-Azad made him understand that it was impossible to mobilize Armenian revolutionaries around the idea of scientific socialism and that the principle of 'economic liberation' was validated and therefore constituted sufficient guarantee of socialist orthodoxy, Nazarbekian rebuked this approach with the argument that 'economic liberation' was an ambiguous expression that could be as much affiliated with dialectical materialism as with the Manchester School (nineteenth century), which followed free trade and laissez-faire liberalism. In these somewhat confused circumstances, it was out of the question for him and his wife, Maro Vardanian, who was even more doctrinaire than him, to associate the SDHP with the ARF. The divorce between the two formations commenced in 1891 in *Hnch'ak*.

A convinced socialist, Khan-Azad understood that both leaders were fighting for the leadership of the Revolution. Mikaelian, a man of the left and sensitive to Durkheim's integrationist ideas, was convinced that socialism could not bring Armenians together and that it was necessary to show pedagogy, so as to remain personally at the centre of the political game. Nazarbekian did not accept being demoted to the periphery of the Revolution while he was the founder of the first Armenian progressive party. He noted that his name did not even appear in the first steering committee of the ARF composed of five people, including Mikaelian,[13] and eschewed any participation of the SDHP in this new federation. He could not be satisfied with the consolation prize of being co-editor-in-chief of *Hnch'ak* with Mikaelian. Throughout the last decade of the nineteenth century, Mikaelian made several attempts to get Nazarbekian and the SDHP on board.[14] Each time he came up against the intransigence of Vardanian, much closer to Leni's Russian Social-Democratic Labor Party (RSDLP) than to the union of Armenian revolutionary forces. Mikaelian went so far as to propose changing the name of the ARF if the SDHP joined its ranks. He suggested 'Federation of Armenian Unified Revolutionaries' or 'Brotherly Federation' or 'Unified Federation', and again he was rejected by the Nazarbekian couple.[15] However, Mikaelian set other conditions since the break-up of the SDHP in 1896 between a Marxist branch (SDHP, Nazarbekian) and a national branch (*Verakazmyal* Hnchakian, Arpiarian, Mihran Damadian).[16] Turning in the first place towards this right-wing split more open to fusion, Mikaelian conditioned the union of the Armenian revolutionaries to two phases: first, the reunification of the Hnchakian currents in a single formation; then, the expulsion of Arpiar Arpiarian from the reunified SDHP. It was a new failure for Mikaelian, who asked his comrades to give up any project of union with the Hnchakians, whom he qualified with sarcasm of *Zournajis* (players of zourna, a traditional Armenian wind instrument, which produces strident and wearing sounds in the long run, a way of saying that the SDHP makes only noise and nothing else).[17] When Mikaelian died in 1905, the project of reunification was only an old memory; his successor did not think about it anymore and Nazarbekian left political life and no one seemed to work for the union of the Armenian forces. This was not exactly true; the initiative would not come from the ARF, as during the lifetime of its founder, but from the Hnchakian leader Stepan Sabah-Gulian (1861–1928), who also came from Nakhichevan, like Mikaelian. Sabah-Gulian was editor-in-chief of the Hnchakian newspaper *Eritasard Hayastan* (1903), as the name of the organization created by Mikaelian before the creation of the ARF. Similar to Mikaelian, this intellectual native of the Caucasus, trained at the Free School of Political Sciences in Paris and former student of future French president Raymond Poincaré, was against any agreement with the Committee of Union and Progress (CUP). He pursued a sociological method in the explanation of social facts; his book 'The Responsible Ones' (*Pataskhanatunerë*), published in 1916, does not only deal with a settling of accounts, in particular against the ARF, but an implacable demonstration of the misjudgments of the ARF leaders during and after the Young Turk Revolution of 1908, which led to the catastrophe of the genocide. Sabah-Gulian advocated the union of all revolutionary forces, stubbornly proposed the holding of a congress of Armenian revolutionaries in 1907 and then in 1913, in the midst of the second Balkan War. He opposed the liquidation of the SD Hnchakian Party in Soviet

Armenia in 1923, before dying a few years later in the United States. Like Mikaelian, he was a fervent defender of centralism, this management technique, which appeared as a modern practice until the Second World War. Like Mikaelian, Sabah-Gulian advocated clandestine action in the Ottoman Empire, regardless of the regime in place.

Towards a world view, a socialism, a type of organization and a contradictory strategy

If the SDHP and the ARF invited Armenians to embrace the world in a dialectics of thought and action, the two organizations did not project themselves in the same way in the contemporary world. In other words, the antagonism Hnchakian-Dashnaktsakan unfolded a confrontation between Nazarbekian's economic and Leninist technique of social transformation and Mikaelian's sociological and Durkheimian technique of global overcoming. It was, so to speak, Marx against Kant.

On the one hand, the SDHP recognized itself in the Russian Marxism of Georgi Plekhanov (1856–1918), theorist of scientific socialism and founder of the social-democratic movement in Russia, and above all of Lenin, leader of the RSDLP, adept of the dictatorship of the proletariat. The SDHP represented the world in a structural relation of forces, a class struggle between those who possessed and those who were possessed, its solidary, internationalist and proletarian dimension. Although the Armenian universe was deprived of all working-class characteristics at the end of the nineteenth century, except perhaps for some industrial hubs in Baku and Tbilisi. This discrepancy provoked inevitable tensions in the ranks, which ended up in the division of 1896. It was the internationalism of the masses coming from different nationalities that would overthrow the bourgeoisie, capitalism and imperialism in favour of world peace. Revolution was an ideology and Marxist dogma of social liberation was its rudder.[18]

On the other hand, the ARF, at least that of Mikaelian, embraced all facets of the Kantian project of perpetual peace through the creation of a world federation free of national units. For Mikaelian, since the world was divided into rival empires, the idea of a world federation could be realized if the number of states was small and the dynamics of re-composition of national units that favoured social integration in a revolutionary mould are in accordance with the precepts of Emile Durkheim. The Dashnaktsakan approach was based on the dialectics of war and peace and social integration. Revolution was not an ideology, but a technique, that of overtaking (*dépassement*), and the Mikaelian dogma of global liberation as its rudder.[19]

From this principled antagonism between Marxist and Kantian perspectives, or between theory and pragmatism, how did the SDHP and the ARF evolve in their goal? While the former advocated sovereignty in order to create a socialist Republic of Armenia – in contrast, the Armenakan party opted for sovereignty in the name of the restoration of the autonomous Armenian kingdom born in the Van region and heir to the Bagratids – the ARF defended a progressive approach to sovereignty: from the outset, Mikaelian's ambition was to create a three-stage system: autonomy, independence and federation. Going beyond independence to reach the threshold of the Kantian project, Mikaelian reinforced this position in the dialectic of statism and federalism, elaborated in the programme of the ARF around independence and emanating from its ninth congress in Yerevan in 1919. Twentieth-century historians have often presented the Armenian revolutionary movement as a force hostile to independence. This is doubly false. On the one hand, the SDHP had favoured the independence of Armenia since its foundation. On the other hand, Mikaelian recognized the usefulness of this stage of independence in his famous article titled *Aybouben* ('A, B, C'),[20] while advocating its overtaking (*dépassement*). However, to go beyond independence is not to be against sovereignty, but to go further than this unavoidable stage of national emancipation. This was the reason for his permanent struggle (*haratew kṛiw*):[21] to liberate his people and his homeland from all foreign domination in order to contribute the Armenian stone to the Kantian edifice of perpetual peace. Everything must be done in the service of this ideal. Everything must be instrumentalized for this purpose. Mikaelian did not choose, but amassed. Kristapor did not decide, but integrated. Mikaelian did not arbitrate, but instrumentalized. We touch there the heart of his know-how: the technique of overtaking. True engineer of power relationship, Mikaelian internalized the whole of the dialectics and then externalized it, covered however with the clothes of the new paradigm. Thus, the religious-political, tradition-modernity, Armenakan-Hnchakian cleavages were all overcome without being disrupted. Mikaelian, for example, never broke with the religious, he had it just replaced by the political in the space of legitimacy, making the latter the new centre of gravity in the writing of history. Mikaelian did not cut the thread with tradition to project himself into modernity but just recovered the heritage of the rich Armenian past to introduce it into the present world and find a place for it in the future. Mikaelian saw the Hnchakian ideal of international socialism, but did not prioritize it; he inserted it into a national and not nationalist dimension. But not all Dashnaktsakan leaders shared this roadmap or diverted it from its original meaning; some stuck only to the independence of Turkish Armenia (Simon Zavarian), others to the ideal of Greater Armenia (Hovnan Davtian), still others were satisfied with Armenian extraterritorial autonomy (Mikayel Varandian) or saw in federation an institutional technique linking Armenia to Russia but by no means the Kantian project (Rostom).

This confrontation between the economic technique of social transformation and the sociological technique of global overtaking found one of its most beautiful expressions in the apprehension of socialism by the two main leaders. A new paradigm of politics, *haitadism* brought Armenians into universalism, reason and revolution, but while composing the basis of a new national and territorialized identity, the absence of sources of sovereignty and its attachment to the religious tradition exposed itself to the modernity of ideas at the end of the nineteenth century, namely nationalism and socialism. But as much as the SDHP identified with an ideology, that of socialism, Mikaelian's ARF defined itself primarily as a technique and distanced itself from socialism. The SDHP claimed to be Marxist socialist and took the necessary steps to join the Second International. It frequented the most left-wing currents and received the sponsorship of Plekhanov and Lenin's RSDLP during its adhesion to the big family of world socialism. On the strength of this membership, the SDHP did its utmost to appear as the only Armenian organization affiliated with the socialism of the International and made a mockery of the Dashnaktsakan leadership. But this did not count on the support that the ARF enjoyed in Europe, notably the Russian SRs (Socialist Revolutionaries) and the French socialists (Jean Jaurès), who pledged to support the ARF's candidacy to the Second International filed in 1905 in the Russian socialist-revolutionary press[22] and validated in 1907 at the Stuttgart Congress. From then on, the struggle between the SDHP and the ARF became a reduced-size version of the struggle between the Russian SDs (Social Democrats) and the Russian SRs, and less explicitly between the orthodox Marxist socialists and the Jaurèsian reformist socialists.

The real question that obsessed activists and observers at the time was how to combine the national ideal and the socialist ideal, or nation and socialism in the same cause? For the SDHP, the question was settled beforehand: the party was created on the basis of socialism and the differences between Europe and the *Yerkir*, between Turkish Armenia and Russian Armenia did not matter; what mattered was to carry out the orders of the Nazarbekian couple. This dogmatism, even sectarianism of Nazarbekian and Vardanian turned against them, because actually the militants of the SDHP did not have much to do with Marxism-Leninism. Essentially implanted in Constantinople, Cilicia and the eastern provinces of the Ottoman Empire, the militants were more infused with national ideas than with dialectical materialism. Indeed, what did Hampartsoum Boyajian, alias 'Murad' (1867–1915) and Mihran Damadian (1863–1945) have to do with Marxist socialism in the depths of Sasun, where they had gone into hiding? Not much; and this discrepancy attesting the limits of the SDHP precipitated, if not the collapse of the Hnchakian movement, at least its inevitable split.[23]

For the ARF, two periods should be distinguished in order to fully grasp the specificity of Dashnakism. In the first period, until his death in 1905, Mikaelian assumed that Armenians were divided and made his federation a laboratory of practical ideas in order to define the contours of such a complex issue as the relationship between nationalism and socialism. Within the federation, he had to deal with nationalists, traditionalists, populists, liberals, anti-Marxist socialists, Marxists and so on. To the question of how to make the particularistic elements of nationalism coexist with the universalist values of socialism, he answered that the battle of ideas is a field that should be similar to political and military battles. Mikaelian did not neglect this battle and knew, that in order to dominate, he should necessarily make the two key vectors of the transformation of the Armenian identity coexist. To reach this stage of coexistence, Mikaelian's method referred to constructivist socialism, that is, a project born from the meeting of different currents. This constructivist socialism constituted an ideological credo, but also a technique of unification of the various tendencies. His constructivist socialism was not a self-fulfilling utopia, but rather a pragmatic dynamic rooted in the field, a kind of elastic field where all ideas are at the service of the Revolution and of national and social integration. It was the birth of *Kristaporism*, which in addition to social sciences and the major ideas, introduced the variables of time and space in its integrationist matrix. Its technique of overtaking marked indeed the points on the ground of the management of the time with a minimum and a maximum programme of the Revolution. Linking short and long time into a single rhythm allowed Mikaelian to give direction, meaning and depth to his ideas, a source of legitimacy to better gather and appear as the master of the clocks of the Revolution. By using the vectors of social and national integration in his constructivist socialism, his whole constituted a syncretic system. Mikaelian's political thought, revealing his instinctive nature, was formed on his own experience. Hence, the ambivalent character of his doctrine, which expressed fluctuations according to the experiences of life and external phenomena. But what his doctrine lost in theoretical rigour, gained in persuasiveness and authenticity. So much so that his articles did not reflect anything of the political origins of the Dashnak movement, except for determinism. Mikaelian thus blurred the cards and did not show any belonging to the political currents, which abounded in the nineteenth century.

Everything changed after Mikaelian's death in the late winter of 1905. How did his political heirs recover his heritage? By their inability to remain faithful to the foundations of *Kristaporism* and to appropriate Mikaelian's coolness and also moved by their concern to save the unity of the federation, his successors uprooted the ARF from its political basis and made it lose its balance. How did they achieve this? By making a shift from the technique of overtaking to the ideology of messianism. Thus, instead of pursuing the sociological method of integration defended by Mikaelian, his successors opted for the ideological dogma of socialism. Instead of mobilizing on the sociology of overtaking (*sociologie du dépassement*), they invested themselves in ideological rhetoric. While Simon Zavarian presented 'the ARF in the guise of humanistic socialism',[24] Rostom replied that 'the ARF has been a socialist party from the very beginning'.[25] While Roupen Der Minassian argued that 'the ARF's socialist program is the Koran, the Talmud and the Bible at the same time',[26] Mikael Varandian retorted that 'one can do socialism without pronouncing the name'.[27] Mikaelian never whispered such nonsense. He never spoke of the ARF in terms of 'party' or 'socialist party' or 'ideology' or 'socialism'. Each one of his successors came up with his own chorus to save the unity of the Federation and the Revolution. Each ideologized the ARF message while Kristapor sociologized it. But in this inability to follow Mikaelian's rational steps, his successors found their feet in dogmatism and moved out of politics into ideology; they moved out of rationality into destructive imagination; they moved out from moderation into excess; they moved out of reality onto the ground. For Mikaelian, the ARF was a technique and a totally social fact; for his successors, the ARF was an ideology and a machine. For Mikaelian, the Dashnaktsakan was a man; for his successors, he was a cog. For Mikaelian, it was the men who made the Federation and the Revolution; for his successors, it was the Federation and the Revolution that made the men. He and his successors did not oppose the ethics of responsibility to the ethics of conviction, but for him, the first prevailed on the second, whereas for his heirs, the second outclassed the first.

From 1905 onwards, Mikaelian's legacy was thus often squandered by his successors who witnessed the Russian (1905), Persian (1906) and Young Turk (1908) revolutions. But instead of remaining faithful to the liberation of Turkish Armenia, the ARF chose Greater Armenia in 1907; instead of the sociological corpus of international relations, the ARF adopted a socialist programme in 1907; instead of the principle of federalism of ideas with regard to minority voices in the ARF, the new leadership imposed an iron discipline, generating multiple dissidences as early as 1905. Instead of remaining faithful to Mikaelian's refusal of any alliance with the Young Turks' CUP, in 1907, just two years after his death, the ARF signed an alliance with Ahmed Rıza, the leader of the exiled CUP. While Kristapor stood as a bulwark against the maximalists, Rostom and Zavarian were unable to confront them. For good reason, they did not get along: where Zavarian defended a fundamental and moral approach to action in which individuals must adapt to institutions, Rostom advocated a radical and autonomous approach to action in which the individual is the only master of his destiny, while Mikaelian preached an instrumental and pragmatic approach. Unable to unite, the two main acolytes of the founder gave ground to the hardliners like Hovnan Davtian. Each time, by passing from Kristaporism to its opposite, the ARF extracted itself from the normative field of reality to become an unavoidable force out of the ground. Now that it publicly adhered to socialism as such, the ARF competed more and more with the SDHP until it left the project of union fallout. If under Mikaelian the ARF tried to merge with the SDHP, since his death the ARF cultivated friction with the SDHP.

As for the mode of organization, there too everything opposed the two formations *a priori*. The Hnchakians constituted themselves as a 'party' on the Leninist model of the vanguard organization, composed of professionals of the revolution. Mikaelian and his followers opted for the 'Federation' out of rejection of the party concept. In other words, if for Nazarbekian, the parties should remain autonomous in a federation of union because the alliances were only temporary, for Kristapor, the parties should merge into the federation, which should remain a federation and not a new party. It was only after his death that the Dashnaktsakan leaders openly described the ARF as a 'party', with the exception of the period of the first congresses of the Socialist International, when, as early as 1896, in London, the ARF participated by presenting pamphlets entitled 'The Dashnaktsutiun party' in accordance with the practices of the leadership of the Second International. But this departure from the federalist principle of the Dashnaktsutiun was more an adaptation to the functioning of the Second International than a desire to transform the ARF into a classical political formation. After Mikaelian's death, Varandian insisted on the formula 'Dashnaktsutiun party' to mimic the European socialist and social democratic parties and be on par with the main organizations of the European left. Rostom used the expression 'Dashnaktsutiun party' by Marxist reflex and alignment with scientific socialism. As for Zavarian, he constantly alternated between 'party' and 'organization' in order to demonstrate that the ARF was above the masses and that it was up to the population to adapt to the message of the Revolution and not the other way around. Finally, for Hovnan Tavtian, the word 'party' had become an essential part of the Dashnaktsakan grammar as a tool for militant and revolutionary integration.

These contradictions could be found both between the SDHP and the ARF and within each formation about the functioning of the organizations. As a good Marxist party of Russian inspiration, the SDHP was a party that advocated democratic centralism.[28] Everything began from the top, from Geneva, from the Nazarbekian couple and nothing was left to chance. To this end, it is necessary to note the prowess of the agents of the SDHP in regions such as Constantinople and its surroundings, Cilicia or even the remote provinces of the Ottoman Empire (e.g. Trabizond), where they created a large number of clandestine cells making them gateways to the subversion of Ottoman society and the delivery of weapons and publications. No doubt the rebellion of Zeytun, in Cilicia, fomented by the SDHP, explains why these provinces near the Taurus Mountains were bastions of 'Hnchakian Marxism'.[29] But this centralism, as modern as it seems, cost the SDHP leadership dearly. Monitored by the imperial police and padlocked by their leadership in Geneva, the militants on the spot were deprived of any freedom of action. Very quickly, the discontent went up to Geneva, which was unable to hear the complaints of its base and stubbornly directed its network with an iron hand. It turned into the inevitable explosion in 1896: in addition to the conflict around Marxist socialism, the Reformed (*Verakazmyal*) branch of the Hnchakian party denounced the democratic centralism of Geneva and advocated the opposite, decentralization. On the Dashnaktsakan side, the debates were apparently calmer: decentralization prevailed in theory thanks to the efforts of Zavarian and Hovnan Davtian, who considered that tactics were the responsibility of the base while the centre was responsible for strategy. Actually, things were much more complex: Mikaelian was not a decentralizer, but a convinced centralizer. Not only did his voluminous correspondence between 1890 and 1905 demonstrate this – he constantly gave orders, demanded accountability and interfered in the affairs of local committees – but he also ensured to be elected to both the Eastern Bureau in Tbilisi and the Western Bureau in Geneva, a fact that would never be repeated in the history of the ARF.

When the leadership created the ARF Council, which included the two world Bureaus and the main central committees of the *Yerkir*, it did so on its own initiative in order to better control the work of its federation. Why does the historiography of the ARF retain only decentralization as a mode of operation? The reason is because it has not admitted the aversion of its founder Mikaelian to decentralization, which he expressed in his letters to his fellow Council members.[30] Although Zavarian and Hovnan Davtian tried to preserve decentralization as a way of making Mikaelian understand that Dashnaktsutiun did not belong to him, the latter replied that he intended to withdraw from the Council's activities now that his authority was being questioned and reminded them that federalism did not mean the erasure of the centre. Any modern organization should operate in a centralized fashion. Its posterity would go even further in worshipping decentralization as a founding principle of the ARF while setting in stone the integrating principle of ideological centralism, the keystone of those who wanted to present the ARF as a party and not as a federation. In reality, the inter-revolutionary and intra-revolutionary debate was reminiscent of the old rivalry in the Armenian dynasty system, with the defenders of the *orinabar* (lawful and decentralized) system on the one hand, that is, that the ruler is the equal of the lords, the *primus inter pares*. This was the wish of the Zavarians, Tavtians (ARF) and Damadians (SDHP), who were opposed to the defenders of the *ishkhanabar* system (authoritarian and centralized), that is, the ruler was above the lords so as to better redistribute his authority. This was the position of Nazaberkian and Mikaelian, for once united in the exercise of power.

The irony of history is that while the debate over the centralization of the SDHP was one of the reasons for its collapse in 1896, Mikaelian's centralism did not cause a split in the party; it was the anchoring in decentralization coupled with ideological centralism that was the source of successive splits in the post-Mikaelian ARF between 1905 and 1991. Centralization or decentralization, the SDHP and the ARF relied on a *haitadist* system that while fighting against the logics of domination (international, religious and economic), in turn became a system of domination of the Armenians, since these two formations of revolutionary and clandestine tradition have occupied almost all the political space and do not have the reflex to be accountable to the people, especially since their experience in terms of democratic elections is slim.

Therefore, from the beginning until the fall of the USSR, Armenians were never able to arbitrate the verbal jousts and incidents between the two organizations. Until the split of the SDHP, the ARF did not recognize itself in the peaceful action of the Hnchakians during the demonstrations in Kumkapı in Constantinople and Erzerum in 1890 to demand from Sultan Abdülhamid II the implementation of the reforms imposed by the Berlin Treaty (1878). Nor did it recognize itself at the Bab-ı Ali demonstration, also peaceful, organized in September 1895, in the midst of the Sasun massacres, with the aim of imposing on the Sultan the execution of the reforms demanded the same year by the European powers in the six eastern provinces of the empire. Two other events fueled the fratricidal struggle and the spirit of competition.[31] In February 1891, on his way back to Geneva, Rupen Khan-Azad arrived in Odessa where, on the instructions of journalist Grigor Artzruni, founder of the newspaper *Mshak* (Tiller) of Tbilisi, he had to visit a certain Mrs. Anoush, who had promised Artzruni, during a meeting in Paris in the spring of 1889, to hand over the sum equivalent to the purchase of 10,000 rifles for the revolution. The meeting between Rupen Khan-Azad, mandated by the ARF, and Mrs. Anoush concluded with an agreement in principle. However, the SDHP refused to join the ARF and Khan-Azad found himself torn between his responsibility to the ARF and his commitment to the SDHP. The Nazarbekian couple demanded that he break with the ARF and give them the contact details of Mrs. Anoush to finalize the arms deal. However, the ARF put strong pressure on Khan-Azad to finalize the agreement as a proxy for Dashnaktsutiun. Torn between two sides, Mrs. Anoush did not know to whom to give the money. In the end, she never paid the sum and none of the 10,000 weapons entered Armenia. In addition to the 'affair of the 10,000 rifles', the SDHP–ARF relations deteriorated a little more a few months later. In August 1891, the assassination of the old revolutionary Khachadur Keresktsian, affiliated with the SDHP, by the young Nechayevian and Dashnaktsakan, Aram Aramian, in Erzerum, threw a cloud over the relations between the Armenian organizations.[32] The ARF leadership publicly condemned the assassination but did not exclude Aram Aramian from its ranks. In 1896, a year after the rebellion of Zeytun fomented by the SDHP, Mikaelian was in Tbilisi, pacing back and forth waiting for news from Constantinople about the seizure of the Ottoman Bank, hoping that a Dashnakstakan commando was behind it as planned and fearing that he had been bypassed by an Hnchakian commando. When he learned that the commando had claimed responsibility for the operation in the name of the ARF, he was exultant, as he understood that the revolution was entering a new dimension, with the ARF taking over from the SDHP in the action of brilliance and the rhythm of the liberation struggle.[33] A few years later, the ARF and the SDHP established contacts with the Young Turk movement, exiled in Paris. The SDHP was in contact with the 'Turkish Girondins' of the Freedom and Accord Party (*Hürriyet ve İtilaf Fırkası*) of Prince Sabaheddin, Murad Bey Mizanci and Damad Mahmoud Pasha. Together, they advocated a modernization of Ottoman society from below, decentralization and equality between nationalities. For its part, the ARF was in contact with the different currents and took note of the failure of talks at the First Congress of the Ottoman Opposition to the Sultan in February 1902, in which the Reformed Hnnchakians participated. But a little more than five years later, in December 1907, two and a half years after Mikaelian's death, the ARF and the 'Turkish Jacobins' led by Ahmed Rıza signed a cooperation agreement that opened the door to the Young Turk Revolution in the Ottoman Empire a year later, in July 1908. There too, Nazarbekian's SDHP refused any alliance with Ahmed Rıza's CUP. The dilemma of whether to form an alliance with the Young Turks or not weighed heavily on the relationship between the SDHP and the ARF, to some extent to this day, as accounts have not been settled between the two parties: the former was always suspicious of the Young Turks but accepted the game of elections in the empire led by the CUP; the latter turned its back on Mikaelian's warnings, hostile to any agreement with the CUP, by signing a partnership with the Ottoman power to the point of swallowing swill during the Adana massacres of 1909, which it attributed to the forces of the *ancien régime* while it knew that the CUP was behind it. The ARF broke its alliance with the CUP in 1912, a pivotal moment that was scorned by the SDHP, whose position was eventually closer to that of Mikaelian. In any case, *fedayees* and Armenian activists of the SDHP and the ARF found themselves hand in hand during the few attempts at armed resistance against the Ottoman armies or in the vanguard of the Russian armies on the Caucasian front during the First World War.

Other sequences have also weighed heavily on bilateral relations, notably the one that began with the Bolshevik Revolution of October 1917. Naturally, the SDHP adhered to the victory of the RSDLP and admitted that its initial objective of the creation of a socialist Armenia was accomplished a few years later with the Sovietization of Armenia in 1920,[34] while during the First Republic (1918–20), the SDHP, joined by the Armenian communists affiliated to Lenin, fought against this young sovereign state led by the ARF. Hnchakians abroad, especially in the United States, did not adopt this position; instead, they welcomed the restoration of Armenia's independence, six centuries after the fall of the Armenian kingdom of Cilicia in 1375. For its part, the ARF generally fought the communists in the Caucasus during these years while negotiating in vain with the Bolshevik power in Moscow to maintain an Armenian Republic confederated with communist Russia. This fundamental rivalry between the pro-communist SDHP and the anti-communist ARF found abroad, in the diaspora, a sounding board of great magnitude, where settling of scores and various incidents have marked their history from the Sovietization of Armenia in 1920 to the fall of the USSR in 1991. Even if the Hnchakians were divided on the steamroller of the Bolshevik Revolution – some like Avetis Nazarbekian being supporters of the dilution in 1923 of the SDHP in the Communist Party of the Soviet Union, while others like Stepan Sabah-Gulian were supporters of autonomy of the SDHP – their network constituted an instrument of Bolshevik influence[35] in the Middle East, Europe and America, in the name of spreading communism and fighting the 'reactionary and bourgeois Dashnaks forces'. It was in Moscow that Avetis Nazarbekian died in 1939, five years after settling in the paradise of the proletarians.

A few years later, the SDHP–ARF relationship also entered the Cold War. In 1947, the ARF sided with the capitalist and American bloc, while the SDHP accentuated its submission to the communist bloc, so that when the Antelias crisis broke out in 1956, each party chose its camp: the ARF was pro-Antelias and defended Zareh I, who was elected Catholicos of the House of Cilicia; the SDHP, pro-Etchmiadzin. The Cold War provoked a religious schism among the Armenians and two years later, the Dashnaktsakans and Hnchakians militias came to an armed confrontation during the 1958 crisis in Lebanon, when the ARF supported the pro-American president Camille Chamoun and the Kataeb, while the SDHP sided with the former prime minister Saeb Salam, Kamal Jumblatt and the Arab nationalist militias commanded by Rashid Karami. These Armenian armed and inter-partisan tensions resurfaced in the 1970s during the Lebanese Civil War and the decade of Armenian terrorism, during which Hnchakian militants joined the ranks of the Armenian Secret Army for the Liberation of Armenia (ASALA), while young Dashnaktsakans formed the basis of the Justice Commandos of the Armenian Genocide (JCAG).

In fact, the SDHP–ARF relations opened a new page in their history on the occasion of the fiftieth anniversary of the Armenian Genocide in 1965, during which the ARF, which had started an ostpolitik towards the USSR, signed a solemn declaration with the SDHP and the Ramkavar Party – founded in 1921 in Constantinople and composed of former Armenian elements from the Verakazmyal and the Liberals – by virtue of which the three so-called traditional Armenian parties undertook to fight as a matter of priority against Turkey, which was responsible for the genocide of the Armenians. To tell the truth, the relationship between the SDHP and the ARF had become the barometer of relations between the ARF, the main Armenian force in the diaspora, and the CPSU (Communist Party of the Soviet Union), which wanted to restore its image abroad, especially since the de-Stalinization in 1956. Thus, when secret negotiations opened positively between the ARF and the CPSU, the ARF-SDHP relationship calmed down and resulted in bilateral collaboration, as it was the case during the commemoration of the Armenian Genocide in 1965 and then during the Lebanese Civil War (1975–90), during which the ARF and the SDHP adopted the progressive Arab principle of 'positive neutrality', and finally during *perestroika* and *glasnost* in the USSR in 1987–8. This was evidenced by the 12 October 1988, call of the three traditional Armenian parties to stop the massive strikes in Soviet Armenia, in the midst of the popular uprising for the annexation of Nagorno-Karabakh to the Armenian SSR. This declaration of the three parties came at a time when the ARF and the CPSU were engaged in serious negotiations with a view to promote the return of the former to the Motherland. A few months after this declaration, the first Armenian self-defence units affiliated with the ARF and the SDHP were noticed on the front line against Azerbaijan. Conversely, when Dashnak-Soviet relations became tense, exchanges between the ARF and the SDHP were frozen and tipped over into violence and confrontation, as it was the case during the settling of scores between Dashnakstakans and Hnchakians leaders between 1981 and 1986 in Lebanon.

Conclusion

The SDHP and the ARF were essentially carriers of several converging innovations: first, they aimed to decentralize the Church-nation and Armenian monism by promoting the empowerment of the political sphere and by introducing Armenians into the social sciences to make them actors of history, their own history. Second, they invited Armenians to stop projecting their future into the cultural sphere and to enter the political sphere in order to face reality because the cultural sphere was seen as a mobilizing instrument to circumvent the balance of power. Through this shift into the space of politics, the revolutionary movement sought to territorialize Armenian identity, which constituted a break with the imperial system in place, by attempting to reinvent the relationship between individuals and territories other than through religious faith alone. Finally, and this is what follows from the first two innovations, the SDHP and the ARF had the ambition to inhabit their world through a universalist discourse based on the Enlightenment (Spencer, Kant, Hegel) and contemporary thoughts (Owen, Marx, Engels, Lavrov, Comte, Durkheim, Bergson, Darwin, Le Bon, Plekhanov, Lenin) that made *haitadism* a topical issue on the global diplomatic agenda.

At the same time, this *haitadist* model carried by the SDHP and the ARF had several limitations. Through its inability to make a definitive break with religion and its lack of a tradition of sovereignty, democracy and freedoms, the forces of *haitadism*, beginning with the SDHP and the ARF, sought to nurture Armenians with their own recipe for education, from their earliest childhood to their last breath, thus verging on totalitarianism in principle, but not necessarily in reality. This totalizing capacity and inability to distinguish between the classical and revolutionary models of *haitadism* is due to the fact that *haitadism* has not moved beyond the proto-system, unable to be confined to a given Armenian institutional framework, and for good reason: *haitadism* predates the state and there is no tradition of sovereignty or geographically delineated prerequisite.

By promoting the emergence of the people as an agent of their own destiny, the primacy of social sciences, making the individual the engine of history, and the strategy of the actors, the SDHP and the ARF clashed with the idea of the Nation, which included other social groups (religious, bourgeoisie) that were themselves sensitive to *haitadism*. But how can we rely on 'the people' as an autonomous actor without undermining 'the nation'? Or, conversely, how to preserve the national ideal if the people did not become autonomous from monism? This was one of the dilemmas of the revolutionary movement, divided between a vast national pole associated with religious and/or bourgeois institutions (ARF, Armenakan) and no less an important popular pole linked to the masses, and which would give rise to a left-wing revolutionary current, itself divided into several rival branches (SDHP, ARF, RSDLP). *Haitadism* would never get out of this dilemma (Figure 11.1).

The revolutionary movement as a whole and the SDHP and the ARF particularly suffered from a legitimacy deficit. All the revolutionary literature that has been produced since the 1870s and 1880s is a sum of examples aimed at justifying the use of violence and weapons among Armenians, the right to freedom and respect for a people in the making, following in the footsteps of other liberation movements, such

Figure 11.1 Stepan Sabah-Gulian. Source: Gidur, *Patmut'iwn S.D. Hnch'akean Kusakts'ut'ean, 1887–1962*, vol. I, 307.

as the Bulgarian *chetes*. But this effort to enter history came across several obstacles: on the one hand, Ottoman Armenians and Caucasian Armenians did not know each other when the Russian and Ottoman Empires opened up to the world with their liberal reforms in the nineteenth century. Despite attempts to bring the Armenian societies of Turkey and Russia closer, the SDHP and the ARF never really overcame those misunderstandings, not to say mistrust, on either side. On the other hand, many Armenians who remained away from the revolutionary movement did not adhere to this positivist approach and considered the revolutionary movement, with its propensity to incorporate the Enlightenment, an intruder in Armenian social reality. For these two reasons, one sociological and the other theoretical, the SDHP and the ARF had difficulty in crossing a certain threshold of legitimacy. Moreover, in need of recognition, the revolutionary movement was struck by a form of disarticulation, the intrinsic opposition of *haitadism* between science and romanticism where politics alternates between these two poles. Like the classical chroniclers of Armenian history, the pioneers of the revolutionary movement did not overcome this difference, knowing that among Armenians novel pre-exists history and that narrative is a coupling between novel and history. The SDHP and the ARF thus brought together in their liberating narrative the tradition of oral history and the modernity of the science of history. From this revolutionary specificity, which suggested that *haitadism* did not break with Armenian monism but was just a new paradigm of identity construction, politics went beyond reason, disrupted in its trajectory of empowerment by the clash between history and novel, and led to a hybrid form where politics romanticized history and historicized the novel. In a passage from the classical to the revolutionary, *haitadism* went, without this being apparent at first sight, from the proto-political to the extra-political, that is, messianism, national genius, Great Armenia, excess, mythology, hubris, the destructive imaginary around the sublimation and sacralization of the territory. Through the centrality of politics, the revolutionary movement updated the old Armenian religious paradigm, and the three places of foundation of the Armenian parties (Van, Geneva, Tbilisi) embodied the political and contemporary version of the spiritual creed of Ephesus-Dvin dear to the faithful of the Armenian Apostolic Church. In other words, if the religious yielded to the political its place at the centre of the game of monism, the ecclesiastic yielded its place to the revolutionary, without seeing the latter break with the sphere of messianism, the outrageous, the memorial, the emotion and so on. On the contrary, in the religious universe, the Armenian Revolution and its instruments, such as the SDHP and the ARF, inspired by the all-political and therefore 'extra-political', were the bearers of catastrophes. In the secular universe, the Armenian Revolution, through the maximalist dimension of politics, was the bearer of devastating utopias and destructive imaginaries. In other words, the revolutionary, whether he is a Hnchakian or a Dashnaktsakan, remained in an extra-political dimension, always wanting more, because he was never satisfied since he was driven by his unlimited imagination. Two men, Mikaelian and Sabah-Gulian, had understood all the risks that this drift of the political involved. By seeking to occupy the space of politics in succession, they rejected ideology as a source of mobilization. Mikaelian's death and Sabah-Gulian's marginalization, crushed by the Bolshevik Revolution, strongly disarticulated *haitadism* since a large part of this proto-system literally broke with the political to huddle in the extra-political: on the one hand, reason has given way to messianism; on the other hand, technique had yielded to ideology. In other words, if the revolution under Mikaelian and Sabah-Gulian embodied rationalism, politics and the technique of the relationship of force, the post-Mikaelian ARF and the SDHP without Sabah-Gulian embodied messianism, extra-politics and ideology. Two excesses, two utopias, one Dashnaktsakan fused with *haitadist* messianism, the other Hnchakian fused with communist messianism, were the object of instrumentalization strategies by successive powers in St. Petersburg and Moscow.

Notes

1 *Drōshak*, 1895, no. 9.
2 Simon Vratsian, *Keank'i Ughinerov: Dēpk'er, Dēmk'er, Aprumner,* vol. I (Beirut: Mshag Press, 1955), 46–51.
3 *Nor Keank',* 18 January 1996, no. 6.
4 This article covers the period from the origins of the two organizations to the fall of the USSR in 1991.
5 See Michael Werner and Bénédicte Zimmermann, *De la comparaison à l'histoire croisée* (Paris: Seuil, 2004).
6 Lousi Nalbandian, *The Armenian Revolutionary Movement: The Development of Armenian Political Parties Through the Nineteenth Century* (Berkley: University of California Press, 1963).

7 See 'Resonances', a publication of *Nouvelles d'Arménie* magazine, numéro 4, 'La pensée politique arménienne, genèse et dilemmes . . .', 2022. https://www.armenews.com/spip.php?page=article&id_article=88407 (accessed 15 November 2022).
8 The expression 'Church-nation' is by Professor Jean-Pierre Mahé.
9 Talcott Parsons, *The Social System* (London: Routledge & Kegan Paul Ltd, 1970).
10 Hratch Dasnabedian, 'The Hunchakian Party', *The Armenian Review* 41 (1988): 17–39.
11 *Drōshak*, 1895, no. 9.
12 Rupen Khan-Azad, 'Hay Heghapʻokhakani mĕ Husherits'', *Hayrenikʻ Amsagir*, no. 8 (June 1927) to no. 7 (May 1929).
13 The first ARF center was formed by Mikaelian, Zavarian, Dastakian, Loris-Melicoff and Sarkissian. See Gaïdz Minassian, *1915: Le rêve brisé des Arméniens* (Paris: Flammarion, 2015).
14 Ibid.
15 Kristapor Mikaelian, *Kʻristap ʻor Mikʻayēleani Namaknerĕ* (Beirut: Hamazkayin Vahe Setian Press, 1993).
16 Dasnabedian, 'The Hunchakian Party', 32.
17 Minassian, *1915: le rêve brisé des Arméniens*, 124.
18 Arsen Gidur, *Patmutʻiwn S.D. Hnchʻakean Kusaktsʻutʻean 1887-1963*, vols. I and II (Beirut: Shirag Press, 1962-3). Dasnabedian, 'The Hunchakian Party', 21–4.
19 Gaïdz Minassian, *Arméniens, le temps de la délivrance* (Paris: CNRS Editions, 2015), 217–47.
20 *Drōshak*, 1893, no. 5 and 1894, no. 6.
21 Kristapor Mikaelian, *Heghapʻokhakani Mĕ Mtkʻer* (Beirut: Hamazkayin Vahe Setian Press, 1981). This work is a collection of Kristapor's articles published in *Drōshak* between 1891 and 1905.
22 Gaïdz Minassian, 'La Fédération Révolutionnaire Arménienne Dachnaktsoutioun: Ethique et Politique, 1959-1998' (Thèse de sciences politiques, Université de Paris X Nanterre, 1999).
23 Dasnabedian, 'The Hunchakian Party', 31–2.
24 Hrach Dasnabedian, *Simon Zawarean: Mahuan Eōtʻanasunameakin Aṙtiw*, vols. I–III (Beirut: Hamazkayin Vahe Setian Press, 1983–97).
25 Hrach Dasnabedian, *Ṛostom: Mahuan Vatʻsunameakin Aṛtʻiw* (Beirut: Hamazkayin Vahe Setian Press, 1979).
26 Rupen, *H.H.D. Kazmakerputʻiwnĕ* (Cairo: Husaper, 1935).
27 Mikael Varandian, *H.H. Dashnaktsʻutʻean Patmutʻiwn* (Paris: Imprimerie de Navarre, 1932).
28 Dasnabedian, 'The Hunchakian Party', 21.
29 Gidur, *Patmutʻiwn S.D. Hnchʻakean Kusaktsʻutʻean 1887–1963*, 586–91.
30 Yervant Pambukian, *Kʻristapʻor Mikʻayēleani Antip Namakner* (Yerevan: Lusagn Press, 2020).
31 Minassian, *1915: Le rêve brisé des Arméniens*.
32 Sergey Gennadiyevich Nechayev (1847–82) was a Russian communist revolutionary and prominent figure of the Russian nihilist movement. He was known for his determination of pursuing revolution by using all available means including that of terror. He was the author of the radical book radical manifesto *Catechism of a Revolutionary* (1869).
33 Leo, *Antsʻyalitsʻ* (Yerevan: Shem Press, 2009).
34 Gidur, *Patmutʻiwn S.D. Hnchʻakean Kusaktsʻutʻean*, vol. I, 486–87.
35 Grigor Yeghikian, 'Hnchʻakeannerĕ ew Bolsheviknerĕ', *Hayrenikʻ Amsagir* 18, no. 10 (August 1940); 19, no. 11 (September 1940); 19, no. 1 (November 1940).

12

The Istanbul Students' Union of the Social Democrat Hnchakian Party and its Periodical *Kaytz* (1911–14)

Yaşar Tolga Cora

Armenian socialists played an important role in the development of socialist thought and activism in the Ottoman Empire. Foundational works by Anahide Ter Minassian on this subject provide insights to researchers concerning the wide scope of this role.[1] However, as she also notes, let alone their content analysis, even inventories of Armenian socialist publications largely remain to be published.[2] This article will analyse the contents of *Kaytz* (Spark), the monthly periodical that was published between 1911 and 1914 by the Istanbul Students' Union of the Social Democrat Hnchakian Party (*SDHP Polsoy Usanoghakan Miut'iwn*) in its first year and a half (Figure 12.1).

Starting with the late-nineteenth century in Europe, America and the Caucasus and after the 1908 Constitutional Revolution in the Ottoman Empire, different Armenian socialist and social democratic groups started to conduct extensive activities and organize. Publishing became an important aspect of these organizing efforts. After 1908, Armenian socialists became significant political and social actors both within the Armenian community and Ottoman society. They claimed to have the right to politically represent the Ottoman Armenian community and through their publications, they contributed to the Ottoman social and intellectual life.

The relationship between the Armenian Revolutionary Federation (ARF, Dashnaktsutiun) and the Committee of Union and Progress (CUP) that had started before 1908 first turned into a relationship of up-and-downs based on interests and cooperation and later into conflict. Another important Armenian socialist party, the Social Democrat Hnchakian Party (SDHP), positioned itself against the CUP and Dashnaktsutiun and within the opposition and began to cooperate with the Freedom and Accord Party (*Hürriyet ve İtilaf Fırkası*) after 1912. In the summer of 1915, twenty SDHP members, including symbolic figures such as Paramaz, were executed with the claim that they had planned to assassinate the CUP leaders.[3]

Despite the differences in their positions in everyday politics, ideologies and styles of organizing, publishing and unionism activities were natural extensions of the party organization for both the ARF and the SDHP. Because of its closeness with the government and because it was more widely organized across the country, the

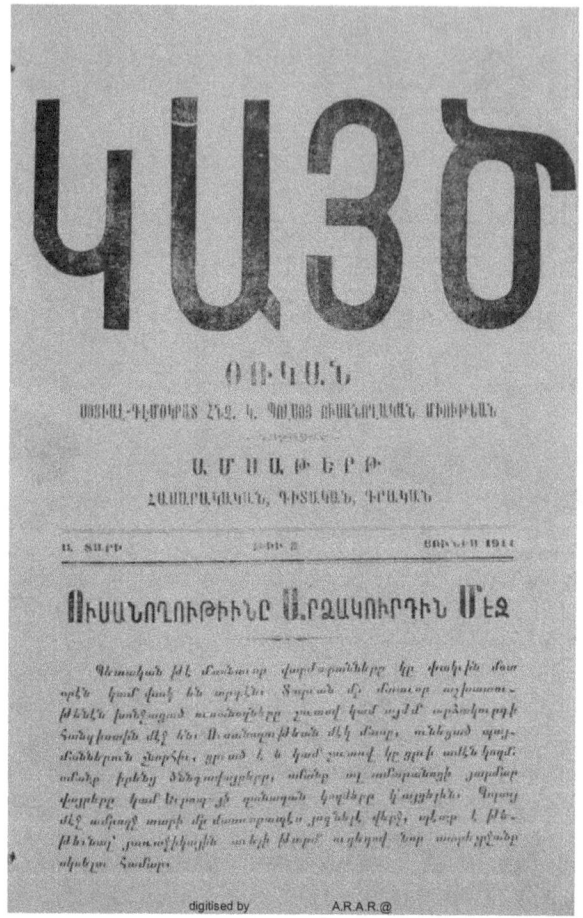

Figure 12.1 *Kaytz* June 1911, no. 2.

ARF was one step ahead of the SDHP in terms of publishing and unionism activities. Starting with 1909, the ARF published *Haṛaj* (Ahead, 1909–14) in Erzurum, *Azatamart* (The Fight for Freedom, 1909–14) in Istanbul and *Ashkhatank'* (Labor, 1910–14, 1915) in Van. Besides these, there were pro-ARF publications such as *But'ania* (Bithynia, 1910–11, 1912) in Izmit and Adapazarı, and *Arōr* (Plow, 1910–11) in Erzincan. Publications of the SDHP or those representing its views included newspapers and periodicals such as *Apaga* (Future, 1910–14) in Istanbul, *Andranik* (1909–11) in Sivas, and *Amasia* (1911–14) in Amasya, both located in the Kızılırmak region where the Hnchaks were traditionally powerful. Besides their objectives of 'reporting', these publications – which published various opinion pieces – analysed the problems of both the Armenian community and the Ottoman society in general in line with party policies and presented suggestions on the basis of their ideology and political tactics. Because of this, as also shown by recent studies on the Armenian political parties, they are crucial for understanding the politics and social life in this period.[4]

Another important point with regard to these publications is that in Istanbul and in the provinces, their administrative and editorial boards and publishing houses were political thought clubs where socialists came together. Another proof of the spatial importance of these publications are activities held in conference salons which had symbolic names (such as the *Zhoghovurd* (People) in Kumkapı) or were named after the publications themselves. Armenian socialists tried to reach and organize different social strata such as women, labourers and non-Armenians through conferences and theatre plays and held activities such as Labor Day (1 May) celebrations.

The youth and university students were another group that both the SDHP and ARF tried to reach and organize through publications and conferences. This was closely related to the larger historical context. During the Second Constitutional Era (1908–18), the youth had become a legitimate social and political actor and gained social visibility and all political parties were trying to reach and organize them.[5] For socialists, organizing high school and university students was especially important, because this group was thought to be more inclined to understand and spread the scientific basis and theoretical aspects of socialism thanks to their high level of education. In its first year and a half, which is examined in this article, and also in its later issues, *Kaytz* tried to help students develop a Marxist thought system by devoting the majority of its pages to the philosophical roots of historical materialism and scientific trends in Europe. The reason for limiting the time period examined in this chapter to May 1911–December 1912 is that there was a structural change after the annual congress of the Students' Union, which convened in late 1912. At this congress, the Students' Union and its publication *Kaytz* amended their charter. Thus, the article stating that the members of the union 'would not engage in political activities' was replaced by the statement that they would 'participate in class struggle'. Instead of defining itself as 'an organization working for the self-development of idealists and students' as stated in the first issue of *Kaytz*, the Union started to define the students who were its members as 'intellectual proletariat', and declared that they would participate in the class struggle as a part of the party alongside with workers.[6]

According to the SDHP's official history, published in 1962 and edited by Arsen Gidur, one of the most important authors of *Kaytz*, the aim behind the establishment of the Students' Union in 1910 was 'to spread Marxism and scientific socialism among a wide array of social strata.'[7] This claim does not only show the importance of socialist students for the party but also indicates that students were seen as people who would develop and spread the theoretical foundations of the party – notwithstanding the criticism often directed against the SDHP that 'despite their claims of being Marxists, they were only able to be populists'.[8]

Articles related to scientific socialism and published in all issues of *Kaytz* prove this point. When we look at the founders of the SDHP Students' Union and the authors of *Kaytz*, we easily see the fluid political geography of the post-1908 era and find Armenians from the Caucasus and Ottoman Armenians side by side. Among the executive staff of the union, there was Jirayr Mirzakhanian, Setrag Karian, Kegham Vanigian, Vahan Zeytuntsian, Hrand Kalikian, who were then students at the Faculty of Law; Hayk Kaldjian, Benyamin Aghoyian, Baghdasar Manuelian, who studied at the Faculty of Medicine, besides Arsen Gidur, who graduated from the Etchmiadzin Djemaran in 1908 and later studied in Istanbul at the Faculty of Education and Yedvard Amaduni, who also studied in the latter.[9]

Kaytz brought together many young socialists under the leadership of its editor-in-chief Kegham Vanigian.[10] It has been argued that *Kaytz* made the emergence of a socialist 'Kaytz Generation' in the Ottoman Armenian intellectual life possible by providing an abstract space in which students interacted through the writings published in the periodical and by providing a material space in which conferences and different activities were held.[11] Just like investigating the impact of any other publication on the reader, it is quite difficult to research the validity of this claim and measure the impact of *Kaytz* on the Armenian youth of high school or university education level. Nonetheless, the importance of the publication of four years of such a periodical, which discussed issues such as the theory of evolution in depth, presented the foundations of scientific socialism at a theoretical level and approached different problems of Ottoman society from a class perspective, is a fact that cannot be denied. Besides, this claim is supported by the fact that high-school student unions that followed the model set by SDHP Istanbul Students' Union were established in provincial towns such as Adapazarı, İzmir, Bardizag, İzmit, Eskişehir, Konya, Merzifon, Sis/Kozan, Van, Erzurum, Adana, Harput (The Euphrates College) and Mamüratü'l Aziz (German and French High Schools) and that some of these unions, such as the one in Bardizag, had manually multiplied periodicals.[12]

In its first issue, published in May 1911, *Kaytz* declared that it started to be published in a context which required the emergence of active forces working for the progress and development of Turkey after 1908 and that it was the manifestation of such a perspective. With regard to its aim, it stated that not only political parties and organizations but also every individual who wanted to serve the society had to strive for this renaissance and for supporting workers' rights. It also claimed that the space for these activities of struggle had to be examined with a 'sound and bright' perspective. This sound and bright perspective was historical materialism and the primary aim of the periodical was 'to examine the current social and public life of Turkey' from this perspective. 'Every other way, which did not examine' the socio-economic problems in this manner 'would be one-sided or deficient'.[13] Another aim of *Kaytz* was to facilitate the self-development of students in the Ottoman Empire and to help them 'understand and internalize science' by making intellectual life in Europe available to them. The periodical would work 'towards victory, aware of its responsibilities and carrying the flag of socialism'.[14]

Starting with the first issue, three types of articles were published in *Kaytz*. First and the most common of these were articles examining European scientific and literary currents, especially the scientific and philosophical foundations of historical materialism. These articles included quotes from European and Russian socialists. The second type of writings were pieces which analysed the political and social situation in the Ottoman Empire and various social issues (worker's rights, social status of women and wars) from a class perspective. Among these are responses penned by Vanigian to the critiques of socialism and pieces reflecting the approach of the periodical to the

Balkan Wars (1912-13). News about socialist politics in Europe and in the world can also be included in this category. The third type of writings were pieces focusing on the SDHP's organizing of students and its activities in Istanbul and in the provinces. News about lectures delivered to students by *Kaytz*'s authors, most importantly Arsen Gidur, can also be counted among these. Apart from these three types of writings, *Kaytz* also published poems and literary criticism on recently published literary works, which examined these works from a historical materialist, class perspective. In the following, I take a closer look at *Kaytz* and the opinions of its authors with references to the political and scientific writings that can be considered within the scope of the first two categories.

Among the first type of writings is the article series titled 'Literary Trends in the Nineteenth Century' penned by Yedvard Amaduni. In this series, various trends such as romanticism, Byronism, realism and naturalism were examined. In a similar vein, the first issue featured an article series titled 'How Do Ideas Develop?' This series, written by Arsen Gidur, analysed the philosophical foundations of historical materialism. Gidur closed the first of these articles, which started with elaborations on ancient Greece and ended with Hegel and Marx, by stating that he 'would examine the wide field of historical materialism and the theories against it in the pages of *Kaytz* in a more extensive and richer way'.[15] Gidur's article series 'History of Philosophy and Historical Materialism', which started to be published in the second issue, expanded this space. This series did not only provide a history of philosophy but also explored the differences between sociology and historical philosophy, history of science and methodology. In the later issues of *Kaytz*, there were pieces such as 'The Theory of Evolution', 'Symbolism' (translation of a piece by Rıza Tevfik, volume 2, issue 1-2), 'The Human Origins' (volume 2, issue 2), 'Comparison of the Thinking Capacity of Humans and Animals' (volume 1, issue 7-8; volume 2, issue 2), 'Animism and Vitalism' (volume 2, issue 6), which were written or translated by Gidur and other authors. It can be argued that among these, the approach of Ernst Haeckel, one of the founders of monism and a leading name in Social Darwinist thought whose works were translated into Turkish and discussed in this period, was presented under the heading of 'The Laws of Existence'.[16]

Among the writings focusing on socialist thought are 'Collectivism' (volume 1, issues 5-7), 'Scientific Socialism', 'Economic Motives According to Marx' (volume 2, issue 1), 'What Is Class?' (volume 2, issue 2), 'Idealism and Materialism' (volume 2, issues 4-6), 'The Relationship between Economy and Ideology' (volume 2, issue 5), which included quotes from 'The Fundamental Problems of Marxism' written by Georgi Plekhanov, with whom the Hnchaks established an affinity (in Ter Minassian's words, 'became friends') and 'The Anarchist Doctrine' (volume 2, issue 5), also with quotes from Plekhanov.

The reader's letters published in the periodical show that these writings were interpreted by, discussed among and even criticized by readers. For example, there were criticisms directed at Arsen Gidur's 'History of Philosophy' and the articles on the relationship between spiritualism and materialism, and extensive responses to these (volume 1, issue 6). Perhaps more importantly, in the memoirs of people who had read *Kaytz*, there are remarks showing that they read these pieces, sent reader's letters which included questions about these topics to the periodical, and received responses to them.[17] This supports the claims that the scientific and theoretical articles about socialism were in fact read and that *Kaytz* had a significant impact on the younger generation.

Similar to many other socialist publications, one of the aims of the SDHP Students' Union was to establish a library; in other words, to publish a book series. In the time period examined in this chapter, two books were published by Kaytz Library. These works reflect the scientific side of the periodical and were similar to the pieces of socialist thought pieces it published. The first was a collection of Arsen Gidur's writings published in the periodical and entitled *The History of Philosophy*. The second was a thirty-two-page brochure entitled *Our Program or Socialism* and written by Wilhelm Liebknecht, one of the founders of the German Social Democrat Party (SDP).

Another group of writings published in *Kaytz* are analyses on the Ottoman Empire. These analyses are writings examining the domestic and foreign policies of the empire on the basis of class. Some of these were about everyday politics. An example of this is the article series titled 'The Future of Turkey', penned by 'S.', which was published in the second and third issues. Examining the approach of international capital against the movement encompassing all Asian countries from China to the Ottoman Empire, and especially the situation of Turkey in terms of Russian-German relations in the aftermath of the Treaty of Potsdam (1911), it underlined the economic dependence of Turkey to imperialist powers. It criticized the CUP, which failed to establish the necessary bourgeois politics in Turkey and used the Parliament as a kitchen serving the appetites of 'prosperous' pashas, beys and gentlemen.

Starting with the third issue, the editor of the periodical Kegham Vanigian, who used the penname Vanig, started to write on socialism and the workers' struggle in Turkey in his articles entitled 'Socialist Activities in Turkey' (*Ěnkerwarakan Gortzuneutʻiwně Tʻurkʻioy Měj*). In one of these writings, published in the fourth issue of the periodical in July 1911, Vanigian elaborated upon the criticisms raised against socialism in Turkey and within the Armenian community and responded to these. These questions and answers are important because they show *Kaytz*'s emphasis on scientific socialism and reflect the efforts of socialists to become legitimate actors in Ottoman political life in the Second Constitutional Era. Against the criticisms that socialism was a utopia and independence and equality were beautiful but non-factual words, Vanigian stated that Marx and Engels developed scientific socialism to replace the utopian socialism of Robert Owen and Charles Fourier and that the foundations of scientific socialism depended on the situation of the working class. In response to the criticism that socialism had come from Europe and developed under the circumstances there, Vanigian argued that socialism was not a flower endemic to Europe, could be adapted to the circumstances all across the world, and the socialist perspective was the only way out of the nationalities problem in Turkey. Finally, responding to the criticism that a ground for socialism had not yet emerged in Turkey because of its level of economic development, he brought to the table the workers' resistance against the working conditions in Istanbul and other regions including Bursa and unionization in Thessaloniki (Salonica). In a similar vein, he showed that a bourgeoise class had already emerged in the country – emphasizing their role in the 1908 Revolution – and claimed that the bourgeoisie defended its own class position.

Vanigian developed these ideas further in his article titled 'Socialist Labor Unions in Constantinople', which was published in the fifth issue of the journal in August. In this article, he examined the relationship between the working class and socialism which he had mentioned in the previous issue. Pointing out to the living conditions of workers, he emphasized the importance of unionization for the formation of a working-class movement. The article provided brief information about the Blazer Sewing Tailors Union, which was established in September 1910 and was the first socialist labour union in Istanbul, the Union of Umbrella Makers, the Tapissier's Union, the Union of Coat Making Tailors, the Union of Mill Workers, the Machinists' Union and the Bookbinders' Union. These labour unions established by Greek, Jewish, Armenian, Bulgarian and a few Turkish workers had a common salon used for conferences. Vanigian highlights the roles of Greek and Bulgarian socialists and the *Irgatis* newspaper published in Greek in facilitating the organizing of these workers. Because of the ARF's activities during the strike at the Tobacco Administration, he discussed the relationship between the ARF and the worker's organizations in a sarcastic way.[18]

The approach of the SDHP Students' Union to the final wars of the Ottoman Empire is also very important. Both during the Tripoli War of 1911 and the Balkan Wars of 1912–13, the Union stood against the war, claiming that war was a result of imperialism and the material interests of the bourgeois class. It is known that the declaration against the war and Italian imperialism, which was published in *Kaytz* during the Tripoli War had also reached different strata of the society.[19] The SDHP Students' Union upheld this anti-war attitude during the Balkan Wars too. In November 1912, the periodical published an editorial titled 'War and Studentship' (volume 2, issue 5). In this editorial, after criticizing the Bulgarian students who formed voluntary battalions, the authors mentioned the pro-war demonstrations of Turkish students and criticized the slogan of these demonstrations: 'Down with article 23, Hail to the War'. It referred to article 23 of the Treaty of Berlin, which was about reform in Rumelia and laid at the basis of 'The Regulation for Rumelian Provinces', which was not put into effect despite being adopted in 1880. In order to prevent the war, the government of Gazi Ahmed Muhtar Pasha proclaimed the adoption of a reform programme for Rumelia in October 1912 on the basis of this article.[20] The SDHP Students' Union especially problematized the slogan 'Down with article 23' and questioned how young people who would govern the country in the future could raise such a demand. It asked whether they too wanted to behave like their fathers who had seen reform as the greatest enemy of the country for many years and to run the country with pillage, loot and blood.[21] Another criticism raised in the article is that the patriotic university students who shouted 'Hail to the War' were not volunteering for the army. It was stated that only around 300 students out of about 7,000 had enlisted, while the others were planning to postpone their military service. According to *Kaytz*, the exploiting class in the country was responsible for this situation of the university youth.

In the following issue (December 1912, volume 2, issue 6), an article titled 'War: Workers and Bourgeoisie' and signed by Vanig[ian] analysed the approach of socialists to the war. The article responded to a question raised by K. Simonian from Bardizag:

'Why socialists thought that the bourgeoisie caused this war and that they themselves would be the losers in the end?' As it was also mentioned at the end of the article, the response was in line with the anti-war perspective adopted at the Basel Socialist Congress:

> The bourgeoisie wants war in order to maintain its class dominance and supports expansionism for its interests... Today's destructive war is between the aggressive Balkan bourgeoisie and the defensive bourgeoisie of Turkey. It is true that this war has been damaging the Turkish bourgeois-feudal class. However, have not Bulgarian, Serbian, Greek, and Montenegrin bourgeoisie expanded and became richer? ... Balkan allies too have things to lose, but the losers are in fact the proletariat, workers and peasants who build the country, not the bourgeoisie who live painlessly.[22]

Kaytz also published news about socialism in Europe and in the world. Examples of these include the news about the Socialist Cooperatives Congress held in France (fourth issue) and the strikes in England (fifth issue). After the suicide of Paul Lafargue (a Cuban-French revolutionary Marxist socialist writer) in October 1911, the seventh issue published an Armenian translation of a letter that the SDHP Students' Union had sent to leading French socialist publications *L'Humanité* and *Le Socialiste*, along with a picture of Lafargue. In the eighth issue, published in November 1911, Lafargue's life and ideas were extensively discussed. In December 1912 (volume 2, issue 6), there was a piece titled 'Socialist Life', informing the reader about the activities of socialist parties and worker's organizations in Europe and China. In the same issue, a piece titled 'Socialism and Intellectuals' examined the German SDP's expulsion of Gerhard Hildebrand, a prominent socialist, who had proposed to cooperate with the Kaiser and supported armament at the party congress held in Chemnitz under a separate heading. The article included extensive quotes from an article published in *Le Socialisme* by Karl Kautsky, which supported this decision. These and similar pieces show that the SDHP Students' Union closely followed and was in touch with the socialist movement in Europe. Moreover, when the aforementioned anti-war stance of the SDHP is taken into consideration, such writings can also be seen as criticisms towards the ARF, which cooperated with the CUP.

In lieu of conclusion

It is clear that an in-depth analysis of *Kaytz*, beyond the limits of this article, will contribute to our knowledge of socialist thought and socialist publications in the Ottoman Empire and especially deepen our understanding of the foundations and development of scientific socialism. In relation to this, it can be argued that one of the roles undertaken by *Kaytz* was to develop a new terminology to explain socialist thought. *Kaytz* did not only contribute to the spreading of the usage of terms such as class, class conflict, proletariat, bourgeoisie, historical materialism and surplus value, which lie at the basis of the socialist thought system and are widely used today but also contributed to the development of language through neologisms used in many science articles it published.

Another topic only briefly mentioned in this article are the criticisms directed towards the ARF in *Kaytz*, which was one of the media outlets of the SDHP. Some of them were related to the everyday politics of the ARF and its cooperation with the CUP. The SDHP had also responded to the criticisms derived from its own alliance with the Freedom and Accord Party and the Greek Constitutional Political League at least once (volume 2, issue 5). Some of those discussions were carried out at an abstract level, within a theoretical framework and socialist thought. These too can be useful for understanding different aspects of the relations among socialists. Another issue that can be further explored through the investigation of the SDHP Students' Union and *Kaytz* is the latter's efforts to organize students and the extent and success of such efforts.

The periodical had a special section titled 'The Student World', which was published regularly. The Charter of the SDHP Students' Union, the activities of the SDHP in high schools and universities, the conferences and the decisions taken at the annual meetings of the Union, which were published in this section, are very important sources in this regard. Another topic that can be explored through *Kaytz* is the relationship among different student unions. A note mentioning that the Students' Association of the Law School did not carry out any significant activities – some authors of *Kaytz* were students at this institution, which gives a different meaning to this criticism – and critical remarks targeting the student periodicals of the ARF and the Armenian Democratic Liberal Party (ADL) can be seen as efforts by the SDHP to lay claim to the political field established by students. In the years following the period examined here, the members of the Students' Union started to work for the party. The significance of this and its impact on *Kaytz* can be another research topic. Such questions would also give us an idea about research on contemporary issues such as the object or subject positions of the youth in politics or the question of their autonomy from the political parties to which they are connected.

Notes

1. Anahide Ter Minassian, '1876-1923 Döneminde Osmanlı İmparatorluğu'nda Sosyalist Hareketin Oluşmasında ve Gelişmesinde Ermeni Topluluğunun Rolü', in *Osmanlı İmparatorluğu'nda Sosyalizm ve Milliyetçilik (1876-1923)* eds. Mete Tunçay and Erik Jan Zürcher (Istanbul: İletişim Yayınları, 1995), 163-238; Minassian, *Ermeni Devrimci Hareketi'nde Milliyetçilik ve Sosyalizm (1887-1912)* (Istanbul: İletişim Yayınları, 2012).
2. Ter Minassian, '1876-1923 Döneminde Osmanlı İmparatorluğu'nda', 176.
3. Kadir Akın, *Ermeni Devrimci Paramaz: Abdülhamid'den İttihat Terakki'ye Ermeni Sosyalistleri ve Soykırım* (Ankara: Dipnot, 2016); Yetvart Çopuryan, *Paramazlar: Beyazıt'ta 20 Darağacı*, trans. Aris Nalcı (İstanbul: Kor, 2018).
4. Bedross Der Matossian, *Shattered Dreams of Revolution: From Liberty to Violence in the Late Ottoman Empire* (Stanford: Stanford University Press, 2016); Ohannes Kılıçdağı, 'Socio-Political Reflections and Expectations of the Ottoman Armenians

after the 1908 Revolution: Between Hope and Despair' (PhD diss., Boğaziçi University, 2014).
5   Yücel Aktar, *İkinci Meşrutiyet Dönemi Öğrenci Olayları, 1908-1918* (Istanbul: İletişim Yayınları, 1990).
6   *Kaytz*, 12 December 1912, no. 6, 2.
7   Arsen Gidur, *Patmut'iwn S.D. Hnch'akean Kusakts'ut'ean*, vol. I (Beirut: Shirag Press, 1962), 339.
8   Ter Minassian, '1876-1923 Döneminde Osmanlı İmparatorluğu'nda', 176.
9   For the founders of the SDHP Students' Union and the editorial board of *Kaytz,* see Gidur, *Patmut'iwn S.D. Hnch'akean Kusakts'ut'ean*, vol. I, 339–40.
10 For a brief biography of Kegham Vanigian, see Çopuryan, *Paramazlar: Beyazıt'ta 20 Darağacı*, 54–69.
11 Gidur, *Patmut'iwn S.D. Hnch'akean Kusakts'ut'ean*, vol. I, 340.
12 Ibid., 341.
13 *Kaytz*, May 1911, no. 1, 1–2.
14 Ibid.
15 *Kaytz*, May 1911, no. 1, 32.
16 Ahmet Nebil translated Haeckel's work *The Evolution of Man*. For a translation of this work into contemporary Turkish, see *İnsanın Kökeni-Beşer Nesli* (Istanbul: Çizgi, 2015).
17 A. Sirvan, '20'lerden İkisi', in Yetvart Çopuryan, *Paramazlar: Beyazıt'ta 20 Darağacı* (İstanbul: Kor, 2018), 121.
18 For these unions and the role of Irgatis see Stefo Benlisoy, *İstanbul'un Irgatları: II. Meşrutiyet'te Sosyalist Bir İşçi Örgütü* (İstanbul: İstos, 2017), 119–40.
19 There are small differences between the text written by P. Dumont and F. Georgon and quoted by Yücel Aktar and the text published in *Kaytz*. Most importantly, contrary to the other text, the emphasis of the text published in *Kaytz* is on the role of 'the present capitalist order' instead of 'the attack of Italian capitalism'. See Aktar, *İkinci Meşrutiyet Dönemi Öğrenci Olayları*, 83.
20 Aktar, *İkinci Meşrutiyet Dönemi Öğrenci Olayları*, 88–97. I am thankful to Cem Yarar who shared his views on this issue with me.
21 *Kaytz*, November 1912, no. 5, 114.
22 *Kaytz*, December 1912, no. 6, 176.

13

In the Footsteps of Hidden History

The Roots of Socialism in the Ottoman Empire

Kadir Akın

When one considers the history of socialism in Turkey, one notices that the greatest harm to the idea of socialism came from nationalism, or the secular nationalism related to the Kemalist ideology in leftist terms.

From the moment when *The Communist Manifesto*'s principle of 'The homeland of proletariat is the whole world' and the socialist parties' common resolution of 'opposition to imperialist war', to which they agreed during the 1912 Basel Conference in Switzerland, were put aside, those ideas that took homeland defence as their pivot led some socialists to become the comprador of the bourgeoisie in the imperialist war. Thus began a betrayal of the history of social democracy, which brought the national battalions of the proletariat face to face. Those socialists who, remaining loyal to the Basel resolutions, went against the war and tried to stop it, alongside those who tried to turn the war into a revolution proceeded with the Communist International (Comintern), otherwise known as the Third International. It was quite obvious that there would not be much left of socialism if internationalism was pulled out of it. Under such circumstances, even those movements whose nationalist orientation one would hardly doubt dared to call themselves 'socialist'.

The socialist movement in Turkey, which was born within this historical framework and ground, could not prevent itself from being shaped in a chauvinistic way by the influence of its own unique history. Unfortunately, so far, the movement has failed to overcome those shortcomings. Turkish socialists have had their fair share from a historical consciousness that was based on hostility towards the 'giaour' (*gavur* means infidel and was usually used to refer to Christians and Jews) and a discourse of hatred that was created through a reversed anti-imperialism. As a result of 'the anti-imperialist National Independence War which was against Seven Great Powers', the new state was established as a republic in Anatolia, which was cleared of non-Muslim populations. While everything was in progress within the axis of Turkification and Islamicization, the conducive basis for fascist reactionism that swept Europe during the great crisis laid the foundations for a distorted historical consciousness that took up an openly racist character in the 1930s. Meanwhile, socialists failed to distinguish themselves from the practical interests of Soviet politics of the time and, instead of criticizing the 'national salvation and foundation' thesis of the Turkish Republic and reaching a conclusion compatible with socialism, they tacitly consented to these problems by engaging with them from a decontextualized 'anti-imperialist' perspective. Even though today they may state it differently, socialists continue to behave in more or less the same way. This behaviour perpetuates an understanding of 'socialism' that is in fact nationalist, even though it talks about internationalism.

Historians of Marxist and socialist movements in the Ottoman Empire did not find much to evince about the socialist movements, organizations, political parties and party programmes within the Ottoman society dating back to before and after 1908,[1] even if it was known that Armenians and Greeks were among the founders of the history of 'the socialist movement of Turkey'. Because the socialist minds of Turkey were formed within the historical circumstances as described above, the movement sought for a Turkish entity to write its own history of struggle and found it in the Communist Party of Turkey (TKP, Türkiye Komünist Partisi), which was set up in 1920 in Soviet Russia. Not mentioning those who defended socialism at the cost of their lives, rendering them invisible by constraining them to footnotes, or ignoring them via denial or ignorance – are all related to the absence of an internationalist perspective.

The beginnings and historical development of the socialist movement in the Ottoman Empire are commonly considered to date back to the Constitutional Era and Hüseyin Hilmi, even though he was neither the first socialist nor was his Ottoman Socialist Party the first socialist organization. The reason why Turkish historians handpick Hilmi as the founder of the socialist movement is because he was Turkish (and also Muslim). Another reason may very well be because those who started the struggle for socialism in those lands were taken away through forced migration and genocide; in that case, this forgetting requires a proper name of its own.

A sequel to the unionists: Kemalism

Neither the Mustafa Suphi–led Communist Party of Turkey (TKP) nor the left-socialist organizations and parties that were set up in the following years made an effort to research this history or confront the past. Undoubtedly, this was due to the impact of Kemalism, which was considered to be the founding ideology of the Turkish Republic and the continuation of the *İttihat ve Terakki Cemiyeti* (The Committee of Union and Progress, CUP)[2] on the left and the fact that the Turkish socialist movement was on the left-wing of the Comintern. Following the order of deportation, many of those who committed crimes of genocide against the Armenians on their death march and were tried by the Courts-Martial (*Örfi İdare Mahkemesi*) in 1918 in Istanbul and sent into exile in Malta as punishment, were personally saved by Mustafa Kemal and took up many important positions, including in the constituent National Assembly during the Republic's founding. Surely it was no coincidence that all founding members of the Kemalist Republic were originally from the CUP. The Republic, founded over the remnants of the Ottoman Empire, was established by the cadres of the CUP which, among all political movements, was inclined to be the most Western-like culture and embodied the most 'modern' cadres. This cadre fostered ideals based on Turkish identity and perpetrated a grave crime against humanity, in order to maintain control over Anatolia and the 'survival of the last Turkish State'.

We have to admit that the deportation of Armenians and Greeks, and the public perception surrounding their deportation, affected Turkey's left-socialist movements for years to come. We could say that Kemalism's effect on Turkey's left-socialist movements and the latter's internationalist weakness led to their brushing aside of 'other' socialists in these lands, their forgetting of the latter's struggle and the lack of transmission of their memories to future generations. Moreover, socialists continue to overlook the claim that genocide-perpetrators like Salih Zeki, who was the governor of Der Zor and who committed crimes against humanity through his participation in the Armenian Genocide, were initially members of the CUP and then joined in the cadre which founded the TKP, which could only cause great shame to socialists. The fact that one of the participants of the Congress of the Peoples of the East in 1920 in Baku was Dr. Bahaeddin Şakir, one of the architects of genocide and a founder of the Special Organization (*Teşkilat-ı Mahsusa*)[3] created to liquidate the Armenians, compels us to carefully scrutinize USSR policies during that period.

When the reality that historians ignore or forget is repeated by socialist organizations, this oblivion does not come to an end. While Armenian, Greek, Bulgarian and Jewish revolutionaries are being ignored, the same fate awaits Hüseyin Hilmi, as the historiography of the socialist movement begins with Mustafa Suphi. The TKP set up in 1920 did not want to accept that a socialist struggle existed before that time, because doing so meant recognizing Armenian, Greek, Bulgarian and Jewish revolutionaries, and obliging them to take positions against their suffering and oppression. That some Armenians participated in the TKP's foundation and its later phases does not absolve the party from overlooking its compliance. Particularly striking is that the discursive-imaginary orientation of the Turkish Left towards its past has never been fully free of such dominant-nationalist modes of approaching history.

The narrative of the past struggles of socialists in Turkey in the twentieth century has predominantly been built on the heroic stories of some prominent political figures who suffered execution, exile, imprisonment or torture. Indeed, such disregard and silence, was not accidental, given the fact that the hegemonic discourse of the Left used to see no harm in starting its historical trajectory with the foundation of the TKP in 1920 and the significant role of its founder Mustafa Suphi. The main goal of my recent book, entitled *Saklı Tarihin İzinde* (*Tracing the Hidden History*) and published in 2021, has been to unearth the truth that Turkish socialists embodied the chauvinist perspective for so long and historically categorized the political Armenian groups as the ones who were in cahoots with the imperialists.

The forgotten and ignored revolutionaries and Social Democrat Hnchakian Party (SDHP)

We should note that all Armenian political parties founded at the end of the nineteenth century were influenced by the contemporary transformations of that age and that their common goal was the freedom of the Armenian people. We can also argue that, besides being engaged with contemporary problems, these political parties, despite their programmatic differences, struggled for the independence of Western Armenians and for the unification of Eastern and Western Armenians living under Russian and Ottoman rule. At the dawn of the twentieth century, there were four active Armenian political parties in the Ottoman Empire: the Armenakan Party, which was set up in 1885 in Van; the Hnchakian Revolutionary Party, which was set up in 1887 in Geneva; the Verakazmyal (Reformed) Hnchakian Party, which broke away from the Hnchakian Revolutionary Party; and the Dashnaktsutiun (Armenian Revolutionary Federation, ARF), which was founded in 1890 in Tbilisi.

Among them, the Hnchakian Revolutionary Party breakaway *Verakazmyal* (Reformed) eventually lost importance. The Dashnaktsutiun and the SDHP, on the other hand, stood out with their socialist party programmes and their membership in the Second International, and carried greater importance in the Ottoman political scene.

Established in 1887 in Geneva, the SDHP was the first Marxist political party organized in the Ottoman Empire. Its network included party branches in the Caucasus, Istanbul and Anatolia. Its founding Central Committee included a woman member, Maro Vardanian. Its members were influenced by Marxist thought, which was spreading across Europe at that time, and collaborated with many notable socialists of the day such as Georgi Plekhanov. Beginning from the early 1900s, the party found a base and spread socialist propaganda among the indigent country people, tobacco workers of the Régie and domestic servants in Istanbul, as well as throughout Anatolia. Party members organized many strikes and the 1 May demonstrations. They published *Hnch'ak* ('Bell' in Armenian), the official organ of the party, the youth magazine *Kaytz* (*Spark*), and *Nor Ashkharh* (New World). Those publications included discussions on socialism and polemical writings by party members regarding organizational issues. According to Engels's preface to the 1888 English edition of *The Communist Manifesto*, an Armenian translation of the manifesto was submitted to a publisher in Istanbul; however, hesitant to publish a book bearing Marx's name, the publisher asked the translator to sign his own, but he refused. Much later, the party founded its own publishing house in Europe and published the works of Marx.

Soon after the Hnchakian Party was established, the party opposition broke away during 1895–6. Headed by Mihran Damadian and Arpiar Arpiarian, they argued that Turkey had no industrial proletariat and therefore no addressee of the socialist programme. They claimed that the Party's efforts could harm the Armenian independence movement. The opposition took the name *Verakazmyal* and appealed to violence in fighting against the centre of the party. According to the newspaper *Gazette de Lausanne* (3 November 1901), the separatist leader Arpiarian, who had also been alleged to be an 'Abdülhamid Spy', was shot in Venice. However, he did not die, in spite of six bullet wounds. Yet, through similar tactics, as reported in *Gazette de Lausanne* (29 October 1903), Mr. Sakouni (Saghatel Kevorkian), chairman of the Armenian Association of Asylum, was murdered by 'Alforist' *fedayeen* (freedom fighters) in front of his house in London.[4] Later, the Verakazmyal faction also made an attempt on the life of Stepan Sabah-Gulian, one of the theorists of the Hnchakian Party, in Boston. During the same year, Nazarbekian, one of the founders of the party, was stabbed in Lausanne; luckily, he survived. That same year, in 1903, while the World Congress was being held in London with the participation of 65 representatives from different countries, Aram Grigorian and Tigran Izmirlian were killed during the break by an Alforist Romanian delegate who then committed suicide. These clashes prevented the Hnchakians from focusing on their internal problems and led to serious disruption of their organizational activities. Furthermore, two Hnchakian newspapers were in court for having the same name, but the local judiciary decided that both had the right to that name.

First demonstration of the indigent and country people

In every geographical place where Armenians lived, Hnchakians began to organize en masse. It is known that Rupen Khan-Azad, who founded the central committee, began the organizational activities in the Ottoman Empire. In 1895, the Hnchakians mobilized 4,000 people to participate in the first demonstration in Istanbul where they presented a petition to Bab-ı Ali (Sublime Porte) about their problems.[5] Most attendees of that protest were Armenians from poor backgrounds and migrant workers from the provinces. This was the first demonstration in the capital city of the Empire and was a challenge to the non-Muslim subjects. Besides protesting the Sasun massacre,[6] this demonstration, which was also supported by the Armenakan Party, aimed at bringing attention to the difficulties experienced by Armenian people living in the Eastern provinces in regard to their civil rights, tax justice, security of life, property and honour. It also aimed at abolishing taxes and taking steps toward eliminating extortion. Another demand they had was to arm themselves as long as the Kurds were armed.[7] When they gathered to take their petition involving their demands to Bab-ı Ali, the Deputy Director of the Security Department, Chief Inspector Mr. Servet, clamped down on the demonstrators, leading to the massacre of Armenians. Both that demonstration and the rebellions of Sasun and Zeytun did not only have national demands, but also economic and social ones as well. The Young Turks, the main opposition group against Sultan Abdülhamid, issued a declaration protesting the Bab-ı Ali demonstration and criticizing the Armenians and their demands.

Another rebellion organized by the Hnchakians was the Zeytun Rebellion (24 October 1895 to 2 February 1896), where they demanded autonomy. At the end of this rebellion, which resulted in the loss of nearly 5,000 Ottoman soldiers and 6,000 Armenians, Abdülhamid gave a tax exemption to the people of Zeytun[8] and agreed that all civil servants, except those of the judicial power, were going to be Armenians. The agreement came into force on 12 February 1896. The most crucial article of the agreement was about the acceptance of a Christian governor to be assigned to the town of Zeytun.

That said, it would be a fallacy to say that Armenians and other nationalities lived 'like a rose' under Ottoman rule, but rather, that the Ottoman Empire was the largest prison of nationalities after Tsarist Russia. 'Şalvarı şaltak Osmanlı, eğeri kaltak Osmanlı. Ekende yok biçende yok, yemede ortak Osmanlı' (Ottoman whose underpants are loose, Ottoman whose saddle is wooden, Ottoman who has neither sower nor reaper but waits for share on the table) was a saying for Ottomans in accordance with their attitude not only for the high taxes applied to non-Muslims, but also due to the humiliation, ignorance and brutality they carried out.

The Hnchakian Party updated its programme during the VI Congress held in Istanbul in 1909. It was no less than the party programmes of the Second International, of which it was a member. The party, which had close relations with the communist leaders of the period, was also in contact with Russian revolutionary leaders, particularly with Lenin. Yet, to be in alignment with other communist parties of the period, the name of the party was amended to Social Democrat Hnchakian Party (SDHP) at its VI Congress. During this congress, two factions emerged in regard to the strategy to follow. The line of thought headed by Hampartsoum Boyajian (*Medzn* Murad) aimed at ending illegal activity and devoting the party's activities to legal struggle. Sabah-Gulian and Paramaz (Matteos Sarkissian), however, argued that the party should not trust the CUP and not enter into any negotations with them. They stressed that the party should continue its illegal activities in order to be prudent. Eventually, Sabah-Gulian and Paramaz stepped back as they did not want to push the party into a deeper schism.

The Hnchakians attempted to develop and promote socialist ideas among Turkish society. Paramaz, a member of the SDHP Central Committee, who was executed in 1915 in Beyazit Square along with nineteen of his comrades, was writing articles telling his party members about the importance of cultivating relations with other nations of the Empire, particularly with Turkish socialists. Paramaz recommended the Hnchakian youth to contact Turkish proletarian socialists and collaborate with them.[9] During his trial, Paramaz gave a speech in court saying: 'We are socialists; our land is the whole world. I tried to spread all my vision in Istanbul among the Turks, as well as in Diyarbakir among the Kurds'.[10]

The 1909 programme of the SDHP

The cornerstones of the programme and the statutes of the SDHP, which were settled at the VI Congress in 1909, include the following:

> Generating the labor class that constitutes the majority of the human society is said to be under the order and power of capitalists and proprietors who are minorities. Gaining the real freedom depends on the possession of all instruments serving for production, circulation of capital and communication, namely land, factories, banks, valuable financial instiutions, railway and similar means of transport. With the expression that the labor class has real freedom it is understood that human societies have complete political and economic freedom, regardless of nationality, tribe and gender. Administrative, financial, economic conditions and various taxes to which the people living in the Ottoman lands (Turkish, Armenian, Kurdish, Arab, Greek, Bulgarian, Syriac and others)(…)are subject to, today will cause the working class to collapse or be destroyed. Today, these people are in such an

economic period that on the one hand, capitalist order emerges in production, and on the other hand, old-style production is slowly coming to an end.

The programme demanded

full administrative authorization on provinces, counties, and sub districts; providing adequate allowance from the national treasury to the public representatives; removing all kind of titles by means of respecting everybody equal by law without any discrimination of nation, race, sectary or gender; freedom of press, speech, conscience and freedom of joining meetings, organizations, election contest, strikes and international labor unions; the expenses of religious organizations are met by donations from those who belong to each denomination; calling for recruitment without any discrimination and establishing a militia system during the peace period; establishing a free, compulsory and secular education system in general; supporting the people who are in need by the government and independent administrative board of each region; maintaining art education for both girls and boys; permission to start schools of each element solely in their own mother tongues in primary, secondary and high levels; providing subventions to all the mentioned schools of the elements by the government and independent local administrative boards if only the mandatory official language teaching is achieved; gaining the right to oral and written expression in mother tongue for every people; respecting the official institutions and public to languages of every element who constitute the people of the state equally; free of charge trials, free assistance for judicial issues and setting up a jury system, paying compensation to the people who are accused, detained or imprisoned wrongfully, suppressing execution; remitting all kinds of debts to the government and unpaid taxes, suppressing forced employment without payment, suppressing *Düyun-ı Umumiye* (Ottoman Public Debt Administration); working at most eight hours a day, a perpetual resting for forty-two hours once a week, not employing children under fourteen and women in any kind of labors which seem to be contrary to their physical features, exemption from services four weeks before and six weeks after maternity and paying the allowance during this period as it is; building up childcare centers for the young and breastfed children in the factories and in other companies where women workers are employed and providing lactation breaks for the lactating women every three hours for thirty minutes; setting up courts of laborers in economic institutions which were composed by representatives elected equally both by the entrepreneurs and laborers; protecting the political justice of the various nations in terms of national cases, entirely refusing the supremacy of a nation over another, protecting absolute equality and originality, and avoiding, socially, economically and politically, the prevention of development and enlargement of a nation as it is a inviolable right under protection.

The idea of living all together on a common land was defined as: 'The Social Democrat Hnchakian Organization completely declines the separation trends from the Ottoman state. Each well behaved person, who completed his twentieth age and who approves and consents to the statute decisions of the Social Democrat Hnchakian Organization, may join the organization without any discrimination of race, sectary and gender'.[11]

This programme was officially established by the appoval of the CUP, the government at the time, in 1909. Most people were not aware of this programme until recently. It resembled the programmes of those parties that called themselves 'socialist' in the following years and, lately, even included more advanced visions. The historical neglect of such a party, established in Istanbul and its programme, must be questioned in order to understand and redirect the orientation of socialists towards their history.

Paramaz and his internationalist attitude

Paramaz's words in court, long before his trial and immediately after he was arrested in an operation in Van in 1897, where he came to rally the organization, provided us with an impressive example in which to understand Hnchakian history. He said in court:

> Our demand is to live on equal terms with Armenians, Turks, Kurds, Greeks, Alevis, Laz, Yazidis, Syriacs, Arabs and Copts. As a revolutionary, I believe we will achieve this goal. (…) We are not nationalists; we are not guided by the 'nation-building motivation'. We are friends of the people, not chauvinistic nationalists. We know that a nationalist rule will maintain the same order. Our demand is that all inhabitants of Armenia, Armenians, Kurds, Turks, Arabs, Laz, Circassians, Assyrians, Yazidis and Copts elect their own rulers by their own will and vote. We demand this future for all inhabitants of Armenia, for all Ottoman peoples.

At the end of his long speech, wherein he defended the idea of a federation of Anatolia, Paramaz touched upon a variety of issues and demanded the improvement of the lives of all Ottoman people: 'Freedom of conscience, press, assembly and speech, security of life, property and honor, annulling the expedient taxes'. He brought forward an example of such taxes, saying:

> A Turk from the village of Ardamet told me, 'They estimated 20 penny tax for a pear of each tree, but I offered to give the tree itself for 10 penny, so I had a severe whipping from the gendarme. After being beaten I paid the taxes.' The weirdest is the tax of grapes. Six kinds of tax are gathered for a load of grapes; the first one is land tax and water tax, then the tax for the fruit of the agrape, juice tax, another tax for dried grapes, another for grape raki, another tax is for selling raki and wine and finally one for employment. Do you see Mr. Chief? There are lots of taxes for only one fruit.[12]

The Hnchakians did not restrict themselves only to national struggle. During the Sasun Rebellion, for example, they also called for social and economic reforms for Armenians engaged in agriculture. Basically, the Ottoman Empire was an agricultural empire and 85 per cent of the population were living in rural areas. Therefore, suggesting that the most significant problem was that of agriculture and land is not an exaggeration. The

Hnchaks played an important role in organizing many strikes in Istanbul, voicing rights and social demands, in the economic struggle, in the organization and celebration of the May Day demonstrations and in the dissemination of Marxist literature and ideas. They were not nationalists but internationalists. They endeavoured to collaborate with Turkish socialists and communists from other nations beside the organization of Armenians. The main goal of the SDHP programme was the socialist organization of the Armenian people and their country. Regarding this main goal, the objective of the programme was to constitute a broad-base democracy and to gain political freedom and national independence for Ottoman Armenia.

All Armenian parties were against Abdülhamid's oppressive and discriminative policies. While they were struggling against Abdülhamid, it was surely impossible not to have come across Turkish opponents and the Young Turks. Before the Committee Union and Progress (CUP) had been set up in Salonica, the Young Turks based in Paris were in contact with Hnchak and Dashnak, who both had strong organizations across Europe. These contacts took place between the years 1891 and 1892. Ahmet Rıza, the Young Turks leader in Paris, held a series of meetings with the SDHP leadership, which did not yield to any results. It was also known that the Hnchakians had a closer relation with Prince Sabaheddin,[13] a proponent of the ideas of decentralization. The Young Turks viewed negatively the Bab-ı Ali demonstration organized by the Hnchaks and the raid on the Bank of Ottoman by the Dashnaks in 1896. They wanted to pursue peaceful means to bring down Sultan Abdülhamid. In addition, the Young Turks were concerned about the demand of Armenians to realize Article 61 of the Treaty of Berlin as they sought to implement the much-needed reforms in the east, instead of the separation of Armenians from the Empire.

Rural and urban *fedayeen* movement

The Armenian parties were influenced by the anarchist movement, the Narodniks of Russia, as well as Marxist movements of the period. In 1904, a group of Hnchak *fedayees*, including Paramaz, attempted to assassinate the Viceroy of the Caucasus, Grigory Golitsyn, for his anti-Armenian policies, specifically for initiating the confiscation of the properties of the Armenian Church. The delay of the reforms that Armenians were expecting and Abdülhamid's efforts to postpone them played an important part in the agenda of the Armenian revolutionary parties. Consequently, the ARF implemented a significant act to draw European attention to the demands of Armenians. On 26 August 1896, twenty-eight members of the ARF led by Bedros Parian, better known by his *nom de guerre* Papken Siuni, occupied the Ottoman Bank. The bank, which was under the control of British and French capital groups, was an important financial centre across Europe. Three SDHP members were also part of the group.

The struggle of the Armenian revolutionary parties was to free Armenians from the shackles of despotism and teach them their basic rights as a nation. If the right to self-determination of nations is accepted as the most important criterion of being a democrat, aside from its contradiction with revolutionism, we can say that defining the struggle of the Armenian parties as 'nationalism' means ignoring their contribution to the struggle for socialism in the Ottoman Empire. The Hnchakian socialists worked to combine the interests of their own nation with those of the oppressor nation's laborers' in the axis of democratic demands. In this context, it is important to remember the words of Rosa Luxemburg on the national struggle problem in the Ottoman Empire: 'The awkwardness of Turkish authority is even insufficient in raising capitalism, other than deriving socialism eventually; therefore the sooner it gets collapsed and divided into its national founder components, the better it becomes. Thus, that underdeveloped region may join the natural process of history dialectics'.[14]

The Socialist Workers' Federation in Thessaloniki

Constantinople (Istanbul), the capital of the Ottoman Empire, was also the capital of politics, but Salonica (Thessaloniki) in the 1900s was a lively business centre, as well as a major hub of intellectual and cultural interactions. The greatest socialist organization was established in the city in the spring of 1909 following Abdülhamid's fall. The spread of the dock workers' strike the previous year opened the door to the foundation of the Socialist Workers' Federation. Business life in the city was about to end due to the strikes that had the participation of Turkish, Armenian, Greek, Bulgarian and Jewish workers. The 120 strikes mostly took place in that city after the proclamation of the Constitution following the Young Turk Revolution of 1908. At the beginning of 1911, the Salonica Socialist Workers' Federation held a meeting and condemned the CUP for its nationalist and militarist policies, and emphasized the need for collective action in favour of the Ottoman proletariat.

Before the 1912 elections, which came to be known as 'Sopalı Seçim' (Election of Clubs) due to CUP's unlawful practices and despotism, the Socialist Workers' Federation of Salonica urged the Armenian parties to join the elections as a bloc. However, this proposal was rejected due to the collaboration agreement signed between the ARF and the CUP. We should note that the Socialist Workers' Federation of Salonica, which consisted of thousands of people from different backgrounds, became confined only to Jewish socialists due to the Balkan Wars. During this period, the CUP's Turkification policies and its desire to create a 'Turkey for Turks' in Anatolia, under which Christians would be cleansed, led the ARF to breakaway from the CUP. As to the SDHP, they would keep their distance from the CUP as they did in the pre-revolutionary period.

Socialist deputies in the Ottoman Chamber of Deputies

In my book *Saklı Tarihin İzinde* (*Tracing the Hidden History*), I have suggested that Turkish society should view the past struggles of socialist deputies – including Krikor Zohrab, Hampartsoum Boyajian, Vartkes Serengülian, Vahan Papazian and Dimitar

Vlahof – who served in the House of Deputies of the Ottoman Empire (1908–15) as the leading actors of a movement dedicated to socialism, equality and freedom for all peoples within the Ottoman Empire.[15] I did so by illustrating how Armenian and Bulgarian deputies believed in the internationalist fight for the workers' fraternity, women's rights, freedom of the press and socialism, which was supposed to break down prejudices between all elements and unite all the people of the Ottoman Empire. *Saklı Tarihin İzinde* offered a proposal to reimagine the unforgotten past, the past-present relations and the future of internationalist-socialist struggle in Turkey. As I discussed in the book, a new appoach to the history of the socialist movement makes it more possible to travel the path of a multicultural, democratic and equal society.

I find it important to raise the following questions: How many of us had knowledge about their existence and struggles? How many of us knew about Vahan Papazian speaking out on education policies (8 May 1911), Vartkes Serengülian defending labour rights against the capitalist class (18 June 1909) or the historic speech of Hampartsoum Boyajian on workers' fraternity (13 May 1909) in the Chamber of Deputies?

When the Chamber of Deputies gathered after 1908, there were socialist deputies, most of whom were Armenian, including Serengülian and Papazian, who worked with Hnchakian deputy Boyajian and Bulgarian revolutionary Vlahof in the 'Deputies Group of Defending Labor Class Rights'. The CUP organ *Tanin*, edited by Hüseyin Cahid, critized the group by publishing an article entitled 'Communists Are Making Propaganda in the Chamber'. *Tanin* accused the four deputies of 'being inspired by a foreign western ideology and participating in destructive activities among the nation and people'.[16]

Boyajian was an important Hnchakian figure who graduated from the Istanbul Faculty of Medicine and completed his master's degree in Geneva. He played an important role in the Sasun rebellion. Through the amnesty decision of the CUP after 1908, he returned to Istanbul from the United States, to where he had escaped after a long period of imprisonment. He became a member of the parliament representing the province of Adana. The speech and the proposal he made in the Chamber in 1909 led to deliberations. While the deliberations on the proposal regarding strikes and labour organizations were held in the Ottoman Chamber, Boyajian took the floor to discuss the constitutional principles of unions and trade associations. He emphasized the need of organizations for the labour class in order to fight against dire living conditions and reiterated the necessity and the importance of unions for them. Boyajian noted:

> There is a struggle of race, religion, and nation among us and we could not prevent this. However, when the labor unions are set up, the feeling of labor class fellowship will be spread and eventually those fights, bigotry and discrimination of religion among Ottomans will come to an end. Dear Minister, please do not assume that we may fail owing to the labor rights struggle, as we all represent 5,000 citizens in poverty.

His speech resulted in a commotion in the parliament, after which Boyajian continued: 'Let me explain. Aren't you aware of how life conditions are expensive? You were paying 5 kuruş while bread was 40 para (one fortieth of a kuruş), now bread is 60 para, will you still pay the same? You want to prohibit laborers to set up their unions and to defend their own rights. You insist not to understand them' (13 May 1909). The discussion in that general session was closed due to the intent for getting permission from the *Şurayi Devlet* (State Council) as an obligation to constitute a union or labour organization.

One year later, a similar discussion took place. This time the proposal for a bill was on the condition and protection of women and child workers in the market. Another subject of the discussions was the sustainability of the unions to act freely. Boyajian reproached,

> During my recent Salonica trip, I saw that Turkish, Armenian, Greek, Jewish, Bulgarian and even Kurdish workers established a labor organization. Those Ottomans, who belong to various ethnic elements, were in harmony. Unfortunately, the government shut down this union and banned its activities. They also banned a similar organization in Kavala. Why do we close them down while we want the unity of Ottoman components?

In the same speech, Boyajian brought the attention of the deputies to the conditions of boys and girls, aged around six, working in wool ateliers in Bursa: 'Children aged six are being employed for ten to twelve hours a day. Why don't we protect children against their employers who deem those conditions proper and who oppress them?'

Unfortunately, the discussion on land tax in the Chamber took up the main portion of the discussions. Three Armenian deputies, Zohrab, Serengülian and Boyajian, agreed that the collection of the land tax was not fair. This matter became the subject of lengthy discussions both in the Chamber and in the public realm. Boyajian and his colleagues proposed to collect land tax in relation to the size of the land and income of the landlord, which was objected by the Minister of Economy Cavit Bey, CUP's Chief of Chamber Ali Bey and Syrian deputy Şefik el Müeyyet, a landlord. This objection was followed by enthusiastic applause from the Chamber. The deputies, who objected to Boyajian's proposal on fair collection of land tax, argued that those ideas were imported Communist thoughts from Europe and that the Ottoman Empire could not be ruled with such foreign ideologies. The Chamber was once again in turmoil as Serengülian shouted at deputies, 'Bullying tyrants!' (*mütegallibeler*), when they attacked Boyajian whilst on the podium for his speech. Armenian deputies and Vlahof could hardly keep themselves from being beaten during the clash in the Chamber.

Ottoman Socialist Party

It is important to discuss Hüseyin Hilmi, who was a contemporary of Armenian, Greek, Bulgarian and Jewish socialists in the Empire. Known as Socialist Hilmi, he was from Izmir. Along with Baha Tevfik, he established the Ottoman Socialist Party in Istanbul. Hilmi began to publish a weekly journal called *İştirak* on 26 February 1910. However, it was temporarily shut down by the court due to an article written by Ahmet Samim in its seventeenth issue. Later, after sharing the news about the establishment of the Ottoman Socialist Party in the eighteenth issue, and publishing the declaration and programme of the party in the following issue, the journal was once again shut down by the court. According to historian Mete Tunçay, the Ottoman Socialist Party was more like a liberal organization than a socialist one. The programme of the party consisted of demands on improving work conditions, political freedom and organizational abilities of labourers in general.[17]

Most accounts of intellectuals who were contemporaries of Hilmi do not contain correct information. Beyond his ignorance about Marxism, it would be appropriate to approach statements made about his liberalism with caution. To Foti Benlisoy and Doğan Çetinkaya, the statements made by Hilmi and his colleagues on freedom of speech and organization were not liberal demands;[18] yet, even his colleagues' 'reformist' side weighed more in time, as they defended a socialist approach based on the labour class and their struggle. Hilmi was always ready to be imprisoned due to his socialist ideology and he was known as someone who was always in solidarity with his friends, whether in prison or in court. Hilmi, who was not very much respected by some of the 'intellectuals' from academic and European educated circles, was in contact with Armenian and Greek revolutionaries, and offered room for their articles in his journal *İştirak*. Nevertheless, even Hilmi did not have a concrete and stable idea on the principle of 'self determination of the nations'.

Socialist Hilmi and his letter to Marx

Hilmi asked the Hnchakians and Greek Ergatis circles[19] to provide him with Marx's address, so he could send him a letter. Even though Marx had died decades before, Hilmi published his letter in *İştirak* under the title of an 'Unsealed Letter to Marx'. This compromised the seriousness of the relations with Armenian socialists, though they acted together many times and succeeded in the organization of successful strikes. The need of the Hnchakian youth to be in relation with Turkish labourers and the socialist youth movement was polemical for the SDHP organ *Nor Aşkharh* (New World) where Kegham Vanigian (executed in Beyazit Square in 1915 with Paramaz), one of the editors of the paper, criticized Turkish socialists about their seriousness by sharing the example of *İştirak*, where Hilmi wrote a letter to Karl Marx twenty-five years after his death. Eventually, Hilmi, who was not on good terms with the CUP, was exiled to Sinop.

Toward war

The CUP's preparations for war in support of Germany led Armenian parties to act. Even though Dashnaks, Ramkavars and Hnchaks held an agreement, following a series of meetings late in 1913, on a common policy towards the war, it would be recorded by history as a late initiative. The Hnchakians convened their VII Congress, just after the Balkan War, in Constanţa, Romania. Discussions about launching an armed struggle took place during the Congress. Hampartsoum Boyajian, who was banned from attending the conference, opposed the decisions of the party along with some representatives from Anatolia. Paramaz, who could not attend the Congress due to security concerns, was chosen for the Central Committee and entrusted with the responsibility of leading the armed struggle. He had already been under surveillance when he returned to Istanbul to keep up preparations for the assassination of CUP leaders. Arshavir Sahagian (who used the alias Artur Yasian and Z. Yaviç), who was a deputy of Egypt, and could not attend the Constanţa Congress as he was late, reported all the decisions he learned to the Ottoman and German security services. Before coming to Istanbul, Paramaz met Sabah-Gulian in Egypt for the last time. When he arrived in Istanbul, he was arrested.

Intellectual accumulation was demolished

After a year in the Istanbul Central Prison and a quick trial, the executions of SDHP member Paramaz and his comrades took place at Beyazit Square three weeks after 24 April, when the most important Armenian intellectuals and professionals were arrested, deported and killed en route. The opportunity for Turkification and assimilation that the CUP had been planning for a long time was eventually consolidated after the Balkan Wars of 1912–13. Enver Pasha's defeat at Sarıkamış, on 17 January 1915, the loss of sovereignty in the Middle East, the threat of a possible defeat in the war in Çanakkale and the danger of losing Istanbul accelerated the CUP's decision to implement the 'Turkification of Anatolia' project against Armenians, along with Greeks, Syriacs and Chaldeans, who were uprooted from their lands where they had lived for thousands of years. They were met by genocide through social engineering in the desert region of Deir-ez-Zor. The Muslim refugees from the Balkans who suffered ethnic cleansing arrived in Anatolia in a miserable condition. They directed their anger and frustration toward Armenians by taking an active role in the genocide. It is clear that the deportation for the 'Turkification of Anatolia', besides being a genocide of hundreds of thousands of Greeks, Armenians, Syriacs and Chaldeans, was also meant to destroy the intellectual legacy and cultural heritage of this land. It harmed the socialist ideology that arose on it.

In his defence during the court martial in Istanbul, Paramaz said:

> There is not one land for us. We are social democrats. We are not fighting only for freedom of Armenians, but also for freedom of humanity; our land is the whole world. What is left that we didn't do for the prosperity of this country? We accepted such altruism to ensure the brotherhood of Armenians and Turks. How much energy we laid and how much blood we sacrificed. The only reason to put up with this was to raise one another by means of trust. And what did we encounter? You did not only ignore our favor, but also tried to destroy us consciously. You forgot that to destroy Armenians means devastation of all Turkey.[20]

The following section from Paramaz's speech is a quality response to those leftist approaches who find Armenian socialist organizations 'nationalist':

> While I was acting in Diyarbekir, I spread my socialist ideas among Kurds, Turks, Syrians, and Arabs as much as Armenians with the same enthusiasm and

excitement... Gentlemen, judge people by their deeds, by their traditions, by the integrity of their ideas. I am not someone who wants to leave this country. On the contrary, it is this country that separates itself from me by refusing to confront the ideas that inspire me.[21]

The story of Paramaz and his comrades being sent to death by an unlawful proceeding just after the deportation is a summary of the injustice and unlawfulness following their slaughter. For many years, people in Turkey were not aware of the twenty Hnchakians who were sentenced to execution without any serious proof or defence. Their words, and motto, were the following: 'You can only kill our bodies, but never our ideas... Tomorrow, Armenians will salute free and socialist Armenia on the east, long live socialism!'[22]

Conclusion: Recalling faithfully the historical reality

In fact, the socialists and revolutionaries who revived the tradition of the twenty Hnchakians on the gallows were unaware that their words and mottos reverberated across the gallows built in Beyazit Square. Deniz, Yusuf, Hüseyin, Necdet Erdal and all who were after them, in addition to the many others who followed Paramaz and his comrades, did so unconsciously. While the revolutionaries of the Generation of '68 from Turkey, who resorted to urban and rural guerrilla actions, were impressed by the guerrilla movements of Latin America, they did not know about the ones who carried out similar *fedayeen* actions on this land. Coming to the Generation of '78, they continued their revolutionary-reformist grouping inside without knowing that they 'borrowed' it from Armenian revolutionaries. Opponents in the revolutionary organizations, who did not see the Central Committee as 'revolutionary' enough, repeated history again while they were 're-building the organization', being unaware of the Hnchakians' and the separated Verakazmyal's conflicts including the raiding of a Congress and the killing of each other. They did not benefit from those experiences that happened before them. Even if it is late in acknowledgement, understanding Paramaz and his comrades with the strength and emotional load of the bond of comradeship between them, while keeping their memories alive and resisting forgetting, should be considered one of the cornerstones of having a democratic consciousness, as well as being an internationalist socialist. The words and mottos that Paramaz and his comrades left us from Beyazit Square, after 100 years, would echo while fighting on Mashtenour Hill against ISIS and the ruptured chain would be replaced by Suphi Nejat.[23]

Not only should the Hnchakians be remembered, but also the Dashnaks, the socialist deputies Boyajian, Zohrap, Serangülian, Papazian and Vlahof who fought for labour rights in the parliament, as well as Ergatis and the Greek revolutionaries. In confronting all of our historical realities, while leaving any kind of concerns aside, we should consider them as our heroes or our revolutionaries both with their rights and wrongs, and we should remove the concepts of 'others' socialists' or 'others' revolutionists' from the Armenian revolutionaries by integrating them into our history of common struggle. For this reason, we must abandon the insistence on starting our history from our values and Mustafa Suphi, who was massacred in the dark waters of the Black Sea.

The struggle of the Kurdish political movement and its climate within recent years led to a 'mind transformation' for some socialist traditions. Even for those groups who see themselves on an 'internationalist' basis, the issue of the Armenian Genocide still stands before them as a test on the axis of internationalism. However, a constant effort into sincerely recalling historical reality, including the memories of Paramaz and other Armenian and Greek revolutionaries who fought for socialism, will not only transform our collective memory, but also expand our capability for building a different country and world ahead.

Notes

1. The Second Constitutional Monarchy was proclaimed in 1908, and thus the Sultanate would irreversibly lose power rapidly.
2. Founded as the continuation of the Young Turks (*Jön Türkler*), the CUP played the leading role in the declaration of the Constitutional Monarchy. They were in power between 1908-1918 and were the architects of the Armenian Genocide, among many other crimes.
3. The first intelligence organization established in Turkey. Besides the genocide, Şakir was also responsible for the assassinations of many dissidents.
4. Alforist refers to Verakazmyal Hnchakian *fedayees*. The name comes from Aldford Street in London, which was the location of their newspaper office.
5. Bab-ı Ali is the name given to the palace of the grand vizier in the Ottoman Period (Government House).
6. Sasun is the name of the region between Diyarbekir and Muş which is connected to Batman province today. It witnessed many Armenian rebellions and massacres in the Ottoman Period.
7. The Hamidiye Regiments, made up of Sunni Kurds, were founded by Abdülhamid in 1890. They were persecuting the Armenians, confiscating their lands and extorting them.
8. Zeytun is an Armenian settlement in Maraş. Just like Sasun, it witnessed many rebellions and massacres in the Ottoman Period.
9. *Nor Ashkharh* (New World), 20 September 1912.
10. Hmayag Aramiants, *Ankakh Hayastan*, vol. 3 (Istanbul: Sanjakjian Press, 1919), 20.
11. Ahmet Tetik, *Arşiv Belgeleriyle Ermeni Faaliyetleri, 1914-1918*, vol. 4 (Ankara: General Staff Press, 2008), 68–76.
12. Stepan Sabah-Gulian, *P'aramazi Charě: Im Datavarut'iwns Tachkastanum 1898 T'uin* (Chicago: Yeridasart Press, 1919).
13. Prince Sabaheddin was the leader of the liberal wing among the Young Turks and also Abdülhamid's nephew.
14. Luxemburg gave this speech in 1896 when the Socialist International Conference, gathered in London, confirmed the principle of 'all nations have the right of self-determination.'

15 Kadir Akın, *Saklı Tarihin İzinde: Osmanlı'da Modernleşme, Anayasa, Sosyalizmin Kökleri ve Ermeni Vekiller* (Ankara: Dipnot Yayınları, 2021).
16 Archives of the Grand National Assembly of Turkey.
17 Mete Tunçay, *Türkiye'de sol akımlar. Cilt 1* (1908–1925) (İstanbul: İletişim Yayınları, 2009), 48.
18 Foti Benlisoy and Y. Doğan Çetinkaya, 'İştirakçi Hilmi', in *Modern Türkiye'de Siyasi Düşünce Cilt 8 Sol* (İstanbul: İletişim Yayınları, 2007), 179.
19 The Socialist Center of Turkey, which was established in Istanbul in 1910 and mostly composed of Greeks, continued its political activities as a working class-based organization almost until 1922. *Ergatis* (Laborer), the first media organ, also made them known by this name.
20 Aramiants, *Ankakh Hayastan*, 42.
21 Ibid.
22 Yetvart Çopuryan, *Paramazlar Beyazıt'ta 20 Darağacı*, trans. Aris Nalci (İstanbul: Evrensel Basım Yayın Kasım, 2015), 15–25.
23 Suphi Nejat died in Kobane, Mashtenour Hill, while he was fighting against ISIS in Syrian Kurdistan side by side with Kurdish forces defending freedom. Suphi Nejat, whose code name was Paramaz Kızılbaş during the fight, had an internationalist approach when he died in 2014.

Biographical notes

Aram (Krikor) Achikbashian (Arabkir, 1867 – Constantinople, hanged on 15 June 1915) was a student at the School of Law of Istanbul in 1886. As a member of the Hnchakian Party he was one of the organizers of the demonstration of Kumkapı in 1890. He was a member of the Central Commission of the SDHP in the third (London, 1903) and fifth (Paris, 1905) conventions. After the Young Turk Revolution of 1908, he became a deputy in the Armenian National Assembly in Constantinople. He was arrested in 1914 under the suspicion of planning an assassination attempt against Artur Yasian.

Aghasi (Karapet Tursarkisian) (Zeitun 1871–1937) was a prominent member of the SDHP. He played a leading role in the Zeytun rebellion. He wrote a history of Zeytun.

Arpiar Arpiarian (Samsun 1852 – Cairo 1908) was the leader of the Verakazmyal (Reformed) Hnchaks. He founded the newspapers *Arewelk'* (East) and *Hayrenik'* (Fatherland) in Istanbul. He was assassinated in Cairo by the Hnchaks.

Grigor Artsruni (Moscow 1845 – Tiflis 1892) was educated in Tiflis, Moscow, St. Petersburg, and Heidelberg. In 1870 he went to Venice to study Armenian with the Mekhitarist fathers. He was the editor of *Mshak* (Tiller) in Tiflis and a leading proponent of liberating Western Armenia.

B. Benne (Bedros Torosian) (1887, village of Huseinig in Kharpert – 15 June 1915) received his education at the Euphrates College in Kharpert. He pursued his higher education at the American University of Beirut (AUB), where he founded the Hnchakian Students' Union. He travelled to the United States and Canada as part of party activities. He was hanged on 15 June 1915, along with the other nineteen Hnchak activists at the Bayazit Square.

Mihran Damadian (Constantinople 1863 – Cairo 1945) was a Hnchak member and one of the main participants of the Kumkapı protests in July of 1890. He was educated at the Murad Rafayelian school in Venice. He resigned from the party after disputes and in 1908 founded the Sahmanadrakan Ramkavar (Constitutional Democrat) party by uniting the Armenakans with part of the Verakazmyal (reformed) Hnchaks. He became the leader of the Ramkavar Azatakan (Armenian Democratic Liberal) party founded in 1921.

Gevorg Gharajian (1861 in Tiflis – 1936 in Yerevan) was one of the founders of the Hnchakian Party. He studied at Geneva University. He was a frequent contributor to Mkrtich Portukalian's *Armēnia*. He was in close contact with Russian socialist Georgi Plekhanov and his Emancipation of Labor group. In 1898 he founded the first Armenian workers Marxist group in Tbilisi and from 1900 to 1901 published the periodical *Banvor* (Worker). In 1901 he became a member of the Russian Social Democratic Workers' Party (RSDWP) Tiflis committee. From 1908 to 1917 he lived in Switzerland and continued his cooperation with Plekhanov. After the establishment of the Soviet regime, he became the director of the revolutionary museum of Tiflis. He taught at the University of Yerevan from 1921 to 1922 and then returned to Tiflis, where he worked for the newspaper *Zarya Vostoka*.

Hrair (Armenak Ghazarian) (Aharonk, Sasun 1864–1904) was a teacher and a graduate of the Surp Garabed and Mush Central schools. At the beginning of his revolutionary career, he joined the Hnchakian Party. Due to ideological disagreements, he left the party in 1893 and joined the Armenian Revolutionary Federation (ARF). He was one of the main leaders of the Sasun Rebellion of 1894. His nom de guerre was *Tzhokhk‛* (hell). He became the main agent of the ARF in Sasun, Bitlis, Mush, and Akhlat between 1895 and 1904. Along with Antranig Ozanian he organized the Sasun resistance of 1904 where he was killed.

Sargis Kasian (S. Ter-Gasparian) (Shushi 1876–1937) received his higher education in Berlin and Leipzig where he was exposed to the German Social Democrat movement. He was a member of the ARF at the beginning and then in 1905 joined the Bolsheviks. He was the president of the Revkom, that declared the Sovietization of Armenia on 29 November 1920. He was the minister of agriculture in the first Soviet Armenian government and a member of the Central Committee of the Transcaucasian Communist Party (1927–31). He was a victim of the Stalinist purges.

Rupen Khan-Azad (Nshan Karapetian) (Yerevan 1862 – Tabriz 1929) received his higher education at the University of Montpellier. He was one of the six founders of the SDHP in Geneva in 1887. He tried to unite the Armenian revolutionary movements under one umbrella. He was very active in both the Ottoman Empire and Transcaucasia. In the mid-1900s he left the Hnchakian Party and retired from political life.

Kristapor Mikaelian (Akulis, Zangezur 1859 – Mount Vitosh, Bulgaria, 1905) was trained as a teacher in Tiflis and became an active member of the *Narodnaya Volya*. He attended the Petrovsky Agricultural Academy in Moscow where he met Simon Zavarian and Stepan Zorian (Rostom). He was the founder of the Young Armenia Society in 1889 and in 1890 along with Rostom and Zavarian founded the Armenian Revolutionary Federation (ARF). He was killed accidentally in 1905 while preparing a bomb in Bulgaria.

Murad (Hampartsoum Boyajian) (Hajin 1867 – Ayash 1915) also known as *Medzn Murad* (Murad the Great), studied medicine in Istanbul and Geneva. While in Istanbul, he founded the Armenian Revolutionary Society in 1885 with a group of friends. In 1887 he and the members of the Society joined the Hnchakian Party. He was the chief organizer of the Kumkapı demonstration of July 1890 and leader of the Sasun revolt in 1894. He was sentenced to life in prison in Tripoli (Fizan) after which he escaped to France. While in exile, he was elected member of the Central Commission of the SDHP by the Sixth Convention held in 1905. In 1906 he appealed to the Armenian revolutionary parties to have a congress and establish a unified front. After the Young Turk Revolution of 1908, he was elected as a deputy for Kozan (Adana). During the Armenian Genocide, he was hanged in Kayseri in 1915.

Avetis Nazarbekian (1866–1936) was one of the main founders of the Hnchakian Party. He studied at St. Petersburg and Paris (Sorbonne) universities. In the beginning, he collaborated with Mgrdich Portukalian and wrote articles for the journal *Armēnia* under the pen name of Avo Lerentz. Later, he broke with Portukalian on ideological grounds and founded the Hnchakian Party along with five fellow students in Geneva in August 1887. He was close to the Russian socialist Georgi Plekhanov and his Emancipation of Labour group. He edited *Hnch'ak*, the organ of the Hnchakian Party, and translated several works of Karl Marx, Friedrich Engels and Plekhanov. In 1903 he survived an assassination attempt by the Verakazmyal Hnchakian Party.

Paramaz (Matteos Sarkissian) (Meghri 1863 – Constantinople 1915) received his education at the Gevorgian Seminary of Etchmiadzin (1878–93) and worked as a teacher in Nakhichevan and Ardabil (Persia) (1884–95). He was a leading member of the Hnchak Party and was involved in transporting *fedayees*, as well as weapons from Salmast to the region of Van. He organized an assassination attempt against Prince Grigory Golitsyn, the viceroy of Transcaucasia. He participated as a delegate in the Sixth Convention of the SDHP in Constantinople in November 1909. He took part in the plans of assassinating members of the CUP leadership. When he returned to Constantinople in 1915, he was arrested and hanged in the Bayazıt Square in 1915 along with the other nineteen Hnchak members.

Mgrdich Portukalian (Kumkapı, Constantinople 1848 – Marseille 1921) was the founder of the Armenakan Party. He received his education in Istanbul after which he pursued his career as a teacher in Tokat in 1867. He was arrested around 1869 for his progressive views. When he was released from prison, he returned to Istanbul, where he edited *Asia* and contributed to *Manzume-i Efkear* (Line of Thoughts) and *Meghu Hayastani* (Bee of Armenia) of Tiflis. He founded the Araratian Society in 1876 which aimed at improving the education level in the provinces. He also found a school in Van, the Kedronakan Varzharan (Central School). He was banished by the government for his activities. From Marseille he continued his activities by publishing the journal *Armēnia* until his death.

Rostom (Stepan Zorian) (Tsghna, 1867 – Tiflis 1919) received his education in Tiflis. In 1889, he left for the Petrovsky Agricultural Academy in Moscow where he met Kristapor Mikaelian and Simon Zavarian and with whom he founded the ARF in the summer of 1890. He worked for the party organ, *Drōshak* (Flag), between 1893 and 1895. He worked in the Balkans with the Macedonian revolutionaries and was active in the Armeno–Tatar conflict of 1905. He also took an active role in the fight for the Iranian Constitutional Revolution of 1905–11.

Stepan Sapah-Gulian (Djahri, a village just north of Nakhichevan, 1861 – Union City, New Jersey, 1928) graduated from the Nersesian Academy in Tiflis. He taught in Nakhichevan, the diocesan school of Yerevan, the seminary of the monastery of St. Garabed in Mush, and the convent of Sts. James in Jerusalem. He received his higher education from the École libre des sciences politiques (ELSP). In Paris he founded the Armenian Students Union, which became very active in promoting the Armenian Question to the French public opinion. In 1889 he was elected as a member of the SDHP Central Commission. He founded and edited a number of journals, including *Eritasard Hayastan* (Young Armenia), *Hnch'ak*, *Veradznund* (Revival), and *Nor Ashkharh* (New World) among others. He was opposed to any type of cooperation with the Committee of Union and Progress (CUP). He wrote several influential ideological and political books.

Mariam Vardanian (also known as Maro Nazarbek) (1864–1941) was one of the founders of the Hnchakian Party. She moved to Paris and then to Vienna to pursue her higher education. She took part in the revolutionary activities in the Russian Empire. She was on the editorial board of *Hnch'ak* journal and a member of the Central Committee of the SDHP. She was banished to Siberia by the Tsarist regime. With the establishment of the Soviet Union, she returned to Tiflis and in 1925 became a member of the Communist Party of the Soviet Union.

P. Varaztad (Hagop Turabian) (Talas, Kayseri, 1876 – Paris, 1967) was a member of the SDHP Central Commission through the Sixth and Seventh Conventions. He edited *Hnch'ak* in 1913–15 and contributed to other periodical publications. He settled in France, where he edited the Hnchakian periodical *Ardzagang P'arizi* (Echo of Paris), 1916–25, and established a printing house.

Simon Zavarian (Igahat, Lori, 1866 – Constantinople 1913) received his education in Tiflis, after which he moved to Moscow to study at the Petrovsky Agricultural Academy. He joined the *Narodnaya Volya*. At the Academy he met Mikaelian and Zorian along with whom he founded the Armenian Revolutionary Federation. Along with Mikaelian, he represented the socialist wing of the party. He was the executive officer of the party's Eastern Bureau. After the Young Turk Revolution of 1908, he was appointed as the inspector-general of all Armenian schools.

Note

Some information in this biographical note is extracted from Christopher J. Walker, *Armenia: The Survival of a Nation* (New York: St. Martin's Press, 1980), 379–428.

Selected bibliography

Archival sources

Başkanlık Osmanlı Arşivi (BOA), İstanbul
Armenian Revolutionary Federation Archives, Watertown, MA
AGBU Nubarian Library (BNu), Paris
Armenian National Archives (ANA), Yerevan
British Foreign Office Documents (FO)
The American Board of Commissioners for foreign Missions (ABCFM) Archives, Cambridge, MA
Ardzanagrut'ean Tomar Haykakan Baregortsakan Ĕndhanur Miut'ean
Ardzanagrut'ean Tomar Hay Gaghut'ayin Kedroni
United States National Archives and Records Administration (USNA), College Park, MD
Curia Generale dei Frati Minori Cappuccini, Instituto Storico, Archivio Generale dei Cappuccini [AGC], Rome.
Sacra Congregazione per le Chiese Orientali, Archivio Storico, Rome
Osterreichisches Staatsarchiv, Die Akten des k.u.k. Ministeriums des Aussern, 1848-1918, Vienna, Archives du Ministère des Affaires Étrangères (AMAE), France

Newspapers and periodicals

Ararat
Aṛawōt
Armēnia
Armenia
Asparēz
Arzhent'inean Mamul
Azatamart
Aṛawōt
Azg
Banvor
Drōshak
Erkir
Erkri Dzaynĕ
Erkunk'
Hayrenik' Amsagir
Hnch'ak
Hayrenik'
Kaytz
Khorhrdayin Hayastan

Koch'nak Hayastani
Kohak
La Prensa
La Razón
Lraber
Mechrutiyet
Mshak
Nor Ashkharh
Nor Keank'
Nor Ōr
Pahak
Rahvira
Sharzhum
Shirak
Vēm
Zang
Zart'ōnk'

Published primary sources

A-Do (Hovhannes Ter-Martirosyan), *Vani, Bit'iti, ew Ērzrumi Vilayet'nerĕ*. Yerevan: Kultura, 1912.

Aghassi, Garabed, *Zeïtoun depuis les origins jusqu'à l' insurrection de 1895*. Paris: Édition du Mercure de France, 1897.

Dasnabedian, Hrach, comp. and ed., *Niwt'er H. H. Dashnakts'ut'ean Patmut'ean Hamar*, vols. 1–4. Beirut: Hamazkayin Vahe Setian Press, 1972–2007.

Evropayi Hay Usanoghakan Miut'iwn, *Apsdamb Sasunĕ*. Geneva, 1903.

Gharajian, G. (S. T. Arkomet), *Rubēn Khanazati Hēk'iat'nerĕ*. Tiflis: n.p., 1928.

Khan-Azat, Rupen, 'Hay Heghap'okhakani Mĕ Husherits", *Hayrenik' Amsagir*, June 1927, 60–72; July 1927, 52–63; August 1927, 56–72; September 1927, 124–38; October 1927, 122–9; November 1927, 122–35; December 1927, 112–24; January 1928, 114–28; February 1928, 123–35; March 1928, 102–14; April 1928, 126–41; May 1928, 147–60; June 1928, 134–48; July 1928, 131–43; August 1928, 136–42; September 1928, 146–56; October 1928, 149–57; November 1928, 146–55; December 1928, 91–100; January 1929, 117–25; February 1929, 99–108; March 1929, 102–14; April 1929, 107–15; May 1929, 147–60.

Khan-Azat, Rupen, *Hushardz'an Nuiruatz Sots'eal Demokrat Hnch'akean Kusakts'ut'ean*. Paris: Imprimerie Turabian, 1930.

Pambukian, Yervant, comp. and ed., *Niwt'er H. H. Dashnakts'ut'ean Patmut'ean Hamar*, vols. 5–12. Beirut: Hamazkayin Vahe Setian Press, 2007–17.

Papazian, Vahan, *Im Husherĕ*, II. Beirut: Hamazkayin Press, 1952.

Sabah-Gulian, Stepan, *Armenak ew Abraham*. Chicago: Eritasard Hayastan Press, 1917.

Sabah-Gulian, Stepan, *Bareri ew Ezreri Pats'atrut'iwnner*. Boston: SDHP Press, 1927.

Sabah-Gulian, Stepan, *Eritasard T'urk'ia*. Paris: [n.p.], 1908.

Sabah-Gulian, Stepan, *Ewropayi K'aghak'akan Drut'iwnĕ Berlini Dashnagrut'iwnits' Hetoy*. Ruschuk, 1898.

Sabah-Gulian, Stepan, *Herder ew Ir K'aghak'akan Hayeatsk'nerĕ*. K. Polis: D. Doghramajian Press, 1909.

Sabah-Gulian, Stepan, *Inkʻnawar Hayastan*. Cairo: Z. Biberian Press, 1915.
Sabah-Gulian, Stepan, *Pʻokʻr Haykʻi Hishatakner*. Chicago: Eritasard Hayastan Press, 1917.
Sabah-Gulian, Stepan, *Pataskhanatunerě*. Providence: Eritasard Hayastan Press, 1916.
Sabah-Gulian, Stepan, *Sotsʻializm ew Hayrenikʻ, A. Prak*. Providence: Eritasard Hayastan Press, 1907.
Turabian, Hagop, 'The Armenian Social-Democratic Hentchakist Party', *Ararat* 3, no. 34 (April 1916), no. 35 (May 1916), and no. 37 (July 1916).
Vratsian, Simon, *Keankʻi Ughinerov: Dēpkʻer, Dēmkʻēr, Aprumner*, vol. I. Beirut: Mshag Press, 1955.

Secondary sources

Adjemian, Boris and Mikaël Nichanian, 'Rethinking the "Hamidian massacres": The Issue of the Precedent', *Études Arméniennes Contemporaines* 10 (2018): 19–29.
Akın, Kadir, *Ermeni Devrimci Paramaz: Abdülhamid'den İttihat Terakki'ye Ermeni Sosyalistleri ve Soykırım*. Ankara: Dipnot Yayınları, 2016.
Akın, Kadir, *Saklı Tarihin İzinde*. Ankara: Dipnot Yayınları, 2021.
Aktar, Yücel, *İkinci Meşrutiyet Dönemi Öğrenci Olayları, 1908–1918*. İstanbul: İletişim Yayınları, 1990.
Altıntaş, Toygun, 'The Abode of Sedition, Resistance, Repression, and Revolution in Sasun (1891–1904)', in *Age of Rogues, Rebels, Revolutionaries and Racketeers at the Frontiers of Empires*, edited by Alp Yenen and Ramazan Hakkı Öztan, 178–207. Edinburgh: Edinburgh University Press, 2021.
Altıntaş, Toygun, 'The Placard Affair and the Ankara Trial: The Hnchak Party and the Hamidian Regime in Central Anatolia, 1892–3', *Journal of the Ottoman and Turkish Studies Association* 4, no. 2 (2017): 309–37.
Artsruni, Ashot, *Taretsʻoytsʻ Har. Amerikahayotsʻ*. Buenos Aires: Ararat, 1943.
Astourian, Stephan, 'The Silence of the Land: Agrarian Relations, Ethnicity and Power', in *A Question of Genocide*, eds. Ronald G. Suny, Fatma Müge Göçek and Norman Naimark, 55–81. Oxford: Oxford University Press, 2011.
Avagyan, Arsen and Gaidz F. Minassian, *Ermeniler ve İttihat Terakki: İşbirliğinden Çatışmaya*. İstanbul: Aras Yayınları, 2005.
Babayan, Yervant, ed., *Pages from my Diary/Archpriest Der Nerses Babayan*. Los Angeles: April Publishers, 2000.
Babloyan, Manvel, *Hay Mamuli Hamahavakʻ Tsʻutsʻak*. Yerevan: ASSR Academy of Sciences Press, 1986.
Barsumian, Kevork H., *Patmutʻiwn Ayntʻapi H. H. Dashnaktsʻutʻean 1898-1922*. Aleppo: Tigris, 1957.
Bayburdyan, Vahan A., *Hay-Kʻrdakan Haraberutʻiwnnerě Ōsmanean Kaysrutʻiwnum*. Yerevan: Hayastan, 1989.
Bdeyan, Sargis, Misak Bdeyan and Aghan Daronetsi, *Harazat Patmutʻiwn Tarōnoy*. Cairo: Sahag-Mesrob Press, 1962.
Berberian, Houri, *The Love for Freedom Has No Fatherland: Armenians and the Iranian Constitutional Revolution of 1905–1911*. Boulder: Westview Press, 2001.
Berberian, Houri, *Roving Revolutionaries: Armenians and the Connected Revolutions in the Russian, Iranian, and Ottoman Worlds*. Berkeley: University of California Press, 2019.

Binayan Carmona, Narciso, *La colectividad armenia en la Argentina*. Buenos Aires: Alzamor Editores, 1974.
Boulgourdjian-Toufeksian, Nélida, 'The Armenian Church and the School Network in Buenos Aires: Channels for the Preservation of Identity', *Journal of the Society for Armenian Studies* 10 (1998–1999 [2000]): 111–24.
Bruinessen, Martin Van, *Shaikh, and State: The Social and Political Structures of Kurdistan Aghas*. London: Zed Books, 1992.
Chormisian, Levon, *Hamapatker Arewmtahayots' Mēk Daru Patmut'ean*, vol. 1, 1878-1908. Beirut: Shirag Press, 1974.
Çopuryan, Yetvart, *Paramazlar: Beyazıt'ta 20 Darağacı*, trans. Aris Nalcı. İstanbul: Kor Kitap, 2018.
Cora, Yaşar Tolga, 'Doğu'da Kürt-Ermeni Çatışmasının Sosyoekonomik Arkaplanı', in *1915: Siyaset, Tehcir, Soykırım*, edited by Fikret Adanır and Oktay Özel, 178–207. İstanbul: Tarih Vakfı Yurt Yayınları, 2015.
Cora, Yaşar Tolga, Dzovinar Derderian and Ali Sipahi, eds., *The Ottoman East in the Nineteenth Century, Societies, Identities, and Politics*. London: I.B. Tauris, 2016.
Damadian, Mihran, *Bir Ermeni Komitecinin İtirafları*. İstanbul: Timaş Yayınları, 2009.
Dasnabedian, Hrach, *Patmut'iwn Hay Heghap'okhakan Sharzhman ew Hay Heghap'okhakan Dashnakts'ut'ean*. Beirut: Hamazkayin, 2009, 1988.
Dasnabedian, Hrach, *Ṛostom: Mahuan Vat'sunameakin Aṛt'iw*. Beirut: Hamazkayin Vahe Setian Press, 1979.
Dasnabedian, Hrach, *Simon Zawarean: Mahuan Eōt'anasunameakin Aṛtiw*, vols. I–III. Beirut: Hamazkayin Vahe Setian Press, 1983–1997.
Dennis, Brad, 'Patterns of Conflict and Violence in Eastern Anatolia', in *War and Diplomacy: The Russo-Turkish War of 1877–1878 and the Treaty of Berlin*, edited by Hakan M. Yavuz and Peter Sluglett, 273–301. Salt Lake City: University of Utah Press, 2011.
Depoyan, Bedros, *Mihran Tamatean*. Cairo: Arewi Terton, 1956.
Der Hagopian, Hagop, *Hayastani Vērjin Aghetě*. Constantinople: M. Der Hagopian Press, 1921.
Der Khachaturian, Ardashes, *Hay Mamuli Ts'uts'ak*. Los Angeles: Hamazkayin Press, 1987.
Der Matossian, Bedross, *The Horrors of Adana: Revolution and Violence in the Early Twentieth Century*. Stanford: Stanford University Press, 2022.
Der Matossian, Bedross, *Shattered Dreams of Revolution: From Liberty to Violence in the Late Ottoman Empire*. Stanford: Stanford University Press, 2016.
Djizmedjian, Manuk G., *Patmut'iwn Amerikahay K'aghak'akan Kusakts'ut'eants': 1890-1925*. Fresno: Nor Or Pess, 1930.
Duguid, Stephen, 'The Politics of Unity: Hamidian Policy in Eastern Anatolia', *Middle Eastern Studies* 9-2 (May 1973): 139–55.
Dündar, Fuat, *Modern Türkiye'nin Şifresi, İttihat ve Terakki'nin Etnisite Mühendisliği*. İstanbul: İletişim Yayınları, 2008.
Eldem, Edhem, Henk de Smaele and Houssine Alloul, eds., *To Kill a Sultan: A Transnational History of the Attempt on Abdülhamid II (1905)*. London: Palgrave Macmillan, 2018.
Fortna, Benjamin, *Learning to Read in the Late Ottoman Empire and the Early Turkish Republic*. Basingstoke: Palgrave Macmillan, 2011.
Genjian, Antranig, *S.D. Hnch'akean Kusakts'ut'iwně ew Kilikean Ink'nawarut'ean Ak't'ě. 1919-1921*. Beirut: Ararat Press, 1958.
Gidur, Arsen, *Patmut'iwn S.D. Hnch'akean Kusakts'ut'ean, 1887–1962*, vol. I and II. Beirut: Shirag Press, 1962–1963.

Gölbaşı, Edip, 'Hamidiye Alayları, Bir Değerlendirme', in *1915, Siyaset, Tehcir, Soykırım*, edited by Fikret Adanır and Oktay Özel, 164–175. İstanbul: Tarih Vakfı Yurt Yayınları, 2015.
Gustave, Rolin-Jaequemyns, *Armenia, the Armenians, and the Treaties*. London and Manchester: John Heywood, 1891.
Hambaryan, Azat, *Agrarayin Haraberut'iwnnerĕ Arewmtean Hayastanum*. Yerevan: Armenian SSR Academy of Sciences, 1965.
Hambaryan, A. A., *Eritt'urk'eri Azgayin u Hoghayin K'aghak'akanut'iwnĕ ev Azatagrakan Sharzhumnern Arevmtean Hayastanum (1908-1914)*. Yerevan: Haykakan SSH GA Hratarakch'ut'yun, 1979.
Hanioğlu, Şükrü M., *The Young Turks in Opposition*. New York and Oxford: Oxford University Press, 1995.
Hartman, Elke, 'The Central State in the Borderlands, Ottoman Eastern Anatolia in the Late Nineteenth Century', in *Shatterzone of Empire, Coexistence and Violence in the German, Habsburg, Russian and Ottoman Borderlands*, edited by Ömer Bartov and Eric D. Weitz, 172–190. Bloomington: Indiana University Press, 2013.
Hovannisian, Richard G., *Armenia on the Road to Independence*. Berkeley and Los Angeles: University of California Press, 1967.
Hovannisian, Richard G., 'The Armenian Question in the Ottoman Empire, 1876-1914', in *The Armenian People from Ancient to Modern Times*, edited by Richard G. Hovannisian, vol. II. New York: St. Martin's Press, 1997.
Hovannisian, Richard G., *The Republic of Armenia*, 4 vols. Berkeley: University of California Press, 1971–96.
Hovhannisyan, Ashot G., 'Hnch'akeanneri Kazmaworman Gaghap'arakan Armatnerĕ', *Patma-Banasirakan Handes* 2 (1968): 19–39.
Hovhannisyan, Gegham, *Hnch'akean Kusakts'ut'ean Patmut'iwn (1887-1915)*. Yerevan: History Institute of the National Academy of Sciences, 2012.
Isgenderian, Zora, *Husher Patmut'ean Hamar*. Beirut: Sevan Printing House, 1974.
Kaligian, Dikran, *Armenian Organization and Ideology under Ottoman Rule: 1908-1914*. New Brunswick: Transaction Publishers, 2009.
Kankrouni, Hrant, *Hay Heghap'okhut'iwnĕ Ōsmanean Bṛnatirut'ean Dēm (1890-1910)*. Beirut: G. Doniguian, 1973.
Ketsemanian, Varak, 'The Hunchakian Revolutionary Party and the Assassination Attempts against Patriarch Khoren Ashekian and Maksudzade Simon Bey in 1894', *International Journal of Middle Eastern Studies* 50, no. 4 (2018): 735–55.
Ketsemanian, Varak, 'Ideologies, Paradoxes, and *Fedayis*: Historiographical Challenges, and Methodological Problems in the Study of the Armenian Revolutionary Movement (1890-1896)', in *Kurds and Armenians in the Late Ottoman Empire*, edited by Ara Sarafian and Ümit Kurt, 119–60. Fresno: The Press at California State University, 2020.
Kévorkian, Raymond, *The Armenian Genocide: A Complete History*. London and New York: I.B.Tauris, 2011.
Kirakosian, Arman, *Britanakan Divanagitut'iwnĕ ew Arewmtahayeri Khndirĕ: 1830-1914*. Yerevan: Gitutyun Publishing, 1999.
Kirakosian, J. *Hayastanĕ Mijazgayin Divanagitut'ean ew Sovetakan Artak'in K'aghak'akanut'ean P'astat'ght'erum*. Yerevan: Hayastan Publishing, 1972.
Klein, Janet, 'Conflict and Collaboration: Rethinking Kurdish-Armenian Relations in the Hamidian Period (1876–1909)', *International Journal of Turkish Studies* 13 (2007): 153–66.
Klein, Janet, *Power in the Periphery: The Hamidiye Light Cavalry and the Struggle Over Ottoman Kurdistan, 1890-1914*. Stanford: Stanford University Press, 2011.

Kochar, Meri, *Armyano-turetskie obshestvenno-politicheskie otnosheniia i Armyanskii vopros*. Yerevan: Yerevan State University Press, 1988.
Koutcharian, Gerayer, 'The History of Armenian-Kurdish Relations in the Ottoman Empire', *Armenian Review* 39 (1986): 1–45.
Kurt, Ümit, 'Reform and Violence in the Hamidian Era: The Political Context of the 1895 Armenian Massacres in Aintab', *Holocaust and Genocide Studies* 32, no. 3 (2018): 404–23.
Kurt, Ümit and Ara Sarafian, eds., *Armenians and Kurds in the Late Ottoman Empire*. Fresno: The Press, at California State University, 2020.
Kushakjian, Mardiros and Boghos Madurian, eds., *Hushamatean Musa Leṛan*. Beirut: Sevan Press, 1970.
Leo, *Ants'yalits'*. Yerevan: Shem Press, 2009.
Libaridian, Gerard J., *Modern Armenia*. New Brunswick: Transaction Publishers, 2004.
Libaridian, Gerard J., 'What Was Revolutionary About Armenian Revolutionary Parties in the Ottoman Empire?', in *A Question of Genocide: Armenians and Turks at the End of the Ottoman Empire*, edited by R. G. Suny, F. M. Göçek and Norman M. Naimark, 82–112. New York: Oxford University Press, 2011.
Lynch, Henry, *Armenia, Travels and Studies, vol. 2, The Turkish Provinces*. London and New York: Longmans, Green, & Co., 1901.
Manoukian, Abel, *Hayrenik'i Azatagrut'ean Banakin Hamozuatz Zinuornerĕ*. Beirut: Araz Printing Press, 2014.
Manoukian, Abel, *The Origins of the Hnchakian Party in Geneva and the Legacy of the Twenty Gallows*. Yerevan: Zangak Publishing House, 2019.
Massayuki, Ueno, 'For the Fatherland and the State, Armenians Negotiate the Tanzimat Reforms', *International Journal of Middle East Studies* 45 (March 2013): 93–109.
Matiossian, Vartan, *Haravayin Koghmn Ashkharhi. Hayerĕ Latin Amerikayi Mēj Skizbēn Minch'ev 1950*. Antelias: Press of the Catholicosate of the Great House of Cilicia, 2005.
Matiossian, Vartan, 'La iglesia armenia en Buenos Aires (1912–1938): bosquejo histórico-organizacional', in *Los armenios en América del Sur. Primeras Jornadas de Estudio*, edited by Vartan Matiossian. Buenos Aires: Instituto de Investigación Armenológica, 1991.
Matiossian, Vartan, *Los armenios en América del Sur. Primeras Jornadas de Estudio*. Buenos Aires: Instituto de Investigación Armenológica, 1991.
Melson, Robert, *Revolution and Genocide: On the Origins of the Armenian Genocide and the Holocaust*. Chicago: University of Chicago Press, 1992.
Mikaelian, Kristapor, *K'ristap'or Mik'ayēleani Namaknerĕ*. Beirut: Hamazkayin Vahe Setian Press, 1993.
Miller, Owen, '"Back to the Homeland" (Tebi Yergir), Or, How Peasants Became Revolutionaries in Mush', *Journal of Ottoman and Turkish Studies Association* 4/2 (November 2017): 287–308.
Miller, Owen, 'Sasun 1894: Mountains, Missionaries and Massacres at the End of the Ottoman Empire', unpublished PhD diss., Columbia University, 2015.
Miller, William, *The Ottoman Empire, and its Successors 1801–1927*. London: Frank Cass, 1966.
Minassian, Gaïdz, *Arméniens, Le temps de la délivrance*. Paris: CNRS Editions, 2015.
Minassian, Gaïdz F. and Arsen Avagyan, *Ermeniler ve İttihat ve Terakki: İşbirliğinden Çatışmaya*. İstanbul: Aras Yayıncılık, 2005.
Nakashian, Avedis, *A Man Who Found a Country*. New York: Crowell, 1940.

Nalbandian, Louis, *The Armenian Revolutionary Movement: The Development of Armenian Political Parties Through the Nineteenth Century*. Berkeley: University of California Press, 1963.

Naltchajan, Nazaret, 'Kaiser Wilhelm II's Visits to the Ottoman Empire: Rationale, Reactions and the Meaning of Images', *Armenian Review* 42, no. 2 (1989): 47–78.

Nazarian, Elie H., *Patmagirkʻ Nazarean Gerdastani (1475-1988)*. Beirut: Atlas, 1988.

Pambukian, Yervant, *Kʻristapʻor Mikʻayēleani Antip Namakner*. Yerevan: Lusagn Press, 2020.

Pambukian, Yervant, ed., *Niwtʻer H.H. Dashnaktsʻutʻean Patmutʻean*, vol. V. Beirut: ARF Publications, 2007.

Papazian, Avetis, *Haykakan Hartsʻĕ ew Mets Egheṛnĕ*. Los Angeles, 1997.

Papazian, Avetis, *Zhamanakarutʻiwn Haykakan Hartsʻi ew Metz Egheṛnĕ*. Yerevan: National Academy of Sciences, 2000.

Pehlivan, Zozan, 'El Niño and the Nomads, Global Climate, Local Environment, and the Crisis of Pastoralism in Late Ottoman Kurdistan', *Journal of the Economic and Social History of the Orient* 63, no. 3 (2020): 316–56.

Petoyan, Vardan, *Sasunn Antsʻealum ew Sasuni Azatagrakan Sharzhumnerĕ*. Yerevan: Lusakn, 2005.

Poghosian, Y., *Hachĕni Ēndhanur Patmutʻiwn ew Shrjaka Gozan-Taghi Hay Giwgherĕ*. Los Angeles: Central Commission of the Compatriotic Union for Reconstruction of Hajin, 1942.

Poghosyan, Haygaz, *Sasuni Patmutʻiwn 1750-1918*. Yerevan: Hayastan, 1985.

Polatel, Mehmet, 'The Complete Ruin of a District, The Sasun Massacre of 1894', in *The Ottoman East in the Nineteenth Century, Societies, Identities, and Politics*, edited by Yaşar Tolga Cora, Dzovinar Derderian and Ali Sipahi, 179–98. London: I.B. Tauris, 2016.

Riegg Badalyan, Stephen, *Russia's Entangled Embrace: The Tsarist Empire and the Armenians, 1801–1914*. Ithaca: Cornell University Press, 2020.

Rupen, H.H.D. *Kazmakerputʻiwnĕ*. Cairo: Husaper, 1935.

Sarafian, Kevork A., ed., *Patmutʻiwn Ayntʻepi Hayotsʻ*, vol. I and II. Los Angeles: Union of the Armenians of Aintab, 1953.

Sarınay, Yusuf, ed., *Osmanlı Belgelerinde Ermenilerin Sevk ve İskanı (1870–1920)*. Ankara: T.C. Başbakanlık Devlet Arşivleri Genel Müdürlüğü Osmanlı Arşivi Daire Bakanlığı, 2007.

Sasuni, Garo, *Hrayri Derĕ Hay Azatagrakan Sharzhman Mēj*. Beirut: Atlas Press, 1964.

Sasuni, Garo, *Kʻiwrt Azgayin Sharzhumnerĕ ew Hay-Kʻrtakan Haraberutʻiwnnerĕ*. Beirut: Hamazkayin Press, 1969.

Sasuni, Garo, *Patmutʻatm Tarōni Ashkharhi*. Beirut: Publications of the Daron-Duruperan Compatriotic Union, 1956.

Seferian, Mihran M., ed., *Druagner Suētioy Antsʻealēn*. Beirut: Ararad, 1957.

Shemmassian, Vahram, 'The Sasun Bantoukhds in Nineteenth-Century Aleppo', in *Armenian Baghesh/Bitlis and Taron/Mush*, edited by Richard G. Hovannisian, 175–91. Costa Mesa: Mazda Publishers, 2001.

Simonian, Harutiun, ed., *Haweluats: Ayntʻapi Hayotsʻ Patmutʻiwn*. Waltham: Mayreni Press, 1997.

Suny, Ronald Grigor, *Looking Toward Ararat: Armenia in Modern History*. Bloomington: Indiana University Press, 1993.

Suny, Ronald Grigor, guest ed., 'The Sassoun Massacres', *Armenian Review* 47, no. 1–2 (Summer 2001).

Suny, Ronald G., Fatma M. Göçek and Norman M. Neimark, eds., *A Question of Genocide: Armenians and Turks at the End of the Ottoman Empire*. New York: Oxford University Press, 2011.
Temo, Ibrahim, *İttihad ve Terakki Cemiyetinin Teşekkülü ve Hidematı Vataniye ve İnkılâbı Millîye Dair Hatıratım*. Mejidiye, Romania: n. p., 1939.
Ter Minassian, Anahide, *Nationalism and Socialism in the Armenian Revolutionary Movement*. Cambridge: Zoryan Institute, 1984.
Tunçay, Mete, *Türkiye'de Sol Akımlar Cilt I -- 1908-1925*. İstanbul: İletişim Yayınları, 2009.
Ünlü, Barış, *Türklük Sözleşmesi, Oluşumu, İşleyişi ve Krizi*. Ankara: Dipnot Yayınları, 2018.
Van Bruinessen, Martin, *Shaikh, and State: The Social and Political Structures of Kurdistan Aghas*. London: Zed Books, 1992.
Varandian, Mikael, *H.H. Dashnakts'ut'ean Patmut'iwn*. Paris: Imprimerie de Navarre, 1932.
Vardanyan, G., *Arevmtahayeri Azatagrut'zat Harts'ě*. Yerevan: Haykakan SSH GA Hratarakch'ut'yun, 1967.
Vartanean, Eznig, *Prazilio Hay Gaghutě*. Buenos Aires: Sipan Press, 1948.
Verheij, Jelle, "'Les frères de terre et d'eau", les massacres arméniens de 1894-1896', in *Islam des Kurdes*, special issue of *Les Annales de l'Autre Islam*, edited by M. van Bruinessen and Joyce Blau. Paris: Institut national des langues et civilisations orientales, 1999.
Walker, Christopher J., *Armenia: The Survival of a Nation*. New York: St. Martin's Press, 1980.

Index

Page numbers followed with "n" refer to endnotes.

Abbas Hilmi II Pasha, Khedive 63, 72 n.64
absolute monarchy 152–3
Achekbashian, Aram 10
ACIA. *See* American Committee for the Independence of Armenia (ACIA)
'Act of Self-Government of Cilicia' 200
Adana massacres. *See* Armenian massacres
Adem-i Markaziyyet movement 51
Adülhamid II, Sultan 6, 41, 42, 47, 51, 56, 93, 94, 99, 108, 112, 118, 119, 121, 133, 134, 220, 241, 245
Afrikian, Poghos 24, 26
AGBU. *See* Armenian General Benevolent Union (AGBU)
Agha, Rifaat 163
Aghasi (Garabed Tursarkisian) 133–4, 149–52, 156, 163
Aharonian, Avetis 48
Ahmed Agha (Deli Ahmed) 138
Aintab 132
    arrest of Hnchak representatives 139
    British occupation and repatriation of Armenians to 139–40
    Hnchakian branch in 133
    'Kelleci Olayı/Kesik Baş Vakası' (The Severed Head Incident) 137–8
    Kemalist-French struggle 140–1
    massacres of November 1895 in 134
    SDHP 133–4
        activities of 134–7
        five-person administrative board 134
        organized groups 139
        Zeytun resistance 133–4
Alawis (Nusayris) 152
Alay Bey 157

Ali, Muhammad 150, 151
Ali Riza 160–2
Amaduni, Yedvard 230, 231
Amasya, pamphleteering in 96
American Committee for the Independence of Armenia (ACIA) 78
ANA. *See* Armenian National Assembly (ANA)
Ankara Trials 99, 119–20
Ansell, W.J. 155
anti-Armenian policies 4
anti-Bolshevik 20, 79
Anti-Christian demonstrations 157
anti-Hamidian forces
    first congress of 47–9
    second congress of 50
anti-imperialism 237, 238
anti-Nazarbekian faction 7
ANU. *See* Armenian National Union (ANU)
Apovian, Khachatur 3
Araradian, Hovhannes 138
Araratian republic 75
Ararat Sport Union 180
Aṟawōt 177
Ardzagang P'arizi 177
ARF. *See* Armenian Revolutionary Federation (ARF)
Argentina 172, 173, 176–7, 181
Argentinean Communist Party 177
Armenakan Organization 1, 2, 4–5
Armenakan Party 207, 208, 210, 214, 240
Armēnia 5, 21–6
Armenian
    Apostolic Church 172, 197–8, 208, 225
    children and youth education 175

genocide   10, 14, 192, 194, 200, 202, 222, 238, 239, 250, 252
independence   75, 79, 96, 195–7, 215, 221
instrumentalization   211
intellectuals   3–4
monism   207, 223, 224
peasants   108–16, 120
reforms   41, 43, 46, 47, 112
refugees   14, 75–8, 139–40
revolution   43, 207, 212, 225
threat   120
Armenian-Alawi relationship   152
Armenian communities
  assassination of   100–1
  SDHP engagement with   98–102
Armenian Community Center   175–6, 179
Armenian General Benevolent Union (AGBU)   78, 79, 172–4, 177
Armenian massacres   9, 39, 41, 42, 44, 46, 49, 59, 83–4, 91, 107, 115, 117, 120–2, 134–9, 148, 150, 153, 154, 158, 159, 195, 197, 199, 200, 211–12, 220, 221, 241
Armenian National Assembly (ANA)   58, 87
Armenian National Union (ANU)   139, 140, 146 n.66, 173–5
Armenian Question   6, 7, 110, 111, 198, 208
Armenian Reform Program   7
Armenian Revolutionary Federation (ARF)   1, 10, 38, 42, 43, 46–51, 75–9, 117, 138, 173–6, 179, 182, 199–201, 206–8, 210, 212–18, 220, 221, 223, 224, 227, 235, 240, 245
  contradictions with SDHP   218
  decentralization   219
  guerrilla warfare   211–12
  ideological centralism   219
  Marxism   209
  publications of   228
  Russian utilization of   211
  socialism   215, 217
  terrorism   211–12
  25 April session of   174

Armenian revolutionary movement   1–2, 12, 207–8, 210, 211, 215, 223–4
Armenian Workers Party   176
Armeno-Kurdish conflicts   107–9, 111, 114
  clashes of 1893   119–20
  Damadian's presence in Sasun   113–15
  massacre of the Armenians   120–2
  Murad the Great and   116–17, 119–21
  resisting pastoralist Kurds   116–17
  from tension to   115–16
Arpiarian, Arpiar   42, 43, 211–13, 240
Arshaluys Youth Union   180
Arslan, Israyel   173
Article 61 of the Treaty of Berlin   2–3, 47, 245
Artzruni, Grigor   4, 220
Arzhent'inean Mamul (Argentinean Press)   176–7
Ashekian, Khoren   198
Astourian, Stephan   110
Autonomous Armenia   9, 61, 69 n.44
Avedis, Baron   154, 158, 162, 163
Azmi Bey   62, 63
Azuri, Nejib   57

Babaian, Khatchig   45
Bab-ı Ali demonstration   6, 7, 41, 83, 119, 220, 241, 245
Bakchejian, Sahag   172, 175–6, 178, 179, 182
balance of power   211
Balkan bourgeoisie   234
Balkan Wars of 1912–13   9, 231, 233, 249, 250
Balta Senesi (The Year of the Ax)   134
Banvor (Worker)   256
Barnham, Henry D.   150, 152
Basmajian, Garabed   48
Bastajian, Soghomon B.   133, 134
Bedirkhan, Bedir Bey   57
Belorian, Mgrdich   182
Bengal, pamphleteering in   91
Benne (Torosian)   10
Beojekian, Nigoghos   151, 154
Blazer Sewing Tailors Union   233
Bolshevik Revolution of October 1917   79, 221, 225

bourgeoisie   76, 83, 201, 208, 210, 214, 232–4
Boyajian, Hampartsoum. *See* Murad the Great
Boyajian, Jirair   93
Brazil   180–1
Brazil, Etienne   174
Buenos Aires   172–4, 177–9, 181, 182
Bulgarian revolution of 1876   4

capitalism   196, 199, 214
Catoni, A.   160
Central Administrative Council of the Armenian Diocese of Uruguay   179
centralization   218–20
Central Turkey College   132, 135
Chamoun, Camille   222
Cheraz, Minas   48
church   194, 197–8, 208, 209
church-nation   207
class struggles   196, 214
Cold War   11, 201, 222
Committee of Aid to Armenia (*Hayastani Ôgnut'ean Komitē*, HOK)   80, 177, 178
Committee of Reconstruction of Soviet Armenia   180
Committee of Union and Progress (CUP)   9, 41–2, 44, 56, 60, 134, 135, 138–9, 199–200, 213, 218, 221, 227, 238, 239, 245, 246
   preparations for war   249
   Turkification of Anatolia   246, 250
Communist Party of Soviet Armenia   201
Communist Party of the Soviet Union (CPSU)   221–2
Communist Party of Turkey (TKP)   238, 239
constructivist socialism   216–17
Cora, Tolga   109
CPSU. *See* Communist Party of the Soviet Union (CPSU)
CUP. *See* Committee of Union and Progress (CUP)
Currie, Philip   43–6, 130 n.131, 155, 161

Damadian, Mihran   43, 113–17, 120, 200, 213, 216, 219, 240
   arrest of   117–19
Dashnaktsutiun. *See* Armenian Revolutionary Federation (ARF)
Dashnaktsutiun Committee   44–5
Da Trieste, Fedele   153–4
da Vallarsa, Marcellino   154, 157–62
Davtian, Hovnan   215, 218, 219
decentralization   219–21
democratic centralism   218–20
demonstrations
   Anti-Christian   157
   Bab-ı Ali   6, 7, 41, 83, 119, 220, 241, 245
   Hnchakian Revolutionary Party   6–7
   Kumkapı   6, 87, 91, 105 n.20, 113, 116, 198, 220
   May Day   240, 245
Dervish *Ağa*   128 n.98
Dowek, Joseph   152, 159
Drōshak   46, 48, 49, 115, 212
Duguid, Stephen   110
Durkheim, Emile   213, 214

Eastern Anatolia
   Armeno-Kurdish conflicts (*see* Armeno-Kurdish conflicts)
   Kurdish feudalism in   109
   in late nineteenth century   108–10
   Ottoman destruction of Kurdish emirates   108
economic liberation principle   212
Engels, Friedrich   98, 232, 240
Enver Pasha   58, 250
Eolmez, Apraham   178, 179
Eṛand   180
Eritasard Hayastan   178
Estado Novo   181
ethnic cleansing   250

FAR. *See* Federation of Armenian Revolutionaries (FAR)
fedayeen movement, rural and urban   245–6
fedayees (freedom fighters)   39, 211, 221
federalism   215, 217, 219
Federation of Armenian Revolutionaries (FAR)   8

Fellaheen, Ansariye   152
feudal nobility   197
First Republic of Armenia   10, 76, 80
   Bolshevik challenge   79
   SDHP and   75–80
   Turkish invasion of   79
   US assistance to   77, 78
first Sasun uprising   39–42
Fourier, Charles   232
Freedom and Accord Party (*Hürriyet ve İtilaf Fırkası*)   9, 58

Gazette de Lausanne   241
Geneva, democratic centralism   218–19
genocide, Armenian   10, 14, 192, 194, 200, 202, 222, 238, 239, 250, 252
Gharajian, Gevorg   5, 23–9, 31–4, 132
Gidur (Kitur), Arsen   77, 78, 93, 229, 231, 232
Gölbaşı, Edip   112
Golitsyn, Grigory   245
Grabill, Joseph   135
Grigorian, Aram   241
Guedjian, Melkon (Harputlu Melkon)   156–7
guerrilla warfare   211–12
Gulbenkian, Hovannes (Onnig)   172

Hagopian, Mgrdich   177
Hagopian, Nerses   136, 137
Haigazian School   179
haitadism   205, 208–11, 215, 223–5
haitadist system   209, 220
Hakkı, Ismail   60
Halâskâr Zâbitân Gurubu (Savior Officers Group)   58
Hamidian massacres. *See* Armenian massacres
Harbord, James G.   76
Harutiunian, Samson   77
Hayrenik'   24, 25, 27, 29
Hayrig, Khrimian   3
Hegel, Friedrich   98, 208, 231
Hildebrand, Gerhard   234
Hilmi, Hüseyin   238, 239, 248–9
   letter to Marx   249
historical materialism   230–1
'History of Philosophy and Historical Materialism' (Gidur)   231, 232

Hnch'ak (Bell)   5, 6, 28, 33–4, 38, 41–3, 48, 49, 57, 94, 98, 113–16, 121, 154, 212, 240
Hnchakian center in London   42, 45–8
Hnchakian paradoxes   193–202
Hnchakian Revolutionary Party   5, 113, 114, 120, 240, 242
   activities   6
   centre of   6
   demonstration   6–7
   formation of   23, 27
   history   21, 28, 29, 31–4
   identity   28
   immediate and final object programme   5
   internal division   7, 42–6, 199
      unification of   49
   photograph of the seven founders   30–2
   programme   5–8, 242
   reconciliation   49–50
   socialism and nationalism   7–9
Hnchak pamphleteering. *See* pamphleteering in Central Anatolia
'How Do Ideas Develop?' (Gidur)   231

Ibrahim, Sheikh   152
ideology
   of SDHP   199–202
   and systems of thought   199
imperialism   199, 214
independence of Armenia   7, 75, 79, 96, 132, 149, 195–7, 215, 221
independent Armenia   39, 87, 96, 152, 196–8, 200
indescribable massacres   162
internationalization of the Armenian issue   198
iron law of wages   98
ishkhanabar system (authoritarian and centralized)   219
Istanbul Students' Union   229, 230, 232–5
İştirak   248–9
Ittihad ve Terakki Cemiyeti. *See* Committee of Union and Progress (CUP)
Izmirlian, Matteos   41

Izmirlian, Tigran 241

Jelaleddin Pasha, Ahmed 49–50
Jumblatt, Kamal 222

Kafian, Gabriel 5, 23–5, 29, 31–2, 34, 132
Kajaznuni, Hovhannes 78
Kantian perpetual peace 214, 215
Karabakh Committee 202
Karami, Rashid 222
Kaytz 178, 180, 181, 227, 240
   analyses on the Ottoman Empire 232
   historical materialism 230–1
   'History of Philosophy and Historical Materialism' (Gidur) 231, 232
   'How Do Ideas Develop?' (Gidur) 231
   library to publish a book series 232
   'Literary Trends in the Nineteenth Century' (Amaduni) 231
   Marxism 229
   news about socialism in Europe and world 231, 234
   poems and literary criticism 231
   reader's letters 231–2
   scientific socialism 229, 230, 232, 234
   social issues from class perspective 230
   'Socialist Activities in Turkey' (Vanigian) 232
   'Socialist Labor Unions in Constantinople' (Vanigian) 233
   socialist thought writings 231
   'The Student World' section 235
   'War and Studentship' 233
   'War: Workers and Bourgeoisie' 233–4
   young socialists 230
Kaytz Youth Union 179
Kazitski 33, 34
Kechejian, Hampartsoum 173, 175
Kefsizian, Mgrdich 149
Kelekian, Diran 49
'Kelleci Olayı/Kesik Baş Vakası' (The Severed Head Incident) 137–8
Kemal, Mustafa 238

Kemal Bey, Ali 137, 138
Kemalism 238–9
Kemalist nationalist movement 140
Keresktsian, Khachadur 220
Keshishian, Garabed 176
Keskin, revolutionary posters in 99–100
Khan-Azad, Rupen 5, 8, 23–34, 43, 119, 132, 212, 213, 220, 241
Khatisian, Alexander 77
Khesulmunian (Khulmunian), Nazaret 173
Khorhrdayin Hayastan 176
Kilikia School of São Paulo 180
Kiwtnerian, Zarmair 176, 177
Kohak 172
Kumkapı Demonstration in 1890 6, 87, 91, 105 n.20, 113, 116, 198, 220
Kurdish
   feudalism 108, 109
   pastoralist tribes 108–14, 116–17, 120
   tribes 108–14

labour class 242
Lafargue, Paul 234
land tax 248
Lassalle, Ferdinand 98
Lavrov, Pyotr Lavrovich 28
Lazo (Hakob Ghazarian) 79
left-socialist movements, Turkey 238, 239
Lenin, Vladimir 213–15, 221
liberation
   economic 212
   nationalist and socialist 87
   Turkish Armenia 8, 217
   of Western Armenia 21, 39, 43
   of the working class 98
'Literary Trends in the Nineteenth Century' (Amaduni) 231
Luxemburg, Rosa 246

Manucharian, Mgrdich 5, 24, 26
Maroukhian, Hrair 205
Marx, Karl 98, 214, 231, 232, 249
Marxism 5, 193–7, 199, 212, 215, 229
Marxism-Leninism 216
Marxist socialism 215–16, 219

massacres
   Armenian 9, 39, 41, 42, 44, 46, 49, 59,
      83–4, 91, 107, 115, 117, 120–2,
      134–9, 148, 150, 153, 154, 158,
      159, 195, 197, 199, 200, 211–12,
      220, 221, 241
   Muslims 95, 102
Matinian, Nikoli 5
Matteos Sarkissian. *See* Paramaz
Maunsell, Francis Richard 49
May Day demonstrations 240, 245
May Reform Project 40–1, 47
Medzn Murad. *See* Murad the Great
Melson, Robert 108
Merrill, John 135
Merzifon, pamphleteering in 100
Mikaelian, Kristapor 4, 8, 208, 212–20, 225
Minassian, Roupen Der 217
Mirzakhanian, Jirayr 229
   theatre group 179
modernity and tradition 209
Montevideo 179
Morgenthau, Henry 78
Mshak (Tiller) 4, 28, 220
Mukhtar Pasha, Ahmed 58
Murad Bey, Mizanci 42, 44
Murad the Great 10, 116–17, 119–21,
      216, 242, 247–9, 251
Musa Dagh 148–50
   Armenians of 151
   SDHP
      administration 152–3
      revolutionaries in 151–64
Mush Valley 110, 111, 113–15
Muslim-Armenian relations 92, 94–5
Muslims
   approval for revolutionary
      pamphleteering 92–8
   massacres 95, 102
   refugees 109, 250

Nadim, Mustapha 157, 160–2
Najarian, Yeghia 11
Nakashian, Avedis 40
Nalbandian, Mikael 3
national haitadism 210
nationalism 196, 197, 215, 216, 245
   socialism and 7–9

Nazarbek, A. 26
Nazarbekian, Avetis 5, 7, 22–4, 26–9,
      31, 32, 34, 43, 116, 132, 212–14,
      216, 218–22, 241
Nazım Pasha, Huseyin 58, 68 n.30, 118
Nejat, Suphi 251, 253 n.23
neologism 208–9
Nivlinsky, Herafion 43
Nor Ashkharh 240, 249
Nor Yerkir 177
Nubar, Boghos 75–7, 79

O Dominante 180
Ohanian, Kristapor 5, 23–6, 29, 31, 32, 34, 132
Ormanian, Maghakia 45
Oshin, M. (Mihran Uzunian) 177
Ottoman Armenians 194–5
Ottoman Chamber of Deputies 246–8
Ottoman Empire 38, 43, 51, 58, 85,
      87, 88, 90, 92–5, 97, 98, 101,
      107, 132, 148, 149, 159, 164,
      192, 196–200, 207, 208,
      210, 211, 224, 232, 234,
      240
   first demonstration in 241–2
   parliamentary elections of 1912 58
   political parties in 240
   socialist deputies 246–8
   socialist movement in 238
   struggle for socialism in 246
Ottoman Socialist Party 248–9
Owen, Robert 232
Ozanian, Antranig (Andranik) 78

pamphleteering in Central Anatolia
   in Amasya 96
   in Colonial Bengal 91
   in Merzifon 100
   and propaganda 89–91
   and revolution 91–2
      appealing to local Muslims 92–8
      SDHP engagement with Armenian
         communities 98–102
      SDHP campaign 97–8
   in Sivas 95–6
pamphlets and posters 91, 92, 99–101
Papazian, Vahan 246, 247, 251
paradoxes 193–202

Paramaz (Matteos Sarkissian)   10, 62, 66 n.1, 135, 242, 245, 249–52
  execution of   250
  internationalist attitude   244–5
  letter to Sabah-Gulian, Stepan   62–5
  theatre group   179
Parian, Bedros (Papken Siuni)   245
Parish Council   173
parliamentary elections of 1912, Ottoman Empire   58
Parsons, Talcott   209–10
Pastermajian, Setrak   45
PDA. *See* Public Debt Administration (PDA)
Pehlivan, Zozan   114
Persian Empire   211
placard affair   93, 94
Plekhanov, Georgi   7, 9, 214, 240
political independence   96, 98, 103
politics   207–9, 224–5
'the politics of unity'   110
Portukalian, Mgrdich   4–5, 22–6, 29
posters   90–4, 98–101
  in Yozgat   101
post-genocide period (1918-22)   139–41
Potton, Albert   154, 157–8, 161, 162
'princes' of Zeytun   196–7
printing press   90
pro-Nazarbekian factions   7
'A Proposal' (Lerents a pseudonym of Nazarbekian)   22
Protestantism   154
Public Debt Administration (PDA)   87

Radio Armenia   179–80
Raffi (Hagop Melik Der Hagopian)   3, 98
Raif Pasha   160
red triumvirate   59, 60
Refik Bey, Manyasizade   20, 57, 67 n.13
religion   194, 198, 207–8
The Republic of Armenia   76
revolutionary committees   92–4, 96, 99–101
revolutionary pamphleteering   91–102
revolutionary society of Geneva   22, 32, 33
  Declaration   23–6
  formation of   25, 26, 34
  preparing the programme   26–9, 34

publishing a paper   26, 29
  tenets   26
revolutionary treasury   22, 24
revolutionary violence   92
Rıza, Ahmed   9, 47–50, 218, 221, 245
Rostom (Stepan Zorian)   208, 217, 218
RSDLP. *See* Social-Democratic Labor Party (RSDLP)
Rupenian, Harutyun   179–80
Russian Armenia   88, 216
Russian Armenians   194–5
Russian Empire   207, 211, 224
Russian populism   5
Russian SDs (Social Democrats)   216
Russian SRs (Socialist Revolutionaries)   216
Russification policies   4
Russo-Turkish War of 1878   2, 109, 207, 211

Sabaheddin (Prince)   47–51, 57, 60, 67 n.8, 221, 245
Sabah-Gulian, Stepan   9, 56, 58–62, 66 n.2, 71 n.62, 76, 213–14, 221, 225, 240, 242, 250
  letter to Paramaz   62–5
  theater group   178, 180
Sadık Bey, Mehmed   58, 60, 62–5, 68 n.24
Safi Bey, Mehmet   111, 113
Sahagian, Arshavir   61, 250
Sahakian, Garo   6, 7
Salmanadir Ramkavar Party   76, 78, 199–201, 206, 222
  declaration of independence   200
Said Halim Pasha, Mehmed   63, 71 n.59
Said Pasha, Mehmed   58, 68 n.26
Şakir, Behaeddin   49–50, 55 n.66, 239
Saklı Tarihin İzinde (*Tracing the Hidden History*, Akin)   246–7
Salam, Saeb   222
Sanders, C.S.   150, 151, 155, 164
São Paulo   180
Sasun   110–11
  Armeno-Kurdish conflict   111, 114
  Boyajian, Hampartsoum in   116-17
  clashes of 1893   119–20
  Damadian, Mihran in   113–15
  first uprising   39–42

Kurdish tribes   111
massacres   83, 120–2, 150, 154, 220, 241
rebellion   6, 7
socio-economic changes   112–13
violence in   13–14, 84, 108, 114
scientific socialism   196, 212, 218, 229–30, 232, 234
SDHP. *See* Social Democrat Hnchakian Party (SDHP)
SDHP-ARF relations   220–2
Seferian, Boghos   149
Serengülian, Vartkes   246–8, 251
Şerif Paha   60, 69 n.42
Şevket Pasha, Mahmut   58, 60, 68 n.31
Shahazizian, Matteos   24, 26
Sharzhum   178–9
Sherif of Mecca   63, 65, 71 n.63
Sherif Pasha   65, 72 n.67
Shkherdemian, Sdepan (Panos)   172, 174, 176, 177
Simonian, K.   233
Siuni, A.   28
Sivas, pamphleteering in   95–6
Social Democrat Hnchakian Party (SDHP)   1, 9–11, 28, 38, 51, 56–7, 87–8, 103, 132–3, 148–50, 173–7, 179, 182, 197, 198, 200, 206–8, 210, 213, 215, 216, 218, 220, 221, 223, 224, 227, 235, 242
  absolute monarchy   152–3
  administration   152–3
  Aintab (*see* Aintab)
  anti-Bolshevik stance   20, 79
  centralization of   219, 220
  and the Church   197–8
  cooperation agreement between WFS and   58
  democratic centralism   218
  engagement with Armenian communities   98–102
  and First Republic of Armenia   75–80
  forgotten and ignored revolutionaries   239–41
  formation and disintegration   39
  guerrilla warfare   211–12
  ideology   199–202
  Istanbul Students' Union   229–30, 232–5
  leader of   133
  leadership   153
  Marxism   193–7, 199, 209, 214, 215
  Musa Daghtsis in   151
  1909 programme of   242–4
  official programme of   132
  pamphleteering campaign   97–8
  paradoxes   193–202
  publications of   228
  revolutionaries in Musa Dagh   151–64
  Russian utilization of   211
  Seventh Convention of   60–1
  Sixth Convention of   57, 59
  socialism   196–7, 199, 200, 215
  terrorism   211–12
Social-Democratic Labor Party (RSDLP)   213–15, 221
social engineering   250
social haitadism   210
socialism   7, 196–7, 199–201, 212, 215–19, 237–8, 240, 246, 247
  and nationalism   7–9
  scientific   196, 212, 218, 229–30, 232, 234
  in Turkey   232
  utopian   232
  working class and   233
'Socialist Activities in Turkey' (Vanigian)   232
socialist deputies in Ottoman Chamber   246–8
'Socialist Labor Unions in Constantinople' (Vanigian)   233
socialist politics   231
Socialist Workers' Federation of Salonica   246
Soviet Armenia   176–7, 200–2
Sovietization of Armenia   221
Stepanian, Levon   5
Students' Union   14, 178–80, 229–30, 232–5
Suphi, Mustafa   238, 252
Svazli, Mihran   43, 52, 77
Sykes-Picot agreement   139
Syrian Agreement   140

Tahsin Pasha (governor of Bitlis)   118–20
'Tax Constitution (*nizamname*) of 1886'   121

territorial haitadism   210
terrorism   211, 212
Thessaloniki, Socialist Workers' Federation in   246
TKP. *See* Communist Party of Turkey (TKP)
Toselli, Augusto   160–2
Treaty of Ankara   141
Treaty of Berlin   2, 46, 198, 220, 233
   Article 61 of the   2–3, 47, 245
Treaty of San Stefano   2, 198
Tripoli War of 1911   233
Turabian (Varaztad), Hagop   8, 9
Turkey
   bourgeoisie of   234
   socialism in   232
   socialist movement in   237–9
Turkification of Anatolia   246, 250
Turkish Armenia   5, 211, 215, 216
   independence of   7, 132, 149
Turkish nationalism   56, 57, 59
Tzhokhk, Hrayr (Armenag Ghazarian)   117, 119, 205, 206, 212

Unión Nacional Armenia (UNA)   173
Uruguay   172, 179
US Senate Foreign Relations Committee   77, 78
USSR   200–2, 222
utopian socialism   232

Vanıgıan, Kegham   229–30, 232, 233, 249
   Student Union   180
Varandian, Mikael   215, 217, 218
Varaztad, P.   61, 70 n.45
Vardanian, Mariam (Maro)   5, 23, 24, 26, 28, 29, 31–4, 43, 132, 151, 200, 212, 213, 216, 240
Vargas, Getulio   181
Vartanian High School for Boys   133

Verakazmyal (Reformed) Hnchakian Party   7, 42, 44, 45, 48–50, 75, 77, 78, 173, 195, 212, 219, 221, 240
violence   83, 88, 91, 107–8, 121–3, 138, 211
   inter-communal and mass   95
   in Sasun   13–14, 84, 108, 114
Vlahof, Dimitar   247, 248, 251
Vratsian, Simon   205, 206

Western Armenia   132, 193, 200
   liberation of   21, 39, 43
WFS. *See* Workers Federation of Salonica (WFS)
Wilhelm II, Kaiser   46–7
Workers Federation of Salonica (WFS)   57–8
working class and socialism   233

yafta   90–1
Yarpuzlian, Sdepan   153, 163
Yasian, Artur   9, 61, 62
Young Armenia Society (*Eritasard Hayastan*)   4
Young Turks   9, 42, 45–51, 134, 199, 241, 245
   Revolution of 1908   9, 13, 51, 56, 145 n.58, 200, 210, 213, 221, 246
   activities of SDHP in Aintab after   134–6
Yozgat, revolutionary posters in   101

Zart'ōnk'   177
Zasulich, Vera   7
Zavarian, Simon   8, 208, 215, 217–19
Zeki, Salih   239
Zeytun   196–7
   rebellion   6–7, 197, 241
   resistance   133–4
Zhoghovrdakan (Democratic) party   76
Zohrab, Krikor   246, 248, 251

www.ingramcontent.com/pod-product-compliance
Lightning Source LLC
Chambersburg PA
CBHW071809300426
44116CB00009B/1258